Getting the Most Out of Free Trade Agreements in Central America

Getting the Most Out of Free Trade Agreements in Central America

J. Humberto López and Rashmi Shankar, Editors

THE WORLD BANK
Washington, D.C.

© 2011 The International Bank for Reconstruction and Development / The World Bank
1818 H Street NW
Washington DC 20433
Telephone: 202-473-1000
Internet: www.worldbank.org

ISBN: 978-0-8213-8712-2
eISBN: 978-0-8213-8713-9
DOI: 10.1596/978-0-8213-8712-2

Library of Congress Cataloging-in-Publication Data
Getting the most out of free trade agreements in Central America / J. Humberto López and Rashmi Shankar, editors.
    p. cm.
  ISBN 978-0-8213-8712-2 — ISBN 978-0-8213-8713-9 (electronic)
  1. Free trade—Central America. 2. Central America—Commercial policy. 3. Central America—Foreign economic relations. I. Lopez, J. Humberto. II. Shankar, Rashmi. III. World Bank.
  HF1782.G48 2011
  382'.90972—dc23

                                                                              2011017660

Cover photos: Crane and cargo containers © Zhang Lianxun/Dreamstime.com;
Trucks on a highway parking place © Ginsanders/Dreamstime.com;
Kindergarten children learning to use computers © Monkey Business Images/Dreamstime.com.

Cover design: Candace Roberts/Quantum Think.

Contents

Box

Figures

Tables

Preface

I still remember my first visit to Central America back in 1988. When I reflect on the dramatic changes that the region has gone through since then, it is difficult not to have a sense of optimism about the prospects of the region for the coming years. It cannot be forgotten that in the late 1980s four Central American countries were still involved in armed conflicts in one way or another, and that it was not until the Esquipulas Agreement (1987) that a framework for peaceful resolution of the conflicts emerged. Then, it was just fifteen years ago that, in 1996, following the Guatemala Peace Accords, Central America managed to build a durable peace that has lasted until today. For this, all Central Americans need to be congratulated.

Peace came accompanied not only by the end to the human drama associated with the conflicts, but also by a significant economic dividend— a much needed development in a region where per capita GDP had stagnated between 1970 and 1990 and where two countries (El Salvador and Nicaragua) had been experiencing negative average growth rates for more than two decades. The social dimension of the dismal growth performance is well captured in the poverty rates. According to World Bank statistics, in the first half of the 1990s the average poverty rate in the region was close to 60 percent in countries such as Honduras and

Nicaragua; almost three-quarters of the population lived on less than US$4 a day.

In contrast, between 1990 and 2010 per capita growth averaged 2.4 percent (across countries and time periods) and the poverty rate declined to 44 percent of the population. In fairness, the economic dividend of the last two decades was due not only to the peace process but also to the significant modernization agenda implemented by all the countries in the region. A key element of these agendas was the promotion of international trade, an implicit acknowledgement that given the size of the different Central American economies in the absence of international trade it would be difficult for domestic firms to specialize in areas of comparative advantage and exploit economies of scale associated with bigger markets. As a result, today Central American countries are very open, with volumes of international trade (exports plus imports of goods and services) ranging from 70 percent of GDP in Guatemala to more than 150 percent of GDP in Panama.

And yet, it is evident that the region aspires to further exploit the opportunities created by international trade. In addition to a significant number of bilateral free trade agreements (FTAs), the past few years have witnessed the conclusion of two important regional agreements: the Dominican Republic–Central America Free Trade Agreement (DR-CAFTA) that is now in effect between the United States, Costa Rica, Dominican Republic, El Salvador, Guatemala, Honduras, and Nicaragua; and the Association Agreement reached in May 2010 between the European Union and Costa Rica, El Salvador, Guatemala, Honduras, Nicaragua, and Panama.

I honestly think that the outward orientation showed by the region and the conclusion of the recent FTAs are part of the answer to the development challenges of Central America. But I also think that, taking into account that 19 million Central Americans still live in poverty, it is not enough to pursue the signature of FTAs. Policy makers in the region have to make an effort to make the best out of them and ensure that their benefits permeate to all segments of the population. This reflection is the motivation of this book.

Several lessons emerge from *Getting the Most Out of Free Trade Agreements in Central America*, but I would like to stress three.

First, Central America should not take the positive results of signed FTAs as a given. As these authors note, trade agreements create opportunities but do not guarantee results. Indeed, the analysis in this book indicates that it is up to the different countries to take the necessary steps to enhance the benefits of the agreements, including improvements in education levels that result in a more productive labor force, in public infrastructure so that the extremely high logistics costs in the region can be reduced, and in the energy matrix to improve access to reliable energy at competitive prices. Admittedly, this is a complex agenda that, realistically speaking, cannot be implemented overnight. And yet, if Central America wants to make the best of its trade agreements, this is the agenda it will need to progress on.

Second, trade promotion needs to be complemented by a strong focus on the poor. In some cases, this focus is because of the challenges brought by additional external competition, which may negatively affect some industries or sectors. Perhaps even more importantly, in other cases, the benefits and opportunities created by an expansion of trade may not be distributed evenly across the population and important groups could be excluded. The evidence in this book indicates that the skill premium may be on the rise in Central America. In other words, ongoing development forces are benefiting the highly educated more than those with fewer skills, therefore potentially contributing to increases in inequality in a region where it is already high.

Third, is the need for more competitive markets. Although many of us tend to think about the benefits of growth in terms of quantities (that is, more exports, more employment, and increased access to goods) many of the welfare effects of FTAs are transmitted through prices (such as lower prices for imported goods). But for this transmission channel to operate, it is important that markets are competitive and that no agent has a predominant market position that offers the possibility of capturing the rents created by lower tariffs. This is a complex issue in small economies where fixed costs may result in too many natural monopolies. This book does not come with a conclusive recommendation on this front, yet, I would like to invite policy makers and practitioners alike to explore whether further regional integration would help address this concern by increasing the market size.

Given that at the time of this book's publication I will have transferred from the position I have held for the past three years, that of World Bank Country Director for Central America, I would like to share one final thought: Central America should, must, and can exploit all the existing opportunities to improve the standard of living of its population. As I mentioned, let's not forget where the region was twenty years ago, and let us not be shy of where the region can be in twenty years.

Laura Frigenti
Director, Strategy and Operations
Latin America and the Caribbean Region
The World Bank
April 2011

Acknowledgments

This report is the result of a collaborative effort of a large team led by J. Humberto López (Poverty Reduction and Economic Management Department) and Rashmi Shankar (Economic Policy Unit) of the Latin America and the Caribbean Region and including Diego Arias, José Barbero, Irene Brambilla, Maurizio Bussolo, César Calderón, Lucio Castro, Juan Miguel Cayo, Bárbara Cunha, Calvin Z. Djiofack, Francisco Estrázulas de Souza, Raquel Fernández, Norbert Fiess, Santiago Flórez Gómez, Mario A. De Franco, Samuel Freije, Leonardo Iacovone, Inessa Love, Muthukumara S. Mani, Teresa Molina Millán, Ana Cristina Molina, Walter G. Park, Virginia Poggio, Guido Porto, Melissa Rodríguez , Patricia Tovar, Riccardo Trezzi, and Henry Vega. Background papers not published in this volume may be found on the World Bank's web site. Patricia Holt and Santiago Flórez Gómez provided invaluable support in all aspects of the production of this manuscript. We would also like to thank Tammy Lyn Pertillar for help on formatting.

We owe a debt of gratitude to our peer reviewers: Chad Bown, Caroline Freund, Carlos Felipe Jaramillo, John Nash, and Jordan Schwartz from the World Bank; David Coady (International Monetary Fund); Pravin Krishna (Johns Hopkins University); and Marcelo Olarreaga, (Département d'Economie Politique Université de Genève) for their suggestions during the preparation of this report. We also thank Patricia Katayama, acquisitions editor, and Janice Tuten, publications production manager in the World Bank's Office of the Publisher.

Finally, we would like to thank Rodrigo A. Chaves (director, Poverty Reduction and Economic Management, Latin America and the Caribbean Region), Laura Frigenti (director, Strategy and Operations, Latin America and the Caribbean Region), and Carlos Felipe Jaramillo (director, Central America Country Management Unit) for overall supervision and guidance to the team.

About the Contributors

Diego Arias is a senior economist in the Agriculture and Rural Development Division of the Latin America and the Caribbean Region of the World Bank. His recent publications have covered topics such as food policy and managing risks in the agriculture sector in Latin America.

José A. Barbero is a senior transport specialist. He has worked in most Latin American countries on freight logistics, urban transportation, infrastructure planning, and transport institutional organization. After several years at the World Bank, he is currently an independent consultant.

Maurizio Bussolo is a senior economist in the Economic Policy Unit of the Latin America and the Caribbean Region of the World Bank. He has been working on quantitative analyses of economic policy and development. Bussolo previously worked at the OECD, at the Overseas Development Institute in London, and at Fedesarrollo and Los Andes University in Colombia. He has published in several international journals and his recent publications include a volume on macro-micro modeling, edited with Francois Bourguignon and Luiz Pereira da Silva. He holds a Ph.D. in economics from the University of Warwick.

César Calderón is a senior economist at the Regional Chief Economist's Office for the Latin America and the Caribbean Region of the World Bank. Prior to this post, he worked in the Research Department at the Central Bank of Chile and the Central Reserve Bank of Peru and was an invited lecturer at the ILADES-Georgetown University Masters Program in Economics in Santiago, Chile. He was awarded his Ph.D. in economics from the University of Rochester in 2002. Calderón has published in the areas of open macroeconomics, growth, and development. He is currently working in issues such as globalization, economic fluctuations, and financial development.

Lucio Castro is the director of International Economics and Productive Development of CIPPEC (Center for the Implementation of Public Policies for Growth and Equity), a think tank based on Argentina. His recent publications have covered topics such as the effects of food prices on development and poverty, price shocks and energy consumption, the determinants of subnational growth and trade, among others.

Juan Miguel Cayo is a senior energy specialist in the Latin America and the Caribbean Region of the World Bank. Before joining the Bank, he worked as the counselor for the executive director for Peru and Chile at the Inter-American Development Bank. He has had a long career in the Peruvian public sector. Cayo was the Vice Minister of Economy (2006) at the Ministry of Economy and Finance, responsible of the macroeconomic, social, and sectorial policies. In 2004 he was appointed Vice Minister of Energy, overseeing the subsectors of electricity and hydrocarbons. He was involved in the reform of the electricity sector in Peru of 2006 and in the development of both the Camisea Gas and the Peru LNG projects.

Bárbara Cunha is an economist in the Economic Policy unit of the Latin America and the Caribbean Region of the World Bank. Her recent work has covered topics such as informality and development and credit shortages in Latin America. She received a Ph.D. in economics from the University of Chicago.

Calvin Z. Djiofack is consultant for the Economic Policy Unit of the Latin America and the Caribbean Region of the World Bank World Bank. His recent publications have covered topics such as trade in services, regional integration, migrations, fiscal policy, natural resources, and CGE models.

Francisco Estrázulas de Souza is an analyst at Castalia, a strategic advisory firm based in Washington, D.C. His latest work has focused on water and energy regulation, public-private partnerships in infrastructure, and management of public utilities. Estrázulas conducted this supply chain analysis as part of his master's degree thesis at the Harvard Kennedy School of Government.

Raquel Fernández is a junior professional associate at the Economics Unit of the Sustainable Development Department of the Latin America and the Caribbean Region of the World Bank. Her work has focused on the linkages between trade logistics and countries' agricultural competitiveness.

Santiago Flórez Gómez is a consultant at the Economic Policy Unit of the Latin America and the Caribbean Region of the World Bank. His work has focused on trade facilitation and competitiveness. He previously conducted research for the Inter-American Development Bank and the European Commission.

Mario A. De Franco is an economic and business consultant for the World Bank and other development agencies. His recent publications have covered the topics of social protection, microfinance, and trade and competitiveness in the Latin American region.

Samuel Freije is senior economist for the Poverty and Gender Unit of the Latin America and the Caribbean Region of the World Bank. His recent publications refer to microsimulation and impact evaluation of social policies as well as to analysis of welfare and income distribution. He is also an associate editor of *Economia*, the journal of the Latin American and Caribbean Economic Association.

Leonardo Iacovone is an economist currently working for the Private and Financial Sector Department of the Africa Region of the World Bank. Before joining the Bank, he served as economic advisor (ODI fellow) for the government of Mozambique and as a consultant for various international organizations (WTO, USAID, UNIDO, UNDP, DfID, and the European Commission). His research focuses on firm-level responses to challenges and opportunities of globalization, industrial dynamics, exports, commodity prices, and regional trade agreements.

J. Humberto López is the lead economist for the Central America Department of the Latin America and the Caribbean Region of the World Bank. His recent publications have covered topics such as remittances and development, and the investment climate in Latin America.

Inessa Love is a senior economist in the Finance and Private Sector Team of the Development Research Group. Since joining the World Bank as a Young Economist in 2001, her research has focused on access to external finance, entrepreneurship, the impact of financial crisis, and development of the domestic financial sector. She holds a Ph.D. in finance and economics from Columbia University Graduate School of Business.

Muthukumara S. Mani is a senior environmental economist in the Sustainable Development Department of the South Asia Region of the World Bank, based in Delhi. Currently, his work focuses mainly on climate change mitigation and adaptation issues in India. He has also worked on country environmental assessments, pollution and natural resources management, environmental institutions and governance, climate change and adaptation, trade, and environment issues. Mani has a number of publications in peer reviewed journals and has a Ph.D. in economics from the University of Maryland.

Teresa Molina Millán is a consultant at the Economic Policy Unit of the Latin America and the Caribbean Region of the World Bank and a Ph.D. student in economics at the Paris School of Economics. Her research interests include access to finance at the firm and at the household level and rural to urban migration in developing countries.

Ana Cristina Molina is an economist in the WTO's Regional Trade Agreements Section. She has been working extensively on trade and development issues. Her areas of expertise include regional integration, export survival, trade diversification, and competitiveness. Among her previous assignments, she worked as a consultant for the World Bank and UNCTAD. Molina holds a Ph.D. in economics from the Graduate Institute in Geneva.

Walter G. Park is an associate professor of economics at the American University. He researches international intellectual property rights (IPRs), measurement, and effects on innovation and technology diffusion. He has conducted projects on IPRs for the World Bank, OECD, European Patent Office, World Intellectual Property Office, and Industry Canada.

Virginia Poggio is a research fellow at the Office of Evaluation and Oversight at the Inter-American Development Bank. Prior to this post, she worked at the Regional Chief Economist's Office for the Latin America and the Caribbean Region at the World Bank. She holds a master's degree in economics from Universidad de San Andrés (Argentina). She is currently working in issues such as infant health, poverty, and economic development.

Guido Porto is a professor of economics at the University of La Plata in Argentina. Before joining the University of La Plata, he was an economist in the research department of the World Bank. He received a Ph.D. in economics from Princeton University. Porto's research focuses on the econometric estimation of the impacts of trade policies in developing countries, including impacts on poverty, household welfare, wages, and the distribution of income, as well as on firm behavior.

Melissa Rodríguez is a consultant for the Poverty Reduction and Gender Unit in the Latin America and the Caribbean Region at the World Bank.

Rashmi Shankar is a senior economist in the Economic Policy Unit of the Latin America and the Caribbean Region of the World Bank. Her recent work has focused on trade and trade facilitation in Central America. She has published widely in several areas including macroeconomics and international finance, growth, and international trade.

Henry Vega is a research fellow at Center for Transportation Policy, Operations, and Logistics at George Mason University. His research has focused on assessing agricultural supply chains and on measuring the effects of air transportation costs on exports of perishables and high-tech goods. He holds a Ph.D. in public policy from George Mason University.

Abbreviations

ADDAPCA	Proyecto de Diseño y Aplicación de Políticas Comunes Centroamericanas
ADF	augmented Dickey-Fuller
ASEAN	Association of South East Asian Nations
ATM	automated teller machine
BEA	Bureau of Economic Analysis, United States
CBTPA	Caribbean Basin Trade Partnership Act
CCHAC	Central America Hydrocarbons Cooperation Committee (Comité de Cooperación de Hidrocarburos de América Central)
CEAC	Central America Electrification Committee (Comité de Electrificación de America Central)
CFE	Comision Federal de Electricidad, Mexico
COCATRAM	Comisión Centroamericana de Transporte Marítimo
COMITRANS	Comité Técnico Regional Permanente de Transportes
CRIE	Comisión Regional de Interconexión Eléctrica
DR-CAFTA	Dominican Republic–Central America Free Trade Agreement
EC	European Community
EKC	environmental Kuznets curve

ENDESA	Empresa Nacional de Electricidad, Spain
ENEE	National Electric Power Company, Honduras
EOR	regional system operator (*ente operador regional*)
EPR	owner of the grid (Empresa Propietaria de la Red)
EPZ	export-processing zone
FDI	foreign direct investment
FTA	free trade agreement
GDP	gross domestic product
GMM	generalized method of moments
HIE	high-income exports
HS	Harmonized System
ICRG	International Country Risk Guide
IPPS	Industrial Pollution Projection System
IPR	intellectual property right
ISA	Interconexión Eléctrica, Colombia
IV	instrumental variable
kilometer	1,000 meters, 0.62 mile
KPSS	Kwiatkowski-Phillips-Schmidt-Shin
LFTTD	Linked-Longitudinal Firm Trade Transaction Database
LPI	logistics performance index
LPM	linear probability model
LSMS	Living Standards Measurement Survey
MAGFOR	Ministry of Agriculture and Forestry, Nicaragua
MER	regional electricity market (*mercado electrico regional*)
MPS	market price support
MWh	megawatt-hour
NAFTA	North American Free Trade Agreement
NRCA	normalized revealed comparative advantage index
OECD	Organisation for Economic Co-operation and Development
OLS	ordinary least squares
OIRSA	Regional International Organization for Farming and Livestock Sanitation
OLI	ownership, location, and internalization
PPP	purchasing power parity
RCA	revealed competitive advantage
R&D	research and development
RICAM	Red Internacional de Carreteras Mesoamericanas
SEDLAC	Socio-Economic Database for Latin America and the Caribbean

SIC	Standard Industrial Classification
SICA	Central American Integration System (Sistema de la Integración Centroamericana)
SIEPAC	Central American Electrical Interconnection System
SLS	standardized logistics survey
SME	small and medium enterprise
TFP	total factor productivity
TIM	Procedimiento Mesoamericano para el Tránsito Internacional de Mercancías
TO	trade openness
TRAINS	Trade Analysis and Information System
TRIPS	Trade-Related Aspects of Intellectual Property Rights
UNCTAD	United Nations Conference on Trade and Development
VAR	vector autoregression
WEF	World Economic Forum
WITS	World Integrated Trade Solut

CHAPTER 1

Getting the Most out of Central America's Free Trade Agreements

J. Humberto López and Rashmi Shankar

Central America has put trade liberalization and the promotion of international trade at the center of its development agenda. Over the past years, the region has witnessed the successful conclusion of negotiations for a significant number of free trade agreements (FTAs). Some of these FTAs have taken the form of bilateral agreements (for example, Costa Rica with Canada, Chile, Mexico, Panama, China, and Singapore; Honduras with Mexico), whereas others have been negotiated as a block. These include the historic Dominican Republic–Central America Free Trade Agreement (DR-CAFTA)[1] between Costa Rica, El Salvador, Guatemala, Honduras, Nicaragua, and the Dominican Republic with the United States and, more recently, the Association Agreement of the CA-6 (Costa Rica, El Salvador, Guatemala, Honduras, Nicaragua, and Panama) with the European Union, which has yet to be ratified. Box 1.1 highlights the priority placed on trade by Central American policy makers and the steady progress made on liberalizing tariffs.

The priority given to trade liberalization in Central America's development strategy is not surprising: trade is generally perceived as being both a benefit for growth and a means of advancement for developing countries. Trade may contribute to faster growth through different channels, all of which are extremely relevant for Central America. First, trade openness

Box 1.1

Trade in Central America

The Central American economies exhibit a high degree of trade openness relative to comparators. The volume of international trade (exports plus imports of goods and services) ranges from 70 percent of gross domestic product (GDP) in Guatemala to more than 150 percent of GDP in Panama. The composition of exports is quite different across the subregion. Nicaragua's exports are dominated by agriculture and agricultural products, while Costa Rica, the Dominican Republic, and El Salvador largely export manufactures. Guatemala and Honduras export a mix of both agricultural and manufactured goods.

The importance of international trade as an engine of growth for Central America was recognized by the region well before the CA-5 (Costa Rica, El Salvador, Guatemala, Honduras, and Nicaragua) and the Dominican Republic signed the DR-CAFTA agreement with the United States. The General Treaty on Central American Economic Integration signed in Managua on December 13, 1960, already called for the creation of a common market and a customs union. The Central American countries have also long enjoyed preferential access to the U.S. market—since 1983—with the Caribbean Basin Initiative. By 2000, Central America had been extended the same terms as Mexico for apparel, and duty-free access was given to approximately 75 percent of Central America's exports to the United States.

In retrospect, the common market had succeeded in unifying external tariffs and removing duties on most products being traded among the member countries, leading to a dramatic increase in trade flows within the member nations. The decrease in tariffs by nearly 50 percent on average between 1995 and 2009 has been accompanied by an increase in trade openness for the region, with exports and imports increasing as a share of GDP for the CAFTA countries by about 30 percentage points. Another noteworthy trend has been the increase in intraregional trade. In 1960, 50 percent of Central American exports flowed toward the United States, and only 7 percent flowed toward other Central American countries. In 2010, the United States was still the main single market of the region, accounting for nearly 40 percent of exports, but the relevance of the region itself as a destination of exports has increased dramatically, and the region now accounts for more than 20 percent of exports.

Source: Author calculations based on World Integrated Trade Solution (WITS), World Bank.

may improve a country's access to foreign markets, allowing domestic firms to take advantage of economies of scale. Second, trade can enhance productivity through technological diffusion and transmission of know-how and managerial practices, thanks to stronger interactions with foreign firms and markets, and may provide innovators with new business opportunities. And third, trade may enhance product market competition, thus reducing anticompetitive practices of domestic firms and leading to higher specialization due to exploitation of the comparative advantages of domestic firms. Beyond the positive impact on growth, trade also contributes to a better standard of living for the population. Empirical evidence supports the theoretical view that trade liberalization will alleviate poverty. There is also evidence that trade results in higher wages for those employed by exporter companies. Thus, the region should be congratulated without reservations for the effort made on this front so far.

At the same time, it is important to recognize that the signing of the FTAs is not the end of the road, but rather the beginning. This is so for several reasons. First, the benefits of trade liberalization and promotion should be considered not in isolation, but rather in the context of the general policy and institutional framework in place in the different countries. As argued by Lederman, Maloney, and Servén (2007) in their evaluation of the North American Free Trade Agreement (NAFTA) after its tenth year of implementation, trade agreements create opportunities but do not guarantee results. Indeed, the benefits associated with trade agreements appear to be related to, among others, the quality of institutions, human capital, infrastructure, and the process of technological upgrading in the country in question. In other words, countries that want to get the most out of trade will have to create an enabling policy and institutional environment, which will entail structural reforms referred to as the "complementary agenda." Lederman, Maloney, and Servén (2007) also argue that the implementation of a sound complementary agenda is more profitable and, at the same time, more urgent in the context of an FTA (particularly if it has the relevance of CAFTA or the Association Agreement with the European Union) given the opportunities and also the challenges associated with trade agreements and trade promotion.

Second, even within a given country, the effects of trade vary widely across regions, firms, and workers. Trade liberalization may therefore need to be complemented with policy actions to ease the transition for those who benefit the least—or even who might be adversely affected. For example, workers with higher skills and education benefited more from NAFTA than those without—a phenomenon referred to as the skill premium—suggesting that a well-targeted policy of investment in educa-tion and training was needed. Similarly, larger firms benefited more from NAFTA than smaller firms, which could be related to, among other factors, differential access to credit. States with higher initial levels of education, better infrastructure, and stronger local institutions did better during the first years of NAFTA, accelerating their rate of convergence toward the more prosperous North. Beyond NAFTA, Harrison (2007) reviews a series of case studies using firm- and household-level data and concludes that the poor are more likely to share the gains from trade integration in developing countries when complementary policies are in place. In the cases of India (Topalova 2005) and Colombia (Goldberg and Pavcnik 2005), the evidence points to the importance of policies that ensure labor mobility and, more generally, facilitate a smoother adjustment for poorer households. For Zambia, Balat and Porto (2007) conclude that poor farm-ers benefit from an increased exposure to international markets only when they also have access to credit, technical knowledge, and other complementary policies. Similarly, Cadot, Dutoit, and Olarreaga (2009) suggest that supply responses to trade-related changes in prices are more likely for rural producers when accompanied by appropriate complemen-tary factors such as access to inputs, information, credit, productive assets and capital, education, and quality land. In the context of developing countries, therefore, the evidence is that the opening of the economy to international trade normally entails access to higher prices for local exporters and potential exporters. However, the extent to which local firms are able to benefit from trade openness is closely related to struc-tural features of the economy that can be influenced by policy—the extent of market competition, for example, or logistical efficiency.

Third, although in principle the overall impact of trade liberalization on the environment is likely to be country specific and could be either positive or negative, even the possibility of trade-related environmental degradation calls for policy attention. This impact may be due to one or a combination of factors. Trade leads to an overall expansion in output and, therefore, to an increase in emissions—also known as the scale effect. Trade liberalization affects resource allocation and production structure by changing the relative prices of goods, leading to either an increase or a decrease in the relative share of output of pollution-intensive sectors—known as a composition effect. Finally, changes in production technolo-gies (including pollution intensity per unit of output) could also affect overall emissions—typically referred to as the technique effect. While trade facilitates the access to and adoption of more efficient (and cleaner) technologies of production, an increase in competition could trigger a race to the bottom on environmental standards, especially in the short run. Therefore, trade promotion needs to be accompanied by policy attention to environmental regulation and enforcement.

This book has been prepared with the main purpose of exploring how the positive impact of trade can be augmented further and how the potential negative effects can be mitigated or offset. It complements and builds on Jaramillo and Lederman (2005), who analyze the challenges of CAFTA and its potential benefits. In our view, the study's timing is highly appropriate given the new agreement with the European Union, yet to be ratified, and the relatively short implementation of DR-CAFTA.[2]

The rest of this chapter reviews the main findings and recommendations of the 12 background papers presented in this volume, which analyze the extent to which (a) trade liberalization and promotion will result in more trade; (b) higher trade flows will result in faster growth; and (c) trade-induced growth can be expected to be inclusive and sustainable.

What Is the Expected Impact on Trade Volumes from Central America's Efforts to Liberalize and Promote Trade?

FTAs—and more generally, trade liberalization—are a means to expand trade. However, one of the findings of this study is that, unless Central America removes existing structural bottlenecks, this expansion will be modest.

The work of Molina, Bussolo, and Iacovone in chapter 2 examines the export behavior of Dominican Republic exporters following implementation of the DR-CAFTA in 2007 using a firm-level data set for the 2002–09 period. The study examines the impact on exports of tariff reductions through (a) the number of new exporters that entered the market, (b) the number of existing exporters that added a new product-market relationship to their export mix, and (c) the probability that an exporter would exit a given market.

The evidence suggests that tariff reductions had a positive but very small effect on the number of new exporters as well as on the behavior of incumbents. This finding is interpreted as signifying that other trade barriers such as standards, phytosanitary requirements, credit constraints, and transport costs are constraining exporters from taking full advantage of the agreement. The Dominican Association of Exporters has identified three major constraints that undermine the ability of Dominican exporters to compete in export markets. These are high electricity costs, high transport costs, as well as difficult credit access conditions. The removal of bottlenecks affecting firm competitiveness would be a necessary policy complement to trade liberalization.

The relationship between export survival and tariff reductions is also positive, but modest. Survival among Dominican exporters is very low, with six out of 10 exporters exiting the export market after one year. Molina, Bussolo, and Iacovone use their model to test whether tariff cuts help exporters to consolidate their position in a market and diminish their probability of exiting. They find that tariff cuts do improve survival rates, but only marginally. Other important results concern the probability of survival for firms located in export-processing zones (EPZs). In general, these firms seem to perform better than their peers in the national territory. The probability of exiting the market after one year is 9 to 18 percent lower for EPZ exporters than for exporters located in the national territory. However, this may be due to self-selection—that is, the fact that better firms choose to locate in EPZs—rather than to the effectiveness of the favorable fiscal regime of EPZs.

Trade liberalization and the associated tariff reductions are therefore generating a positive payoff in terms of additional trade flows in Central America. However, other factors are limiting the potential impact of trade liberalization on the expansion of trade flows. An important corollary is that these factors should be the focus of policy attention.

One reason often used to justify trade policy is that exporters are more productive than nonexporters. For example, table 1.1 reports the estimated total factor productivity (TFP) premiums of exporters (that is, the difference in the productivity level enjoyed by an exporter over a nonexporter) for several Latin American countries. As the table indicates, all estimated premiums are positive. For the South American countries and Mexico, the average premiums are on the order of 39 percent. Although lower for Central America, suggesting scope for improvement in incumbent exporters, the estimated premium is still significant at about 13 percent. This, however, is just a correlation and tells us little about the direction of causality. In fact, the interesting question is whether exporters become good firms or whether instead good firms become exporters. This issue is discussed by Brambilla, Castro, and Porto in chapter 3.

Under the first hypothesis (exporters become good firms), exporting improves productivity. The most common explanation, known as "learning by exporting," is that exporters acquire information from foreign

Table 1.1   TFP Premiums of Exporters

Region and country	Premium
Latin America and the Caribbean	0.39
Argentina	0.60
Brazil	0.35
Chile	0.48
Colombia	0.30
Ecuador	0.09
Mexico	0.00
Peru	0.52
Uruguay	0.68
Central America	0.13
Costa Rica	0.01
El Salvador	0.36
Guatemala	0.15
Honduras	0.22
Nicaragua	0.02
Panama	0.02

Source: Casacuberta and others 2007.

customers on how to improve the product design, the manufacturing process, or the quality of the good.[3] Foreign demand also allows domestic firms—particularly in small countries—to take advantage of unexploited economies of scale. Under the second hypothesis (that is, good firms become exporters), the best firms self-select into export markets. One rationale for this self-selection is that important entry barriers exist in export markets because of the higher costs associated with selling in foreign markets (transport, but also distribution, marketing, and even production costs when firms need to adapt their product to foreign standards). Thus only the more productive firms can enter foreign markets, and the observed differences between exporters and nonexporters can then be explained by preexisting differences.

These two hypotheses are not mutually exclusive and are likely to be relevant to a different extent, creating a virtuous circle. But depending on which is the most important force, the policy implications can be very different. On the one hand, export promotion activities such as those already discussed are often justified on the basis of the learning-by-exporting explanation. On the other hand, the self-selection explanation would suggest that policy makers should focus on the internal determinants of productivity growth. The existing literature offers no clear-cut answer regarding the relative strength of the self-selection hypothesis versus the learning-by-exporting hypothesis. Moreover, by nature, this literature is country specific, and, depending on the country examined, studies seem to reach different conclusions.

As discussed by Brambilla, Castro, and Porto in chapter 3, the work of Casacuberta and others (2007) surveys 54 studies (covering 70 countries) that look at the productivity premium associated with export activity, finding that the main reason behind the positive correlation of exports and productivity is self-selection: good firms become exporters, suggesting that penetrating foreign markets may require higher productivity. Casacuberta and others (2007) also find something relevant to the Central American region, namely that exporting is more likely to create productivity premiums in small countries, perhaps because of an economies-of-scale rationale for productivity premiums. Once again, the message that emerges from chapter 3 is that FTAs are potentially beneficial for the Central American countries, but they need to be complemented with actions aimed at improving firm productivity (such as an enabling business environment).

What Is the Expected Impact on Growth from an Increase in Central America's Trade?

Given that trade has a positive, though modest, impact on growth, how can this impact be enhanced? The empirical literature on trade and growth has typically argued that growth is positively correlated with higher trade volumes, even after accounting for a variety of growth determinants. Edwards (1992), Dollar (1992), Ben-David (1993), Sachs and Warner (1995), Ades and Glaeser (1999), Frankel and Romer (1999), and Alesina, Spolaore, and Wacziarg (2000) are examples of this sort. However, a recent paper by Chang, Kaltani, and Loayza (2009) finds that, although trade stimulates growth, this effect appears to be dependent on the reforms undertaken in the economy. The authors specifically find that interactions among trade and structural factors such as human capital, financial depth, infrastructure, and economic regulations are statistically and economically significant and robust to changes in specification, econometric method, and openness measure.[4]

Calderón and Poggio further explore these issues in chapter 4 with a focus on Central America. These authors rely on an empirical growth model that is estimated using a sample of 136 countries over the period 1960–2010. Beyond allowing for an estimate of the impact of trade flows on the growth of Central American countries, the model also allows the estimation of interactions between trade and other key structural factors. In practice, this is equivalent to an assessment of how the growth impact of trade changes when the policy environment changes—or, in other words, when countries make progress on what could be termed the "complementary agenda." What are the main findings of chapter 4? As in the discussion in the previous section, Calderón and Poggio find that increases in Central American trade flows are associated with faster growth. Yet the estimates are quite modest. For example, they estimate that a 30 percent increase in the volume of regional international trade in Central America could result, on average, in a 0.16 percentage point increase in the annual growth rate of the region—hardly a dramatic increase. However, when Calderón and Poggio explore the impact on growth of a trade expansion that is accompanied by progress in, for example, improving infrastructure or raising educational attainment to the level of the benchmark countries, the model predicts that growth projections could be twice as large.

What Is the Complementary Agenda for Promoting Trade?

In this section, we review the findings presented in this book regarding the need to pay attention to key areas in the complementary agenda. These include infrastructure (differentiating between energy and logistics and transportation), human capital, access to finance, competition policy, and enforcement of intellectual property rights.

Infrastructure

Since the need to improve infrastructure may be too broad to implement in practice, chapters 5 to 7 dig deeper into three main areas: energy and logistics and transport-related infrastructure.

Energy. Energy is a key input for production; as such, high energy prices put firms at a competitive disadvantage. The issue is particularly relevant in Central America, where energy prices tend to be high by regional standards. In chapter 5, Cayo explores what Central American countries can do to address this problem and argues that several structural problems need to be overcome in regional energy markets. These include (a) a tight balance between power generation and demand, which adversely affects the reliability of supply and its quality; (b) significant exposure to oil price volatility and shocks due to excessive dependence on oil imports, which have increased with the growing reliance on thermal power stations; (c) significant inefficiencies in the institutional and regulatory framework of several countries, which affect the financial sustainability of power utilities and their operations; and (d) relatively low levels of access in certain countries, affecting rural areas in particular.

Facilitation of the energy trade—and there are several integration initiatives, particularly in electricity—is perceived in Central America as being potentially effective for achieving cost competitiveness. International exchange of electricity could bring three major advantages: (a) lower operating costs through the use of the most economic energy resources, particularly through coordinated management of hydropower and thermal systems, (b) the possibility of balancing generation with current needs and accounting for seasonal variations through exporting or importing and pooling of reserve capacity, thereby improving efficiency and avoiding the extra cost of emergency power contracts, and (c) better risk management once the market is no longer constrained by the size of individual domestic economies, thereby improving investment in the sector and supporting lower prices. The Central American Electrical Interconnection System project—without doubt the most ambitious integration initiative so far—physically links the six Central American countries (including Panama).

However, for the intraregional power trade to increase significantly, there are four preconditions: political will, regional institutional capacity, harmonized regulatory frameworks, and investment in generation and transmission capacity.

On the whole, the potential for improvement in energy collaboration in Central America is clear, as are the prospective benefits in terms of energy cost competitiveness. The main message is that strengthening institutionality and regulation are as important as attracting more investment, and none of these actions is possible without significant political will and consensus. Strengthening domestic markets is part of the complementary agenda required to generate a strong, integrated power system.

Logistics and Transport. Global competition has intensified the need for efficiency in transport and logistics systems, from the point of manufacture to delivery to the customer. Studies on the share of logistics costs in the final price of delivered goods reveal that these costs represent a greater barrier to trade than import tariffs, especially in the light of free trade agreements such as the DR-CAFTA. In fact, the World Bank has estimated that on average, ad valorem tariffs for food imports have decreased in the Latin America and Caribbean region from 2005 to 2008 and currently range from 3 to 12 percent of product value. Transport and logistics costs, in contrast, measured in this case by the international maritime and road haulage components alone, can total about 20 percent of the free-on-board value of goods.

These issues are explored by Fernández, Flórez Gómez, Estrázulas de Souza, and Vega in chapter 6, where the authors describe the results of an analysis of eight supply chains that follow the entire distribution process to shed light on the share of logistics in total costs for a few products in Central America. This analysis was undertaken for Costa Rica's exports of tomatoes to Nicaragua by a big and a small exporter and U.S. exports of rice, wheat, and corn to Nicaragua and Honduras. Trade in tomatoes presents an opportunity to study the difficulties in distributing perishable goods that require refrigeration. Moreover, by differentiating between a large and a small firm, one can observe whether small firms are particularly affected by logistics costs. Rice, wheat, and corn dominate the Central American food basket and are imported into Nicaragua and Honduras largely from the United States.

The analyses in chapter 6 show that overall high domestic transportation costs, along with bottlenecks at land border crossings, present the biggest hurdle to intraregional trade, such as between Costa Rica and Nicaragua, and to extraregional imports, such as grain shipments from the United States. The surveyed Central American exporters point to the lack of good-quality paved secondary roads, especially for linking farms with cities, which impedes intraregional commerce notwithstanding the relatively good condition of the major transit arteries. The poor road quality, in turn, causes direct losses from delays in shipments and breakage of 8 to 12 percent of the sales value of exported goods and is seen by a large share of local firms as presenting a severe obstacle to growth. Additionally, the costs related to the reception of the grains at the port of entry, including those stemming from phytosanitary and sanitary revisions, are important in some cases and are a potential source of cost saving through trade facilitation.

On the whole, estimates of the logistics costs for the eight value chains in chapter 6 would range from 17 percent for a big Costa Rican tomato exporter to Nicaragua to 48 percent for yellow corn imports to Nicaragua, with typical logistics costs in the range of 30 percent or more for the other value chains (see figure 1.1). This compares negatively with Latin America, where logistics costs are estimated at about 25 percent, and with the Organisation for Economic Co-operation and Development

Figure 1.1 Supply Chain Diagram of the Cost Contributions to the Average Price of Yellow Corn Used for Animal Feed in Nicaragua

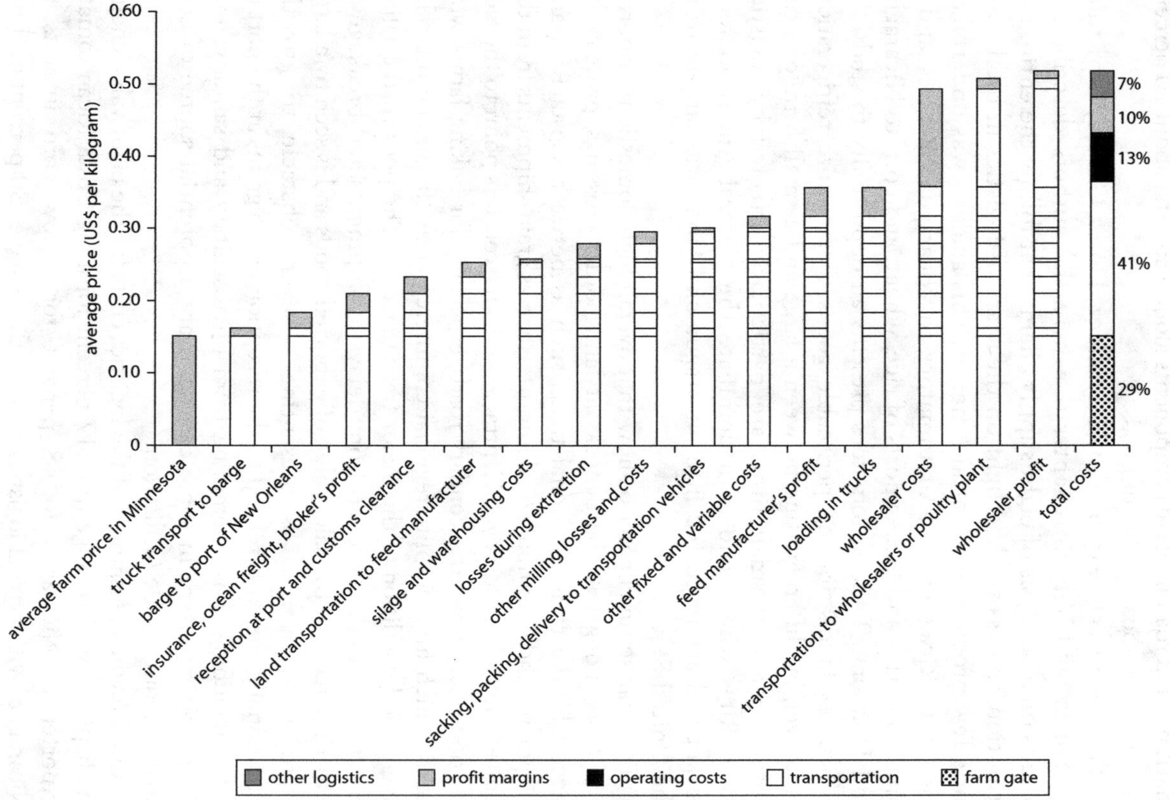
0.60
0.50
0.40
0.30
0.20
0.10
0
average price (US$ per kilogram)
7%
10%
13%
41%
29%
average farm price in Minnesota
truck transport to barge
barge to port of New Orleans
insurance, ocean freight, broker's profit
reception at port and customs clearance
land transportation to feed manufacturer
silage and warehousing costs
losses during extraction
other milling losses and costs
sacking, packing, delivery to transportation vehicles
other fixed and variable costs
feed manufacturer's profit
loading in trucks
wholesaler costs
transportation to wholesalers or poultry plant
wholesaler profit
total costs
other logistics
profit margins
operating costs
transportation
farm gate

Source: Authors' calculations.

Note: The lines on each bar refer to the addition to costs from each category listed on the horizontal axis.

(OECD), where logistics costs appear to be below 10 percent. It also suggests that the improvement of regional competitiveness may require a strong emphasis on policy interventions that target the distribution of goods after they leave the firm and that factor productivity at the firm level may offer just a very partial picture of the competitiveness problematic in the region.

Against this background, Barbero argues in chapter 7 that a strategy to address logistics costs in Central America should consider a combination of elements including ports, transport services, freight security, and customs modernization. More specifically, the most serious deficiencies are found in the quality and connectivity of roads and ports, domestic and regional surface transportation (mainly trucking), and security of surface freight. Border management and border-crossing facilities also reveal gaps, as do airports, international transport services (air and maritime), carriers' ability to manage their supply chain efficiently, and logistics operators and intermediaries.

Human Capital

Firm productivity and exports are closely related, as discussed earlier in this chapter. A related question is how trade affects returns to individual skill endowments. This is a critical question for Central America since one potential channel through which trade liberalization can lead to important changes in the structure of an economy is by affecting factor rewards. For example, trade can result in shifts in production technology that favor goods with a higher component of skilled labor over unskilled labor. This is an important issue from a policy perspective because to the extent that trade liberalization is skilled biased—that is, favors skilled labor—policy makers may need to think of investing in people as a critical complement to trade liberalization.

Brambilla, Castro, and Porto also explore in chapter 3 whether the implementation of CAFTA has resulted in any change in the skill premium (that is, the ratio of skilled to unskilled wages) so far. They find empirical evidence consistent with an increase in the skill premium in Central America in recent years, which is not observed in other Latin American non-CAFTA countries. Chapter 3 also takes the additional step of exploring whether the estimated increase in the skill premium is driven by within-sector changes or between-sector compositional shifts in the skilled labor force, concluding that the former factor dominates. The authors also find that the export share of GDP seems to affect the skill premium positively and that both per capita GDP and skill composition are significant determinants of the industry-skill premiums: richer countries seem to have greater disparities between skilled and unskilled wages, and, as expected, countries with a greater fraction (supply) of skilled workers pay smaller skill premiums.

On the whole, the results call for investment in human capital if the region is to be in a better position to exploit the income-generating opportunities created by trade. This message is fully aligned with that of Calderón and Poggio in chapter 4 regarding the role of education as a necessary complement to using trade to boost growth in Central America. Additionally, although not uniform across the six countries of Central America or across all years, there is evidence of high and sometimes rising returns to higher education in the subregion. At the same time, the coverage of tertiary education systems in Central America has increased, albeit starting from a comparatively low base, leading to an increasing supply of skilled labor. A rise in the skill premium in the presence of an increase in the supply of skilled workers is seen as evidence of skill-biased technical change. An increase in the supply of higher education graduates seems to be called for, especially as many middle-income Central American countries have lower educational attainment than other middle-income comparator countries.

However, there are other factors to consider. Increasing returns may reflect the fact that there is a shortage of higher education graduates of good quality; hence, while coverage has expanded, not all higher education graduates have the necessary skills and knowledge. Much of the recent expansion of tertiary education in Central America has been through the private sector, and in the absence of rigorous accreditation standards the quality of courses is known to be variable. The majority of courses in the public universities are also not accredited. A second issue is that there can be imbalances in demand for and supply of specific disciplines, such as technology and engineering. Enrollments in Central American universities are highly skewed toward disciplines such as law, literature, and the arts, with enrollment in applied science, engineering, and technology courses representing only a small fraction of the total. The content, teaching methodology, and assessment system in these courses are not aligned with international standards, leading to low quality. Reorganizing and modernizing higher education is thus a priority even if expanding coverage is necessary. More detailed follow-up of graduates of different disciplines and their labor market performance is also required to better understand the demand for skills.

Access to Finance

Access to credit remains limited in Central America, and this is a critical issue, as there is now a growing literature that emphasizes the role of the financial sector in enhancing the positive impacts of trade. Love, Molina Millán, and Shankar explore in chapter 8 the relationship between productivity, access to finance, and exports, noting the growing evidence of the comparative advantage that financial development provides to exporters or firms entering foreign markets. For example, trade finance is found to be a critical part of the institutions that countries need if they are to take full advantage of trade-related opportunities. The work of Rajan and Zingales (1998), Demirgüç-Kunt and Maksimovic (1998), and Beck, Demirgüç-Kunt, and Levine (2001) shows that a well-developed financial sector helps countries to secure access to external finance for investment projects and puts them in a better position to execute new ideas and therefore innovate. More recently, Beck, Demirgüç-Kunt, and Levine (2003) and Svaleryd and Vlachos (2005) find a positive relationship between financial sector development and the specialization pattern of international trade and comparative advantage.

The main findings of Love, Molina Millán, and Shankar are that in the Central American context (a) access to credit and productivity are positively associated and (b) productivity and exports are also positively associated. Although it must be admitted that due to data limitations, chapter 8 does not allow interpretation of these correlations as signifying unidirectional causality from financial access to firm productivity, the analysis is suggestive of a close relationship between these variables. Moreover, there is now considerable empirical evidence justifying a focus on the financial sector, especially given that access to credit remains limited in Central America. For example, the composite indicator developed by Beck, Demirgüç-Kunt, and Martínez Peria (2007), which measures the percentage of the adult population with access to an account with a financial intermediary, indicates that the entire Central American region, especially Nicaragua, is well below the median of Latin America, suggesting that measures to improve financial access, especially of smaller firms, could facilitate trade.

From a policy perspective, the work by Love (2009) gives two clear ideas of how to expand access levels. One is to make progress on the judicial front. Love presents empirical evidence indicating that the quality of courts is positively correlated with a number of measures of access (having a checking account, using credit, and so forth) and concludes that court reform should promote wider use of the courts for resolving disputes and improve outcomes in terms of the percentage of cases that result in court judgments.

Second, even though financial development cannot be equated with financial access, Love presents evidence indicating that higher levels of financial development are associated with longer loan maturity, larger size of loans relative to sales, and more likely use of land and buildings as collateral and that this trend appears to be driven by the access of small and median firms. In other words, measures aimed at modernizing the financial sector can not only have a positive impact on overall access, but also be biased toward small and medium firms (which, as noted, have less access than larger firms).

Competition Policy

Trade allows improved resource allocation, enabled by the transmission of price signals to producers and consumers, which sets into motion a chain of adjustments—in production and consumption baskets and therefore in labor markets. As noted earlier, the labor market adjustments allow workers to realize the benefits of a skill premium, provided the institutional environment permits the necessary reorientation in human capital formation. To understand the potential supply and demand responses, De Franco and Arias estimate in chapter 9 the degree of transmission of international prices to domestic prices of key agricultural commodities in Nicaragua and Honduras, analyzing the extent to which a change in the international price of a given food product affects the domestic price of that same good, at the level of the consumer and producer as well as in different regions within each country. De Franco and Arias examine markets for key agricultural commodities (sugar, coffee, meat, beans, maize, rice, and vegetable oil) in Nicaragua and Honduras. The goods in the analysis represent a mix of imported and exported products and are highly traded in the subregion.

The main finding is that price transmission is imperfect and has been persistently weak, with little improvement over time. The weakness of price signals suggests that welfare impacts of trade liberalization may not be fully realized and that the failure of price signals to transmit can lead to sluggish growth and reduce the gains to consumers, who would normally benefit from the competition offered by cheaper imports. Imperfect price transmission can be explained by several factors, but the two most plausible explanations for Central America are (a) the existence of noncompetitive market structures, where one agent has significant market power, or (b) the costs of price adjustments at some point within the supply chain. This would, in turn, suggest a need not only to improve logistics (in line with the discussion above), but also to introduce competition in relevant markets.

Enforcement of Property Rights

So far the discussion has centered on the benefits of trade. FTAs can also have a positive impact by encouraging foreign direct investment (FDI). FDI can not only enhance Central America's opportunities to secure financing for private sector development, but also be a key instrument to transfer technology to the region. Yet this will be unlikely unless firms perceive that their intellectual property rights (IPRs) are protected. IPRs have traditionally been regarded as a means to encourage research and development. However, they are increasingly seen as a means to encourage technology transfers through an expansion of FDI, particularly through licensing, which may have positive implications for knowledge spillover. De Ferranti and others (2003) report findings associating improved IPRs with higher FDI through licensing from the United States, for example.

How can Central America use its FTAs to attract FDI? The negotiated FTAs already devote significant attention to IPRs, but legal copyright protection can be meaningless unless investors perceive that enforcement is effective. In chapter 10, Park examines intellectual protection in CAFTA countries and finds that the Dominican Republic and El Salvador have the strongest protection in the region and are the only CAFTA members above the Latin America mean (admittedly a poor benchmark). Both countries rank well below Chile and the United States, for example. However, investor survey results published in the *Global Competitiveness Reports* suggest that enforcement is perceived as being weak in El Salvador. Estimates by the Business Software Alliance suggest that piracy rates in 2008 ranged from 59 percent in Costa Rica to 74 percent in Honduras and about 80 percent in all the remaining DR-CAFTA members, implying that legal protection in the Dominican Republic and El Salvador is virtually meaningless in the software market segment. A useful benchmark is the United States, where piracy rates are 20 percent. The study also finds that the substantive IPR reforms envisaged under the DR-CAFTA are likely on balance to encourage investment and technology transfer in the longer run, but only if institutions evolve so that they are strong enough to enforce the new regulations.

What Are the Expected Welfare Effects of Trade Liberalization and Promotion in Central America?

As already discussed, exporters pay higher wages (see table 1.2), and therefore an expansion of trade should be welcomed from a welfare perspective. However, not everybody benefits equally from these higher wages. The existing evidence highlights that these higher wages are associated with a skill premium (that is, exporters hire a more skilled labor force), suggesting that the beneficiaries of higher wages are those with higher levels of human capital (who are not likely to be at the bottom of the income distribution to start with). This, however, should not be understood as implying that trade is likely to create jobs only in sectors where the poor are disproportionately underrepresented. In the Central American context, changes in wages due to tariff cuts appear to lead to welfare gains that are distributionally progressive in Guatemala and Honduras. In contrast, Costa Rica, El Salvador, and Nicaragua seem to generate regressive welfare effects, suggesting adverse impacts for poorer unskilled and rural workers. Higher trade may therefore result in higher wages but also may cause greater inequality in countries that already have inequitable income distributions. These findings reinforce the need to increase the levels of human capital, but in this case stressing the need

Table 1.2   Wage Premiums of Exporters

Region and country	Premium
Latin America and the Caribbean	0.20
Argentina	0.09
Brazil	0.27
Chile	0.26
Colombia	0.27
Ecuador	0.02
Mexico	0.12
Paraguay	0.05
Peru	0.30
Uruguay	0.46
Central America	0.27
Costa Rica	0.54
El Salvador	0.30
Guatemala	0.35
Honduras	0.21
Nicaragua	−0.02
Panama	0.26

Source: Casacuberta and others 2007.

to expand access to opportunities for all rather than just to increase average skills.

The welfare impact of lower prices caused by tariff cuts varies depending on whether we consider net producers or net consumers. This is therefore more an empirical than a theoretical question. Estimates of the welfare impact of tariff cuts in Central America indicate that for all countries (with the exception of Nicaragua), the resulting price changes lead to positive welfare gains. These welfare gains are either distributionally neutral or slightly progressive in the sense that they are marginally larger for households at the bottom than at the top of the income distribution. The welfare impact of wage changes shows considerably more variation across the subregion: it is progressive in the Dominican Republic, Guatemala, and Honduras and regressive elsewhere; in fact, for Costa Rica and Nicaragua, these effects are actually negative. Since the skill content of net exports is a key determinant of these changes, the bottom line for policy makers is that investing in people and in flexible labor markets is a priority.

Trade may also affect male and female workers differently. Due to social norms and discrimination outside as well as inside the household, women and men differ not only in terms of education, but also in terms of access to labor markets, remuneration, sectoral employment, control over resources, and roles within the household. While price changes are the main mechanism by which trade affects gender outcomes, many factors mediate this impact—resource endowments, labor market institutions, systems of property rights, access to markets and information, and other socioeconomic characteristics. This implies that the impact of trade on gender gaps can be highly heterogeneous across countries. Because of these gender differentials, which tend to be higher in poorer households, men and women may not be uniformly able to take advantage of the opportunities created by trade liberalization.

These issues are explored by Bussolo, Freije, Djiofack, and Rodríguez in chapter 11 for Central America. They find two counterbalancing forces in the countries under analysis. On the one hand, the impact of trade on returns to employment in the tradable sector implies that lower tariffs in the United States (that is, increased market access and potentially increased export orientation) would reduce the gender wage gap. On the other hand, a reduction of own tariffs imposed on exports to the United States would increase the gender wage gap for skilled workers in all sectors and for skilled and unskilled workers in tradable sectors. Reducing own tariffs induces wage increases for skilled and unskilled workers in the tradable sector. But it does so more among males than females, particularly among the skilled, hence increasing the gender wage gap. Besides, exposure to external competition (import shares from the United States) can also cause a larger relative decline in male wages in the sector. An increase of 1 percentage point in the share of imports within sector GDP also brings about a fall in the gender wage gap of about 1 percentage point. In the end, the final impact of trade openness is an empirical matter and one that will likely be country specific.

The simulations show very different patterns depending on the country. Trade would narrow the gender wage gap in Costa Rica and widen it in the Dominican Republic. For example, trade would have reduced the gender wage gap by 1.1 and 4.6 percentage points in urban and rural areas, respectively, in Costa Rica. This reduction would have been through a decline of about 3 percentage points in the gender wage gap between unskilled workers in urban areas and even larger reductions in the gap for rural workers. This simulation does not match the actual trend of increasing wage-gender gaps in Costa Rica in recent years but highlights that trade can have a beneficial impact in the future as trade liberalization and promotion continue. Trade expansion, however, would have slowed the decline in the gender wage gap actually observed in El Salvador, Guatemala, and Honduras in recent years (that is, it would have contributed ceteris paribus to a higher gender wage gap). In Nicaragua, as in Costa Rica, trade is potentially beneficial in this context.

On the whole, these differential impacts would call for policies that enhance female participation in the tradable sector, while promoting the acquisition of skills through schooling and training. In addition, the effective implementation of institutional measures that prevent discrimination in the workplace is a priority—as industries become profitable, the best jobs should not be male biased. Also, to the extent that some of these effects are associated with the penetration of imports and hence may be associated with job losses or other competitive pressures on the labor market of workers in the tradable sector, remedial policies, which could include mechanisms to facilitate reallocation from declining sectors unable to face external competition and investment in human capital— education, training, and retraining of the labor force, particularly in areas associated with tradables—are clearly necessary.

One additional finding of chapter 11 is the puzzling absence of a statistically significant association between trade liberalization and job reallocation, for both males and females. This is both a surprise and a cause for concern, given that the benefits of trade to individual workers depend to a large extent on their ability to exploit new opportunities. Excessive informality in the labor market and lack of employment creation in trade-related activities are perhaps signs of a labor market that is not responding to the incentives of trade. In the countries of the region, this lack of responsiveness may be associated with rigidities in labor markets, leading to lack of mobility from one activity to another, lack of retraining opportunities, and inability to reallocate labor services.

In addition to the welfare effects that emerge from the creation and destruction of jobs, tariff reductions can also have welfare implications by leading to changes in prices that affect both producers and consumers. Thus a natural question that emerges in this context is related to the likely overall welfare impact in the Central American context of price and wage effects associated with FTAs. Bussolo, Freije, Djiofack, and Rodríguez address this question in chapter 12 by simulating the impact of trade openness on household welfare—through both consumption prices and labor markets for the Central American countries.

In principle, the consumption price–related welfare gain is positive for all countries (except Nicaragua, where prices increased after DR-CAFTA), suggesting that all population groups benefit from falling prices in consumer goods due to trade openness. The net gain varies between 2 and 6 percent. These gains, however, can be easily lost if macroeconomic mismanagement leads to inflation and depreciation of the exchange rate, all of which nullifies the gains of lower prices through lower tariffs. This part of the analysis assumes perfect pass-through, which, as discussed in chapter 9, does not hold, at least for Nicaragua and Honduras.

The welfare impact of wage changes shows considerably more variation across the subregion. These welfare gains are progressive in the Dominican Republic, Guatemala, and Honduras and are the result of the structure of exports and the kind of demand for labor that arises from higher trade given this structure. In these countries, exports favor unskilled workers, who tend to be members of poorer households, and are therefore distributionally progressive. The other three countries (Costa Rica, El Salvador, and Nicaragua) demonstrate regressive changes in labor income; in fact, for Costa Rica and Nicaragua, these effects are actually negative. Again this is a result of the trade shock that, in these cases, produces adverse effects for poorer unskilled and rural workers. In the case of El Salvador, unskilled labor earnings rise, but trade favors skilled and urban workers. The percentage net gain by the average household varies by country as well: more than 15 percent for the Dominican

Republic, 10 percent for Guatemala, and more than 13 percent for Honduras compared to 5 percent for El Salvador, a marginal loss of about 0.5 percent for Costa Rica, and a larger loss of 2.4 percent for Nicaragua. These findings support the message emphasized in this volume that investing in people and promoting labor mobility through training and flexible market policies can help households to realize potential gains from trade.

A final issue that needs particular attention in this context is the potential impact of trade liberalization and promotion on the environment. The seminal work of Grossman and Krueger (1993) ignited the debate on the impact of international trade on the environment. The existing empirical studies on the relationship between trade and the environment have found varying results. For example, Grossman and Krueger (1993), who examine the environmental impacts of NAFTA, find no evidence that a comparative advantage was being created by lax environmental regulations in Mexico. This result is confirmed by Stern (2005), who finds only small pollution effects of NAFTA on Mexico shortly after the agreement, followed by an improvement in environmental quality. In a related work, Gamper-Rabindran and Jha (2004) analyze the empirical relationship between trade liberalization and the environment in the Indian context. Their findings indicate that exports and FDI grew in the more polluting sectors relative to the less polluting sectors between the periods before and after liberalization. Mani and Jha (2006) find similar results for Vietnam and Turkey, respectively. This evidence provides some support for concerns raised about the environmental impact of trade liberalization.

Mani and Cunha review these issues in chapter 13, noticing that there is significant heterogeneity in the environmental regulatory regimes of the region (see table 1.3). In fact, while the United States and Costa Rica appear to be above the international average, Guatemala and Honduras are at the bottom of the international classifications. These differences could potentially favor the rise of pollution havens within the region.

In this regard, the analysis by Mani and Cunha assesses the pollution effects related to implementation of the DR-CAFTA along different dimensions or channels. One of these channels is the *scale effect* associated with trade-related acceleration of growth causing an expansion in production. The idea is that scaling up (holding constant the mix of goods produced and production techniques) would lead to an increase in pollution emissions. A second channel is the *composition effect* that may result from the impact that changes in relative prices may have on the structure of

Table 1.3   Environmental Regulatory Regime Index

Rank[a]	Country	Index
1	Finland	2.303
14	United States	1.184
36	Costa Rica	−0.078
60	Dominican Republic	−1.014
62	Nicaragua	−1.164
63	El Salvador	−1.215
66	Honduras	−1.300
69	Guatemala	−1.532

Source: Esty and Porter 2005.
a. Out of 71 countries.

production. This effect can either increase or decrease relative output in pollution-intensive sectors, depending on the changes in relative prices. Finally, changes in production technologies (including pollution intensity by unit of output) tend to follow trade liberalization. This *technique effect* can result from different forces: while trade facilitates access to and adoption of more efficient (and cleaner) technologies of production, stronger competition can trigger a race to the bottom of environmental standards, favoring the adoption of cheaper, dirtier technology in the short run. Nevertheless, as income grows, the demand for environmental quality tends to increase. By adopting both tighter environmental policies and more advanced, cleaner technologies, countries can afford to reduce emissions after they attain a certain level of income.

By comparing average annual emissions of different types of pollutants before and after implementation of the agreement, chapter 13 concludes that the scale effect outweighs the composition and technique effects, with most of the variation in pollution resulting from a scaling up in production. Composition effects appear to be small and vary across member countries with similar regulatory frameworks, mainly since implementation varies considerably. A policy implication is that all countries could benefit from closing the gaps in their environmental regulatory framework in terms of actual regulations, capacity, and monitoring. Countries such as El Salvador, where there has been a relative expansion of more polluting industries, should go beyond the legal requirements of the environmental agenda of the DR-CAFTA, for example, and work on strengthening implementation in the short run. For poorer countries such as Nicaragua and Honduras, environmental regulation does not seem to play an important role in the current allocation of production. Nevertheless, as these economies grow, this situation will change. For this reason, these countries should start planning and implementing a medium-term environmental agenda that will mitigate risks down the road.

Notes

1. Throughout the book, references to the "region" or to Central America are used loosely to include Costa Rica, El Salvador, Guatemala, Honduras, Nicaragua, and Panama (not a DR-CAFTA signatory) and, in some cases, the Dominican Republic (not an Association Agreement signatory).

2. The agreement has been effective only for a year and half in Costa Rica and for two to three years in the remaining countries—years that have been complicated by the food and fuel crisis (2007–08) and the global financial crisis.

3. The expected effects from learning by exporting could occur either at the time of entry into exporting (a one-time effect) or every year after entry (a continuous effect).

4. The empirical growth literature offers some related examples of nonlinear specifications considering interaction effects. Borensztein and others (1998) and Alfaro, Chanda, and Kalemli-Ozcan (2006) find that the growth benefits from foreign direct investment are attained when the host country has sufficiently high levels of human capital and financial development, respectively.

References

Ades, A. F., and E. L. Glaeser. 1999. "Evidence on Growth, Increasing Returns, and the Extent of the Market." *Quarterly Journal of Economics* 114 (3): 1025–45.

Alesina, A., E. Spolaore, and R. Wacziarg. 2000. "Economic Integration and Political Disintegration." *American Economic Review* 90 (5): 1276–96.

Alfaro, L., A. Chanda, and S. Kalemli-Ozcan. 2006. "How Does Foreign Direct Investment Promote Economic Growth? Exploring the Effects of Financial Markets on Linkages." NBER Working Paper 12522, National Bureau of Economic Research, Cambridge, MA.

Balat, J., and G. Porto. 2007. "Globalization and Complementary Policies: Poverty Impacts in Rural Zambia." In *Globalization and Poverty*, ed. A. Harrison, 373–416 Chicago: University of Chicago Press.

Beck, T., A. Demirgüç-Kunt, and R. Levine. 2001. "Legal Theories of Financial Development." *Oxford Review of Economic Policy* 17 (4): 483–501.

———. 2003. "Law, Endowments, and Finance." *Journal of Financial Economics* 70 (2): 137–81.

Beck, T., A. Demirgüç-Kunt, and M. S. Martínez Peria. 2007. "Reaching Out: Access to and Use of Banking Services across Countries." *Journal of Financial Economics* 85 (1): 234–66.

Ben-David, D. 1993. "Equalizing Exchange: Trade Liberalization and Income Convergence." *Quarterly Journal of Economics* 108 (3): 653–79.

Borensztein, E., J. De Gregorio, and J. W. Lee. 1998. "How Does Foreign Direct Investment Affect Economic Growth?" *Journal of International Economics* 45 (1): 115–35.

Cadot, O., L. Dutoit, and M. Olarreaga. 2009. "Barriers to Exit from Subsistence Agriculture." World Bank, Washington, DC.

Casacuberta, C., N. Gandelman, M. Olarreaga, G. Porto, and E. Rubiano. 2007. "Exporter Premiums." In *The Latin American and Caribbean Regional Study on Microdeterminants of Growth*, ch. 7. Washington, DC: World Bank.

Chang, R., L. Kaltani, and N. Loayza. 2009. "Openness Can Be Good for Growth: The Role of Policy Complementarities." *Journal of International Economics* 90 (1): 33–49.

De Ferranti, D., G. Perry, I. Gill, L. Guasch, W. F. Maloney, C. Sánchez-Páramo, and N. Schady. 2003. Closing the Gap in Education and Technology, The World Bank, Washington, DC.

Demirgüç-Kunt, A., and V. Maksimovic. 1998. "Law, Finance, and Firm Growth." *Journal of Finance* 53 (6): 2107–137.

Dollar, D. 1992. "Outward-Oriented Developing Economies Really Do Grow More Rapidly: Evidence from 95 LDCs, 1976–85." *Economic Development and Cultural Change* 40 (3): 523–44.

Edwards, S. 1992. "Trade Orientation, Distortions, and Growth in Developing Countries." *Journal of Development Economics* 39 (1): 31–57.

Esty, D., and M. Porter. 2005. "National Environmental Performance: An Empirical Analysis of Policy Results and Determinants." *Environment and Development Economics* 10 (4): 391–434.

Frankel, J. A., and D. Romer. 1999. "Does Trade Cause Growth?" *American Economic Review* 89 (3): 379–99.

Gamper-Rabindran, S., and S. Jha. 2004. "Environmental Impact of India's Trade Liberalization." Working Paper, University of North Carolina at Chapel Hill, Department of Public Policy.

Goldberg, P. K., and N. Pavcnik. 2005. "The Effects of the Colombian Trade Liberalization on Urban Poverty." NBER Working Paper 11081, National Bureau of Economic Research, Cambridge, MA.

Grossman, G. M., and A. B. Krueger. 1993. "Environmental Impacts of a North American Free Trade Agreement." In *The Mexico–U.S. Free Trade Agreement*, ed. P. Garber, 13–56. Cambridge, MA: MIT Press.

Harrison, A., ed. 2007. *Globalization and Poverty*. Chicago, IL: University of Chicago Press.

Jaramillo, C. F., and D. Lederman. 2005. "Challenges of CAFTA." World Bank, Washington, DC.

Lederman, D., W. Maloney, and L. Servén. 2007. *Lessons from NAFTA for Latin America and the Caribbean*. Palo Alto, CA: Stanford University Press.

Love, I. 2009. "What are the Determinants of Financial Access in Latin America" Chapter 5 in Does the Investment Climate Matter?, The World Bank, Washington, DC.

Mani, M., and S. Jha. 2006. "Trade Liberalization and the Environment in Vietnam." Policy Research Working Paper 3879, World Bank, Washington, DC.

Rajan, R., and L. Zingales. 1998. "Financial Dependence and Growth." *American Economic Review* 88 (3): 559–86.

Sachs, J. D., and A. M. Warner. 1995. "Economic Reform and the Process of Global Integration." *Brookings Papers on Economic Activity* 1: 1–118.

Stern, D. I. 2005. "The Effect of NAFTA on Energy and Environmental Efficiency in Mexico." Working Paper in Economics 0511, Rensselaer Polytechnic Institute, Troy, NY.

Svaleryd, H., and J. Vlachos. 2005. "Financial Markets, the Pattern of Specialization, and Comparative Advantage: Evidence from OECD Countries." *European Economic Review* 49 (1): 113–44.

Topalova, P. 2005. "Trade Liberalization, Poverty, and Inequality: Evidence from Indian Districts." NBER Working Paper 11614, National Bureau of Economic Research, Cambridge, MA.

World Economic Forum. Various years. *Global Competitiveness Report*. Geneva: World Economic Forum.

CHAPTER 2

The DR-CAFTA and the Extensive Margin: A Firm-Level Analysis

Ana Cristina Molina, Maurizio Bussolo, and
Leonardo Iacovone

Regional trade agreements have spread rapidly around the world since the 1990s, and Latin America is no exception. Today all countries in the region are signatories of at least one regional trade agreement. This new economic environment has created new challenges and opportunities for exporters in the region. Yet despite its importance to policy makers, the dynamics of exporters following a regional trade agreement have been poorly documented. Previous studies have looked at the effects of such agreements on export flows and especially at the trade creation and diversion effects (for a theoretical and empirical review, see Freund and Ornelas 2009). These studies use product, sectoral, or country-level data and thus provide little insight as to the effects on exporters' activities and performance. Using a novel firm-level data set of trade transactions for the Dominican Republic covering the period 2002–09, we examine exporters' responses to the Dominican Republic–Central America Free Trade Agreement (DR-CAFTA). The agreement entered into force in 2007[1] and includes the United States—the Dominican Republic's main trade partner—Costa Rica, El Salvador, Guatemala, Honduras, and Nicaragua. We test whether DR-CAFTA has had a positive impact on the extensive margin—that is, whether it has increased exports through the entry of new exporters and the introduction of new product-market relationships. Finally, we analyze whether the agreement has improved exporters' survival in foreign markets.

The adjustments across the four margins (that is, firms, products, markets, and survival) are particularly important. First, exports generated by the entry of new firms and the introduction of new products or markets are a source not only of growth, but also of export diversification, both key elements of a country's development strategy. Second, exporters' survival in foreign markets is crucial for sustained export growth. Finally, it is essential to understand the effects of market access on exporters in order to design policies aiming to help exporters reap all the benefits from trade liberalization.

For our analysis, we follow the theoretical frameworks outlined in Melitz (2003) and Bernard, Redding, and Schott (2009). Melitz's influential paper describes firms' dynamics following trade liberalization. In his framework, firms differ in their productivity (that is, marginal costs) and have to pay a fixed cost to enter the export market, thus implying that only the most productive firms will export. One of the main implications of the model is that a reduction in trade costs (that is, tariffs) will lead to the entry of new exporters, as more firms will be able to afford to enter the export market. An indirect implication of the model is that lower tariffs will raise the profits of incumbent exporters, thus increasing their likelihood of staying in the market and decreasing their exit rates. Bernard, Redding, and Schott (2009) refine the Melitz model to account for firms with multiple products and destinations.[2] In their framework, a decrease in variable trade costs induces surviving exporters to start selling products that were not profitable before, thus increasing the number of goods exported by each firm.[3] We test these predictions in the case of the Dominican Republic exporters.

Using the export firm–level data set provided by the Dominican Republic Customs Agency for the period 2002–09, we estimate the effect of tariff reductions on the number of new exporters and on the number of incumbents that introduce a new product or enter a market within the CAFTA area.[4] In addition, we evaluate the effect of tariff cuts on the probability of exiting a market. We find that tariff preferences have a positive effect on the number of new exporters and on the number of exporters that introduce new product-market combinations. The effect is, however, very small, which would suggest that other factors may be preventing exporters from taking advantage of improved market access. Finally, we find that tariff cuts reduce the probability of exiting a CAFTA market. The effect is also very small.

This chapter contributes to the burgeoning literature on firm-level export dynamics. Most studies have focused on the relationship between export participation and firm productivity (that is, firm selection and learning by exporting). Some others have explored the effects of trade liberalization on the productivity of import-competing plants (see, for instance, Pavcnik 2002; Trefler 2004), but only very few have looked at the effects of tariffs on firms' export behavior. Bernard, Jensen, and Schott (2003) analyze the effect of tariff reductions on the participation of firms in export markets using survey data for U.S. manufacturing plants for three years over the period 1987–97. They find that firms in industries with declining export costs face lower probabilities of death and higher probabilities of becoming exporters. Baldwin and Gu (2004) study Canadian manufacturing firms and find that the tariff cuts following the U.S.-Canada Free Trade Agreement (of 1988) promoted the entry of Canadian plants into export markets. Their data, however, do not include a destination dimension. Their estimates are therefore "aggregate" estimates—that is, they are not market specific.

This chapter also relates to studies exploring the relationship between tariff cuts and the extensive margin. These studies use trade data at the product level and suggest that lower tariffs have a positive effect on the exports of new goods (see, among others, Kehoe and Ruhl 2009; Gómez and Volpe 2008; Debaere and Mostashari 2005). Given the level of disaggregation of the data, such studies can investigate the effect of tariffs only on the range of products, not on firms' dynamics.

The rest of the chapter is organized as follows. It begins by presenting the data and then describes the pattern of aggregate exports and the firm-level extensive margin of the Dominican Republic. It then looks at tariffs and exporters' behavior and presents the empirical exercise and the results. A final section concludes.

The Data

Our study employs a unique, very detailed export firm–level data set provided by the Dominican Republic Customs Agency. The data contain all transactions (that is, amount and quantity) by product at the Harmonized System (HS) 12-digit level and by destination for all exporters for the period 2002–09.[5] The sample includes 135,016 exporter-destination-product relationships. The universe of firms during this period consists of 8,706 firms, among which not all export in every year.[6] Table 2.1 reports the number of exporting firms, products, and markets for select years.

Table 2.1   Summary Statistics, Select Years, 2003–09

Indicator	2003	2005	2007	2009
Exports by firm (US$, millions)				
Mean	1.4	1.5	1.4	1.5
Standard deviation	9.4	9.9	9.0	9.8
Products by firm				
Mean	6.3	5.2	6.5	6.2
Standard deviation	10.7	8.9	13.1	13.1
Markets by firm				
Mean	2.1	2.1	2.1	2.2
Standard deviation	2.7	2.9	2.9	3.1
Number of firms	2,660	2,622	3,237	3,031
Number of products	2,035	2,049	2,937	2,812
Number of markets	133	131	147	147
Total exports (US$, millions)	3,742	3,969	4,474	4,563

Source: Authors' calculations based on data provided by the Dominican Republic Customs Agency.

The data show that the number of exporters, products, and markets increased until 2007, before declining in the next years (except for the number of markets). The number of exporters rose from 2,660 in 2003 to 3,237 in 2007, which is a 21.6 percent increase. In addition, the number of products rose 44.3 percent for the same period, from 2,035 in 2003 to 2,937 in 2007. The change in the number of both products and firms was more significant during 2005–07 than during 2003–05. As for the number of markets, it rose 10.5 percent between 2003 and 2007.

Each year about 60 percent of firms are multiproduct exporters (that is, they export more than one product). Half of them export to a single market, while the other half export to multiple markets.[7] For the remaining firms, about 37 percent export only one product to one destination and 3 percent export one product to multiple destinations. Almost all exports come from multiproduct firms. These findings are similar to those in Bernard, Redding, and Schott (2009) and show that exports are concentrated within multiproduct exporters.

Another important characteristic of our data set is that it distinguishes between exporters in export-processing zones (EPZs) and exporters in the national territory. This is an important feature, as it allows us to control for the firms' location in our empirical exercise. In terms of value, EPZ exporters are particularly important: their exports account for 74 percent (2009) to 84 percent (2002) of total exports. About 20 percent (545) of the total number of exporters operate in an EPZ each year.

Finally, we exclude from our analysis reexports, ferronickel exports,[8] occasional exporters, couriers, as well as firms whose partners are not identified. These exclusions reduce our sample by 18 percent to 110,702 trade relationships.

Export Trends

With the purpose of identifying any major change in export patterns following the DR-CAFTA, we briefly review in this section the evolution of exports from Dominican firms to the United States and the other CAFTA members (that is, El Salvador, Honduras, Guatemala, and Nicaragua).[9]

Figure 2.1 reports the exports from the Dominican Republic by destination from 2002 to 2009 (in millions of U.S. dollars). The United States is by far the largest partner of the Dominican Republic, with average exports amounting to US$2.6 billion each year. Other main destinations for the shipments of Dominican exporters are Puerto Rico (10.2 percent

Figure 2.1   Dominican Exports, by Destination, 2002–09

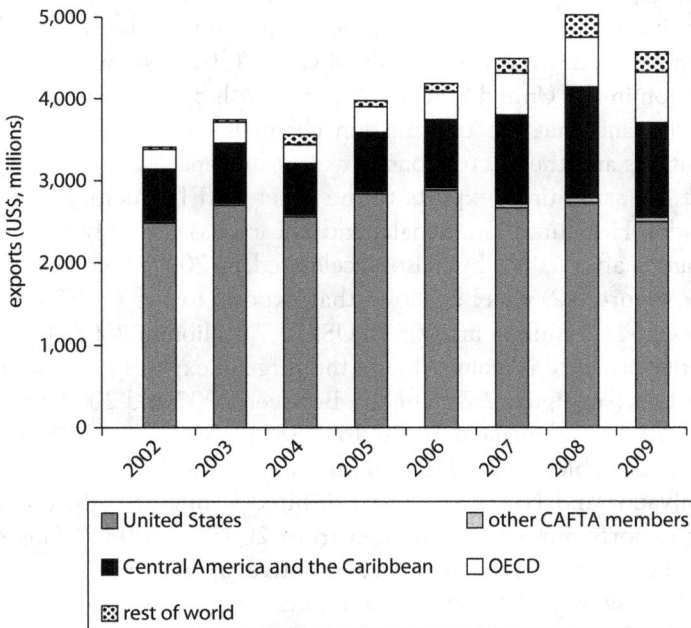

Source: Authors' calculations.

in 2008), Haiti (9.9 percent), Belgium (2.1 percent), Spain (2 percent), and the Netherlands (1.9 percent). Exports to the other CAFTA members account for only 1 percent of total exports from the Dominican Republic in 2008, and this share has been relatively stable since 2002.

Two main features of the Dominican trade with the United States can be highlighted. First, the share of exports to the United States has declined since 2002 as a result of market diversification and a slowdown in exports to this market. Between 2002 and 2008, exports to other countries in the Caribbean (for example, Haiti and Jamaica) as well as to other developed countries (for example, Spain and Belgium) expanded rapidly, growing some 150 percent, while exports to the United States expanded a modest 10 percent.

Second, exports to the United States are relatively volatile. They exhibit alternating periods of modest growth and decline. Following a decrease in 2004, exports picked up, before falling again in 2007 and in 2009. As a result, the years after the DR-CAFTA have been characterized by slow export growth. In 2009, the demand for Dominican exports fell across all regions (except for exports to the developed countries), and exports to the United States were almost at the same level as in 2002. However, this does not necessarily reflect the effectiveness of the agreement, but rather the difficult business conditions in the U.S. market during this period. In a recent study, Swiston (2010) shows that the 2008 recession in the United States reduced growth by 4–5 percent in Central America and that the transmission channels were mainly the financial conditions and the fluctuations in export demand.

At the same time, exports to the other CAFTA members (that is, El Salvador, Honduras, Guatemala, and Nicaragua) not only expanded significantly after 2005, but also accelerated in 2007, before declining in 2009. Figure 2.2, panel a, shows that exports to the CAFTA area went from US$21.5 million in 2005 to US$57.7 million in 2008. This remarkable performance is mainly due to the surge in exports to Guatemala and Honduras (see figure 2.2, panel b). Between 2005 and 2008, the value of exports to Guatemala doubled to US$11.8 million, while exports to Honduras trebled from US$10.9 million to US$32.8 million. Exports to El Salvador and Nicaragua also exhibited strong growth: the value of their exports more than doubled from 2005 to 2008.[10] This suggests that the tariff preferences were effective in boosting exports to the CAFTA members.[11] Moreover, Dominican exporters seem to have anticipated the agreement and started to expand their exports to the CAFTA area in 2006.

Figure 2.2   Dominican Exports to CAFTA Members in Select Years, 2002–09

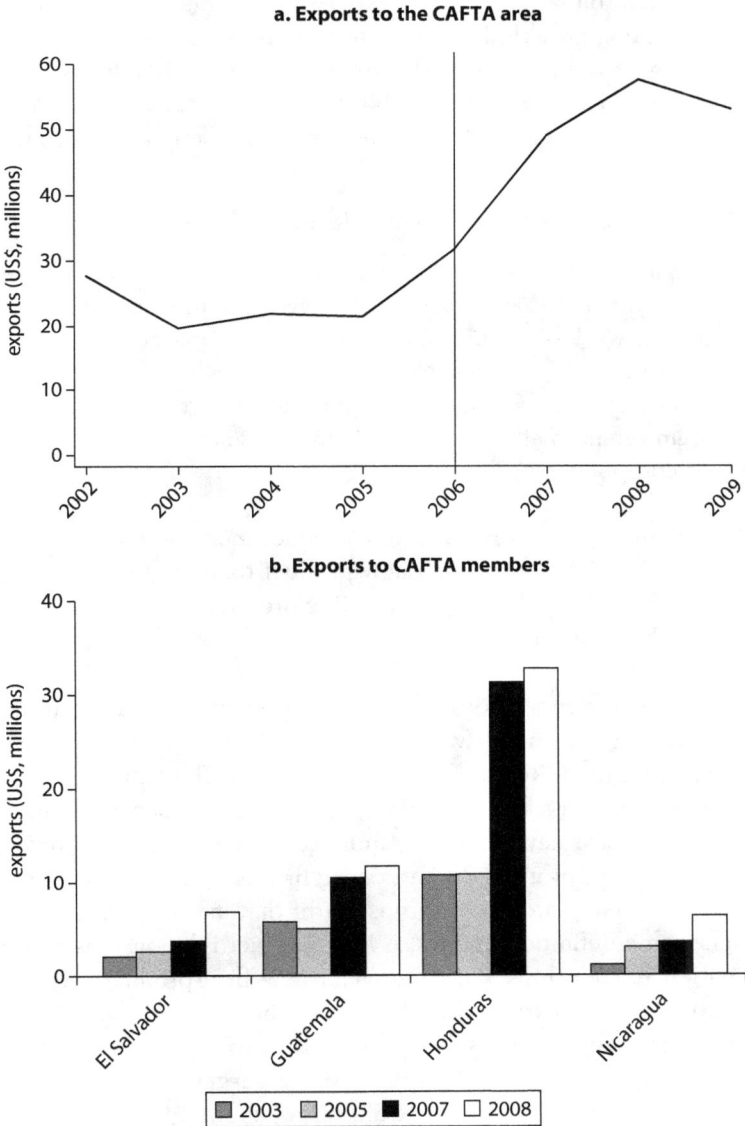

a. Exports to the CAFTA area

b. Exports to CAFTA members

2003   2005   2007   2008

Source: Authors' calculations.

To summarize, following the DR-CAFTA, exports to the United States stagnated in absolute terms, while exports to the other CAFTA members exhibited strong growth, but their share still represents only 1 percent. This highlights the potential for further trade expansion among Central American countries. However, in both cases, exports dropped in 2009, probably as a consequence of the global economic crisis at that time.

Firm-Level Patterns of Extensive Margin

Having analyzed the aggregate pattern of exports, we now examine the exporters' dynamics that lie behind the aggregate movement of exports. In particular, we look at firms' export extensive margin to the United States and the CAFTA area to assess whether there were significant changes in exporters' behavior subsequent to the agreement. The extensive margin refers to all new trade relationships and can be decomposed into four components[12]:

- Exports by existing firms of a new product to a new market
- Exports by existing firms of a new product to an existing market
- Exports by existing firms of an existing product to a new market
- Exports by new firms.

Using this decomposition, we sketch exporters' behavior during this period and can determine whether they reacted as predicted in Melitz (2003) and Bernard, Redding, and Schott (2009). To identify each of the components, we classify firms, products, and markets according to three different statuses: new, existing, and exit. A *new* firm is a firm that exports in t, but not in $t - 1$. An *existing* firm is a firm that exports in t and in $t - 1$. Finally, an *exiting* firm is a firm that exports in $t - 1$, but not in t. The same definition applies to firm-product relationships and firm-destination relationships. For example, a new firm-product relationship refers to a product exported by firm i in t, but not in $t - 1$. Figure 2.3 reports the number of firms by year according to their export status.

The number of newly exporting firms surged in the year when DR-CAFTA took effect. As for exiting firms, about 1,000 firms stopped exporting in any given year during the 2002–09 period, except in 2007 and 2008. From 2006 to 2007, the number of exits dropped significantly to 766, before reaching their high (that is, 1,595) in 2008. Two events may explain this result. First, the large number of entries during the DR-CAFTA year may have boosted the number of exits in 2008. Short

Figure 2.3   Number of Firms, by Export Status, 2003–09

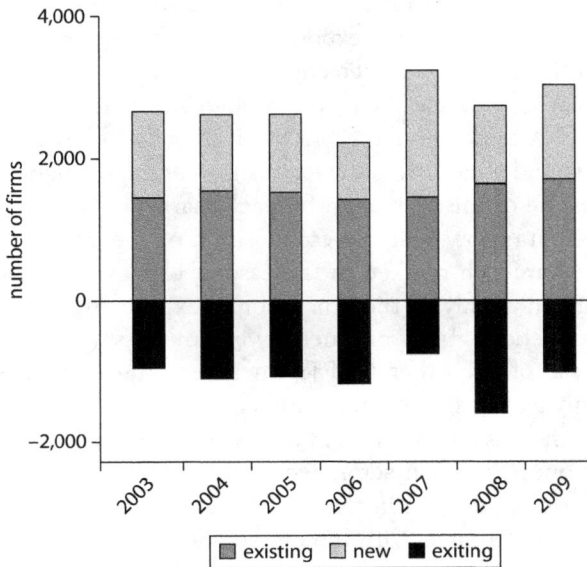

Source: Authors' calculations.

survival among new exporters has been well documented in the literature (see, among others, Besedes and Prusa 2006, 2007; Eaton and others 2007; Cadot and others 2010) and recently modeled in Albornoz and others (2009). In their framework, firms discover their export profitability only once they become exporters. Experienced exporters entering a new market are therefore better informed than new exporters about their skills and their chances of success. As a consequence, new exporters are more likely to exit than experienced ones. It could be that, drawn by the more attractive conditions created by the agreement, many exporters entered the market in 2007, only to realize their true export performance, which forced them to exit in mass the next year. But in addition to the inherent low survival of exporters, the global economic crisis that started at the end of 2007 could have amplified this phenomenon, increasing even more the likelihood to exit of both experienced and new exporters.

The weight of the extensive margin in total exports varies across the United States and the CAFTA area.[13] In the case of exports to the United States, the extensive margin is volatile and accounts for a small share of total trade to this country, about 5 to 13 percent of total exports. As for exports to the CAFTA area, their extensive margin has been growing since 2005, and so has their share in total exports. In 2007, the extensive margin trebled, accounting for about 55 percent of total exports to the region. In both cases, the data suggest that the extensive margin expanded during the year the DR-CAFTA came into force, but declined in the following years.

To understand what drives the extensive margin, see figure 2.4, which decomposes the extensive margin for each market.

First, the data show that the composition of the extensive margin is very different in each market. In the case of U.S. exports, the extensive margin is driven mainly by the generation of exports by new entrants and by the introduction of new products by incumbents.

In the case of the other CAFTA members, the extensive margin is driven mainly by the exports of incumbent exporters—in particular since 2007, when there is a clear jump in the extensive margin. In this year and in the next ones, the main actors were incumbent exporters who either introduced a new product in the CAFTA area or exported for the first time to the CAFTA area. With the marked decline in the extensive margin in 2008 and 2009, only exports generated by the introduction of a new product remained (approximately) at the level of 2007.

These figures suggest that new exporters played a more important role in the expansion of the extensive margin in the U.S. market than in other CAFTA markets. This could reflect the preferences of new exporters for the United States, which see this destination as a market with more opportunities, given its size and wealth. Yet this could also reflect the existence of nontariff barriers to entry into the CAFTA markets.

Relationship between Tariff Reductions and Exporters' Behavior: Preliminary Evidence

In this section, we describe the tariffs and the tariff reductions that followed the introduction of DR-CAFTA. We then examine the relationship between the extensive margin and tariff cuts.

Tariffs and Tariff Cuts

The data on tariffs come from the tariff schedules that were negotiated in 2004 by each CAFTA member. Each country has its own tariff schedule in which goods are classified in eight to 12 different categories[14] according to the time frame over which tariffs will be eliminated. While most

Figure 2.4   Decomposition of the Firm-Level Extensive Margin, 2003–09

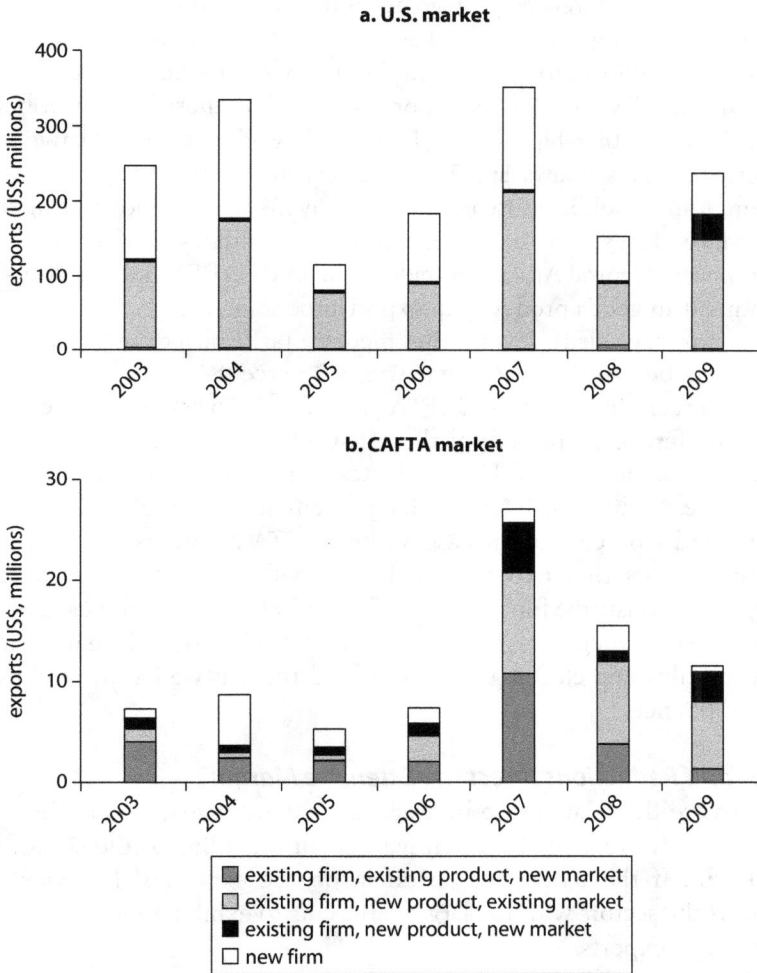

a. U.S. market

b. CAFTA market

■ existing firm, existing product, new market
▨ existing firm, new product, existing market
■ existing firm, new product, new market
□ new firm

Source: Authors' calculations.

Dominican products could enter the U.S. market duty free immediately after the agreement, between 15 percent (Guatemala) to 40 percent (El Salvador) of the total number of products in the other CAFTA markets were subject to a duty. Products whose tariffs were not eliminated immediately after the agreement are being phased out progressively over a five- to 20-year period.[15]

For the Dominican Republic–U.S. trade, the agreement consolidates the existing preferences and grants duty-free treatment to almost all products entering the U.S. market,[16] except for some agricultural products that are subject to quotas.[17] In the case of textile and apparel exports, the DR-CAFTA provisions are more flexible than those in the Caribbean Basin Trade Partnership Act (CBTPA), as they allow for cumulative rules of origin.[18] This allows apparel exporters in Central America and the Dominican Republic to use inputs from any member, without losing their duty-free access to the U.S. market (Hornbeck 2008). For the Dominican–Central American trade,[19] the DR-CAFTA extends duty-free treatment to goods produced in export-processing zones.

As for the tariff levels, the median tariff faced by Dominican exporters before the agreement was 3.2 percent in the United States and 5 percent in the other CAFTA members.[20] To assess the size of the tariff preferences granted by the DR-CAFTA, we compute the tariff cuts by product for the United States[21] and the other CAFTA members. The median tariff cut is 3.1 percent in the case of the United States and 1 percent in the case of the CAFTA members. In the United States, sectors that experienced high tariff cuts include agriculture, prepared foodstuffs, footwear, textiles, and clothing. In the case of the other CAFTA members, important tariff cuts also took place in agriculture, textiles, and clothing, prepared foodstuffs, as well as in machinery and appliances.

Did Tariff Reductions Affect the Extensive Margin?

To explore the relationship between the extensive margin and the tariff reduction, we look at the extensive margin according to the size of the tariff cut. If the tariffs had an effect on the exporters' behavior, one expects the sectors with the larger tariff cuts to exhibit a relatively bigger increase in exports.

We first classify sectors (HS two-digit) according to whether they had a low or a high tariff cut. A sector is a high-cut sector if its median tariff cut is larger than the overall median tariff (that is, 3.1 percent in the case of the United States and 1 percent in the case of the other CAFTA members). We use tariffs at the sector level (HS two-digit) rather than at the product level, to have the largest product concordance between exports of the Dominican Republic and those of its partners. Exports by tariff cuts are reported in figure 2.5.

In the case of exports to the Central American countries, the extensive margin behaves as expected. The growth in the extensive margin between

Figure 2.5   Extensive Margin, by Tariff Cut, 2003–09

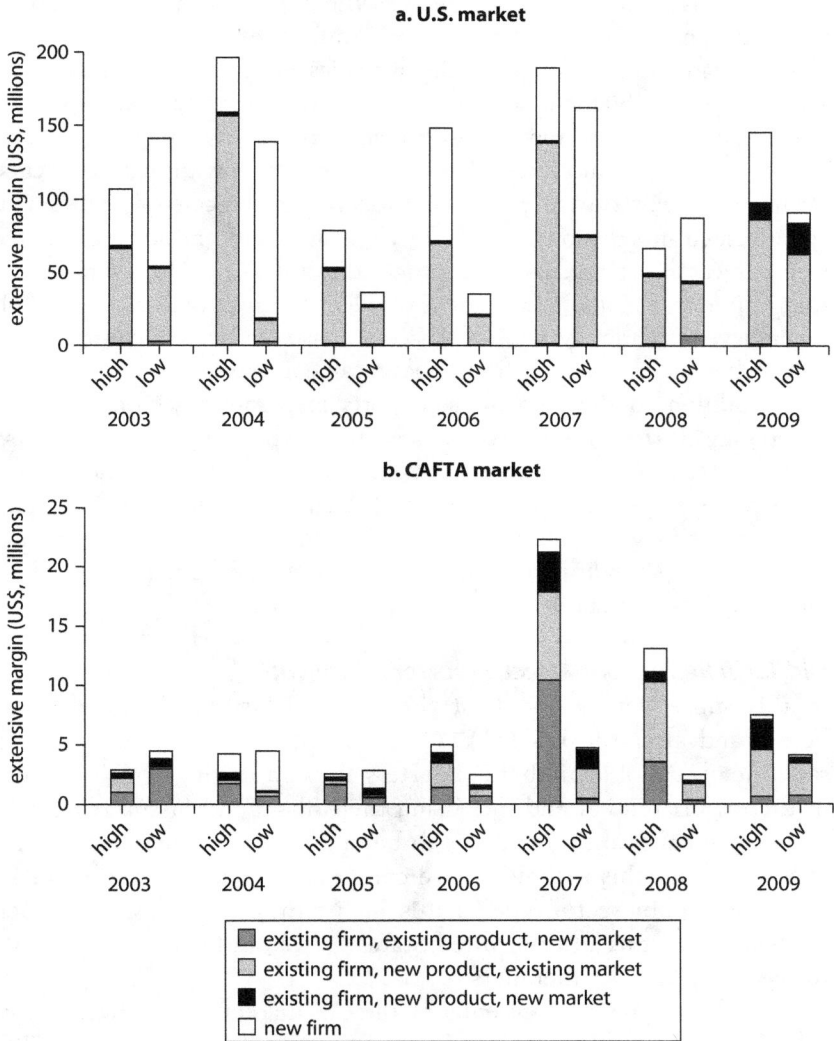

a. U.S. market

b. CAFTA market

- ▦ existing firm, existing product, new market
- ▢ existing firm, new product, existing market
- ■ existing firm, new product, new market
- ☐ new firm

Source: Authors' calculations.

2007 and 2009 is driven by the export growth in sectors that experienced high tariff cuts. This suggests that the DR-CAFTA did promote new exports to the CAFTA members, and incumbent exporters seem to have benefited the most. These sectors include cotton, tobacco, and apparel. However, the effect seems to vanish with time, as the extensive margin in both low- and high-cut sectors exhibits a progressive decline from 2008 onward. This could reflect the effects of the 2008 economic crisis rather than a decline in the exporters' enthusiasm for the agreement.

In the case of the U.S. market, the dynamics are less clear. From 2005 to 2007 exports in high-cut sectors grew rapidly, suggesting that exporters may have anticipated the agreement and started exporting before the agreement entered into force. New exports in sectors with high tariff cuts include apparel, footwear, plastic, and tobacco. In the case of textiles and apparel, such anticipation effect is very likely, as textiles and apparel exports were subject to a retroactivity rule provided by the DR-CAFTA. Under this rule, importers can apply for refunds of duties when DR-CAFTA's rules of origin have been met. As a result this could have created a major incentive to start buying immediately from Dominican exporters.

In addition to the increase in exports in high-cut sectors, we also observe in 2007 an impressive expansion of exports in low-cut sectors. This is driven mainly by the sales from new exporters. This should not come as a surprise, as it could suggest that even if the tariff cut was low, it was big enough to modify the decision to export in that year. The extensive margin in both low- and high-cut sectors dropped in 2008, but picked up again in 2009.

Did Tariff Reductions Affect Exporters' Survival?

In this subsection, we look at the exporters' survival probabilities before and after the DR-CAFTA agreement. A tariff reduction will raise the profits of incumbent exporters, thus improving firms' position in the export market and increasing their likelihood of surviving. We expect the survival probabilities to be larger in high-cut sectors.[22] To check whether this is the case, we compute the survival probabilities by cohort and by sector type (that is, high tariff cut and low tariff cut) for firms exporting to the United States, as well as for firms exporting to the other CAFTA members.

First, the number of firms entering the U.S. market in any given year is considerably larger than the number of firms entering any other CAFTA market. This is not necessarily surprising considering the size of the U.S. market relative to the other markets. Second, the number of firms entering sectors with high tariff cuts between 2006 and 2009 is larger than the number entering sectors with low tariff cuts. This is true for the U.S. market, except for 2008. Third, the survival probabilities in 2007 and 2008 are higher for exporters in sectors with high tariff cuts than for exporters in sectors with low tariff cuts, for all markets, regardless of the year of entry. There were only very few cases, in both the United States and the other CAFTA members, where this is not observed. Finally, the survival probabilities before 2006 and in 2009 do not exhibit any particular pattern in any of the sectors, unlike in subsequent years.

This constitutes preliminary evidence that tariffs do affect the pattern of firms in terms of survival, especially in sectors with high tariff cuts, where survival seems to be higher in the first years of the DR-CAFTA.

Empirical Strategy and Results

In this section, we formally test the relationship between tariff cuts and exporters' dynamics. We are particularly interested in examining whether the tariff reductions implemented by the DR-CAFTA promoted (a) the participation of firms in the export market and (b) the introduction of new product-market relationships. In the third part of this section, we also look at whether the tariff cuts improved (c) the survival of Dominican exporters by preventing firms from exiting the export market.

Before proceeding to the empirical exercise, a few caveats related to our data set need to be mentioned. First, the observations in our data set are likely to be subject to left and right censoring. In the case of left censoring we cannot determine whether a firm with a positive trade value in 2002 started exporting in 2002 or before (that is, whether it is a new exporter or not). So we only consider firms that started exporting strictly after 2002 when estimating the effects of tariffs (a) on the number of new exporters and (b) on the decision to exit the export market. Similarly for right-censored observations, we cannot determine whether exporters reporting a positive trade in 2009 exited the next year or not. Only the exits that took place before 2009 can be assessed.

A second caveat concerns the period covered by our study. We observe only three years after the agreement, namely 2007, 2008, and 2009, and thus our empirical exercise considers only the short-term adjustments of the DR-CAFTA. Moreover, this period coincides with the economic crisis that broke in the United States, which could have undermined the effects of the agreement on Dominican exports.

Finally, given the nature of our data (that is, customs data) we can observe only the firms that exported at least once during our period of observation and not the total number of firms that potentially could have exported but didn't. This selection problem could be a major handicap if one would like to estimate the probability of entering the export market (that is, becoming an exporter). However, this is not the empirical strategy adopted in the present study.

New Exporters

One of the main implications of the Melitz model is that lower trade costs will induce the entry of new firms into the export market. To test this, we estimate the effect of tariff cuts on the number of new exporters according to the following equation:

$$\text{New Exporters}_{jpt} = \beta_1 \Delta tariffs_{jpt} + \alpha Controls + \eta_k + \delta_j + \gamma_t + \varepsilon_{jpt}. \quad (2.1)$$

The dependent variable is the number of new entrants in the national territory and in export-processing zones exporting product p (at the HS eight-digit level) to country j in time t. $\Delta tariffs_{jpt}$ is the duty reduction (in percentage points) in product p implemented in period t by country j.[23] The coefficient β_1 will be positive if the change in tariffs has a positive effect on the number of new entrants.

We also include two proxies for information spillovers: the number of firms that exported product p in $t - 1$ and the number of exporters that served market j with product p in $t - 1$. Potential exporters may see the participation of other Dominican firms in foreign markets as a signal of profitability. We therefore expect these two covariates to have a positive effect on the decision of new entrants to export.

Additionally, we control for the exporters' location by adding a dummy EPZ that equals 1 for firms operating in an export-processing zone, and 0 otherwise.

To account for the benefits of a reduction in import costs due to the bilateral feature of the agreement, we introduce the cut of the import-weighted tariff. This variable was calculated at the sector level (HS two-digit) using as weights the coefficients observed in the 2005 input-output table of the Dominican Republic.[24] The rationale is that following implementation of the DR-CAFTA, firms in the Dominican Republic could have access to cheaper inputs. If this is the case, implementation of the DR-CAFTA would reduce their costs, improve their competitiveness, and therefore increase their propensity to export.

We also add a measure of comparative advantage, namely the normalized revealed comparative advantage index (NRCA) suggested by Laursen (1998) to assess whether new exporters start in sectors with a comparative advantage. The NRCA is based on the revealed competitive advantage (RCA)[25] and was computed for each year at the HS four-digit level according to $\text{NRCA}_{kt} = (\text{RCA}_{kt} - 1) / (\text{RCA}_{kt} + 1)$. The main advantage of the NRCA is its symmetry: it ranges between −1 and 1. An $NRCA_{kt}$ between −1 and 0 suggests a comparative disadvantage in sector k in period t, while an $NRCA_{kt}$ between 0 and 1 indicates a comparative advantage. We also add an interaction term between the NRCA and the tariff cuts to determine whether the tariff preferences promoted the entry into sectors of comparative advantage to the Dominican Republic more than the entry into nontraditional sectors.

Finally, fixed effects for time (γ_t), country (δ_j), and sectors (η_k), at the HS two-digit level, are included. By their inclusion, we expect to control for any market, sector, and year characteristic that could affect our results, such as the difficult business environment of 2008 and 2009. ε_{jpt} is the usual idiosyncratic error term.

We also estimate equation 2.1 using the actual applied tariffs enjoyed by Dominican exporters in foreign markets instead of the tariff cuts. By including the tariff levels, we can distinguish between the short-term effects (that is, tariff reductions or adjustments) and the long-run effects (that is, levels) of tariffs. Tariff levels should negatively affect the number of new exporters. The data for applied tariffs (HS six-digit) comes from TRAINS/WITS and is incomplete for the period 2002–09, which reduces the number of observations for our empirical exercise.[26]

Table 2.2 presents the results. The three first columns contain the estimations using the tariff cuts, while columns 4 to 6 show the results using tariff levels. In each case there are three specifications. In the first one, we include only the market access proxy. In the second specification, we control for information spillovers and exporters' location. In the last one, we add the weighted import tariff cut, the comparative advantage index, and its interaction term.

As shown in table 2.2, the coefficient of the tariff cuts is positive and statistically significant in all three specifications. Ten additional percentage points in the tariff cut will increase by 1 the number of new exporters of product p. This implies that sectors with large tariff cuts attract a larger number of new exporters, but the effect is small. The effect of the tariff levels is also significant and negative, as expected. This suggests that sectors with relatively low tariffs attract more exporters. The effect is, however, almost negligible. As for the effect of the information spillovers, the fact that other firms export product p does not affect the behavior of potential exporters in the same sector. In contrast, the number of new entrants selling product p in a given destination rises with the number of Dominican firms in the same market. The behavior of other exporters in a market seems

Table 2.2   OLS Estimates of the Number of New Exporters

Variable	(1)	(2)	(3)	(4)	(5)	(6)
Tariff cut	0.100**	0.097***	0.081***			
	(0.040)	(0.036)	(0.027)			
Tariff				−0.017***	−0.018***	−0.016***
				(0.006)	(0.005)	(0.005)
Number of exporters, same product ($t-1$)		0.001	0.000		−0.000	−0.001
		(0.002)	(0.002)		(0.003)	(0.003)
Number of exporters, same product and market ($t-1$)		0.126***	0.122***		0.126***	0.125***
		(0.012)	(0.011)		(0.013)	(0.013)
EPZ		−0.918***	−0.963***		−1.337***	−1.378***
		(0.177)	(0.189)		(0.302)	(0.310)
Dominican Republic import-weighted tariff cut			−0.149***			−0.123**
			(0.054)			(0.061)
Comparative advantage			0.204***			0.464***
			(0.070)			(0.130)
Comparative advantage x tariff cut			0.126***			
			(0.039)			
Comparative advantage x tariffs						−0.009
						(0.006)
Number of observations	14,187	14,187	14,179	5,730	5,730	5,729
R^2	0.301	0.437	0.452	0.281	0.402	0.403

Source: Authors' calculations.
Note: Time, country, and sector fixed effects are used in all specifications, but are not reported. Errors are clustered by product. Robust standard errors are in parentheses.
** $p < .05$, *** $p < .01$.

therefore to affect the decision of new entrants. As for the exporters' location, there is a negative and statistically significant relationship between the number of new exporters and export zones. This suggests that the entry of new exporters takes place mainly in the national territory. This should not come as a surprise since the requirements needed to start a firm in an export zone are more demanding. The effect of the import tariff cuts is negative and statistically significant. Having access to cheaper inputs does not seem to benefit new exporters. One possible reason for this could be that sectors with large import tariff cuts were highly protected sectors in the past, and not necessarily competitive, thus explaining the lack of new entries. Finally, our results suggest that the number of new exporters is larger in sectors where the Dominican Republic has a comparative advantage. As for the interaction term, only the interaction between the NCRA and the tariff cut is significant. Its effect is positive, thus implying that the tariff cuts had an additional and positive effect on the number of new exporters in a comparative advantage sector.

The results suggest that both tariff reductions (that is, short-run adjustment) and lower tariffs levels (that is, long-run equilibrium) do induce the entry of new exporters.[27] However, both effects seem to be very small. This result could reflect the existence of other factors including, but not limited to, high transport costs and phytosanitary and standards requirements.

Introduction of New Product-Market Relationships in the Export Mix

The second effect that we are interested in is whether a tariff decline encourages incumbent firms to export an additional product to the CAFTA area. For this exercise, we consider only existing firms and test the effect of tariffs and tariff cuts on the number of exporters that introduce a new product in a given market (that is, a new product-market combination). The equation to be estimated is the following:

$$\text{Add}_{jpt} = \beta_1 \Delta tariffs_{jpt} + \alpha Controls + \eta_k + \delta_j + \gamma_t + \varepsilon_{jpt}, \qquad (2.2)$$

where Add_{jpt} is the number of incumbent exporters in the national territory and in export-processing zones that start shipping product p to market j in year t. $\Delta tariffs_{jpt}$ is the tariff cut (in percentage points) in product p implemented in period t. We expect that the number of firms adding product p to their export mix is the largest for products exhibiting large tariff reductions. Table 2.3 reports the results. The first three specifications use the tariff cuts (columns 1 to 3), while columns 4 to 6 show the results using tariff levels. As for the control variables we include the same covariates as for equation 2.1, namely, information covariates, exporters' location, import-weighted tariff cuts, and a comparative advantage measure. Time (γ_t), country (δ_j), and sector (η_k) fixed effects are also included. ε_{jpt} is an idiosyncratic error term.

The effect of the tariff cut is positive and statistically significant, but very small (that is, 0.007 to 0.009). The effect of tariffs is negative and significant, but also small. This suggests that in the short and long run, low tariffs can promote the participation of existing exporters by inducing them to add new product-market relationships in their export mix. The effect is, however, very small, which could indicate the existence of other nontariff barriers.

As for the information spillovers, both the number of exporters of a given product and the number of exporters of a given product in a given destination have a positive effect on the number of new trade relationships

Table 2.3   OLS Estimates of the Number of Exporters Adding New Product-Market Relationships

Variable	(1)	(2)	(3)	(4)	(5)	(6)
Tariff cut	0.009*	0.009**	0.007*			
	(0.005)	(0.004)	(0.004)			
Tariff				−0.007**	−0.007**	−0.005**
				(0.003)	(0.003)	(0.003)
Number of exporters, same product ($t-1$)		0.003***	0.002***		0.005***	0.004***
		(0.000)	(0.000)		(0.001)	(0.001)
Number of exporters, same product and market ($t-1$)		0.111***	0.110***		0.097***	0.096***
		(0.007)	(0.007)		(0.006)	(0.006)
EPZ		−0.078	−0.093		0.117	0.094
		(0.076)	(0.077)		(0.141)	(0.142)
Dominican Republic import-weighted tariff cut			0.038***			0.076**
			(0.015)			(0.033)
Comparative advantage			0.161***			0.359***
			(0.024)			(0.055)
Comparative advantage x tariff cut			0.019***			
			(0.006)			
Comparative advantage x tariffs						−0.009***
						(0.003)
Number of observations	37,486	37,486	37,435	13,629	13,629	13,621
R^2	0.487	0.627	0.629	0.480	0.603	0.606

Source: Authors' calculations.
Note: Time, country, and sector fixed effects are used in all specifications, but are not reported. Errors are clustered by product. Robust standard errors are in parentheses.
* $p < .1$, ** $p < .05$, *** $p < .01$.

introduced by existing exporters. Compared to the effect for new exporters, the effect of a cut in the import tariff is also positive for existing exporters. The exporters' location seems not to have an effect on the number of new product-market relationships. Finally, more new trade relationships are created in comparative advantage sectors. The interaction term between NRCA and tariff cuts is statistically significant and positive, which indicates that the effect of a larger tariff cut is amplified when the product belongs to a comparative advantage sector. A similar result is found in the case of the interaction term between NRCA and the tariff levels.[28]

Exporter Exit

According to Melitz (2003), we could expect that, as tariffs fall, the profits of incumbent exporters rise, thus improving exporters' chances of survival. This implies that lower tariffs could help incumbent exporters to consolidate their market position and prevent them from exiting foreign markets.

We examine this implication by estimating the effect of tariffs and tariff cuts on the probability that a firm will exit the export market. As mentioned at the beginning of this section, we consider only firms that start exporting and then exit during the 2002–09 period. The probability[29] for firm i to stop exporting product p to country j in year t is given by:

$$\Pr(Exit_{ijpt} = 1) = \beta_1 \Delta tariffs_{jpt} + \alpha Controls + \eta_k + \delta_j + \gamma_t + \varepsilon_{jpt}, \quad (2.3)$$

where the dependent variable $Exit_{ijpt}$ is a dummy that equals 1 if firm i stops exporting product p to market j in t and 0 otherwise. As before, $\Delta tariffs_{jpt}$ refers to the tariff reductions in product p in time t applied by country j. We also include three measures of export experience. Our first measure is the number of years a firm has been an exporter. Market experience is proxied by the number of products firm i exports to country j in $t - 1$. Product experience is given by the number of markets firm i serves with product p in $t - 1$. To account for the weight of product p in the exports of firm i, we also add the share of product p in the sales of firm i in $t - 1$. We expect that, as the share of a product increases, the probability that the firm will stop exporting the product declines. We also introduce a dummy that takes 1 if the firm is a multiproduct firm in $t - 1$ and 0 otherwise. Finally, as in the previous estimations, we control for the exporters' location and add a measure of comparative advantage and an interaction term. We estimate three specifications. The first one is the baseline regression, which includes the tariff cuts and the share of product p in total sales. The second one includes measures of the exporters' experience. The last one controls for the exporters' location as well as for sector characteristics. We estimate each specification using the tariff cuts as well as the tariff levels. Results are reported in table 2.4.

While the tariff levels do not seem to affect the probability of exiting export markets, the coefficient of the tariff cuts is negative and statistically significant. However, its effect is very small (0.001).

The coefficients of the other covariates are very similar and statistically significant across all specifications. The size of previous sales has a negative effect on the probability of stopping exports of product p. But the effect is very small (that is, 0.001 to 0.002). Products with a small share in the export mix have a higher probability of exit. This is in line with the model of Bernard, Redding, and Schott (2009), which predicts that firms will stop producing or selling products that are not in their core competencies.

Table 2.4   Estimates of the Probability of Exit

Variable	(1)	(2)	(3)	(4)	(5)	(6)
Tariff cut	−0.001***	−0.001***	−0.001***			
	(0.000)	(0.000)	(0.000)			
Tariff				0.000	0.000	0.000
				(0.000)	(0.000)	(0.000)
Share in sales ($t − 1$)	−0.001***	−0.002***	−0.002***	−0.000***	−0.002***	−0.002***
	(0.000)	(0.000)	(0.000)	(0.000)	(0.000)	(0.000)
Market experience ($t − 1$)		−0.003***	−0.003***		−0.005***	−0.004***
		(0.000)	(0.000)		(0.000)	(0.000)
Product experience ($t − 1$)		−0.018***	−0.016***		−0.020***	−0.018***
		(0.001)	(0.001)		(0.001)	(0.001)
Years as an exporter		−0.014***	−0.014***		−0.010***	−0.009***
		(0.001)	(0.001)		(0.002)	(0.002)
Multiproduct exporter ($t − 1$)		−0.206***	−0.187***		−0.232***	−0.208***
		(0.010)	(0.009)		(0.015)	(0.014)
EPZ			−0.093***			−0.134***
			(0.006)			(0.009)
Comparative advantage			−0.052***			−0.045***
			(0.004)			(0.006)
Comparative advantage x tariff cut			−0.000			
			(0.000)			
Comparative advantage x tariffs						0.000
						(0.000)
Number of observations	90,261	90,223	90,149	47,145	47,113	47,102
R^2	0.720	0.736	0.738	0.693	0.711	0.715

Source: Authors' calculations.
Note: Time, country, and sector fixed effects are used in all specifications, but are not reported. Errors are clustered by product. Robust standard errors are in parentheses.
*** $p < .01$.

Market and product experience decreases the probability of exiting foreign markets. The more experienced a firm is, the lower is the probability of stopping the sale of product p in market j. But product experience seems to matter more than market experience when it comes to exit. As for the number of years as an exporter, the probability of stopping the sale of a product in a given market decreases 1 percentage point with an additional year of export experience. Also being a multiproduct exporter in $t − 1$ decreases the probability of dropping a product-market combination in t by 18.7 to 23.2 percent. This is the covariate with the largest effect on the probability of stopping the sale of a product in a given market.

Firms located in an export-processing zone show a lower probability of exiting from market j. This is not surprising, as the requirements to be located in an EPZ are more stringent than those to be located in the national territory. Larger fixed costs in the EPZ could therefore explain the better survival of EPZ firms through a hysteresis mechanism (Baldwin and Krugman 1989; Dixit 1989).[30] Another explanation could be that the firms in export zones are the most productive ones (that is, firms self-select into export zones) and therefore also exhibit higher survival rates.

Finally, exporters operating in a comparative advantage sector have a lower probability of discontinuing the sale of a product in a given market. Yet no significant effect is found for the interaction term between the comparative advantage measure and the tariff cuts (*tariff levels*).

Recent studies have documented the low survival of trade relationships in their first years of activity. Eaton and others (2007) show that during the 1996–2005 period, most Colombian exporters survived only one year. In another recent study, Cadot and others (2010) also document the short duration of the export activity for exporters in four African countries and look at its determinants. These firm-level analyses as well as other studies at the product level (Besedes and Prusa 2006, 2007) highlight the importance of surviving in those first years. Dominican exporters are no exception. On average, 63 percent of the new exporters last only one year (that is, exit after one year). We perform the same exercise as before, but this time we consider only new entrants. We test whether the probability of stopping the export of product p to market j in t of firm i that started exporting in $t - 1$ diminishes with a decline in tariffs.[31] We find that only tariff cuts affect the probability of exiting after one year. However, its effect is very small (0.001), and it disappears once we control for the exporters' location and sector characteristics. Young exporters located in an EPZ show an exit probability that is 18 percent lower than those in the national territory. As for the remaining variables, they are in most cases similar to those in our previous exercise.

Conclusions

Thanks to the implementation of the DR-CAFTA in 2007, Dominican exporters face better market access not only in the United States, but also in El Salvador, Guatemala, Honduras, and Nicaragua. Using an original firm-level data set with exports by product and destination for the 2002–09 period, this chapter looks at the Dominican exporters' responses following the agreement and analyzes whether increased market access supported the expansion of the extensive margin and improved exporters' survival. Based on the theoretical findings of Melitz (2003) and Bernard, Redding, and Schott (2009), we test the effect of tariff reductions on (a) the number of new exporters, (b) the number of existing exporters that added a new product-market relationship to their export mix, and (c) the probability of exiting a given market.

Our results suggest that tariff reductions have had a positive, but very small, effect on the number of new exporters. A similar result is found in the case of incumbent exporters. Tariff preferences seem to affect their behavior, but the effect is also fairly small. Such results could suggest that other trade barriers such as standards, phytosanitary requirements, credit constraints, and transport costs, among others, could be preventing exporters from taking full advantage of the agreement. This implies that beyond tariffs, further efforts must be undertaken to identify the factors that are constraining exporters from benefiting from the agreement. This is also essential for the design of complementary policies aiming to stimulate export participation.

Finally, we also look at the relationship between export survival and tariff preferences. Survival among Dominican exporters is very low: six out of 10 firms exit the export market after one year. We test whether tariff cuts help exporters to consolidate their position in a market and diminish their probability of exit. We find that tariff cuts improve survival rates, especially among experienced exporters, although the effect is very small. Our findings also highlight the great challenge that export survival represents for young exporters and therefore the need for policies that help them to develop and grow in foreign markets.

Other important results concern the exporters located in EPZs. In general, these seem to perform better than their peers in the national territory when it comes to surviving in export markets. Our results suggest that the probability of exiting the market is 9 to 18 percent lower for EPZ exporters than for exporters located in the national territory; however, this may be due to self-selection—that is, better firms may choose to locate in EPZs—rather than to the effectiveness of the favorable fiscal regime for EPZs.

Our findings provide some preliminary insight into the effects of the DR-CAFTA on Dominican exporters, in particular into the effects of improved market access on the extensive margin in the Dominican Republic. However, trade liberalization may also affect exporters' performance through other channels such as access to cheaper inputs. Our future research will look at these effects, as well as those on the exporters from other CAFTA members. The purpose is to get a more complete assessment of the effects of the DR-CAFTA on exporters in the region.

Notes

1. The agreement was signed in 2004, but it was ratified only in 2007. Compared to earlier agreements with the United States, the Caribbean Basin Initiative, and the CBTPA, the DR-CAFTA covers almost all products and, unlike its predecessors, is based on reciprocal trade preferences. In 2008, the Dominican trade policy with the European Union also changed. The Cotonou Agreement, which granted nonreciprocal trade preferences to the Dominican Republic, was replaced by Economic Partnership Agreements, a reciprocal trade regime.

2. Their setup generates not only firm selection, but also product selection by including a product-market fixed cost and by taking into account (product-country) demand heterogeneity.

3. A similar result is also predicted in Eckel and others (2009).

4. In our study, we do not classify Costa Rica as part of the group of countries that are signatories of the DR-CAFTA, since this country ratified the agreement only in 2009.

5. Exporters are identified through their names.

6. From this universe, only 459 export in every year.

7. Calculations are available from the authors on request.

8. We exclude ferronickel exports because they involve only one exporter and account on average for 13 percent of the Dominican Republic's total exports. Moreover, their export value is heavily dependent on international price fluctuations, which could also bias our results. Ferronickel exports accounted for 26 percent of total exports in 2007, but only 9 percent in 2008 as consequence of a price decline.

9. We exclude Costa Rica from the CAFTA country group, as it ratified the treaty only in 2009.

10. Exports to Costa Rica also experienced an important expansion since 2005, rising from US$6 million to US$31 million. This suggests that Costa Rican exporters may have anticipated the ratification of the DR-CAFTA.

11. Sectors (HS two-digit) with the largest exports to the CAFTA area in 2008 were plastics (22 percent), cotton (20 percent), and tobacco (19 percent). In the case of the United States, the main export sectors were apparel (20 percent), medical and surgical instruments (16 percent), machinery and electrical appliances (14 percent), and jewelry (14 percent).

12. A trade relationship is defined as the combination of a firm, a product, and a destination. A new trade relationship can therefore be generated by the participation of new firms, the introduction of new products, or the introduction of new markets. Our unique data set contains information at the firm, product, and destination level, which allows for such decomposition.

13. Calculations are available from the authors on request.

14. The United States has eight categories. El Salvador, Nicaragua, and Honduras have 12 categories, and Guatemala has 11 categories.

15. There are also cases in which duty-free treatment is delayed and will not begin until seven or 12 years after the agreement enters into force. All tariffs will be eliminated in 20 years.

16. According to the U.S. International Trade Commission, before the agreement about 80 percent of exports from the Dominican Republic had preferential access in the U.S. market.

17. Sugar in the case of the Dominican Republic.

18. The provision was retroactive to January 1, 2004.

19. The Central American countries (that is, Costa Rica, El Salvador, Guatemala, Honduras, and Nicaragua) and the Dominican Republic signed a free trade agreement in 1998, which entered into force in all countries between 2001 and 2002. The agreement guaranteed duty-free entry to almost all goods that comply with the rules of origins and transformation criteria, excluding goods from export-processing zones.

20. To compute the median tariff in the case of the Central American members, we first compute the median tariff by product across the five countries and then calculate the overall median tariff. The median tariff cut by product and the overall median tariff cut are computed in the same way. These computations are possible using eight-digit data since countries in Central America share the same product classification at this level of disaggregation, namely the Sistema Arancelario Centroamericano.

21. U.S. tariff figures exclude products whose tariff scheme depends on the characteristics (weight, length, and so forth) of the good, as well as some tobacco products whose tariffs are equal to 350 percent. In total, we exclude 963 products.

22. The effect of tariffs on export survival could have an ambiguous lagged effect if we take into account the survival behavior of new entrants. Consider a decline in tariffs in t; according to the theoretical evidence this would increase unambiguously the survival of incumbent exporters in t and in subsequent years, but also increase the number of new exporters. Yet the empirical evidence shows that most new exporters live only for one year; that is, most of the new exporters will exit in $t + 1$. If the number of new entrants is very large in t and so is the number of exits in $t + 1$, the export

survival could be lower than in previous years, unless the survival of new exporters also improves.

23. To have the largest product concordance between tariff data and exports, tariffs are averaged at the HS six-digit level. To compute the tariff cuts, we further assume that there are no changes in the trade policy of other countries vis-à-vis the Dominican Republic during the period under consideration.

24. The input-output table comes from http://www.bancentral.gov.do/publicaciones_economicas.asp.

25. The RCA index for a given year is given by $RCA_{jk} = (x_{ik}/X_i) / (x_{wk}/X_w)$, where x_{ik} and x_{wk} are the values of country i's exports of product k and world exports of product k and where X_i and X_w refer to the country's total exports and the world's total exports. The RCA ranges between zero and infinity. An RCA lower than 1 suggests that the country has a revealed comparative disadvantage in the product. Similarly, if the index exceeds unity, this implies that the country has a revealed comparative advantage in the product. Moreover, the RCA is a static concept and does not allow for comparison across time. One way to deal with this is to demean the RCA using the average RCA in each year. This is not necessary in the present study, as we have incorporated time fixed effects in the regression.

26. TRAINS/WITS is the Trade Analysis and Information System/World Integrated Trade Solution, developed by the World Bank and United National Conference on Trade and Development.

27. The effect of tariffs seems to be larger in the short run than in the long run.

28. We also estimate equations 2.1 and 2.2 in their log-linear version (that is, dependent variable in logs); results remain very similar for tariffs and tariff cuts, although not always significant. Another possibility would have been to employ a fixed-effect poisson estimator. However, this model does not allow us to evaluate the effect of time-invariant variables such as the firm location, EPZ (Cameron and Trivedi 2005, ch. 23). As a robustness check, we run equations 2.1 and 2.2 using the poisson estimator (ML and QLM), but excluding the variable EPZ. The results are very similar to those of the ordinary least squares (OLS) model: the effects of tariffs are very small (in terms of incidence ratios). We also estimate equations 2.1 and 2.2 using the negative binomial model, but the latter is subject to stronger distributional assumptions and does not converge for all specifications.

29. The main drawback of the linear probability model (LPM) is that the predicted probabilities can be negative and larger than 1. But despite this, the LPM estimator remains a good indicator of the size of the effect. Moreover, as a robustness check, we test the model using a logit estimator with fixed effects—that is, conditional logit (not shown here). In this type of model, only the signs of the coefficients can be interpreted (see Wooldridge 2001, ch. 15).

The results on the signs of the coefficients are similar to those obtained with the LPM model.

30. Hysteresis refers to the persistency of a firm's export participation as a consequence of the sunk costs associated with entry into new markets (Baldwin 1988). Entry into new markets is generally costly, so if a firm enters a market following a shock (that is, an exchange rate depreciation) it will not necessarily exit once the shock disappears.

31. Results are not shown due to space considerations but are available on request.

References

Albornoz, F., H. Calvo Pardo, G. Corcos, and E. Ornelas. 2009. "Sequential Exporting." CEP Discussion Paper dp0974, London School of Economics, Centre for Economic Performance, London.

Baldwin, J., and W. Gu. 2004. "Trade Liberalization: Export-Market Participation, Productivity Growth, and Innovation." *Oxford Review of Economic Policy* 20 (3, Autumn): 372–92.

Baldwin, R. 1988. "Hysteresis in Import Prices: The Beachhead Effect." *American Economic Review* 78 (4): 773–85.

Baldwin, R., and P. Krugman. 1989. "Persistent Trade Effects of Large Exchange Rate Shocks." *Quarterly Journal of Economics* 104 (4): 635–54.

Bernard, A., J. B. Jensen, and P. Schott. 2003. "Falling Trade Costs, Heterogeneous Firms, and Industry Dynamics." NBER Working Paper 9639, National Bureau of Economic Research, Cambridge, MA.

Bernard A., S. J. Redding, and P. Schott. 2009. "Multi-Product Firms and Trade Liberalization." Working Paper 09-21, U.S. Census Bureau, Center for Economic Studies, Washington, DC.

Besedes, T., and T. J. Prusa. 2006. "Ins, Outs, and the Duration of Trade." *Canadian Journal of Economics* 39 (1): 266–95.

———. 2007. "The Role of Extensive and Intensive Margins and Export Growth." NBER Working Paper 13628, National Bureau of Economic Research, Cambridge, MA.

Cadot, O., L. Iacovone, F. Rauch, and D. Pierola. 2010. "Success and Failure of African Exporters." World Bank, Washington, DC.

Cameron, A. C., and P. Trivedi. 2005. *Microeconometrics: Methods and Applications.* Cambridge, U.K.: Cambridge University Press.

Debaere, P., and S. Mostashari. 2005. "Do Tariffs Matter for the Extensive Margin of International Trade? An Empirical Analysis." CEPR Discussion Paper 5260, Centre for Economic Policy Research, London.

Dixit, A. 1989. "Entry and Exit Decisions under Uncertainty." *Journal of Political Economy* 97 (3): 620–38.

Eaton, J., M. Eslava, M. Kugler, and J. Tybout. 2007. "Export Dynamics in Colombia: Firm-Level Evidence." NBER Working Paper 13531, National Bureau of Economic Research, Cambridge, MA.

Eckel, C., L. Iacovone, B. Javorcik, and P. Neary. 2009. "Multi-product Firms at Home and Away." Centre for Economic Policy Research, London. http://www.cepr.org/meets/wkcn/1/1721/papers/Neary.pdf.

Freund, C., and E. Ornelas. 2009. "Regional Trade Agreements." CEP Discussion Paper dp0961, London School of Economics, Centre for Economic Performance, London.

Gómez, S., and C. Volpe. 2008. "Trade Policy and Export Diversification: What Should Colombia Expect from the FTA and the United States?" Working Paper 05, Inter-American Development Bank, Washington, DC.

Hornbeck, J. F. 2008. "The Dominican Republic-Central America-United States Free Trade Agreement (CAFTA-DR)." Congressional Research Service Report for the U.S. Congress, Washington, DC. http://www.nationalaglawcenter.org/assets/crs/RL31870.pdf.

Kehoe, T. J., and K. J. Ruhl. 2009. "How Important Is the New Goods Margin in International Trade?" Staff Report 324, Federal Reserve Bank of Minneapolis.

Laursen, K. 1998. "Revealed Comparative Advantage and the Alternatives as Measures of International Specialisation." DRUID Working Paper 98-30, DRUID, Copenhagen Business School, Department of Industrial Economics and Strategy, Copenhagen; Aalborg University, Department of Business Studies, Aalborg.

Melitz, M. 2003. "The Impact of Trade on Intra-Industry Reallocations and Aggregate Industry Productivity." *Econometrica* 71 (6): 1695–725.

Pavcnik, N. 2002. "Trade Liberalization, Exit, and Productivity Improvement: Evidence from Chilean Plants." *Review of Economic Studies* 69 (1): 245–76.

Swiston, A. 2010. "Spillovers to Central America in Light of the Crisis: What a Difference a Year Makes." IMF Working Paper WP35, International Monetary Fund, Washington, DC.

Trefler, D. 2004. "The Long and Short of the Canada-U. S. Free Trade Agreement." *American Economic Review* 94 (4): 870–95.

Wooldridge, J. 2001. *Econometric Analysis of Cross Section and Panel Data.* Cambridge, MA: MIT Press.

CHAPTER 3

Exports, Wages, and Skills: Implications for CAFTA

Irene Brambilla, Lucio Castro, and Guido Porto

This chapter explores whether implementation of the Dominican Republic–Central America Free Trade Agreement (DR-CAFTA) has as yet resulted in changes in the skill premium (that is, the ratio of skilled to unskilled wages). We find that the evidence is consistent with an increase in the skill premium in Central America in recent years, but not in other Latin American non-CAFTA countries. We also explore whether the estimated increase in the skill premium is driven by within-sector changes or by between-sector compositional shifts in the skilled labor force. We find that the former factor dominates, and, in fact, the empirical evidence indicates that the service sector, which is the largest employer of skilled workers, has increased its share of this type of worker. In contrast, half of the changes observed in the skill premium in the non-CAFTA comparison group are explained by shifts in the composition of skilled labor across sectors. Given these trends, this chapter seeks to provide evidence on the overall link between exports, wages, and skill utilization to illustrate the likely impacts of the DR-CAFTA on workers, employment, and skill composition (as well as on the skill premium). This evidence can help guide policy makers in designing a set of policies to boost the gains from the CAFTA agreement.

Our analysis is based on a detailed review of the literature, including results from recent research on this topic. We first review a paper by

Bernard and others (2007), who use different types of data to characterize exporters and importers in international trade. Their paper provides a summary of the literature and is thus a natural starting point in our analysis. We then describe some of the available results for Latin America. To this end, we review a paper by Casacuberta and others (2007). This paper focuses on exporting firms and provides a full characterization of the exporter premium in the region, including a productivity premium and a wage premium. We then discuss recent research by Brambilla and others (2010) and Brambilla, Lederman, and Porto (2010), who look at the overall link between exports and wages as well as between export destinations, wages, and skill utilization. This research is relevant for CAFTA because it suggests that exporting to high-income countries typically requires higher skills than either exporting to low- or middle-income countries or producing for the local market. Since DR-CAFTA implies access to U.S. markets, which are high-income markets, the agreement may have implications for skill utilization and the skill premium that are worth discussing in detail.

Firms in International Trade

This section is based on Bernard and others (2007), who provide a nice overview of the main features of exporting firms vis-à-vis firms devoted to the local market. The authors also review some of the characteristics of importing firms.

A basic feature of the data is how rare firm exporting is. Table 3.1 illustrates this point with data from the 2002 U.S. Census of Manufactures. Column 1 reports the distribution of firms across three-digit industries; column 2 displays the share of firms in each industry that actually do some exporting. Two conclusions emerge: while the overall share of U.S. manufacturing firms that export is only 18 percent, there are wide differences within industry categories. At the top, in sectors like computer and electronic products and electrical equipment and appliances, 38 percent of firms export; at the other end, only 5 percent of firms export in printing and 8 percent export in apparel manufacturing or wood product manufacturing.

Moreover, even among those exporting, export sales are only a small fraction of the firms' activities. This information is in the last column of table 3.1. The average share of exports is 14 percent (which is lower than the 18 percent share of exporting firms). There is also a lot of heterogeneity across sectors, with the highest shares observed in computer and electronic products (21 percent) and the lowest shares in beverages and tobacco (7 percent) and paper manufacturing (9 percent).

Table 3.1   Exporting by U.S. Manufacturing Firms, 2002

NAICS industry	% of firms	% of firms that export	Mean exports as % of total shipments
311 Food manufacturing	6.8	12	15
312 Beverage and tobacco products	0.7	23	7
313 Textile mills	1.0	25	13
314 Textile product mills	1.9	12	12
315 Apparel manufacturing	3.2	8	14
316 Leather and allied products	0.4	24	13
321 Wood product manufacturing	5.5	8	19
322 Paper manufacturing	1.4	24	9
323 Printing and related support	11.9	5	14
324 Petroleum and coal products	0.4	18	12
325 Chemical manufacturing	3.1	36	14
326 Plastics and rubber products	4.4	28	10
327 Nonmetallic mineral products	4.0	9	12
331 Primary metal manufacturing	1.5	30	10
332 Fabricated metal products	19.9	14	12
333 Machinery manufacturing	9.0	33	16
334 Computer and electronic products	4.5	38	21
335 Electrical equipment and appliances	1.7	38	13
336 Transportation equipment	3.4	28	13
337 Furniture and related products	6.4	7	10
339 Miscellaneous manufacturing	9.1	2	15
Aggregate manufacturing	100	18	14

Source: Bernard and others 2007.
Note: The first column of numbers summarizes the distribution of manufacturing firms across three-digit NAICS (North American Industry Classification System, U.S. Census Bureau) manufacturing industries. The second reports the share of firms in each industry that export. The final column reports mean exports as a percentage of total shipments across all firms that export in the noted industry.

Clearly, exporting is a relatively rare phenomenon, and it is thus not surprising to learn that exporters are very different from nonexporters in various characteristics. Using U.S. data, Bernard and others (2007) calculate the export premiums in U.S. manufacturing in 2002 for different firm characteristics, and we report those in table 3.2. If we focus on unconditional differences (column 1), we see that exporting firms have 119 percent more employment, 148 percent more shipments, 26 percent higher value added per worker, 2 percent higher productivity, 17 percent higher wages, 32 percent higher capital-labor ratios, and 19 percent higher skill per worker.

Column 2 reports results from a regression model that includes industry fixed effects in the explanatory variables. This allows us to control for

Table 3.2   Exporter Premiums in U.S. Manufacturing, 2002

Variable	(1)	(2)	(3)
Log employment	1.19	0.97	n.a.
Log shipments	1.48	1.08	0.08
Log value added per worker	0.26	0.11	0.10
Log TFP	0.02	0.03	0.05
Log wage	0.17	0.06	0.06
Log capital per worker	0.32	0.12	0.04
Log skill per worker	0.19	0.11	0.19

Source: Bernard and others 2007.
Note: TFP = total factor productivity. All results are from bivariate ordinary least squares (OLS) regressions of the firm characteristic in the first column on a dummy variable indicating the firm's export status. Regressions in column 2 include industry fixed effects. Regressions in column 3 include industry fixed effects and log firm employment as controls. TFP is computed as in Caves, Christensen, and Diewert (1982). Capital per worker refers to capital stock per worker. Skill per worker is the share of nonproduction workers in total employment. All results are significant at the 1 percent level. n.a. = Not applicable.

the basic inherent heterogeneity of firms across industries. The same differences between exporters and nonexporters can still be seen (although the differences are now smaller because export participation is positively correlated with industry characteristics). Within industries, exporters are larger than nonexporters: employment is 97 percent higher, and shipments are 108 percent higher. Exporters are also more productive by 11 percent in value added per worker and by 3 percent in total factor productivity (TFP).

Exporters also pay higher wages, by about 6 percent, and are more capital intensive (12 percent) and skill intensive (11 percent). While these results are based on U.S. data, they are representative of the literature. We show below similar results for select outcomes (namely, wages and productivity) for Latin American countries.

The evidence discussed so far has focused on exporters, mainly because of data limitations. It is, however, interesting to ask whether importers also have special characteristics. Bernard and others (2007) are in a unique position to shed some light on this matter; they have information on U.S. importers from the Linked-Longitudinal Firm Trade Transaction Database (LFTTD), which is based on data collected by the U.S. Census Bureau and the U.S. Customs Bureau. This data set captures all U.S. international trade transactions between 1992 and 2002.

The main results are reported in table 3.3, which shows that importers and exporters have basically the same characteristics. First, the act of importing is rare, and it is even rarer than the act of exporting. In the

Table 3.3　Exporting and Importing by U.S. Manufacturing Firms, 1997

NAICS industry	% of all firms	% of firms that export	% of firms that import	% of firms that import and export
311 Food manufacturing	7	17	10	7
312 Beverage and tobacco products	1	28	19	13
313 Textile mills	1	47	31	24
314 Textile product mills	2	19	13	9
315 Apparel manufacturing	6	16	15	9
316 Leather and allied products	0	43	43	30
321 Wood product manufacturing	5	15	5	3
322 Paper manufacturing	1	42	18	15
323 Printing and related support	13	10	3	2
324 Petroleum and coal products	0	32	17	14
325 Chemical manufacturing	3	56	30	26
326 Plastics and rubber products	5	42	20	16
327 Nonmetallic mineral products	4	16	11	7
331 Primary metal manufacturing	1	51	23	21
332 Fabricated metal products	20	21	8	6
333 Machinery manufacturing	9	47	22	19
334 Computer and electronic products	4	65	40	37
335 Electrical equipment and appliances	2	58	35	30
336 Transportation equipment	3	40	22	18
337 Furniture and related products	6	13	8	5
339 Miscellaneous manufacturing	7	31	19	15
Aggregate manufacturing	100	27	14	11

Source: Bernard and others 2007.

Note: The first column of numbers summarizes the distribution of manufacturing firms across three-digit NAICS industries. Remaining columns report the percentage of firms in each industry that export, import, and do both.

LFTTD data, about 27 percent of firms export (this figure is higher than the census data), while only 14 percent import. As before, these shares vary significantly across industries. There is a strong correlation (0.87) between industries with a high share of importers and those with a high share of exporters. Moreover, 41 percent of exporting firms also import, while 79 percent of importers also export.

Table 3.4 reports the "trading premium" for both exporters and importers. As shown, exporters and importers share a variety of positive attributes: they are both bigger and more productive, they pay higher wages, and they are more skill and capital intensive than nonexporters and nonimporters. This is consistent with all the previously available evidence.

The Latin American Experience

The data presented in Bernard and others (2007) are based on U.S. data. Many of the patterns found here are representative of the behavior of firms worldwide. In particular, we are interested in characterizing the export premiums in Latin America. To do this, we review results first reported in Casacuberta and others (2007), who focus on exports and wages and exports and productivity.

Casacuberta and others (2007) estimate productivity and wage exporter premiums using the enterprise surveys available for Latin American and Caribbean countries. They regress measures of TFP and average wages on firms' age, size (number of employees), foreign ownership, unique establishment, log of capital per worker, and region and industry dummies. They carry out two exercises. First, they run one regression for each of the

Table 3.4   Trading Premiums in U.S. Manufacturing, 1997

Variable	Exporter premium (1)	Importer premium (2)	Exporter and importer premium (3)
Log employment	1.50	1.40	1.75
Log shipments	0.29	0.26	0.31
Log value added per worker	0.23	0.23	0.25
Log TFP	0.07	0.12	0.07
Log wage	0.29	0.23	0.33
Log capital per worker	0.17	0.13	0.20
Log skill per worker	0.04	0.06	0.03

Source: Bernard and others 2007.
Note: All results are from bivariate OLS regressions of the firm characteristic listed on the left on a dummy variable noted at the top of each column as well as industry fixed effects and firm employment as additional controls. Employment regressions omit firm employment as a covariate. TFP is computed as in Caves, Christensen, and Diewert (1982).

16 countries for which data are available. Second, they run a regression with all countries pooled together and country dummies to account for country heterogeneity. Results are reported in table 3.5.

Exporters are indeed better than nonexporters in Latin America, too. First, exporters are more productive. In 14 of the 16 Latin American countries in the sample, there is a positive TFP exporter premium. The exporter premium also shows up in the pooled regression. Second, exporters pay higher wages. Again, in 15 of the countries, the regressions capture a positive wage exporter premium. This wage exporter premium also shows up in the pooled regressions. Notice that only about half of these positive exporter premiums are statistically different from 0 (eight in the case of TFP and 12 in the case of wages), which indicates that they are not estimated very precisely. However, they tend to be very large. For Latin America and the Caribbean as a whole, the productivity exporter premium is about 34 percent, and exporters tend to pay wages that are about 20 percent higher.

An Exploration into the Exporter Premium

The exporter premiums documented above indicate that firms that export are much more productive and pay much higher wages to their workers than other firms. This, however, is just a correlation and tells little about the direction of causality: do exporters become "good" firms, or do "good" firms become exporters?

Under the first hypothesis (that is, exporters become good firms), exporting improves productivity. The most common explanation, known as "learning by exporting," is that exporters acquire information from foreign customers on how to improve the product design, the manufacturing process, or the quality of the good (Westphal, Rhee, and Pursell 1984).[1] Foreign demand also allows domestic firms—particularly in small countries—to take advantage of unexploited economies of scale.

Under the second hypothesis (that is, good firms become exporters), the best firms self-select into export markets. One rationale for this self-selection is that important entry barriers exist in export markets because of the higher costs associated with selling in foreign markets (transport, but also distribution, marketing, and even production costs when firms need to adapt their product to foreign standards). Thus, only the more productive firms can enter foreign markets, and the observed differences between exporters and nonexporters can then be explained by preexisting differences.

These two hypotheses are obviously not mutually exclusive, but depending on which is the most important force, the policy implications

Table 3.5   Productivity and Wage Exporter Premiums in Latin America and the Caribbean

Premium country	TFP	Log of wages
Latin America and	0.339***	0.203***
the Caribbean	(0.035)	(0.026)
Argentina	0.597***	0.09
	(0.111)	(0.074)
Bolivia	−0.353*	0.084
	(0.193)	(0.163)
Brazil	0.478***	0.274***
	(0.070)	(0.054)
Chile	0.427***	0.262***
	(0.135)	(0.090)
Colombia	0.304***	0.275***
	(0.083)	(0.071)
Costa Rica	0.011	0.538***
	(0.009)	(0.177)
Ecuador	0.091	0.017
	(0.259)	(0.173)
El Salvador	0.357***	0.305***
	(0.126)	(0.092)
Guatemala	0.153	0.347**
	(0.148)	(0.143)
Honduras	0.22	0.208*
	(0.163)	(0.126)
Mexico	0.001	0.124
	(0.132)	(0.096)
Nicaragua	−0.02	−0.019
	(0.109)	(0.080)
Panama	0.024	0.257
	(0.362)	(0.125)
Paraguay	0.485	0.052
	(0.297)	(0.179)
Peru	0.520***	0.297**
	(0.160)	(0.121)
Uruguay	0.678***	0.465***
	(0.185)	(0.105)

Source: Casacuberta and others 2007.
Note: Standard errors are in parentheses. An OLS regression is run for each country, as well as a pooled regression labeled for Latin America and the Caribbean. Only the coefficient on the exporter dummy is reported. All regressions include as control variables firm-, region-, and industry-level characteristics (see text for more details).
* $p < .10$, ** $p < .05$, *** $p < .01$.

can be very different. On the one hand, export promotion activities, which are quite common in Latin America, are often justified on the basis of the learning-by-exporting explanation. On the other hand, the self-selection explanation suggests that policy makers should focus their efforts on the internal determinants of productivity growth.

The existing literature offers no clear-cut answer regarding the relative strength of the self-selection hypothesis versus the learning-by-exporting hypothesis. By nature, this literature is country specific, and depending on the country examined, studies seem to reach different conclusions. A survey follows. We begin with the productivity premium, and we then turn to the wage premium.

In their paper, Casacuberta and others (2007) survey 54 studies (covering 70 countries) that look at the productivity premium associated with export activity. In 86 percent of these studies, exporters are found to be more productive than nonexporters. Most of these studies—with rare exceptions (see, for example, the results for the Republic of Korea in Aw, Chung, and Roberts 2000)—find evidence of self-selection: good firms become exporters, suggesting that penetrating foreign markets may require higher productivity. About 60 percent of the studies test the learning-by-exporting hypothesis, but the evidence is mixed. Half of the studies find support for it, and the other half find no evidence of differences in productivity growth between firms that just became exporters and nonexporters.

Thus, the general messages coming from the literature are that exporters are indeed more productive that nonexporters, that firms do self-select into the export market, but that exporting does not always improve productivity (or does so only half the time). These findings suggest that a lot of heterogeneity exists across studies in terms of the learning-by-exporting hypothesis.

To illustrate in which types of countries exporting leads to productivity gains at the firm level, Casacuberta and others (2007) run probit regressions in which the explained variable is a dummy that takes the value of 1 when the study finds that in a particular country exports cause productivity gains and 0 when the study finds that exports do not cause productivity gains (any study in which the question of causality is not addressed is excluded from this regression). A regression is also run that explores in which types of countries learning by exporting is more likely. The dummy is regressed on country characteristics, such as the degree of trade openness of the country, its level of development, its size, and variables capturing the investment climate.

The purpose of this exercise is to illustrate the type of countries in which causality running from exports to productivity is most likely to be found. One would expect exports to be more likely to cause productivity increases in poorer countries with a smaller domestic market. Indeed, poorer countries tend to be further away from the technological frontier, and they have potentially much more to learn from foreign buyers. Similarly, in small countries, firms may count on foreign demand to take advantage of unexploited economies of scale. Openness to trade and a good investment climate may have ambiguous signs. A better investment climate allows firms to take advantage of business opportunities more freely, but may make it more difficult for exporters to appropriate these productivity gains when barriers to enter or exit are small. Obviously, this possibility does not necessarily mean that there are no productivity premiums or that exporting does not allow firms to become productive. The point is that it is difficult or impossible for the statistician to identify this effect if the benefits created by the exporter are easily captured by all other firms in the economy.

Table 3.6 reports results from these probit regressions. Each column is run with a different investment climate variable taken from the World Bank's Doing Business database. They are not all included simultaneously because they tend to be highly collinear. The clear message of table 3.6 is that exporting is more likely to create productivity premiums in small

Table 3.6   Exporting and Productivity Gains, by Investment Climate

Variable	Difficulty of entry procedures	Difficulty of closing a business	Difficulty of paying taxes	Difficulty of firing workers
Openness ($[M + X]$)/GDP)	−0.47	−0.64	−1.73	−1.25
	(0.97)	(1.01)	(1.32)	(1.19)
Level of development	0.05	0.01	0.05	0.20
(GDP per capita)	(0.16)	(0.15)	(0.16)	(0.2)
Size (GDP)	−0.31**	−0.41**	−0.57**	−0.38**
	(0.15)	(0.17)	(0.23)	(0.19)
Investment climate[a]	0.13	−0.41	−0.98**	0.40
	(0.73)	(0.36)	(0.50)	(0.31)
Pseudo R^2	0.22	0.15	0.25	0.22

Source: Casacuberta and others 2007.
Note: Standard errors are in brackets. All regressions are estimated using probit where the left-hand-side variable takes the value of 1 when a study finds that export causes growth and 0 when it does not find any evidence of causality. Each column runs this regression using a different variable to capture the investment climate. Each regression has 34 observations. All regressions include a dummy equal to 1 when the period under examination is in the 1990s or later. This dummy is never significant.
a. See the variables in the top row.
** $p < .05$.

countries. This finding somehow gives more prominence to the economies-of-scale rationale for productivity premiums than to the knowledge-acquisition hypothesis, although this specification clearly does not allow disentanglement of these two forces.

Probably because of the conflicting forces, the level of development does not seem to be an important determinant of the causality between exports and productivity: poorer countries have much more to learn from foreign buyers, but absorbing this knowledge may be more difficult. The degree of trade openness is also always statistically insignificant. The investment climate variables give an ambiguous picture, but the only result that is statistically significant tends to suggest that a cumbersome business environment is not likely to help exporters to take advantage of some of the potential benefits in foreign markets.

Finally, two important points should be kept in mind. First, the determinants of self-selection remain an open question, and little work has been done to explain the sources of productivity growth before entry into the export market. As Yeaple (2005) argues, productivity is likely to be an endogenous decision, and trade opportunities may induce some firms to adopt new technologies. The expected future entry into export markets may well encourage firms to invest in new technology and product design and to benefit from the experience and know-how of potential foreign buyers. Thus, the increase in productivity observed before entering export markets may well be due to this export potential. Alvarez and López (2005) call this *conscious self-selection*, and they find evidence using plant-level data from Chile that self-selection is indeed a conscious process, where firms increase productivity with the objective of becoming exporters.[2]

Second, regardless of whether exports cause firm-level productivity gains, the fact that exporters are more productive and larger (perhaps exclusively because of self-selection) suggests that, as countries increase their export orientation, larger and more productive firms will produce a larger share of national output. This reallocation of resources from less productive and smaller firms to more productive and larger firms in itself is a source of aggregate gross domestic product (GDP) growth.

Turning now to the wage premiums, Casacuberta and others (2007) review 30 studies that explore wage premiums associated with export activity. In two-thirds of the studies analyzed, there is evidence of an overall wage premium. In all but two studies, evidence exists of large skilled-wage premiums,[3] whereas unskilled workers in the export sector benefit from a premium in only 45 percent of the studies. Thus, the big-picture message emerging from this review is that exporters pay higher wages to skilled workers and sometimes pay higher wages to less-skilled workers.

The issue of causality is seldom addressed in the literature, however. Although many of the papers are based on panel data that allow for controls of fixed effects and unobserved heterogeneity at the firm level, the issue of causality from exports to wages remains largely unsolved. One exception is Feenstra and Hanson (1997), who set up an instrumental variables estimator of the effects of foreign direct investment and outsourcing on wages and wage inequality. Another exception is Verhoogen (2008), who uses the Mexico peso devaluation to establish that exporting leads to higher wage payments in Mexican manufacturing. Below, we review recent research that addresses the issue of causality.

Before turning to the causality problem, we again explore the heterogeneity in the findings regarding overall wage premiums and unskilled wage premiums to see whether some country characteristics are associated with a higher likelihood of finding a wage premium associated with exports (regardless of whether self-selection or causality is involved). Again, for the same reasons as before (the productivity channel), one may expect the wage premium to be especially likely in small and poor countries. A better and more competitive investment climate should in principle help transmit these gains from firms to workers, but the same caveat discussed earlier applies. One would also expect unskilled wages to have a higher premium in countries with an abundant supply of skilled workers. Indeed, because unskilled workers are the rare factor in skill-abundant countries, one would expect them to benefit later from these wage premiums.

Table 3.7 shows the results of the probit regressions. The first two columns explain the presence of an overall wage premium using two investment climate variables; the second two columns explain the presence of an unskilled wage premium, again using two different investment climate variables. The regression could not be run for the skilled wage premium because almost all the studies surveyed find that a skilled wage premium exists.

The clear message coming out of table 3.7 is that wage premiums are more likely to be observed in small countries. This finding again provides tangible evidence of the importance for firms in small countries of being able to take advantage of unexploited economies of scale in world markets. Unskilled wage premiums are also more likely to be observed in skill-abundant countries. This finding may be because exporters may need to pay higher wages to attract the rare factor (unskilled workers) to their firms in countries where skilled workers are relatively abundant.

Table 3.7 Wage Premiums, by Investment Climate

	Overall wages		Unskilled wages	
Variable	Difficulty of entry procedures	Difficulty of firing workers	Difficulty of entry procedures	Difficulty of firing workers
Openness ([M + X]/GDP)	-0.40	-0.23	-1.36	-1.53
	(0.96)	(1.04)	(0.86)	(1.14)
Level of development	1.49	0.64	-0.90	-0.90
(GDP per capita)	(1.37)	(0.65)	(0.67)	(0.68)
Size (GDP)	-2.43*	-0.69	-1.45**	-1.23**
	(1.39)	(0.54)	(0.57)	(0.61)
Unskilled abundance (unskilled workers to skilled workers)	0.92	-0.24	-4.16**	-4.51**
	(0.95)	(0.77)	(1.45)	(2.07)
Investment climate[a]	-2.76*	-0.36	-0.55	0.05
	(1.46)	(0.56)	(0.39)	(0.35)
Pseudo R^2	0.36	0.13	0.38	0.35

Source: Casacuberta and others 2007.

Note: Standard errors are in parentheses. All regressions are estimated using probit where the left-hand-side variable takes the value of 1 when a study finds that there are wage premiums (overall wage premiums for the first two columns and unskilled wage premiums for the last two columns). Each of the two columns runs the regression using a different variable to capture investment climate: either the difficulty of entry procedures or the difficulty of firing workers. Only 17 observations in the overall wage regression and 26 in the unskilled wage regression reflect the number of studies surveyed that tried to answer these questions. All regressions include a dummy equal to 1 when the period under examination is in the 1990s or later. This dummy is never significant.

a. See the variables in the top row.

* $p < .10$, ** $p < .05$.

The Skill Premium in Exporting

To complete our discussion of the wage premium due to exporting, this section explores the wage-skill premium. We discuss scenarios in which exporting may lead to the existence of a skill premium, and we review evidence on this for Latin America. To this end, we summarize some of the key findings in a recent paper by Brambilla and others (2010). The authors work with 64 household surveys for 16 countries covering more than 5 million workers in the region. The countries included in the study are Argentina, Brazil, Chile, Colombia, Costa Rica, the Dominican Republic, Ecuador, El Salvador, Guatemala, Honduras, Mexico, Nicaragua, Panama, Paraguay, Peru, and Uruguay. Following the literature on industry wage differentials (Dickens, Katz, and Lang 1986; Dickens and Lang 1988; Gibbons and Katz 1992), the authors allow the skill premiums to vary across industries, as in Galiani and Porto (2010). Then they study econometrically the relationship between the industry skill premiums and the level of sectoral exports. Once the superior performance of exporting firms (as well as importing firms) has been established (see above), the analysis in Brambilla and others (2010) is useful to illustrate the existence of an exporter *skill* premium.

Two leading theories explain this potential link between industry exports and skill premiums. One argues that the act of exporting requires activities that are skill intensive, although the production of the good may require unskilled labor. Exporting firms, and therefore industries with more exports in general, will thus demand higher skills and pay a higher skill premium. The alternative theory argues that exporting is associated with higher profits (because more productive firms self-select into exports) and these higher profits are shared with the workers via profit-sharing rules.

The theory focusing on the need to engage in skill-intensive activities to export a product is based on Brambilla, Lederman, and Porto (2010). If skilled labor is imperfectly mobile and unskilled labor is perfectly mobile, unskilled labor earns an economywide competitive wage, while industries using skilled workers pay more. Exporting requires both the production of the physical units of the product and the provision of export services. These services include labeling, marketing, technical support, and consumer support (web page, e-mail, warranty) and are assumed to be skill intensive.[4] The high-export sector pays higher wages to their skilled workers, therefore, since the wage offered to the unskilled workers is assumed to be the same across industries (given the competitive national market for unskilled labor). An alternative theory is based on profit-sharing mechanisms. Skilled workers demand a wage premium to exert the necessary effort because it is considered fair to share the profits of the firms. In consequence, while marginal firms pay the competitive outside wage, more profitable firms pay increasingly higher wages. In equilibrium, if high-export firms are high-profit firms, they offer higher wages to their skilled workers. Under both hypotheses, the industry-specific skill premium is an increasing function of the level of sectoral exports.

Country and Industry Effects

Brambilla and others (2010) estimate two-digit industry skill premiums for 16 Latin American countries and exploit these estimates to provide evidence in support of the claim that the premiums depend positively on sectoral exports. As a first step, we assess the role of country and industry dummies. More specifically, the industry skill premium is explained by (a) country dummies alone, (b) industry dummies alone, and (c) country and industry dummies. For each of these models, we calculate the R^2 (adjusted) and the F-test of joint significance of each set of dummies. We do this for all sectors, for the manufacturing sectors, and for the nontradable (and services) sectors. If we include all sectors, country dummies alone account for 20 percent of the variance in the skill premium, while industry dummies alone account for almost 48 percent. Both sets of dummies jointly explain about 69.2 percent of the variation in the industry skill premium. The dummies are always jointly statistically significant. In this case, it appears that the industry dummies play a more important role than the country dummies. It should be kept in mind, however, that the comparison of R^2 is a descriptive assessment of the role of the dummies in explaining the variance in the dependent variable.

Exports and the Skill Premium

As mentioned above, sectoral exports could be an important determinant of the industry-specific skill premiums. To assess this claim, Brambilla and others (2010) regress the skill premium for sector j in country c on the log of the ratio of sectoral exports to GDP together with country and industry dummies. The model is estimated with weighted least squares to account for the fact that the industry-specific skill premiums are estimated. The weights are thus the inverse of the standard errors. Naturally, these estimates do not provide any causal evidence; instead, they suggest a clear reduced-form interpretation to illustrate whether the data support any link between sectoral exports and sectoral skill premiums.

Table 3.8 presents the results. Column 1 shows the estimate of the model when the skill premiums are regressed on a constant and the log of the ratio of exports over GDP. The estimate is positive and significant, suggesting that the skill premium rises with exports. The estimate in column 1 implies that doubling a sector's share of exports over GDP (a change in the log of exports over GDP equal to 1) is associated with an increase of 0.0028 in the skill premium, that is, the wage differential between skilled and unskilled workers rises by 0.28 percentage point. Notice that the simulated shock of a change of 1 in the log of exports over GDP is reasonable because the standard deviation of the variable in our sample is about 2.1. Thus this association is positive and significant, but it is not very large.

In columns 2 to 5 of table 3.8, we perform several robustness tests. The incidence of industry exports remains significant, with a similar magnitude as in column 1. Column 3 includes country dummies only, and the link between exports and the skill premium disappears. In column 4, we include both sets of dummies, and the link disappears, too. Controlling for both country and industry dummies might be too restrictive, however. Country fixed effects explain about a third of the variation in the skill premium, and both country and industry dummies account for about 60 percent. This leaves little room for exports to explain the skill premium because much of the variation in the dependent variable is attenuated by the dummies. To learn more about the role of sectoral exports, we work with a more parsimonious version of the regression model where, instead

Table 3.8   Exports and the Industry Skill Premium

Variable	(1)	(2)	(3)	(4)	(5)
Log exports to GDP	0.0028***	0.0033***	0.0004	−0.0002	0.0027**
	(0.001)	(0.0011)	(0.0011)	(0.0015)	(0.001)
Log GDP_pc					0.0284***
					(0.004)
Log skilled to unskilled					−0.014***
					(0.004)
Country dummies	No	No	Yes	Yes	No
Industry dummies	No	Yes	No	Yes	Yes
Number of observations	273	273	273	273	273
R^2	0.03	0.31	0.43	0.58	0.46

Source: Authors' calculations.
Note: Standard errors are in parentheses.
** $p < .05$, *** $p < .01$.

of country dummies, we control for country characteristics—namely, the log of per capita GDP and the ratio of skilled (completion of high school) over unskilled labor. These results are reported in column 5 of table 3.8. Both per capita GDP and the skill composition are statistically significant determinants of the industry skill premiums with the expected signs: richer countries seem to have greater disparities between skilled and unskilled wages, and, as expected, countries with a greater fraction (supply) of skilled workers pay smaller skill premiums. The significance of these variables supports their use in lieu of country fixed effects. Also the R^2 of the model remains high at 0.46, which is higher than the R^2 from the model with country dummies. In these models, the coefficient of exports as a fraction of GDP is positive and statistically significant (column 5), and the estimate is of similar magnitude as the one reported in columns 1 and 2.

Exporting, Productivity, and Wages: Causality

The main goal of this section, which closely follows Porto (2007), is to generate evidence on the causality of exports to wages with an application to Argentina. The empirical strategy exploits the Brazilian devaluation of 1999. Argentina and Brazil are major trade partners, and the Brazilian devaluation greatly affected Argentine exports. Having an exogenous shock to exports is crucial in identifying a causal relationship between exports and wages. The combination of the panel data set and the devaluation shock is an important instrument with which to address this problem because the same firm can be considered before and after the devaluation to see how the wages paid by this firm changed when an exogenous change occurred in exporting opportunities. This situation presents the opportunity to determine causality from exports to wages.

Regression Model: Exports and Export Destinations

This section examines whether wages and the share of nonproduction workers (an approximation of the percentage of skilled workers) depend on exports and on the country of destination of exports. Some of the following hypotheses are tested: (a) whether exporting firms pay higher wages and have higher ratios of nonproduction workers than firms producing for the domestic market; (b) whether the composition of export destinations of a firm matters (that is, whether firms that export to rich countries pay higher wages and have higher ratios of nonproduction workers than firms that either produce for the domestic market or export to low-income countries); and (c) whether product quality is one of the factors behind the wage-employment effect of exports.

The following regression models are set up to test these hypotheses:

$$\ln w_{it} = \alpha_1 Exp_{it} + \mathbf{x}'_{it}\,\beta_1 + \phi_t^w + \phi_i^w + \varepsilon_{it}^w$$
$$\ln s_{it} = \alpha_{12} Exp_{it} + \mathbf{x}'_{it}\,\beta_2 + \phi_t^s + \phi_i^s + \varepsilon_{it}^s, \tag{3.1}$$

where w is average wage paid by firm i at time t, and s is the share of skilled workers (nonproduction workers). Controls in x are industry dummies; location dummies; year dummies; indicators of whether the firm is foreign; the percentage of foreign ownership; the firm size, as measured by total number of workers and, alternatively, by sales; materials consumption as a proxy for productivity shocks; and age of the plant. The error terms have a firm fixed effect ϕ_i^u and ϕ_i^s. The variable Exp captures exports and export destinations. Concretely, we include the share of exports in sales (to account for export status) and the share of exports to high-income destinations in total exports (to account for the role of export destinations).

The model in equation 3.1 includes firm fixed effects that control for time-invariant unobserved heterogeneity. However, these regressions may still suffer from endogeneity or omitted variable biases. An instrumental variable approach is followed to address these issues and the issue of causality. The strategy is to explain both the level of exports of the firms and their composition of countries of destination by the exogenous exposure to the Brazilian devaluation of 1999. Notice that heterogeneity exists in the exposure to this shock because firms and industries that exported more to Brazil before the devaluation were more likely to be affected by the shock.

Two endogenous variables are used in the model. One is the HIE variable—the share of exports to high-income countries—which is related to the export destinations of the firm. The other is the share of exports in sales, which is related more closely to export status. The instrument for the HIE share is built by interacting a post-devaluation dummy with the share of the industry's exports that were destined for Brazil in 1998. More specifically, two specifications are adopted. In the nonparametric model with dummies, the impacts of the devaluation are allowed to vary from one year to the other (as the economy adjusted, exposure in 1999 was different from exposure in 2000). Consequently, this instrument is built by interacting the level of exposure to Brazil before the devaluation—that is, the share of exports to Brazil in 1998—with a 1999 dummy variable and a 2000 dummy. In the second specification, an alternative instrument is built, which is the interaction of the pre-devaluation share of exports to Brazil (at the firm level) with the exchange rate of the Brazilian currency in 1999 and 2000. This instrument is a parametric model of the exposure to the shock. Support for these instruments comes from the preview of patterns of exports in Argentina. The argument is that, following the devaluation, firms that were most exposed to the Brazilian devaluation had to adjust and move away from this market, exploring new markets in high-income countries.

A similar strategy is followed to deal with the endogeneity of the ratio of exports to sales. More concretely, the share of exports to Brazil in total sales is used as an instrument for the share of total exports in total sales. Two arguments support this instrument. One claim is that firms with a larger share of exports to Brazil in total sales had smaller shares of exports in sales because part of the effect of the devaluation was to make them retrench into local markets. Another argument is that, conditional on the share of exports to Brazil in total exports, firms with a higher ratio of exports to Brazil in total sales had a lower base from which to divert exports to high-income countries. As before, exposure is measured non-parametrically with a dummy for 1999 and another for 2000, using the Brazilian exchange rates.

First-stage regressions reveal that the instruments work well (see Porto 2007 for more details). They have substantial explanatory power and are statistically significant in all the regressions. Furthermore, the results imply that, in fact, following the Brazilian devaluation, firms that were more exposed to it switched to high-income destination countries but faced lower export-to-sales ratios, as expected. Also, the correlations persist even after including year effects to account for the macroeconomic impacts of the devaluation (and other time effects that affected all firms in the same fashion).

Now this chapter turns to the main results: the instrumental variable coefficients of exports on wages. These results are reported in table 3.9, which lists the two potential endogenous variables and has nine columns. These columns correspond to the three models: only exports-to-sales ratio, only share of exports to high-income countries, and both export to sales and HIE together. We work with different specifications: without year effects and nonparametric dummy instruments (columns 1 to 3), with year effects and nonparametric dummy instruments (columns 4 to 6), and with year effects and parametric instruments using exchange rates

Table 3.9 Exports, Export Destination, and Wages: Wage Regression with Instrumental Variables

dependent variable: log average wage

Variable	(1)	(2)	(3)	(4)	(5)	(6)	(7)	(8)	(9)
Exports to sales	-0.979		-0.343	-0.735		-0.259	-0.543		-0.075
	(0.638)		(0.478)	(0.594)		(0.513)	(0.546)		(0.495)
High-income exports		0.365***	0.357***		0.317***	0.305***		0.296***	0.293***
		(0.106)	(0.111)		(0.108)	(0.107)		(0.107)	(0.110)
Log sales	0.054***	0.054***	0.055***	0.064***	0.057***	0.058***	0.063***	0.057***	0.058***
	(0.019)	(0.018)	(0.018)	(0.020)	(0.020)	(0.020)	(0.021)	(0.020)	(0.020)
Number of firms	901	901	901	901	901	901	901	901	901
Number of observations	2,544	2,544	2,544	2,544	2,544	2,544	2,544	2,544	2,544

Source: Authors' calculations.

Note: All regressions include firm fixed effects. Robust standard errors are in parentheses. Year effects are included in columns 4–9, but not in columns 1–3. The instruments are dummies for columns 1–6 and the exchange rate for columns 7–9.

*** $p < .01$.

(columns 7 to 9). The major conclusion of this work is that, although exporting to high-income countries improves wages, the ratio of exports to sales does *not* affect them. Thus exporting per se is not a significant channel toward higher wages, but exporting to high-income countries is. That is, what appears to matter is the composition of exports.

The magnitudes are important, too: firms with average shares of exports to high-income countries pay wages between 8.79 (29.3 × 0.30) and 9.51 (31.7 × 0.30) higher than firms with no exports to high-income countries. It is difficult not to overemphasize this fact: the results are very robust and survive the inclusion of firm fixed effects (using the panel data) and the use of instrumental variables.

Conclusions and Policy Implications

Export firms are more productive and pay higher wages than other firms. There is also evidence that exporters pay a higher skill premium at the industry level. These exporter premiums have two explanations that are not mutually exclusive. Either more productive firms self-select into export activities, because only highly productive firms could face the entry costs associated with selling in foreign markets, or learning by exporting occurs, in which case participation in the export market allows firms to become more productive.

The existing empirical evidence strongly supports the self-selection hypothesis; learning by exporting is observed in only some countries. More than 80 percent of the studies surveyed for this chapter find evidence that exporting firms were more productive than other firms before entering the export market, whereas only half the studies find that the productivity of exporting firms grew faster than the productivity of non-exporting firms after the former entered the export market.

Learning by exporting is more likely to be observed in small countries, suggesting that the ability to exploit economies of scale in foreign markets may be part of the explanation behind learning by exporting. In contrast, trade openness, the investment climate, and the level of development do not explain why learning by exporting occurs, suggesting that they are not important determinants of learning by exporting.

Wage export premiums (that is, the fact that exporters pay higher wages than nonexporters) are more likely in small economies, whereas trade openness, the investment climate, and the level of development do not seem to matter. Recent research shows that exporting is also associated with an industry skill premium. In the presence of some sort of labor immobility, so that skilled workers earn a premium that can vary by industry, this premium is larger in those industries that are more oriented toward export markets in general. This evidence is very strong for Latin American countries.

The existing literature on exports and wages stops at identifying whether a wage export premium is present and does not address the issue of causality. More recent studies, including Verhoogen (2008), Porto (2007), and Brambilla, Lederman, and Porto (2010), provide stronger evidence of a causal effect of exports on wages. Furthermore, the evidence in the last paper also suggests that export destination matters and that, in particular, exporting to high-income countries matters. This paper finds, in a panel of manufacturing firms in Argentina, that exporting to high-income countries is associated with higher wages and higher skill utilization. This may be due to two major reasons. First, the act of exporting (rather than the act of producing) may require skills. Second, accessing high-income destinations may also require quality upgrades that are, in turn, skill intensive.

The results are consistent with both a quality and a profit-sharing story. High-income countries tend to demand higher-quality goods, a situation that allows firms to pay higher wages. However, Porto (2007) cannot rule out the existence of profit-shifting mechanisms, whereby firms that export to high-income countries tend to share part of the excess profits with their workers.

But what determines the rapid productivity growth observed by firms before they enter the market? Little is known about this growth, and some authors, such as Alvarez and López (2005), argue that an important part of the explanation—at least among Chilean manufacturing plants—is conscious self-selection. Firms become more productive with the objective of becoming exporters. So export activity may be the cause of the jump in productivity before firms enter the export market.

An important point to keep in mind is that, regardless of whether exports cause firm-level productivity gains, the fact that exporters are more productive and larger (perhaps exclusively because of self-selection) suggests that, as countries increase their export orientation, larger and more productive firms will produce a larger share of national output. This reallocation of resources from less productive and smaller firms to more productive and larger firms in itself is a source of aggregate GDP growth.

Depending on which is the most important force, however, the policy implications can be very different. On the one hand, offshore export promotion activities, which are quite common in Latin America, are often justified on the basis of learning by exporting. On the other hand, the self-selection explanation suggests that policy makers should focus their efforts on the internal determinants of productivity growth. Evidence elsewhere indirectly suggests that the latter is probably more important in developing countries. In a recent paper, Lederman, Olarreaga, and Payton (2006) show, with the help of a recent survey on export promotion activities, that in developing countries the returns to onshore export promotion activities, such as technical assistance and training for (large) domestic firms on how to enter foreign markets, are much larger than the returns to offshore export promotion activities, such as country image, fair participation, and other marketing activities abroad, including foreign offices. They also find that, to maximize the effect on aggregate exports, export promotion activities should focus on large domestic firms that are not yet exporting rather than on established exporters. These findings are consistent with the idea that self-selection plays an important role in explaining export premiums.

Notes

1. The expected effects from learning by exporting could occur either at the time of entry into exporting (a one-time effect) or every year after entry (a continuous effect).

2. Hallward-Driemeier, Iarossi, and Sokoloff (2002) show that part of what self-selection may be capturing is the idea that exporters invest in retooling for foreign markets in advance of entering the market and that therefore self-selection may be associated with export activity.

3. These two studies (Breau and Rigby 2006; Schank, Schnabel, and Wagner 2007) match employer-employee data, which allows them to control for workers' characteristics, such as education, age, and experience, that are unobservable when working with firm (employer) data only. It is probably too early to conclude anything, but a large share of what is captured as an exporter skill premium seems to result from the "superior" characteristics of workers in the export sector.

4. In Verhoogen (2008), exporting requires quality upgrades.

References

Alvarez, R., and R. López. 2005. "Exporting and Performance: Evidence from Chilean Plants." *Canadian Journal of Economics* 38 (4): 1384–400.

Aw, B., S. Chung, and M. Roberts. 2000. "Productivity and Turnover in the Export Market: Micro-level Evidence from the Republic of Korea and Taiwan (China)." *World Bank Economic Review* 14 (1): 65–90.

Bernard, A., B. Jensen, S. Redding, and P. Schott. 2007. "Firms in International Trade." *Journal of Economic Perspectives* 21 (3, Summer): 105–30.

Brambilla, I., R. Carneiro, D. Lederman, and G. Porto. 2010. "Skills, Exports, and the Wages of Five Million Latin American Workers." Policy Research Working Paper 5246, World Bank, Washington, DC.

Brambilla, I., D. Lederman, and G. Porto. 2010. "Exports, Export Destinations, and Skills." World Bank, Washington, DC.

Breau, S., and D. Rigby. 2006. "Is There Really an Export Wage Premium? Case Study of Los Angeles Using Matched Employee-Employer Data." Working Paper 06-06, U.S. Census Bureau, Washington, DC.

Casacuberta, C., N. Gandelman, M. Olarreaga, G. Porto, and E. Rubiano. 2007. "Exporter Premiums." In *Latin American and Caribbean Regional Study on Microdeterminants of Growth*, ch. 7. Washington, DC: World Bank.

Caves, D. W., L. R. Christensen, and W. E. Diewert. 1982. "The Economic Theory of Index Numbers and the Measurement of Input, Output, and Productivity." *Econometrica* 50 (6): 1393–1414.

Dickens, W. T., L. F. Katz, and K. Lang. 1986. "Are Efficiency Wages Efficient?" NBER Working Paper Series w1935, National Bureau of Economic Research, Cambridge, MA.

Dickens, W., and K. Lang. 1988. "Labor Market Segmentation and the Union Wage Premium." *Review of Economics and Statistics* 70 (3): 527–30.

Feenstra, R., and G. Hanson. 1997. "Foreign Direct Investment and Relative Wages: Evidence from Mexico's Maquiladoras." *Journal of International Economics* 42 (3–4): 371–93.

Galiani, S., and G. Porto. 2010. "Trends in Tariff Reforms and Trends in the Structure of Wages." *Review of Economics and Statistics* 92 (3, August): 482–94.

Gibbons, R., and L. F. Katz. 1992. "Does Unmeasured Ability Explain Inter-Industry Wage Differences?" *Review of Economic Studies* 59 (3): 515–35.

Hallward-Driemeir, M., G. Iarossi, and K. Sokoloff. 2002. "Exports and Manufacturing Productivity in East Asia: A Comparative Analysis with Firm-Level Data." NBER Working Paper 8894, National Bureau of Economic Research, Washington, DC.

Lederman, D., M. Olarreaga, and L. Payton. 2006. "Export Promotion Agencies: What Works and What Doesn't." Policy Research Working Paper 4044, World Bank, Washington, DC.

Porto, G. 2007. "From Exports to Wages: Evidence from Panel Data in Argentina." Background paper for *Latin American and Caribbean Regional Study on Microdeterminants of Growth*, World Bank, Washington, DC.

Schank, T., C. Schnabel, and J. Wagner. 2007. "Do Exporters Really Pay Higher Wages? First Evidence from German Linked Employer-Employee Data." *Journal of International Economics* 72 (1): 52–74.

Verhoogen, E. 2008. "Trade, Quality Upgrading, and Wage Inequality in the Mexican Manufacturing Sector." *Quarterly Journal of Economics* 123 (2): 489–530.

Westphal, L., Y. Rhee, and G. Pursell. 1984. "Sources of Technological Capability in South Korea." In *Technological Capability in the Third World*, ed. M. Fransman and K. King, 279–300. London: Macmillan.

Yeaple, S. 2005. "A Simple Model of Firm Heterogeneity, International Trade, and Wages." *Journal of International Economics* 65 (1): 1–20

CHAPTER 4

Trade and Economic Growth: Evidence on the Role of Complementarities for the DR-CAFTA Countries

César Calderón and Virginia Poggio

One of the salient features of the world economy has been the important surge in trade and financial globalization in the past two decades. Multiple free trade agreements and regional integration agreements are being celebrated—with more than 400 regional trade agreements in force by December 2008 according to the World Trade Organization. In addition, world trade has grown at least twice as fast as world output over the past two decades, thus deepening economic integration.

Theoretically, it has long been argued in the literature that trade stimulates long-term growth and that it can do so through multiple channels. International trade would allow countries to specialize in areas where they possess comparative advantage, expand potential markets, allow firms to exploit economies of scale, enable the diffusion of technological innovation and frontier managerial practices, and reduce incentives for

The authors would like to thank their peer reviewers, J. Humberto López and Rashmi Shankar, for invaluable comments.

firms to conduct rent-seeking activities through higher market competition. Empirically, earlier works find evidence in support of the growth-enhancing effects of trade. However, Rodríguez and Rodrik (2001) suggest that most of the evidence is not robust due to measurement issues of trade openness and trade policy as well as econometric problems (that is, endogeneity of trade measures and collinearity of trade and institutions). Rodrik (2005) also argues that policies toward trade openness may not render the same results for all countries since there is no unique mapping from economic principles to economic packages. Most of these criticisms have been tackled in recent empirical efforts by developing new identification strategies (Frankel and Romer 1999), developing new trade indicators (Wacziarg 2001), examining the trade-growth correlation around episodes of policy changes (Wacziarg and Welch 2008), and addressing the issue of mapping from principles to policies by assessing the role of complementarities between trade and other structural reforms in stimulating growth (Calderón, Loayza, and Schmidt-Hebbel 2006; Calderón and Fuentes 2009; Chang, Kaltani, and Loayza 2009).

The goal of this chapter is to assess the growth effects of trade among Dominican Republic–Central America Free Trade Agreement (DR-CAFTA) countries and, more specifically, to evaluate the structural areas that might become a constraint to reaping the benefits from growth. In this context, the chapter argues that policy complementarities are a cornerstone of growth. Pro-growth policies should mutually reinforce—for example, trade openness will have positive and substantial effects on growth in countries with higher levels of human capital. At the same time, policy complementarities may also impose severe restrictions on the design of an optimal growth strategy—especially among countries with less favorable initial conditions.

To accomplish this task, we gather annual information for a sample of 136 countries over the period 1960–2009 and construct a panel database of five-year nonoverlapping observations. We run our cross-country regressions using econometric techniques suitable for dynamic panel data models that account not only for the presence of unobserved components, but also for the likely endogeneity or reverse causality of the growth determinants. Our results find that trade has indeed promoted growth, and our result is robust to the specification and technique used. However, the growth benefits of rising trade openness are conditional on the level of progress in structural areas such as education, innovation, infrastructure, institutions, regulatory framework, financial development, and international financial integration. Indeed, we find that lack of progress in these areas can restrict the potential benefits of trade.

We discuss the implications of our regression analysis for the DR-CAFTA nexus, putting emphasis on the impact of trade openness on growth per capita and identifying the structural areas that may represent a constraint to growth. To do so, we calculate the impact of trade on growth among DR-CAFTA countries over the past 15 years and the potential growth gains from raising trade openness to the levels of a benchmark country or region (in our case, the East Asian tigers, EAP-7). In both cases, we find that there is room for trade to stimulate growth, but special attention should be placed on reforms in structural areas that are complementary to the trade reform efforts launched by DR-CAFTA countries, mainly in the areas of education, institutional quality, and infrastructure.

This chapter is divided into five sections. It begins with a brief review of the literature on trade and growth with some emphasis on the channels of transmission, the problems in the empirical literature, and the complementarities between trade and other structural factors in driving growth. It then describes the data and outlines the econometric methodology used to estimate our cross-country growth regressions. This is followed by a presentation of the empirical evidence on trade and growth and a test of whether the impact of the former on the latter is enhanced by advances in structural areas such as education, domestic financial market development, institutional quality, infrastructure, financial integration, innovation, and regulatory framework. We also discuss the economic implications of our statistical analysis for DR-CAFTA countries. A final section concludes.

Literature Review

The classical paradigm of international trade argues that trade promotes growth by increasing the relative price of the good that is intensive in the relatively abundant factor (see, for example, Deardorff 1974). The standard theory predicts an effect of trade openness on the long-run level rather than on the long-run growth of GDP (Lucas 1988; Young 1991). The new trade literature, in contrast, argues that long-term growth from trade can be channeled through more intense research and development (R&D) activity (see Romer 1990; Grossman and Helpman 1991). In this context, trade promotes long-term growth by raising the availability of resources for R&D and, thus, increasing the availability of specialized inputs and the size of the market, among other things. More broadly speaking, the theoretical literature is ambiguous about the impact of trade on long-run growth. A strand of the literature suggests that the growth effects are positive when trade specializes in increasing returns-to-scale activities (Grossman and Helpman 1991; Young 1991). Others suggest that the effect is either negligible or negative whenever there are market or institutional imperfections (Rodríguez and Rodrik 2001), underutilization of human or capital resources, focus on extractive activities (Sachs and Warner 1995), or specialization away from technologically intensive sectors with increasing returns to scale (Matsuyama 1992).

The literature suggests that trade may affect economic growth through different channels. First, trade openness may increase a country's market size and, thus, may provide innovators with new business opportunities and allow domestic firms to take advantage of scale economies (Alesina, Spolaore, and Wacziarg 2005). Second, trade can enhance technological diffusion and transmit know-how and managerial practices thanks to stronger interactions with foreign firms and markets (Coe and Helpman 1995; Sachs and Warner 1995; Coe, Helpman, and Hoffmaister 1997). Relatedly, Lewer and van den Berg (2003) find that the strength of trade as an engine of growth depends on the composition of trade—that is, countries that import mostly capital goods and export consumer goods tend to grow faster than those that export capital goods. Third, trade may enhance product market competition, thus reducing the anticompetitive practices of domestic firms and leading to higher specialization due to exploitation of the comparative advantages of domestic firms (Trefler 2004; Aghion and others 2008). Finally, the literature on the effects of trade liberalization can also be classified into two strands: (a) the long-run productivity benefits of free trade policies (for example, Tybout, de Melo, and Corbo 1991; Levinsohn 1993; Krishna and Mitra 1998; Head and Ries 1999; Pavcnik 2002) and (b) the impact of freer trade on short-run worker displacement and earnings (for example, Gaston and Trefler 1995; Levinsohn 1999; Krishna, Mitra, and Chinoy 2001).

The empirical literature on trade and growth typically argues that growth is positively correlated with higher trade volumes, even after accounting for a variety of growth determinants. Dollar (1992), Edwards (1992), Sachs and Warner (1995), Ades and Glaeser (1999), and Alesina, Spolaore, and Wacziarg (2000) are examples of this sort. However, Rodríguez and Rodrik (2000) argue that most of these findings are less robust than claimed due to (a) difficulties in measuring openness and

especially trade policy, and (b) the statistical sensitivity of the specifications and other econometric difficulties—among them, collinearity of
protectionist policies with other bad policies and likely endogeneity of
trade openness. These authors argue that the literature focuses on the
growth effects of trade volumes rather than trade policy and that the former is plagued by severe endogeneity problems. Moreover, indicators of
trade openness are deemed as controversial proxies for trade barriers.
Finally, a critical assessment is issued on the inadequacies of the literature for addressing endogeneity as well as controlling for other structural
factors—notably institutions.

Frankel and Romer (1999) tackle the issue of endogeneity by using the
gravity model to instrument for trade openness. Here, trade flows
between countries depend on geographic and cultural characteristics of
trading partners (say, distance, remoteness, common border, landlocked,
among others) as well as their size. Using gravitational variables, they
attempt to establish a causal link between trade and growth and find that
the impact of the former on the latter is positive and statistically significant. Wacziarg and Welch (2008), in contrast, study the contingent relationship between trade policy and growth by examining the evolution of
growth, investment, and openness around episodes of trade liberalization.
Growth rates in countries that liberalized their trade regimes were, on
average, 1.5 percentage points higher after than before liberalization,
whereas investment rates were almost 2 percentage points higher. Finally,
the ratio of trade to GDP rose 5 percentage points due to liberalization.
In sum, trade and growth have a positive co-movement, with investment
being a channel of transmission.

Although it is suggested that, on average, trade openness appears to be
beneficial to economic growth, its effect may vary considerably across
countries. It is argued that the growth benefits from open trade may kick
in after the country surpasses a "minimum critical threshold" associated
with the level of development (Helleiner 1986) or the structure of trade
(Kohli and Singh 1989). Recently, Chang, Kaltani, and Loayza (2009)
find that, although trade stimulates growth, this effect can be enhanced
by complementary reforms undertaken in the economy—especially in
the areas of education, financial development, infrastructure, and regulatory framework. Finally, Bolaky and Freund (2004) find that trade
openness is effective in promoting an expansion of income in countries
that are not excessively regulated—that is, resource allocation toward
the most productive sectors and companies is prevented in highly regulated countries.

The Data

We have collected a panel data set of 136 countries organized in five-year nonoverlapping observations over the period 1970–2010, with each country having at most eight observations. Given that the availability of data is different across variables, we have an *effective* sample of 99 countries with at least four consecutive observations for all variables involved in our analysis. This subsection describes the construction and sources of the data used in our empirical analysis.

Our dependent variable is the average annual growth rate in real GDP per capita within the five-year period, which is computed as the simple average of log differences in real GDP per capita over the five-year period. Real GDP per capita is expressed in 2005 international dollars (adjusted by purchasing power parity, PPP) from Heston, Summers, and Aten (2009). Our set of control variables includes the (log) level of real GDP per capita at the beginning of the five-year period to test for the existence of *transitional convergence*. Our set of long-run growth determinants follows Loayza, Fajnzylber, and Calderón (2005): human capital, financial depth, institutional quality, lack of price stability, infrastructure, financial openness, and our variable of interest, trade openness.

Human capital is approximated by the initial gross rate of secondary schooling (in logs), and the data are obtained from Barro and Lee (2001).[1] *Financial development* is measured by the ratio of domestic credit to the private sector to GDP, and the data are collected from Beck, Demirgüç-Kunt, and Levine (2000) and from Beck and Demirgüç-Kunt (2009) and are updated using data from the International Monetary Fund's International Financial Statistics and the World Bank's World Development Indicators. For the sake of robustness, we use other proxies of financial development: domestic credit provided by domestic money banks and liquid liabilities of the financial sector. Both variables are expressed as a percentage of GDP and in logs. *Institutional quality* comprises different dimensions such as absence of corruption, rule of law, enforcement of contracts, quality of the bureaucracy, and democratic accountability, among others. We use the International Country Risk Guide (ICRG) index of political risk as our indicators of institutional quality, and the data are published in the ICRG by the Political Risk Services Group. The *lack of price stability* is approximated by the average consumer price index inflation rate. This variable typically reflects the quality of monetary and fiscal policies and is directly related to other indicators of poor macroeconomic management. The data on the inflation rate are gathered from the International Monetary Fund's International Financial Statistics.

Infrastructure is a multidimensional concept. To account for this, we use principal component analysis to build synthetic indexes summarizing information on the quantity of different types of infrastructure assets (see Calderón and Servén 2004). These synthetic indexes combine information on three core infrastructure sectors—telecommunications, power, and roads—and help address the problem of high collinearity among their individual indicators.[2] We denote IK the synthetic quantity indexes that result from this procedure. The indexes can be expressed as linear combinations of the underlying sector-specific indicators, and hence their use in a regression context is equivalent to imposing linear restrictions on the coefficients of the individual infrastructure indicators. We define the synthetic infrastructure quantity index IK_1 as the first principal component of three variables: total telephone lines (fixed and mobile) per 1,000 people (Z_1/L), electric power installed capacity expressed in megawatts per 1,000 people (Z_2/L), and the length of the road network in kilometers per 1,000 people (Z_3/L). Each of these variables is expressed in logs and standardized by subtracting its mean and dividing by its standard deviation. All three infrastructure stocks enter the first principal component with roughly similar weights:

$$IK_1 = 0.603 * \ln\left(\frac{Z_1}{L}\right) + 0.613 * \ln\left(\frac{Z_2}{L}\right) + 0.510 * \ln\left(\frac{Z_3}{A}\right). \tag{4.1}$$

The index accounts for almost 80 percent of the overall variance in the three underlying indicators. As a robustness check, we compute an alternative index IK_2, which uses main telephone lines instead of the combined main lines and mobile phones employed in the first index.[3]

Financial openness is approximated by the data on holdings of foreign assets and liabilities from Lane and Milesi-Ferretti (2001, 2007). Specifically, we use summary measures of financial openness $FO_{it} = (FA_{it} + FL_{it}) / GDP_{it}$ and $FO(L)_{it} = FL_{it} / GDP_{it}$, where FA and FL refer to the stock of foreign assets and liabilities—expressed as a ratio to GDP. Note that FA and FL include the stock of assets and liabilities in foreign direct investment, portfolio equity, financial derivatives, and debt (portfolio debt, bank debt, and trade-related lending).

Our variable of interest, *trade openness*, is measured as the ratio of real exports and imports to real GDP (all these magnitudes are expressed in local currency at constant prices), and the data are collected from the World Bank's World Development Indicators. We also use an alternative measure of openness that adjusts the volume of trade over GDP for the size (area and population) of the country and for whether the country is landlocked or an oil exporter.[4] Loayza, Fajnzylber, and Calderón (2005) argue that this structure-adjusted volume of trade may be preferable to the unadjusted ratio given that the econometric analysis is based on cross-country comparisons. Unadjusted measures of trade volume may unfairly attribute to trade policy what is merely the result of structural country characteristics—for example, smaller countries are more dependent on foreign trade than larger countries, oil exporters may have large trade volumes and also impose high import tariffs, and landlocked countries tend to trade less than other countries due to higher transport and trading costs.

Finally, we describe two sources of data for which we lack extensive time series, but have good cross-country coverage: R&D and economic regulations. We argue that positive complementarities between trade and innovation can trigger higher and sustained growth. Our proxies for innovation are R&D spending as a percentage of GDP, R&D scientists (per 1 million people), and R&D technicians (per 1 million people). We summarize these three measures in an aggregate R&D index. In addition, we use the share of high-tech exports to manufacturing exports as a proxy for innovation.

Econometric Methodology

Having an *effective* cross-country and time-series data set for 99 countries over the period 1970–2010 requires us to use an estimation method that accounts for the dynamic specification of our growth equation, for unobserved time- and country-specific effects, and for likely endogeneity or reverse causality among the explanatory variables. In short, we use the generalized method of moments (GMM) for dynamic panel data models developed by Arellano and Bond (1991), Arellano and Bover (1995), and Blundell and Bond (1998).

We regress the growth in real output per capita on a standard set of growth determinants that includes our variable of interest, trade openness. Our basic set of control variables comprises information on the level of human capital, domestic financial depth, institutional quality, lack of price stability, financial openness, and infrastructure stocks. In addition to our baseline regression, we explore the role of complementarities between trade and structural factors in driving growth. In short, our dynamic regression equation can be specified as follows:

$$y_{it} - y_{it-1} = \alpha y_{it-1} + \phi' K_{it} + \gamma' Z_{it} + \mu_t + \eta_i + \varepsilon_{it} \qquad (4.2)$$
$$= \alpha y_{it-1} + \beta' X_{it} + \mu_t + \eta_i + \varepsilon_{it},$$

where y denotes the real GDP per worker (in logs), K is a set of standard growth or inequality determinants, and Z is our variable of interest: trade openness. The terms μ_t and η_i, respectively, denote an unobserved common factor affecting all countries and a country effect capturing unobserved country characteristics. The second equality follows from defining $X_{it} = (K'_{it}, Z'_{it})'$ and $\beta = (\phi', \gamma')'$.

The econometric challenges posed by our growth equation are tackled as follows. First, we control for unobserved time effects by including period-specific dummies in our regressions, while accounting for unobserved country effects by differencing and instrumentation. Second, we address joint endogeneity by instrumentation. More specifically, the assumption of *strong exogeneity* of the explanatory variables is lifted by allowing them to be correlated with current and previous realizations of the error term, e. Since no obviously exogenous instruments are available, the methodology relies primarily on *internal instruments*—that is, suitable lags of the explanatory variables (Arellano and Bond 1991). Rather than using internal instruments for our variable of interest, we use *external instruments*. We are concerned that future shocks to growth may lead to an expansion in foreign trade, thus invalidating our moment conditions. To do so, we follow Loayza, Fajnzylber, and Calderón (2005) and Chang, Kaltani, and Loayza (2009) and consider measures of size and geography as instruments of trade openness—that is, (actual and lagged values of) population, surface area of the country, and dummies for oil-exporting countries and landlocked countries. The consistency of the GMM-IV (instrumental variable) estimator relies on the validity of these moment conditions.[5]

Empirical Assessment

We first present the basic panel correlations and then the baseline regression.

Simple panel correlations between trade openness and growth are calculated for a sample of 136 countries with five-year nonoverlapping observations spanning the period 1960–2010. The positive correlation,

+0.08, is significant and larger in countries with higher levels of income per capita, human capital, infrastructure, and financial openness.[6] The correlation between growth and trade openness is larger in the 2000s, 0.21 compared with 0.08 for the full sample of countries. Zooming in on the DR-CAFTA countries, we observe that most of these countries are close to or below the medians of both trade openness and growth, and they have a flatter relationship than the rest of the sample (see figure 4.1).

Plotting the trade-growth nexus in countries with high versus low levels of structural policies (say, human capital, financial development, institutions, financial openness, infrastructure, and regulations) shows that the trade-growth correlation is stronger in countries with more educated people, stronger institutions, an improved infrastructure network, and more flexible regulations (see figure 4.2).[7]

Table 4.1 reports the coefficient estimates for our baseline regressions using different estimation techniques. The coefficient estimate of our variable of interest, trade openness, is positive and significant (at least at the 10 percent level) regardless of the technique used. In column 1, we run a pooled ordinary least squares (OLS) regression, while

Figure 4.1   Correlation between Growth and Trade Openness in DR-CAFTA Countries

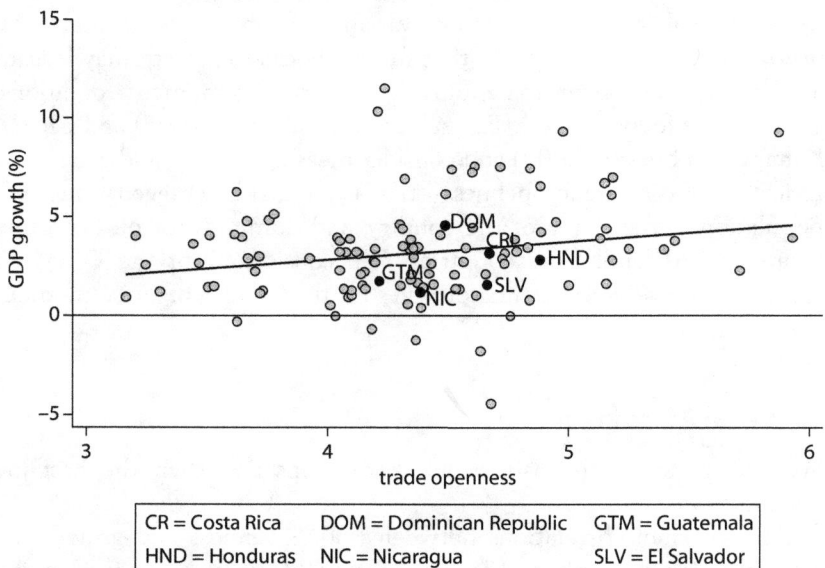

| CR = Costa Rica | DOM = Dominican Republic | GTM = Guatemala |
| HND = Honduras | NIC = Nicaragua | SLV = El Salvador |

Source: Authors' calculations.

Figure 4.2   Correlations between Trade Openness and Growth, by Select Indicators of Economic Development

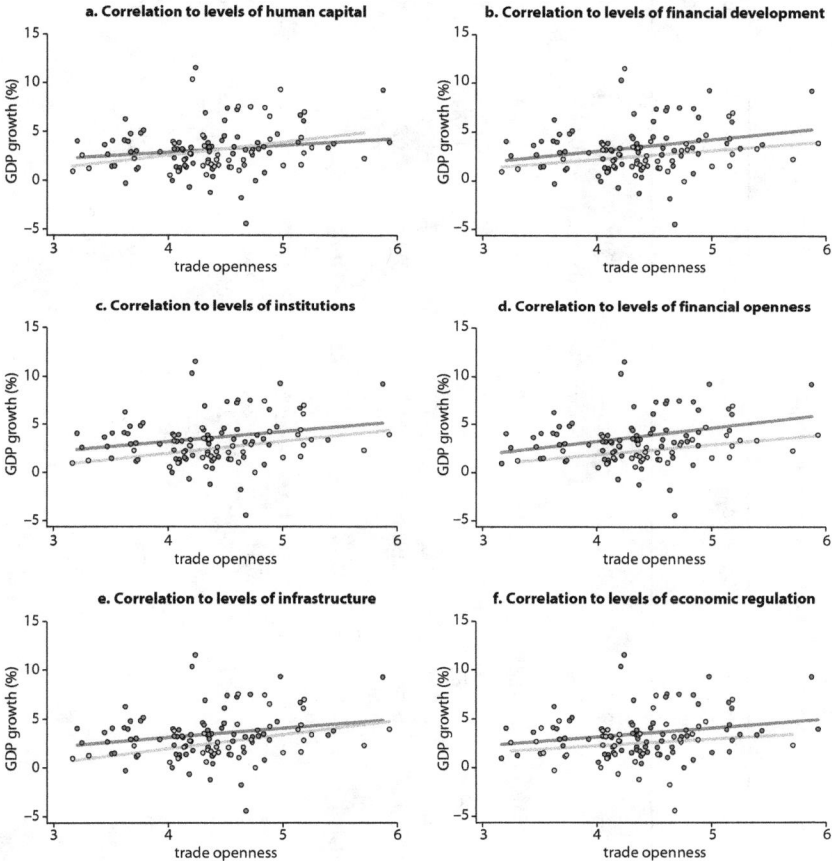

Source: Authors' calculations.

column 2 controls for time dummies, and column 3 controls only for country dummies. We apply the Arellano and Bover (1995) GMM-IV difference estimator in column 4, thus controlling for unobserved components and endogeneity and instrumenting the differences in the explanatory variables using their lagged levels. However, the GMM-IV difference estimator may face the problem of weak instruments if the explanatory levels are highly persistent. Hence, columns 5 and 6 estimate our baseline regression using the GMM-IV system estimator (Arellano and Bover 1995; Blundell and Bond 1998). While the estimation

Table 4.1 Trade and Growth: Baseline Regression under Different Estimation Techniques
dependent variable: growth in real GDP per capita (annual average, %)

Variable	Pooled OLS (1)	OLS time dummies (2)	Within group (3)	GMM-IV difference (4)	GMM-IV system (5)	GMM-IV system (6)
Variable of interest						
Trade openness (exports and imports as % of GDP, log)	0.5756* (0.319)	0.4860* (0.322)	1.7448** (0.757)	5.8530** (1.053)	0.3614** (0.134)	0.6245** (0.143)
Control variable						
Transitional convergence (initial GDP per capita, log)	-1.7788** (0.394)	-1.9137** (0.437)	-6.4594** (0.852)	-7.4420** (0.760)	-2.1768** (0.343)	-2.1263** (0.218)
Human capital (gross secondary enrollment rate, log)	0.7783** (0.350)	0.9918** (0.327)	-1.3719** (0.575)	1.0505* (0.597)	1.8700** (0.285)	1.5336** (0.207)
Financial depth (credit to private sector, % GDP, log)	0.2492 (0.299)	0.1963 (0.305)	0.4415 (0.378)	0.6054** (0.281)	0.2939* (0.158)	0.6229** (0.148)
Institutional quality (ICRG political risk index, log)	0.6914 (0.725)	0.9657 (0.713)	0.4272 (0.854)	0.6872 (0.732)	1.0118** (0.345)	1.5695** (0.418)
Lack of price stability (CPI inflation rate, log)	-2.5916** (0.610)	-2.4343** (0.642)	-2.9280** (0.526)	-3.4301** (0.823)	-3.6547** (0.134)	-3.7073** (0.184)
Infrastructure stock (principal component)[a]	0.6284** (0.169)	0.5882** (0.187)	1.2285** (0.244)	-0.2651 (0.293)	0.4335** (0.139)	0.2987** (0.146)
Financial openness (foreign assets and liabilities, % GDP, log)	-0.6767** (0.281)	-0.4241 (0.303)	-0.2343 (0.279)	-1.2307** (0.380)	-0.3706** (0.123)	-0.5876** (0.129)
Time dummy						
Dummy: 1976–80 period	..	0.0138	..	..	-0.1739	-0.2339
Dummy: 1981–85 period	..	-2.4998**	..	-1.4681**	-2.6141**	-2.5612**
Dummy: 1986–2000 period	..	-1.2370**	..	0.7218**	-1.4532**	-1.3186**

Dummy: 1991–95 period	..	−1.6349**	−0.5876*	−1.8917**	−1.6285**
Dummy: 1996–2000 period	..	−1.7096**	−0.5278	−1.9168**	−1.5804**
Dummy: 2001–05 period	..	−1.5078**	0.3271	−1.9714**	−1.5529**
Dummy: 2006–09 period	..	−0.6260	1.0000**	−1.0186**	−0.5994*
Number of countries	99	99	99	99	99
Number of observations	646	646	547	646	646
Country effects	No	No	Diff	Diff	Diff
Time effects	No	Yes	Yes	Yes	Yes
Instruments[b]	No	No	Internal	Internal	External
Specification tests (p-value)					
Sargan test (overidentifying restrictions)	..	(0.044)	(0.072)	(0.310)	(0.256)
Second-order serial correlation	(0.082)	(0.273)	(0.181)	(0.182)	(0.211)

Source: Authors' calculations.

Note: Numbers in parentheses are robust standard errors. Regression includes constant. .. = negligible.

a. The aggregate stock of infrastructure is computed as the first principal component of (a) main telephone lines and mobiles, (b) electric power installed capacity (in megawatts), and (c) length of the road network (in kilometers). All these physical indicators of infrastructure are expressed in their corresponding units per 1,000 people.

b. The set of "internal instruments" corresponds to lagged levels and differences of the corresponding explanatory variables in our regression analysis. In contrast, "external instruments" include variables that instrument for trade openness such as lagged population, surface area of the country, dummy for landlocked countries, and oil-exporting countries.

* $p < .10$, ** $p < .05$.

in column 5 uses internal instruments, the estimation in column 6 uses external instruments to account for the likely endogeneity of trade openness. As pointed out earlier, those external instruments are the (actual and lagged levels of) population (in logs), the surface area of the country (in logs), and dummies for landlocked and oil-exporting countries. Our preferred estimation is the one reported in column 6, and we discuss these results for our baseline regressions.

We find a negative and significant coefficient for the initial (log level of) GDP per capita, thus providing evidence of conditional convergence. Growth is enhanced by a faster accumulation of human capital (as proxied by rising gross rates of secondary schooling), deeper domestic financial markets (as measured by higher ratios of domestic credit to the private sector to GDP), and better institutions (as approximated by higher levels of the ICRG political risk index). Lack of price stability, measured by higher rates of consumer price inflation, hinders growth. A faster accumulation of infrastructure stocks (as proxied by deeper penetration of telecommunications, larger installed capacity for electricity, and a longer road network) promotes long-term growth. Financial openness, however, seems to have an adverse effect on growth rate.

Our variable of interest, trade openness, has a positive and significant coefficient. This result implies that long-run growth is enhanced by a more outward orientation in goods markets. Our coefficient estimates suggest that doubling trade openness would raise the growth rate by 43 basis points a year—that is, more than 4 percentage points over a decade. Finally, the coefficient estimate of trade openness may vary according to the extent of the outward orientation of the country and over time.

Some extensions of the sensitivity of growth to trade are explored in Calderón and Poggio (2010). First, they investigate whether the effect of trade openness on growth depends on the extent of integration with world goods markets. That is, they test whether the growth effects of openness increase as the extent of integration increases. Their results show that trade openness exerts a positive impact on growth despite the extent of outward orientation of the country; however, it is statistically significant only for countries with deeper trade integration (that is, countries with trade openness beyond the sixty-seventh percentile of the world distribution). Second, they test whether the impact of trade openness on growth has changed over time. The authors find that, while the coefficient estimate for the 1980s is negative and significant in most cases, it is positive and significant for the 2000s.[8]

Trade and Growth: The Role of Complementarities

Since the growth elasticity of trade appears to vary over time and across countries, we proceed to estimate the growth regression in equation 4.3:

$$y_{it} - y_{it-1} = \alpha y_{it-1} + \phi' K_{it} + \gamma_{it}' Z_{it} + \mu_t + \eta_i + \varepsilon_{it}, \qquad (4.3)$$

where the trade openness (TO) coefficient, γ_{it}, is allowed to vary across countries and time. Thus, the existence of complementarities between trade and structural factors (F) is modeled as $\gamma_{it} = \gamma_0 + \gamma_1 F_{it}$, where the coefficient of trade openness depends directly on TO as well as its interaction with structural factors. In this section we consider the complementarities between trade openness and the following factors: human capital, financial development, institutions, infrastructure, financial openness, R&D, and certain aspects of the regulatory framework.

Complementarities between Trade and Structural Factors

Table 4.2 presents regression estimates that test for the significance of complementarities between trade openness and human capital (regression 2), trade openness and financial development (regressions 3 to 5), and trade openness and institutional quality (regression 6). The impact of trade openness on growth now depends on the level of the specific structural factor in each country at a determined period of time.

Regression 1 in table 4.2 includes the interaction between trade openness and the level of income per capita in our baseline regression. While the TO coefficient (γ_0) is negative and significant, its interaction with income per capita is positive and significant (γ_1). This finding suggests that opening up the current account would require a minimum development threshold to generate positive growth effects. Economically speaking, our regression suggests that a 1 standard deviation increase in trade openness—that is, the ratio increases approximately 75 percent—would lead to a decline in the growth rate of 30 basis points a year for countries with lower levels of income per capita (approximately US$2,500 at 2005 PPP prices—Mongolia in 2005), while it would raise growth of output per capita by almost 1 percentage point (more precisely, 97 basis points) in countries with higher levels of income per capita (US$22,000— Republic of Korea in 2005). The first panel of figure 4.3 reports the growth effects of rising trade openness for different levels of income per capita—that is, selected percentiles of the distribution (tenth, twenty-fifth, thirty-third, the median, sixty-seventh, seventy-fifth, ninetieth percentiles), regions (CAFTA, Latin America and the Caribbean excluding

Table 4.2 Trade and Growth: Interaction with Structural Factors and Policies

dependent variable: growth in real GDP per capita (annual average, %)

Variable	Baseline regression	Ancillary regressions					
		(1)	(2)	(3)	(4)	(5)	(6)
Variable of interest							
Trade openness, *TO* (exports and imports as % of GDP, log)	0.6245** (0.143)	−8.2487** (1.627)	−9.8907** (1.105)	−0.6676 (0.474)	−1.2141 (0.873)	−2.5225** (1.251)	−10.0006** (2.054)
TO * *ypc*	:	0.9916** (0.183)	:	:	:	:	:
TO * *human*	:	:	2.6520** (0.282)	:	:	:	:
TO * *findev1*	:	:	:	0.4230** (0.129)	:	:	:
TO * *findev2*	:	:	:	:	0.4382** (0.216)	:	:
TO * *findev3*	:	:	:	:	:	0.8046** (0.312)	:
TO * *instq*	:	:	:	:	:	:	2.5798** (0.492)
Control variable							
Transitional convergence, *ypc* (initial GDP per capita, log)	−2.1263** (0.218)	−7.7486** (0.864)	−3.8154 (0.213)	−2.7008** (0.239)	−2.2621** (0.261)	−1.8939** (0.301)	−3.3400** (0.186)
Human capital, *human* (gross secondary enrollment rate, log)	1.5336** (0.207)	1.5093** (0.205)	−9.0224** (1.116)	1.6259** (0.212)	2.1980** (0.198)	1.9878** (0.232)	1.5617** (0.181)
Financial depth, *findev1*, (domestic credit to private sector, % GDP, log)	0.6229** (0.148)	0.7660** (0.128)	0.7449 (0.120)	−1.2707** (0.549)	:	:	0.6589** (0.127)

Financial depth, findev2, (banking credit private sector, % GDP, log)	..	..	..	-2.0794** (0.823)	..	..
Financial depth, findev3, (liquid liabilities—M3—% GDP, log)	..	..	..	..	-3.0230** (1.260)	-8.7044** (1.942)
Institutional quality, instq (ICRG political risk index, log)	1.5695** (0.418)	1.3471** (0.303)	1.4749 (0.274)	0.2013** (0.334)	0.1840 (0.356)	1.8149 (0.424)
Number of countries	99	99	99	99	99	99
Number of observations	646	646	646	646	646	646
Specification test (p-value)						
Sargan test (overidentifying restrictions)	(0.256)	(0.243)	(0.196)	(0.226)	(0.280)	(0.299)
Second-order serial correlation	(0.211)	(0.213)	(0.181)	(0.201)	(0.193)	(0.261)

Source: Authors' calculations.

Note: Numbers in parentheses correspond to robust standard errors. The full regression includes as control variables: the initial GDP per capita (log), gross secondary enrollment rate (log), domestic credit to the private sector as a percentage of GDP (log), ICRG political risk index (log), consumer price index inflation rate, the aggregate index of infrastructure stock (in logs, see definition in note a of table 4.1), foreign assets and liabilities as a percentage of GDP (log). The regression also includes constant and time (five-year period) dummies. We control for endogeneity using lagged levels and differences for all the variables other than trade openness. The latter variable, in turn, is instrumented using lagged population, surface area of the country, and dummies for landlocked and oil-exporting countries. .. = Negligible.

$* p < .10, ** p < .05.$

Figure 4.3   Growth Response to a 1 Standard Deviation Increase in Trade Openness, by Level of Select Indicators of Development

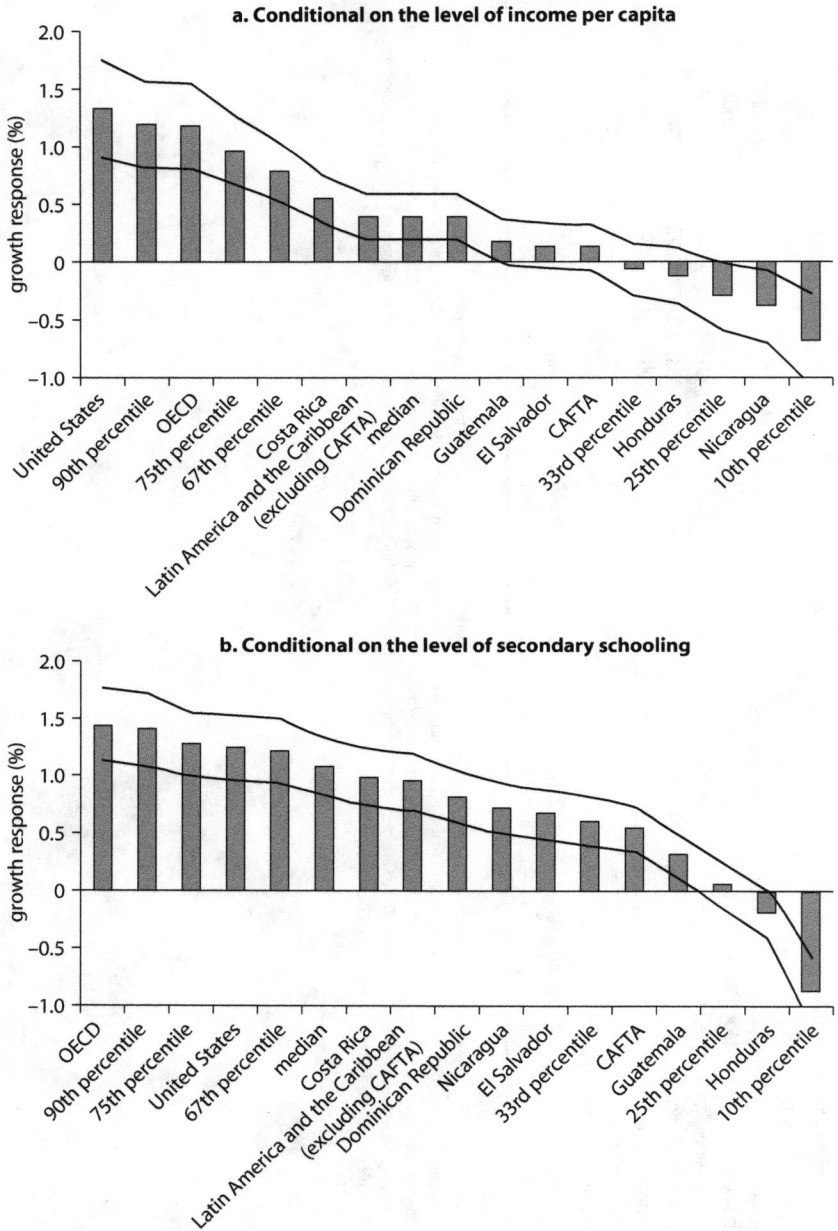

a. Conditional on the level of income per capita

b. Conditional on the level of secondary schooling

(continued next page)

Figure 4.3   *(continued)*

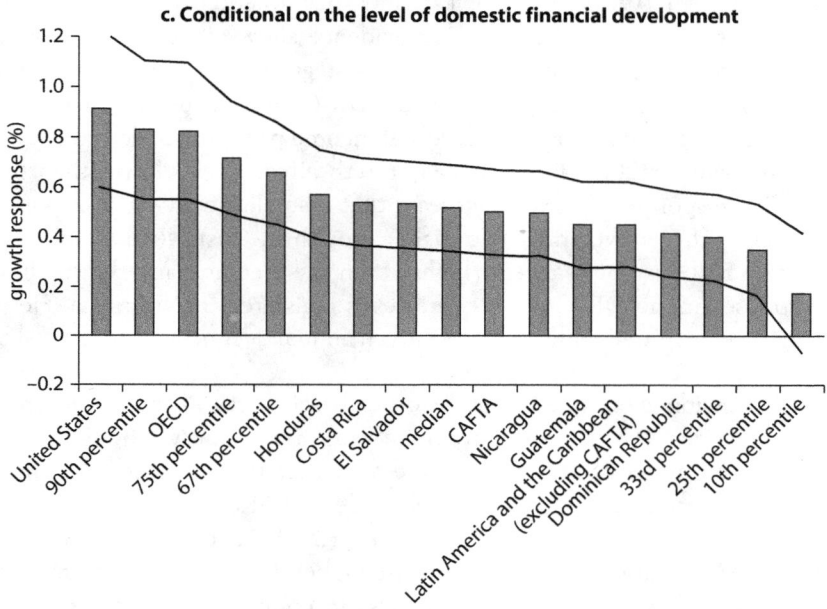

c. Conditional on the level of domestic financial development

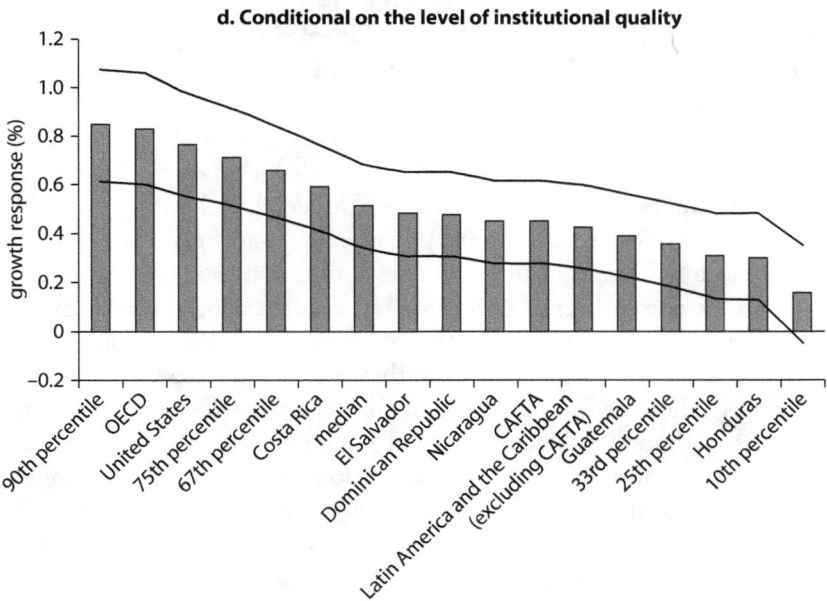

d. Conditional on the level of institutional quality

Source: Authors' calculations.
Note: The computed responses were obtained using the estimated coefficients in table 4.4 as follows: for panel a, column 1; for panel b, column 2; for panel c, column 3; and for panel d, column 6.

CAFTA countries, the Organisation of Economic Co-operation and Development [OECD] countries), and specific countries (DR-CAFTA countries, the United States). Our evidence shows that countries with higher income per capita reap the largest growth benefits from rising trade openness. We also find that all DR-CAFTA countries (with the exception of Costa Rica) have levels of income per capita below the sample median for 2005 and, hence, a growth effect that is lower than the median response—that is, an increase that is smaller than 40 basis points a year in the growth rate. The higher growth in Costa Rica is approximately 55 basis points a year (higher than the median), and the smallest response among DR-CAFTA countries is registered in Nicaragua. Here, the increase in trade openness leads to an annual decline in growth of output per capita of 38 basis points.

Regression 2 of table 4.2 adds to our baseline regression the interaction between TO and the enrollment rate of secondary schooling (our proxy of human capital). Again, we find that the coefficient of trade openness is negative and significant, while that of the interaction is positive and statistically significant. Hence, growth benefits from trade are positive and larger in countries with higher levels of human capital. More specifically, rising trade openness in countries with low rates of enrollment in secondary schooling (43 percent—for example, Bangladesh and Ghana, in the twenty-fifth percentile of the 2005 sample) would have negligible effects on growth (almost 5 basis points a year). However, a 1 standard deviation increase in TO would raise the growth rate almost 1.3 percentage points a year in countries with higher levels of secondary schooling (96 percent—for example, the Slovak Republic and Slovenia in the seventy-fifth percentile).

Regressions 3 through 5 report the interaction between trade openness and measures of financial development such as domestic credit to the private sector, domestic credit provided by domestic money banks, and liquid liabilities, respectively. All of these variables are expressed as a percentage of GDP and in logs, and they are interacted with trade openness. Regardless of the indicators of financial development used in our analysis, we find that the coefficient of TO is negative and not statistically significant in most cases, but the interaction with financial development is robustly positive. Our estimation suggests that countries with deeper domestic financial markets may reap the largest growth benefits from trade. Economically, countries with low financial development (say, with domestic credit to the private sector of 20 percent of GDP—for example, the average for the 2006–08 period in Paraguay and Botswana at the twenty-fifth percentile of the distribution for that period) would raise their growth per capita by 35 basis points if trade openness were to increase by a 1 standard deviation. An analogous increase in TO would raise growth by 72 basis points in countries with high financial development (for example, Israel, with average domestic credit of 90 percent of GDP in 2006–08).

Finally, regression 6 interacts trade openness and the level of institutional quality. We use the ICRG index of political risk (in logs) as our indicator of institutional quality. Again, the interaction between TO and institutions is positive and significant, while the coefficient of TO is negative (although statistically significant). This implies that a minimum institutional threshold is required to reap the benefits from trade. It is consistent with the finding that trade reforms may lead to higher growth per capita in countries with stronger institutional quality (Calderón and Fuentes 2006, 2009; Chang, Kaltani, and Loayza 2009). Economically speaking, growth per capita would increase by only 30 basis points a year in countries with weak institutions (say, Bolivia and Honduras, at the twenty-fifth percentile of the sample distribution for the 2006–09 period), whereas the annual growth per capita benefit for a country with strong institutions (Poland and the Slovak Republic, at the seventy-fifth percentile) is approximately 72 basis points a year.

Complementarities between Trade and Infrastructure

There is ample evidence in the literature that an enlarged and more efficient infrastructure network will promote long-term growth (Sánchez-Robles 1998; Calderón and Servén 2004, 2010), while improved access to this network may help to reduce income inequality (Calderón and Chong 2004; Calderón and Servén 2004; Galiani, Gertler, and Schargrodsky 2005). Recent work also finds that the efficient provision of infrastructure is crucial for the success of trade liberalization strategies aimed at optimal resource allocation and export growth (Lederman, Maloney, and Servén 2007).

Table 4.3 includes the interactions between trade openness and a battery of infrastructure indicators (either at the aggregate level or by sector). We have constructed two aggregate indexes of infrastructure, IK_1 and IK_2, that summarize information on telecommunications, electricity, and roads. Regressions 1 and 2 in table 4.3 include the interaction between trade openness and the aggregate indexes of infrastructure, IK_1 and IK_2, respectively. In both cases, we find that the coefficient of TO is negative and significant, whereas that of the interaction between TO and

Table 4.3 Trade and Growth: The Role of Physical Infrastructure

dependent variable: growth in real GDP per capita (annual average, %)

Variable	Baseline regression (1)	Ancillary regressions (2)	(3)	(4)	(5)	(6)	(7)	(8)	(9)
Variable of interest									
Trade openness. *TO* (exports and imports as % of GDP, log)	0.6245** (0.143)	−1.7379** (0.225)	−1.1129** (0.186)	0.0076 (0.236)	1.2848** (0.140)	−0.5840** (0.123)	−1.6612** (0.389)	1.9481** (0.216)	−2.3922** (0.271)	−2.4914** (0.454)
$TO * IK_1$	0.7038** (0.066)	⋮	⋮	⋮	⋮	⋮	⋮	⋮	⋮
$TO * IK_2$	⋮	0.4733** (0.049)	⋮	⋮	⋮	⋮	⋮	⋮	⋮
$TO * TC_1$	⋮	⋮	0.1188** (0.048)	⋮	⋮	0.5174** (0.072)	⋮	⋮	⋮
$TO * EGC$	⋮	⋮	⋮	0.4285** (0.038)	⋮	⋮	1.2333** (0.132)	⋮	⋮
$TO * RD$	⋮	⋮	⋮	⋮	0.0246** (0.012)	⋮	⋮	1.8601** (0.149)	⋮
$TO * TC_2$	⋮	⋮	⋮	⋮	⋮	⋮	⋮	⋮	0.7101** (0.096)
Control variable									
Index of aggregate infrastructure, IK_1 (first principal component: *TC, EGC, RD*)	0.2987** (0.146)	−1.6361** (0.228)	⋮	0.3848** (0.158)	0.0341 (0.138)	−1.2645** (0.117)	⋮	⋮	⋮
Index of aggregate infrastructure, IK_2 (first principal component: *TC, EGC, RD*)	⋮	⋮	−0.2592* (0.166)	⋮	⋮	⋮	⋮	⋮	⋮
Telecommunications 1, TC_1 (main lines and mobiles per 1,000 people, log)	⋮	⋮	⋮	⋮	⋮	⋮	−1.5394** (0.285)	⋮	⋮

	(1)	(2)	(3)	(4)	(5)	(6)	(7)	(8)	(9)	(10)
Electric power, EGC (installed capacity, in megawatts per 1,000 people, log)	..	..	..	..	..	..	..	−4.5521** (0.508)	..	..
Roads, RD (length of total network, in kilometers per 1,000 people, log)	..	..	..	..	..	..	..	..	−7.3920** (0.608)	..
Telecommunications 2. TC_2 (main telephone line per 1.000 people, log)	..	..	..	..	..	..	..	..	..	−2.0130** (0.374)
Number of countries	99	99	99	99	99	99	99	99	99	99
Number of observations	646	646	646	646	646	646	646	646	646	646
Specification test (p-value)										
Sargan test (overidentifying restrictions)	(0.256)	(0.222)	(0.377)	(0.221)	(0.252)	(0.246)	(0.206)	(0.283)	(0.214)	(0.192)
Second-order serial correlation	(0.211)	(0.177)	(0.162)	(0.173)	(0.184)	(0.180)	(0.195)	(0.163)	(0.172)	(0.142)

Source: Authors' calculations.

Note: Numbers in parentheses correspond to robust standard errors. .. = Negligible.

a. The full regression includes as control variables: the initial GDP per capita (log), gross secondary enrollment rate (log), domestic credit to the private sector as a percentage of GDP (log), ICRG political risk index (log), consumer price index inflation rate, the aggregate index of infrastructure stocks (in logs, see definition in note a of table 4.1), foreign assets and liabilities as a percentage of GDP (log). The regression also includes constant and time (five-year period) dummies. We control for endogeneity using lagged levels and differences for all the variables other than trade openness. The latter variable, in turn, is instrumented using lagged population, surface area of the country, and dummies for landlocked and oil-exporting countries.

$* p < .10$, $** p < .05$.

infrastructure is positive and significant. Our evidence suggests that a better infrastructure network would enhance the impact of trade on growth. Using the estimates of regression 1 we find that a 1 standard deviation increase in trade openness would increase the growth rate per capita by 16 basis points in countries with a poor infrastructure network (that is, India and Pakistan, with an average index of infrastructure at the twenty-fifth percentile of the distribution for the 2006–08 period), while growth per capita would be higher by 1.4 percentage points for countries with a better infrastructure network (both for Taiwan, China, and for Singapore, with levels of infrastructure provision in the seventy-fifth percentile of the distribution).

Note that when sectoral measures of infrastructure are included separately—rather than the aggregate measures—the results hold (see regressions 3–5 and 7–10 in table 4.3). Hence, an adequate supply of telecommunications and electricity and an improved road network may help raise the growth benefits from trade.

Complementarities between Trade Openness and R&D

Table 4.4 further investigates the complementarities between trade and human capital by examining the interaction between trade openness and innovation. Among proxies of innovation, we consider R&D spending (as a percentage of GDP), number of R&D scientists (per 1 million people), number of R&D technicians (per 1 million people), and high-technology exports (as a percentage of manufacturing exports). We also explore the interaction between trade and an index of R&D that summarizes information on R&D spending, R&D technicians, and R&D scientists.

Regression 1 incorporates the interaction between trade openness and the index of innovation—the latter being measured as the first principal component of spending and the number of scientists and technicians in R&D. Higher values of this index indicate more resources devoted to R&D. We find that the coefficient of TO and its interaction are positive and significant, thus implying that trade openness enhances growth and that this effect is larger in countries with higher levels of innovation—as proxied by more resources devoted to R&D.

When assessing the individual impact of the components of our index, we find that the interaction between TO and R&D is positive and significant only for R&D spending (regression 2) and R&D scientists (regression 3). Our estimates suggest that a 1 standard deviation increase in TO would lead to growth per capita higher by 90 basis points a year in countries with low R&D (that is, Colombia and Thailand, with 1.2 percent

Table 4.4 Trade and Growth: The Role of Innovation

dependent variable: growth in real GDP per capita (annual average, %)

Variable	Baseline regression	Ancillary regression				
		(1)	(2)	(3)	(4)	(5)
Variable of interest						
Trade openness, TO (exports and imports as % of GDP, log)	0.6245** (0.143)	2.4385** (0.874)	1.5130** (0.216)	3.5576** (0.055)	1.5577** (0.748)	0.7394 (0.161)
TO * R&D index (R&D aggregate index)	..	0.0002* (0.000)	..	..	..	..
TO * R&D spending (R&D spending as % of GDP)	..	..	0.1989** (0.041)	..	..	..
TO * R&D scientists (scientists in R&D per 1 million people)	..	..	..	0.0004** (0.000)	..	..
TO * R&D technicians (technicians in R&D per 1 million people)	..	..	..	..	0.0001 (0.000)	..
TO * high-tech exports (high-tech exports, % manufacturing exports)	..	..	..	..	..	-0.0062 0.013
Number of countries	99	67	82	78	72	98
Number of observations	646	446	545	519	472	641
Specification test (p-value)						
Sargan test (overidentifying restrictions)	(0.256)	(0.693)	(0.311)	(0.318)	(0.638)	(0.164)
Second-order serial correlation	(0.211)	(0.394)	(0.219)	(0.263)	(0.641)	(0.188)

Source: Authors' calculations, using the GMM-IV System Estimator from Arellano and Bover 1995; Blundell and Bond 1998.

Note: Numbers in parentheses correspond to robust standard errors. The full regression includes as control variables: the initial GDP per capita (log), gross secondary enrollment rate (log), domestic credit to the private sector as a percentage of GDP (log), ICRG political risk index (log), CPI inflation rate, the aggregate index of infrastructure stock (in logs, see definition in note a of table 4.1), foreign assets and liabilities as a percent of GDP (log). The regression also includes constant and time (five-year period) dummies. We control for endogeneity using lagged levels and differences for all the variables other than trade openness. The latter variable, in turn, is instrumented using lagged population, surface area of the country, and dummies for landlocked and oil-exporting countries. The aggregate index of R&D is calculated as the first principal component of the following variables: R&D spending as a percentage of GDP, scientists in R&D per 1 million people, and technicians in R&D per 1 million people. .. = Negligible.

* $p < .10$, ** $p < .05$.

of GDP at the twenty-fifth percentile of the sample distribution in 2000–09). And the impact is 101 basis points a year in countries with higher spending (say, Ireland and New Zealand, with 3.2 percent of GDP at the seventy-fifth percentile).

Complementarities between Trade Openness and Regulations

Table 4.5 presents evidence on the complementarities between trade openness and economic regulations—that is, firm entry regulations and labor market regulations. Previous research shows that trade openness is unable to promote growth in heavily regulated economies (Bolaky and Freund 2004).

We have constructed an index of economic regulations that comprises two subcategories: firm-entry regulations (the number of procedures to start a business, the number of days to start that business, and its cost) and labor regulations (difficulty of hiring, difficulty of firing, and rigidity of hours). Each subindex includes three variables. We construct this index and its two subindexes using either simple averages or principal components. The results are robust to either method of aggregation. Hence, for the sake of brevity, we discuss the results using simple averages, that is, regressions 1 through 3. In these regressions, we find that the coefficient of TO is positive and significantly different from 0, whereas that of the interaction between TO and regulations is negative and significant. This confirms existing evidence that more stringent regulations in the economy may hinder economies from reaping the growth benefits of rising trade openness. Our estimates suggest that rising trade (a 1 standard deviation increase in TO) in countries with more flexible regulations (for example, Colombia, in the twenty-fifth percentile of the sample distribution) would lead to higher growth per capita by almost 50 basis points. The increase in growth is lower (30 basis points) in countries that are heavily regulated (for example, France, in the seventy-fifth percentile of the sample distribution).

Are Trade and Financial Openness Complementary in the Growth Process?

Calderón and Poggio (2010) explore the complementarities between trade and financial openness in the growth process. The authors find that the interaction between trade openness and financial openness is positive and significant and that this effect may be driven by the higher accumulation of equity-related foreign assets and liabilities. These results suggest that the structure of external assets and liabilities may have a role in catalyzing the

Table 4.5 Trade and Growth: The Role of Regulations

dependent variable: growth in real GDP per capita (annual average, %)

		Ancillary regressions					
		Aggregation method: simple averages			Aggregation method: principal components		
Variable	Baseline regression	(1)	(2)	(3)	(4)	(5)	(6)
Variable of interest							
Trade openness, TO (exports and imports as % of GDP, log)	0.6245** (0.143)	0.7914** (0.144)	1.0219** (0.171)	0.6772** (0.192)	0.6950** (0.135)	0.7087** (0.184)	0.8693** (0.230)
TO * index of regulations	‥	−0.5878** (0.224)			−0.3190** (0.055)		
TO * index of firm entry regulations			−1.6636** (0.276)			−0.4504** (0.178)	
TO * index of labor regulations				−0.6731** (0.135)			−0.3388** (0.096)
Number of countries	99	99	99	99	99	99	99
Number of observations	646	646	646	646	646	646	646
Specification test (p-value)							
Sargan test (overidentifying restrictions)	(0.256)	(0.250)	(0.194)	(0.321)	(0.201)	(0.282)	(0.211)
First-order serial correlation	(0.000)	(0.000)	(0.000)	(0.000)	(0.000)	(0.000)	(0.000)
Second-order serial correlation	(0.211)	(0.181)	(0.158)	(0.311)	(0.194)	(0.251)	(0.192)

Source: Authors' calculations using the GMM-IV System Estimator from Arellano and Bover 1995; Blundell and Bond 1998.

Note: Numbers in parentheses correspond to robust standard errors. The full regression includes as control variables the initial GDP per capita (log), gross secondary enrollment rate (log), domestic credit to the private sector as a percentage of GDP (log), the ICRG political risk index (log), consumer price index inflation rate, the aggregate index of infrastructure stock (in logs, see definition in note a of table 4.1), foreign assets and liabilities as a percentage of GDP (log). The regression also includes constant and time (five-year period) dummies. We control for endogeneity using lagged levels and differences for all the variables other than trade openness. The latter variable, in turn, is instrumented using lagged population, surface area of the country, and dummies for landlocked and oil-exporting countries. Our indexes of regulations comprise information on the following dimensions: (a) firm entry regulations: number of procedures to start a business, time to start (in days), and its cost (as a percentage of income per capita), and (b) labor market regulations: difficulty of hiring, rigidity of hours and difficulty of firing. All these indexes are constructed such that higher values indicate more obstacles to entry and industry and more rigidities in the labor market. Our index of regulations comprises information for all six indicators, and it is aggregated either using simple averages or the principal components analysis (that is, we take the first principal components). Analogously, we compute the aggregate index of regulation for firm entry regulations and labor market regulations by either taking simple averages or the first principal component of the three indicators in each category. ‥ = Negligible.

* p < .10, ** p < .05.

effects of trade on growth. Hence growth benefits from trade openness may be larger in countries that accumulate more equity than debt assets and liabilities. The results are largely discussed in Calderón and Poggio (2010) and are available from the authors on request.

Economic Implications of Our Estimates: Discussion for DR-CAFTA

We now discuss the economic implications of the regression analysis for the DR-CAFTA countries. We conduct this analysis along three dimensions: (a) plot the growth response to a 1 standard deviation increase in trade openness conditional on the DR-CAFTA country's level of determined structural factors, (b) calculate the growth effects of an increase in trade openness in 2006–10 vis-à-vis 1991–95, and (c) assess potential growth benefits of trade openness if DR-CAFTA countries reach the extent of trade openness in a benchmark region (EAP-7).

Growth Implications of Rising Trade in DR-CAFTA

Figure 4.3 depicts the growth response to a 1 standard deviation increase in trade openness (that is, an increase in the trade ratio of approximately 75 percent during the period 2006–09) conditional on the level of income per capita (panel a), human capital (panel b), financial development (panel c), and institutional quality (panel d). We calculate the response for all DR-CAFTA countries (Costa Rica, Dominican Republic, El Salvador, Guatemala, Honduras, and Nicaragua), select regions and countries (CAFTA, Latin America and the Caribbean excluding CAFTA, OECD, and United States), and select percentiles of the sample distribution in 2006–09. The bars represent the growth response (in percentage points), and the lines represent the 95 percent level of confidence interval. Growth benefits from trade vary greatly across DR-CAFTA countries. For instance, the growth benefits of DR-CAFTA countries conditional on the level of secondary schooling are below the median of our sample distribution (that is, below 1.1 percentage points a year), with Costa Rica close to the median, Honduras below the twenty-fifth percentile of the distribution, and the model predicting a contraction in growth per capita of 19 basis points. However, the growth benefits of rising trade conditional on the depth of domestic financial markets among DR-CAFTA countries cannot surpass those of the sixty-seventh percentile of the sample distribution (66 basis points a year). Indeed, growth in Costa Rica, El Salvador, and Honduras rises between 53 and

57 basis points a year. The lowest benefits from trade are registered by the Dominican Republic (42 basis points), which is closer to that of countries in the thirty-third percentile of the sample distribution. Finally, the growth effects of trade openness conditional on institutional quality are also below that of the sixty-seventh percentile of the sample distribution for DR-CAFTA countries.

Figure 4.4 plots the growth response to rising trade openness conditional on the level of infrastructure. We depict the response conditional on the aggregate index of infrastructure stock IK_1 (panel a) and the stock of telecommunications (panel b), electricity (panel c), and roads (panel d). For the sake of brevity, we focus on the results for the aggregate index of infrastructure. The growth effect of rising trade in DR-CAFTA countries ranks below that of the country with the median level of infrastructure. Costa Rica and the Dominican Republic enjoy the largest benefits from trade (with increases in growth per capita of 95 and 84 basis points, respectively), thanks to their relatively better infrastructure network than other DR-CAFTA countries. Nicaragua is the country with the lowest gains from growth (below 50 basis points) among DR-CAFTA countries.

Finally, figure 4.5 displays the growth response to trade openness conditional on spending on research and development (panel a) and regulatory indexes for firm entry (panel b) and labor markets (panel c). Although growth response to rising trade is always positive, we fail to find significant differences between countries with low levels of innovation and regulation vis-à-vis those with high levels—especially in the case of labor market regulations. For instance, differences in the growth response to trade openness of Costa Rica (close to the R&D sample median) and El Salvador (below the tenth percentile in R&D spending) is not significant (91 and 88 basis points, respectively). The same can be said for regulations. On average, DR-CAFTA countries have regulations that are more restrictive than those of the representative country in our sample. However, growth effects are not large when comparing the countries with the most stringent regulations and those with the most flexible regulations among DR-CAFTA countries (see panels b and c).

Assessing the Growth Benefits from Open Trade in DR-CAFTA

We evaluate the growth effects of a 1 standard deviation increase in trade openness for DR-CAFTA countries conditional on structural factors and policies. If we denote α_0 as the coefficient estimate of trade openness (TO) and α_1 as the interaction between TO and a determined structural

Figure 4.4   Growth Response to a 1 Standard Deviation Increase in Trade Openness, by Aggregate Stock of Select Infrastructure

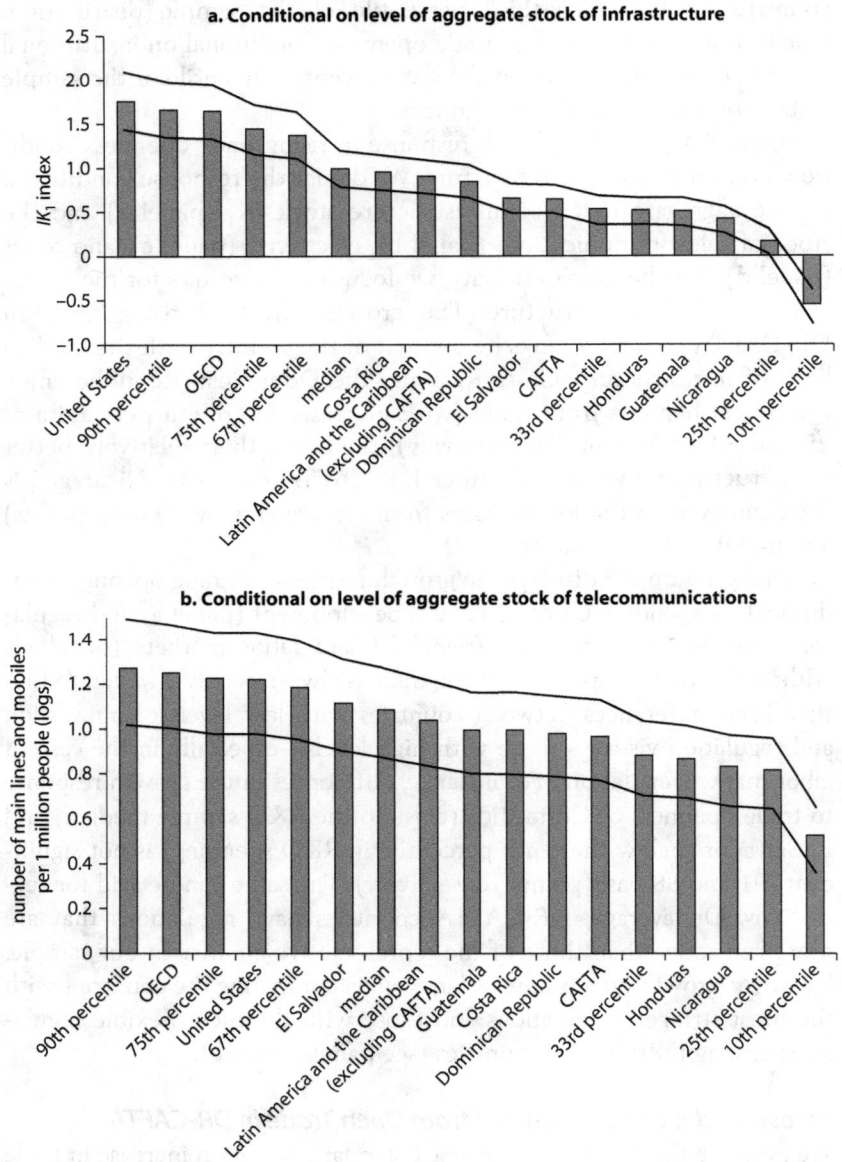

a. Conditional on level of aggregate stock of infrastructure

b. Conditional on level of aggregate stock of telecommunications

(continued next page)

Figure 4.4   *(continued)*

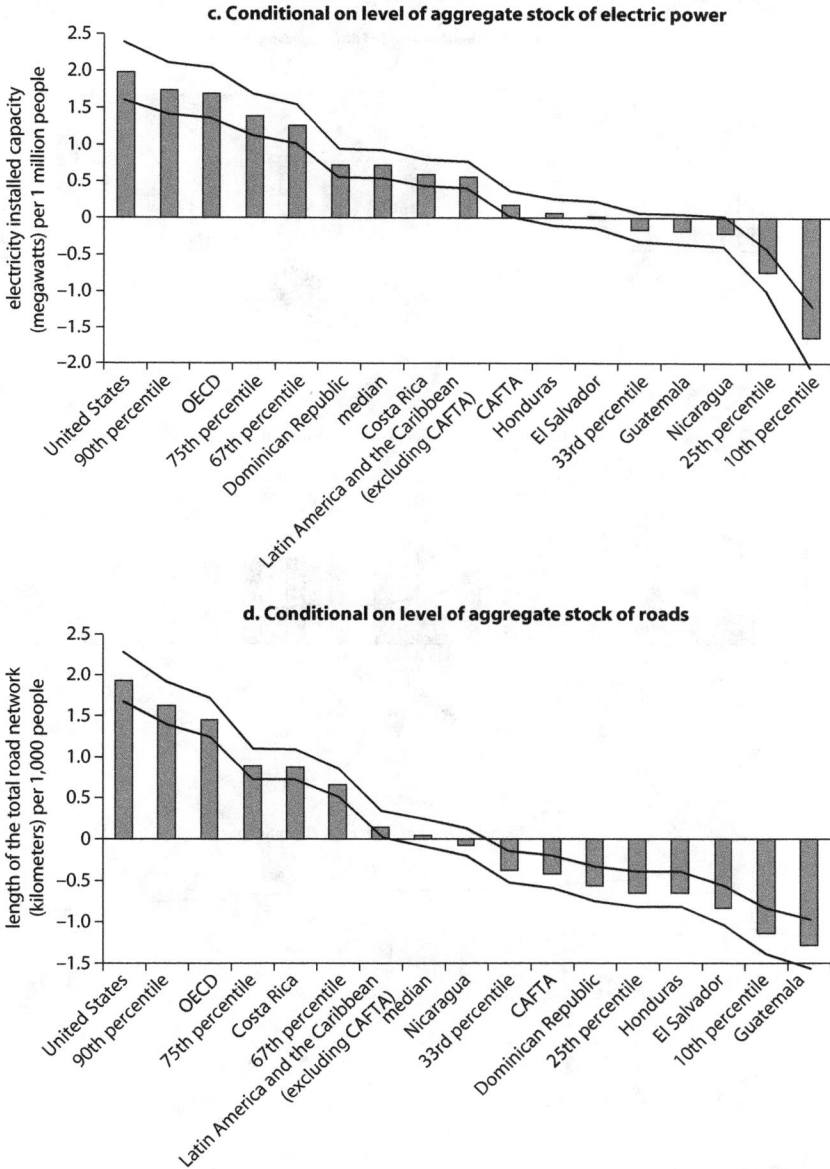

c. Conditional on level of aggregate stock of electric power

(y-axis: electricity installed capacity (megawatts) per 1 million people)

x-axis categories: United States, 90th percentile, OECD, 75th percentile, 67th percentile, Dominican Republic, median, Costa Rica, Latin America and the Caribbean (excluding CAFTA), CAFTA, Honduras, El Salvador, 33rd percentile, Guatemala, Nicaragua, 25th percentile, 10th percentile

d. Conditional on level of aggregate stock of roads

(y-axis: length of the total road network (kilometers) per 1,000 people)

x-axis categories: United States, 90th percentile, OECD, 75th percentile, Costa Rica, 67th percentile, Latin America and the Caribbean (excluding CAFTA), median, Nicaragua, 33rd percentile, CAFTA, Dominican Republic, 25th percentile, Honduras, El Salvador, 10th percentile, Guatemala

Source: Authors' calculations.
Note: The computed responses were obtained using the estimated coefficients from table 4.3: column 2 for panel a; column 7 for panel b, column 8 for panel c, and column 9 for panel d.

Figure 4.5   Growth Response to a 1 Standard Deviation Increase in Trade Openness, by Level of R&D Spending and Regulations

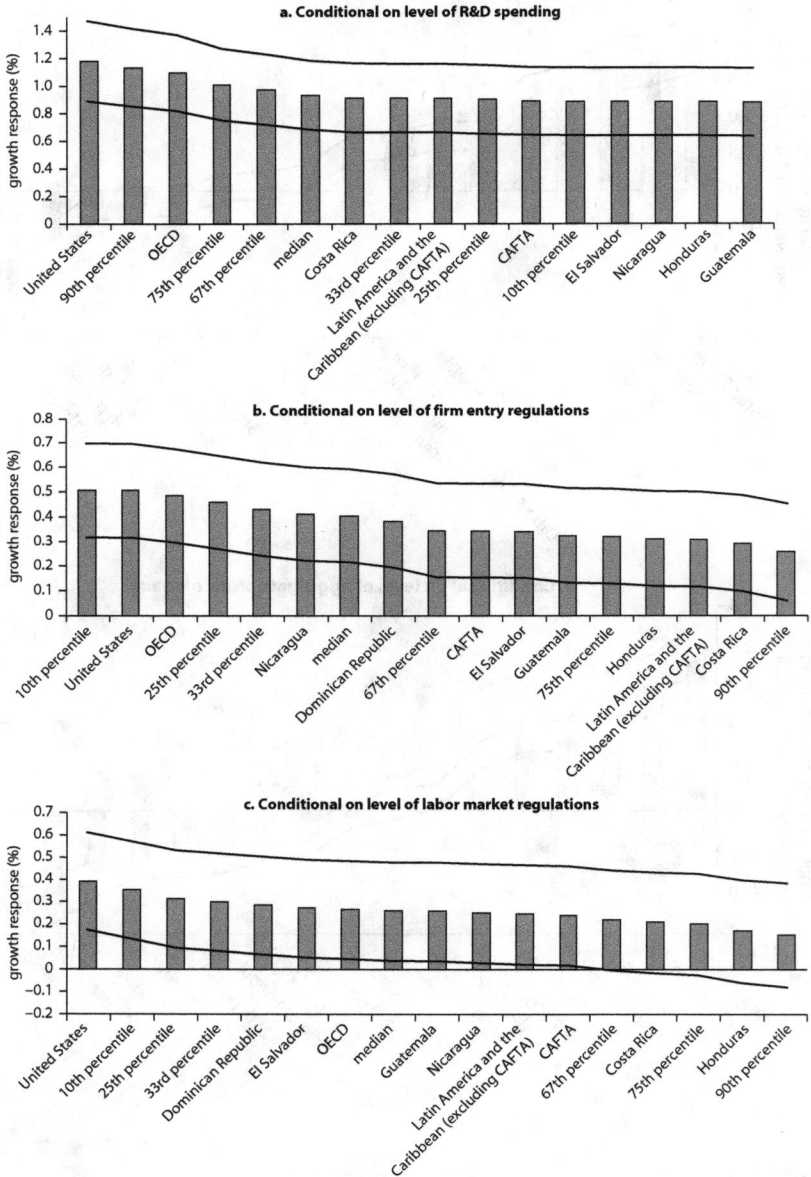

Source: Authors' calculations.
Note: The computed responses were obtained using the estimated coefficients from column 2 of table 4.4 for panel a and from column 2 of table 4.5 for panel b. R&D spending is the average ratio of R&D expenditure as a percentage of GDP for the 2000–09 period. Firm entry regulations are calculated as the simple average of the following measures: number of procedures, time, and cost.

factor SF, then the response of growth to a change in trade openness is as follows:

$$dg = \left(\alpha_0 + \alpha_1 \cdot \overline{SF}\right) \cdot dTO, \qquad (4.4)$$

where dTO is the standard deviation increase in the ratio of trade to GDP for each country over the sample period and $\overline{SF}$ is the level of the structural factor. Table 4.6 reports the growth response to rising trade openness conditional on the following structural factors: human capital, financial development, institutional quality, infrastructure stock, financial openness, innovation, and regulations. Panel a of table 4.6 assumes that $\overline{SF}$ is the level of the structural policy in the DR-CAFTA country in the period 2006–10. Panel b calculates the growth benefits that DR-CAFTA countries could potentially obtain if their structural policies were at the level of the seventy-fifth percentile of the sample distribution in 2006–10. Finally, panel c presents the growth gains for DR-CAFTA of shifting their structural policies to those of the leaders (seventy-fifth percentile) in the face of rising trade openness.

The first column of table 4.6 shows the growth effects of a 1 standard deviation increase in trade openness for DR-CAFTA countries. The countries in the region reaping the largest benefit in our baseline model (without interactions) are Costa Rica (25 basis points), Nicaragua (25 basis points), and El Salvador (22 basis points), whereas the Dominican Republic and Honduras obtain the lowest benefits (7 basis points). Next we report the contribution in the models with interactions. If the growth benefits are higher than those reported in the baseline model, then the complementarities at work enhance rather than hinder the impact of trade openness on growth.

Conditional on the level of human capital in the corresponding DR-CAFTA countries, we find that Costa Rica obtains the largest benefits (67 basis points a year), while human capital in Honduras offsets the effect of rising trade integration on growth. Financial development, in contrast, does not amplify the growth effect of openness as much as human capital. Again, Costa Rica is the winner, with a growth rate higher by 37 basis points, while the Dominican Republic obtains the lowest benefits from growth. The same is found for infrastructure; in Costa Rica, the large network of infrastructure allows the country to raise the growth rate by 41 basis points a year, while in Honduras the growth rate increases by a meager 6 basis points.

Table 4.6 Growth Effects due to Changes in Trade Openness

	Baseline model	Trade openness interacted with						
		Human capital	Financial development	Institutional quality	Infrastructure stock	Financial openness	Research & development	Economic regulations
a. Conditional on the structural factors of the DR-CAFTA country in 2006–10								
Costa Rica	25	67	37	41	65	30	62	22
Dominican Republic	7	17	8	10	17	8	..	8
El Salvador	22	41	32	29	39	28	53	22
Guatemala	10	8	12	11	13	5	24	9
Honduras	7	-4	12	6	10	10	18	6
Nicaragua	25	49	34	31	28	33	60	25
b. Conditional on the structural factors of the 75th percentile of the world distribution in 2006–10								
Costa Rica	25	88	49	49	98	54	69	23
Dominican Republic	7	26	15	15	29	16	21	7
El Salvador	22	77	43	43	86	47	61	20
Guatemala	10	35	19	19	39	21	27	9
Honduras	7	26	15	15	29	16	21	7
Nicaragua	25	88	49	49	98	54	69	23
c. Growth gains due to a 1 standard deviation increase in trade if the structural factors improve to 75th percentile of distribution								
Costa Rica		20	12	8	34	24	7	1
Dominican Republic		10	6	5	12	8	0	
El Salvador		36	11	14	47	19	7	0
Guatemala		26	7	9	25	16	4	0
Honduras		30	3	8	19	6	3	0
Nicaragua		39	15	18	70	21	9	0

Source: Authors' calculations.

Note: .. = Negligible.

Panel b presents the growth effects of trade evaluated in the seventy-fifth percentile of the structural policies in the sample distribution. In most cases, given the distance to the frontier by DR-CAFTA models, the growth effects are larger. Panel c summarizes these differences by calculating the potential growth gains of a 1 standard deviation increase in trade openness if DR-CAFTA countries were to reach the level of structural policies of the top quartile of the sample distribution.

The results show that human capital and infrastructure are the sectors with the largest potential to realize the growth effects from trade openness. Whereas the growth rate would increase between 10 and 39 basis points a year if the level of human capital were to increase in DR-CAFTA countries, it would increase between 12 and 70 basis points if the improvement would occur in infrastructure. Of course, reaching these levels implies a large amount of investment that is likely to be implausible to undertake in a short time horizon.

Finally, other exercises are presented in Calderón and Poggio (2010): (a) growth effect of the change in trade openness in 2006–10 vis-à-vis 1991–95, conditional on the structural policies of DR-CAFTA countries; and (b) potential growth benefits of DR-CAFTA countries of attaining the trade integration levels of the East Asian tigers. The results, although not reported, are available from the authors on request.

Concluding Remarks

The goal of this study is to evaluate the growth effects of trade openness among DR-CAFTA countries and, more specifically, to examine whether these growth effects are stimulated or hindered by advances in structural policies and institutions. Following recent empirical literature, we evaluate the role of complementarities between trade openness and the following factors: human capital, financial development, institutional quality, infrastructure, financial openness, innovation, and economic regulations.

Using our effective regression sample of 99 countries with five-year nonoverlapping observations over the period 1960–2010, we find the following results.

First, there is a robust causal link between trade and growth. Regardless of the set of instruments used in our regression analysis, we find that trade openness stimulates growth. In fact, our estimates are not only statistically but also economically significant: a 1 standard deviation increase in the ratio of trade to GDP (that is, an increase of roughly 75 percent in the ratio) would lead to an increase in the rate of growth per capita of 35 basis points a year (and an accumulated increase of 5.5 percentage points over 15 years).

Second, we find strong evidence that the impact of trade openness on growth depends on country-specific conditions in structural areas such as education, financial development, institutional quality, infrastructure, financial openness, innovation, and regulations. In general, we find that growth benefits from trade openness will be larger in countries that surpass a certain threshold in the structural areas mentioned above.

Third, trade stimulates growth in countries with higher levels of human capital, deeper domestic financial markets, stronger institutions, more developed infrastructure networks, high integration with world financial markets, higher intensity in R&D investment, and less stringent regulations.

Fourth, although our baseline model (without) interactions predicts growth benefits from trade for DR-CAFTA countries, we find that not accounting for complementarities between trade openness and structural factors may overstate these results. In fact, we find that human capital, infrastructure development, and institutional quality may play an important role in enhancing the growth benefits from trade.

Finally, there is ample room among DR-CAFTA countries for reaping the growth benefits from trade. However, a larger role should be played by further reforms in areas such as education, infrastructure, international financial integration, and the development of domestic financial markets.

Notes

1. This "flow" measure more closely captures current policies on schooling and human capital investment than "stock" measures related to educational attainment of the adult population or life expectancy (Loayza, Fajnzylber, and Calderón 2005).

2. The sector-specific indicators of infrastructure quantity and quality employed below, while standard in the literature, are subject to caveats regarding their homogeneity and international comparability. For example, the quality and condition of a "paved road" can vary substantially across countries—even within the same country. More homogeneous measures of infrastructure performance would clearly be preferable, but unfortunately they do not exist, at least with any significant coverage across countries and time periods.

3. The correlation between the two synthetic quantity indexes is over 0.996. This is not surprising given the similarly high correlation between the two indicators of telephone density underlying the respective synthetic indicators.

4. A similar adjustment is presented in Pritchett (1996).

5. For details, see Arellano and Bover (1995); Blundell and Bond (1998).

6. The results are presented in Calderón and Poggio (2010) and are available from the authors on request.

7. Although these scatter plots are not reported, they are available from the authors on request.

8. A more detailed presentation of these results is provided by Calderón and Poggio (2010).

References

Ades, A. F., and E. L. Glaeser. 1999. "Evidence on Growth, Increasing Returns, and the Extent of the Market." *Quarterly Journal of Economics* 114 (3): 1025–45.

Aghion, P., J. Fedderke, P. Howitt, C. Kularatne, and N. Viegi. 2008. "Testing Creative Destruction in an Opening Economy: The Case of the South African Manufacturing Industries." Documents de Travail 2008-23, Observatoire Français des Conjonctures Economiques, July.

Alesina, A., E. Spolaore, and R. Wacziarg. 2000. "Economic Integration and Political Disintegration." *American Economic Review* 90 (5): 1276–96.

———. 2005. "Trade, Growth, and the Size of Countries." In *Handbook of Economic Growth*, ed. P. Aghion and S. N. Durlauf vol. 1, part 2, 1499–542. Amsterdam: Elsevier North-Holland.

Arellano, M., and S. Bond. 1991. "Some Tests of Specification for Panel Data: Monte Carlo Evidence and an Application to Employment Equations." *Review of Economic Studies* 58 (2): 277–97.

Arellano, M., and O. Bover. 1995. "Another Look at the Instrumental-Variable Estimation of Error-Components Models." *Journal of Econometrics* 68 (1): 29–52.

Barro, R. J., and J. W. Lee. 2001. "International Data on Educational Attainment: Updates and Implications." *Oxford Economic Papers* 53 (3): 541–63.

Beck, T., and A. Demirgüç-Kunt. 2009. "Financial Institutions and Markets across Countries and over Time: Data and Analysis." Policy Research Working Paper 4943, World Bank, Washington, DC, June.

Beck, T., A. Demirgüç-Kunt, and R. Levine. 2000. "A New Database on Financial Development and Structure." *World Bank Economic Review* 14 (3): 597–605.

Blundell, R., and S. R. Bond. 1998. "Initial Conditions and Moment Restrictions in Dynamic Panel Data Models." *Journal of Econometrics* 87 (1): 115–43.

Bolaky, B., and C. Freund. 2004. "Trade, Regulations, and Growth." Policy Research Working Paper 3255, World Bank, Washington, DC, March.

Calderón, C., and A. Chong. 2004. "Volume and Quality of Infrastructure and the Distribution of Income: An Empirical Investigation." *Review of Income and Wealth* 50 (1): 87–105.

Calderón, C., and R. Fuentes. 2006. "Complementarities between Institutions and Openness in Economic Development: Evidence for a Panel of Countries." *Cuadernos de Economía* 43 (127): 49–80.

————. 2009. "Removing the Constraints from Growth: Some Guidelines." Working Paper 366, Instituto de Economía, December, Pontificia Universidad Católica de Chile, Santiago.

Calderón, C., N. Loayza, and K. Schmidt-Hebbel. 2006. "External Conditions and Growth Performance." In *External Vulnerability and Preventive Policies*, ed. R. Caballero, C. Calderón, and L. F. Cespedes, 41–70. Series on Banking, Analysis and Economic Policies. Santiago: Central Bank of Chile.

Calderón, C., and V. Poggio. 2010. "Trade and Economic Growth: Evidence on the Role of Complementarities for CAFTA-DR Countries." Policy Research Working Paper 5426, World Bank, Washington, DC, September.

Calderón, C., and L. Servén. 2004. "The Effects of Infrastructure Development on Growth and Income Distribution." Policy Research Working Paper 3400, World Bank, Washington, DC, September.

————. 2010. "Infrastructure in Latin America." Policy Research Working Paper 5317, World Bank, Washington DC.

Chang, R., L. Kaltani, and N. Loayza. 2009. "Openness Can Be Good for Growth: The Role of Policy Complementarities." *Journal of International Economics* 90 (1): 33–49.

Coe, D. T., and E. Helpman. 1995. "International R&D Spillovers." *European Economic Review* 39 (5): 859–87.

Coe, D. T., E. Helpman, and A. W. Hoffmaister. 1997. "North-South R&D Spillovers." *Economic Journal* 107 (440): 134–49.

Deardorff, A. V. 1974. "Factor Proportions and Comparative Advantage in the Long Run: Comment." *Journal of Political Economy* 82 (4): 829–33.

Dollar, D. 1992. "Outward-Oriented Developing Economies Really Do Grow More Rapidly: Evidence from 95 LDCs, 1976–85." *Economic Development and Cultural Change* 40 (3): 523–44.

Edwards, S. 1992. "Trade Orientation, Distortions, and Growth in Developing Countries." *Journal of Development Economics* 39 (1): 31–57.

Frankel, J. A., and D. Romer. 1999. "Does Trade Cause Growth?" *American Economic Review* 89 (3): 379–99.

Galiani, S., P. Gertler, and E. Schargrodsky. 2005. "Water for Life: The Impact of the Privatization of Water Services on Child Mortality." *Journal of Political Economy* 113 (1): 83–120.

Gaston, N., and D. Trefler. 1995. "Union Wage Sensitivity to Trade and Protection: Theory and Evidence." *Journal of International Economics* 39 (1–2): 1–25.

Grossman, G. M., and E. Helpman. 1991. *Innovation and Growth in the Global Economy*. Cambridge, U.K.: MIT Press.

Head, K., and J. Ries. 1999. "Can Small-Country Manufacturing Survive Trade Liberalization? Evidence from the Canada-U.S. Free Trade Agreement." Perspectives on North American Free Research Publication 1, Industry Canada, April.

Helleiner, G. 1986. "Outward Orientation, Import Instability, and African Economic Growth: An Empirical Investigation." In *Theory and Reality in Development: Essays in Honor of Paul Streeten*, ed. S. Lall and F. Stewart, 139–53. London: Macmillan.

Heston, A., R. Summers, and B. Aten. 2009. "Penn World Table Version 6.3." Center for International Comparisons of Production, Income and Prices, University of Pennsylvania, Philadelphia.

Kohli, I., and N. Singh. 1989. "Exports and Growth: Critical Minimum Effort and Diminishing Returns." *Journal of Development Economics* 30 (2): 391–400.

Krishna, P., and D. Mitra. 1998. "Trade Liberalization, Market Discipline, and Productivity Growth: New Evidence from India." *Journal of Development Economics* 56 (2): 447–62.

Krishna, P., D. Mitra, and S. Chinoy. 2001. "Trade Liberalization and Labor Demand Elasticities: Evidence from Turkey." *Journal of International Economics* 55 (2): 391–409.

Lane, P. R., and G.-M. Milesi-Ferretti. 2001. "The External Wealth of Nations: Measures of Foreign Assets and Liabilities for Industrial and Developing Countries." *Journal of International Economics* 55 (1): 263–94.

———. 2007. "The External Wealth of Nations Mark II: Revised and Extended Estimates of Foreign Assets and Liabilities, 1970–2004." *Journal of International Economics* 73 (2): 223–50.

Lederman, D., W. F. Maloney, and L. Servén. 2007. *Lessons from NAFTA for Latin America and the Caribbean*. Latin American Development Forum Series. Palo Alto, CA: Stanford University Press, Stanford Economics and Finance; Washington, DC: World Bank.

Levinsohn, J. 1993. "Testing the Imports-as-Market-Discipline Hypothesis." *Journal of International Economics* 35 (1–2): 1–22.

———. 1999. "Employment Responses to International Liberalization in Chile." *Journal of International Economics* 47 (2): 321–44.

Lewer, J., and H. van den Berg. 2003. "Does Trade Composition Influence Economic Growth? Time Series Evidence for 28 OECD and Developing Countries." *Journal of International Trade and Economic Development* 12 (1): 39–96.

Loayza, N., P. Fajnzylber, and C. Calderón. 2005. "Economic Growth in Latin America and the Caribbean: Stylized Facts, Explanations, and Forecasts." Latin American and the Caribbean Studies. Washington, DC: World Bank, April.

Lucas, R. E. Jr. 1988. "On the Mechanics of Economic Development." *Journal of Monetary Economics* 22 (1): 3–42.

Matsuyama, K. 1992. "Agricultural Productivity, Comparative Advantage, and Economic Growth." *Journal of Economic Theory* 58 (2): 317–34.

Pavcnik, N. 2002. "Trade Liberalization, Exit, and Productivity Improvement: Evidence from Chilean Plants." *Review of Economic Studies* 69 (1): 245–76.

Pritchett, L. 1996. "Measuring Outward Orientation in LDCs: Can It Be Done?" *Journal of Development Economics* 49 (2): 307–35.

Rodríguez, F., and D. Rodrik. 2001. "Trade Policy and Economic Growth: A Skeptic's Guide to the Cross-National Evidence." In *NBER Macroeconomics Annual 2000*, ed. B. Bernanke and K. Rogoff, 261–335. Cambridge, MA: MIT Press.

Rodrik, D. 2005. "Growth Strategies." In *Handbook of Economic Growth*, vol. 1, ed. P. Aghion and S. Durlauf, 967–1014. Amsterdam: Elsevier.

Romer, P. M., 1990. "Endogenous Technological Change." *Journal of Political Economy* 98 (5, pt. 2): S71–S102.

Sachs, J. D., and A. M. Warner. 1995. "Economic Reform and the Process of Global Integration." *Brookings Papers on Economic Activity* 1: 1–118.

Sánchez-Robles, B. 1998. "Infrastructure Investment and Growth: Some Empirical Evidence." *Contemporary Economic Policy* 16 (1): 98–108.

Trefler, D. 2004. "The Long and Short of the Canada-U.S. Free Trade Agreement." *American Economic Review* 94 (4): 870–95.

Tybout, J. R., J. de Melo, and V. Corbo. 1991. "The Effects of Trade Reforms on Scale and Technical Efficiency." *Journal of International Economics* 31 (3–4): 231–50.

Wacziarg, R. 2001. "Measuring the Dynamic Gains from Trade." *World Bank Economic Review* 15 (3): 393–429.

Wacziarg, R., and I. Welch. 2008. "Trade Liberalization and Growth: New Evidence." *World Bank Economic Review* 22 (2): 187–231.

Young, A. 1991. "Learning by Doing and the Dynamic Effects of International Trade." *Quarterly Journal of Economics* 106 (2): 369–405.

CHAPTER 5

Power Integration in Central America: From Hope to Mirage?

Juan Miguel Cayo

Energy is a key input for production, and as such high energy prices put firms at a competitive disadvantage. The question then is, why are energy prices so high in Central America (see figure 5.1), and what can be done to address this problem? According to a recent study by the World Bank (2010), several obstacles remain in the path to energy security in Central America. These include (a) a tight balance between power generation and demand, which adversely affects the reliability of supply and its quality; (b) significant exposure to oil price volatility and shocks due to overdependence on oil imports, which have increased with the region's growing reliance on thermal power stations; (c) significant inefficiencies in the institutional and regulatory framework of several countries, which affect the financial sustainability of power utilities and their operations; and (d) relatively low levels of access in certain countries, which affect rural areas in particular.

The six Central American countries of Costa Rica, El Salvador, Guatemala, Honduras, Nicaragua, and Panama share a long tradition of regional integration, including a common market, substantial intraregional trade, as well as coordinated commercial policies, such as the Central America Free Trade Agreement (CAFTA) with the United States. In the electricity subsector, the most significant example of regional

Figure 5.1   Electricity Tariffs in Select Cities[a]

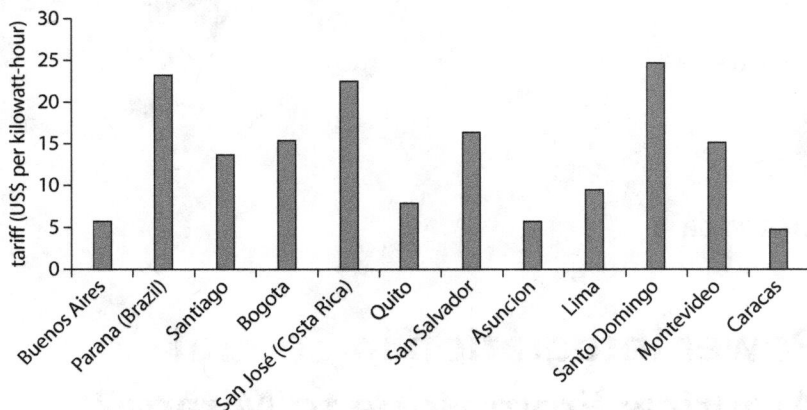

Source: CIER 2010.
a. Industries using less than 50,000 kilowatt-hours a month.

integration consists of the SIEPAC (Central American Electrical Interconnection System) interconnection line, which is expected to fully link the six countries by 2011; Costa Rica and Panama were connected in November 2010. The interconnection has been a long-term effort, starting in the early 1990s with the support of the Inter-American Development Bank and the government of Spain.

SIEPAC was designed to bring the benefits of integration to the six countries and to improve their national power systems. Due to the relatively small size of the power system in each of the region's nations, the opening of the regional market was seen as a means for creating a larger market to enhance competition among power producers and for providing a secure supply of power to all individual countries at the same time. The goal is for the regional market to allow qualified agents to buy or sell electricity no matter where they are located in the Central American region. Additionally, a regional market with clear and uniform rules is expected to offer incentives for building larger and more efficient power plants, sparking investments that would help to reduce the costs and increase the reliability of electricity systems in the region. However, as the national markets evolve toward integration and increased trade, important barriers still hinder the full implementation of the regional electricity market (MER).

This chapter identifies some of the barriers to the development of a truly enhanced regional electricity market in Central America. As this book is aimed at a nonenergy public, the chapter begins by explaining some of the complexities of modern electricity markets and the challenges of power trade and integration. Then it presents some of the key political economy considerations around power integration. In particular, the trade-off between energy integration and sovereignty is a fact that governments participating in integration initiatives will have to deal with and solve. Next the paper presents a brief history of the SIEPAC project and the harmonization efforts to date. Finally, it identifies the remaining obstacles to power integration that the governments of Central America will have to overcome for success in this important effort. The year 2010 may be crucial to determining the success or failure of the SIEPAC project. The measure of how far the region is able to advance in the near future will determine whether power integration in Central America will fulfill the expectations of its designers or will convert into a wasteful effort.

What Does Power Integration Mean?

The physical properties of electricity production, transmission, and distribution make the challenge of matching supply and demand at every moment especially difficult. Because storing electricity is virtually impossible (at least in economical terms) and capacity constraints on production from a plant cannot be breached for significant periods without incurring extreme risks, the amount of energy that can be delivered at any particular moment is essentially fixed. Any failure to equate demand and supply endangers the stability, not only of the market participants that caused the imbalance, but of the system as a whole. Moreover, an action that could be profitable to one market participant but simultaneously degrades the system's reliability can negatively affect the ability of other buyers or suppliers to fulfill their contractual obligations (that is, there are important externalities as a result of being interconnected). For this reason, modern electricity markets usually have a system operator that controls the operation of the flows generated (dispatch) to preserve adequate functioning—and avoid major oscillations in tension—throughout the transmission network.

One major feature of modern electricity markets is that, while electrons flow according to the laws of physics, energy payments flow according to the terms of financial contracts.[1] This means that the laws governing the flow of energy are totally independent of the financial flows. When consumer A signs a contract to purchase energy from generator B, it does not necessarily mean that the energy received by consumer A was physically produced by generator B. On the contrary, this generally is not the case. As Wolak (2004) clearly states,

> Contrary to common perception, a buyer of electricity is not purchasing megawatt-hours (MWhs) of energy produced by a specific generation unit. A buyer is only purchasing the right to withdraw that quantity of MWhs from a specific location in the network, and a seller is paid for injecting a certain quantity of MWhs into the grid at a specified location in the network.

In the spot or wholesale market, generators can buy or sell energy among themselves as long as the system is ultimately balanced. For example, if the system operator who administers system dispatch instructs one generator to generate less energy than the amount agreed in its contracts, it becomes a "deficit generator" and has to buy the rest of the energy needed to complete its contracts in the spot market. On the contrary, if a generator is made to generate more energy than it is contracted to provide, it becomes a "surplus generator," so it has to sell surplus energy in the spot market. The spot market price is given by the marginal cost of the system, in other words, by the variable cost of the most expensive generator that is dispatched.

The supply curve of the industry is—as usual—the aggregation of all of the marginal cost curves, which is represented by a stairway profile because the marginal cost of the system jumps up every time a new power plant enters the dispatch merit order. The market price is determined by the marginal cost of the last plant that is generating power to meet the demand for energy in that precise moment in the very short term. In peak hours (typically in the evenings) when demand increases, the spot price jumps because the more expensive plants are required to generate.

Originally, electric power systems were developed as small isolated monopolies with a few generating units under central control. Gradually these isolated systems were interconnected to allow power trading and reserve sharing. As interconnections grew, so did the scope and complexity of the control system. No real-time pricing of grid interactions was established, but there was little reason to do so because neighboring generators (monopolies) essentially bartered energy and reserves and cooperated to maintain system reliability.

Eventually, simple contract trading developed among neighboring monopolies, but this trading did not include any actual pricing of network interactions. Pressure for competitive generation developed only in the

1970s and 1980s, when independent power producers could also be paid for delivering energy to the local monopoly utility. But real competition, in which a generator could compete to sell directly to a consumer or to a distributor not affiliated with the local monopoly utility, did not develop until the 1990s (see Hunt 2002).[2]

In modern electricity markets, there are multiple participants; a large number of generators; and a large number of consumers, whether regulated (that is, small household and commercial consumers that are served by distribution utilities) or not regulated (that is, big industrial plants, mines, and so forth that can purchase energy directly from suppliers at negotiated prices). As mentioned, the control of this complex system relies on a centralized system operator, which manages the dispatch of several power plants according to their marginal costs, either "real" costs or "bid prices," depending on the regulatory framework, in the best manner to ensure the stability and proper functioning of the transmission grid. The financial flows linked to contracts among participants in the market are independent of the physical flows, so a market administrator is needed to function as a clearinghouse for net energy flows so that payments can clear accordingly.[3]

Interconnection Is Not Equal to Integration

There are many examples of electricity interconnections between two or more national power systems in the Latin American region. For example, the Colombia-Ecuador interconnection started operations in late 1998, but due to the physical configuration of the transmission line, it is just a "radial" interconnection—meaning that it is impossible to attain a synchronized operation of both systems.[4] Under these circumstances, it would be difficult to assert that Colombia and Ecuador have an integrated power system; they just trade power.

Another example is the interconnection of Brazil and Paraguay through the co-owned Itaipu power plant. Itaipu is owned on a 50-50 basis by Brazil and Paraguay, but 90 percent of its production goes to Brazil and only 10 percent goes to Paraguay. The Paraguayan energy surplus—that is, the difference between its right to access 50 percent of the plant's energy and domestic consumption—is obligated to be sold to Brazil through the Brazilian electricity monopoly, which acts as a single buyer.[5] Again, it would be fair to say that the Paraguayan power system is linked to Itaipu (almost 90 percent of Paraguay's domestic demand is provided by this plant), but not necessarily to the Brazilian power system. The reverse is even more true: the Brazilian power system is not really integrated with the Paraguayan system; they just share a common power plant. Hence, the difference between interconnection and integration is analogous to the difference between trading goods and having a common economic market.

One important feature of power integration is that it is a very long process with multiple stages. The first stage is, of course, to create the physical interconnection through a transmission line across the border. But from that point onward, power integration can take different modalities or degrees of "integration." In its most basic form, a generator in one country can provide electricity to consumers in another country at a contract price. Itaipu is an example of this basic form of trade, which would not be referred to as "integration." Neither system is working in coordination nor does the dispatch of different plants on either side of the border affect the energy flows of this plant.

The next stage is to integrate the two systems so that they work with a coordinated dispatch that allows participants in both markets to know the spot prices in each market at every moment.[6] The higher-price country will always import from the lower-price country and vice versa. These are the so-called short-term international transactions; contracts are not between specific suppliers or consumers but rather between the two wholesale markets (the Colombia-Ecuador trade operates through this modality). In the case of the existence of a long-term contract between a supplier in country A and a consumer in country B (for instance, a distribution company), the fact that a contract exists does not mean that the supplier will necessarily generate its own energy to comply with the contract. It may well honor its contract by buying energy in the domestic spot market (if $P_A < P_B$) or in the foreign spot market (if $P_A > P_B$).

One important feature of this level of integration is that, whenever the low-price country is exporting, the domestic spot price will rise as a consequence of having additional demand that will have to be met with its installed capacity. As a result of export activity, higher-cost plants will have to be ordered to dispatch power, as the new demand (from the import country) exerts pressure on the domestic system. Conversely, the spot market price in the import country will decline as the new supply (coming from across the border) partially meets the domestic demand, thereby displacing high-cost plants in the local market. This is a basic idea that is important to have in mind when promoting power trade: prices will rise in the export country as a consequence of the power trade. This is why some countries find it politically difficult to convince domestic consumers that exporting power is beneficial. By analogy, power generators in the import country are prone to lobby the government, as imports of cheap energy from abroad can erode their profits.

The third stage of integration is the integrated market—or power pool—in which the two systems behave as one, with a single centralized dispatch and no difference between market participants, whether nationals or foreigners. In this integrated market, a unique supply curve is determined by the marginal costs of all the power plants in both systems,[7] and the aggregate demand for power is the sum of all consumption on both sides of the frontier. Consequently, there is only one price in the spot market for this integrated system. This is the last stage and what most people have in mind when they talk about "integration." Of course, this level of integration (attained, for example, in the Nordpool system of the Nordic countries) requires an impressive amount of political will, substantial investments in information technology systems, and an advanced level of regulatory harmonization.

Potential Benefits of Power Integration
In theory, international exchange of electricity brings four major advantages: (a) trade allows countries to make better use of complementary resources—for example, exchanging hydropower for thermal power when individual countries do not have both resources; (b) international interconnection allows countries to balance variations in annual demand—for example, Ecuador and Colombia have asynchronic rainy seasons, so they can exploit water resources efficiently throughout the year through trading; (c) power trade allows countries to balance generation with current needs, exporting or importing to match their requirements without incurring emergency power contracts; and (d) international trade allows countries to pool their reserve capacity, thereby reducing costs for extra power stations and limiting the inefficient dispatch of power plants required for the provision of spinning reserves.

In a developing-country context, as is the case of the Central American MER, the creation of a regional power system by a group of smaller market economies can reduce the risks and help the region to match supply and demand more efficiently. The existence of an enlarged power system enhances a project developer's ability to finance and construct regional power-generating facilities that would be impossible if relying exclusively on the domestic demand of smaller market economies. Consequently, it can make the development of a country's or a subregion's capital-intensive power projects more attractive to both domestic and international investors and lenders, reducing risks by creating a broader demand pool of utilities and off-takers of potential generating facilities. The result would benefit all consumers in the region by lowering prices and improving the quality and safety of the power supply and would eventually result in a lower environmental impact relative to power development (World Bank 2001). In the medium to long term, the main benefits would be (a) lower operating costs from using the most economically favorable energy resources, particularly through the integration and coordination of hydropower and thermal systems, which reduce operating costs by generating hydropower in off-peak periods, and (b) lower investment costs in the long term from using integrated planning on a multisystem basis, realizing economies of scale, and reducing total reserve requirements (USAID 2008).

The benefits arising from cross-border interconnection facilities, once built and put into operation, are derived primarily from the multiplication of energy exchanges among national power utilities. In economic terms, such growth in cross-border energy exchanges should increase until the marginal benefits from displacing more expensive capacity or from making additional sales equal the marginal costs of transmission across the interconnected networks. The same applies to expansion of an interconnection, for which the costs of new generation and transmission must be taken into account (World Bank 2008).

However, as Robinson (2009) asserts, much of the literature on the benefits of regional power pools is more advocacy than serious analysis. Establishing a causality relationship between power integration and higher investments based on least-cost projects is problematic in practice. Despite regional generation and transmission optimization, exercises show significant gains over the sum of national plans. The problem is that politicians equate *energy security* with having *domestic generation* capacity (that is, there is a bias toward national power development plans). Countries remain unwilling to surrender sovereignty to regional bodies or to depend on other countries' ability or willingness to provide the power needed to supply domestic demand. The recent epsiodes in Europe with regard to the Russian gas supply and the problems between Argentina and Chile with regard to gas contract compliance illustrate the difficulties that energy integration (whether gas or electricity) can entail and their implications for energy security. As a general proposition, Robinson (2009) states that, even though the benefits from *power trade* are clear and accountable with regard to electricity exchanges, most of the theoretical benefits from *power integration* are yet to be demonstrated.

Power Trade: Contracts and Spot Transactions

When two electricity systems are interconnected, energy is transmitted from the low-price country (zone) to the high-price country (zone). In the exporting country, prices increase because additional, more expensive generators are required to dispatch, whereas in the importing zone, prices decrease because expensive plants are no longer required to generate. In equilibrium and assuming infinite transmission capacity, price equalizes between the two zones, creating potential savings in the importing country and potential costs in the exporting country.

However, in practice, most of the transmission interconnections are subject to capacity constraints, so there are no conditions for price equalization because the demand for exchange constitutes only a relatively small portion of total demand in the import zone system. As a result, the price gap between the two power zones does not vanish. There is, in other words, a price differential between the importing and exporting countries. This price differential, multiplied by the total energy traded, generates "congestion rents." There has been a lot of debate on how to share these congestion rents between the two zones. In the case of the Colombia-Ecuador power exchanges, the rents go to the export country to compensate for the additional costs incurred by its consumers.[8] In other international power exchanges, these rents have been shared equally between both countries. In fact, the lack of agreement about how to share these congestion rents has been the main obstacle to starting operation of the Peru-Ecuador interconnection.[9] In the case of Central America, the sharing of congestion rents has not posed an issue because the 50-50 formula has been the rule in the region's power trade during the past few years.

In markets that show high price volatility—such as the power spot markets—it is common for buyers and sellers to smooth out their transaction prices through long-term contracts. Under forward power purchase contracts, the buyer is obliged to purchase a certain amount of power from the seller under a predefined price and for a sufficiently long-term tenure (typically, 10 to 15 years). International experience has shown that the main supply-side benefit of industry restructuring is the competitive procurement of long-term power purchase contracts that have sufficient magnitude and duration to allow suppliers to fund the construction of new generation facilities. These power purchase agreements are very important to making the construction of new power facilities "bankable." This fact is of paramount importance when discussing the feasibility of regional power plants in Central America.[10]

The Political Economy of Integration

National policies toward energy security have a significant impact on how countries approach power integration. The perception of whether regional energy trade is seen as contributing to energy security through diversification and cost reduction or, on the contrary, as reducing energy security through the creation of dependencies and disruption risks is critical to the way that power trade develops. If the latter view is true, countries would need to overcome the inclination to equate self-sufficiency (and the bias toward national expansion plans) with energy security, at the expense of trade. The key point here is to recognize that the trade-off between integration and sovereignty is real.

For starters, power integration means that governments are not allowed to do a few things anymore, such as (a) prioritize national consumers versus foreigners, (b) cut supply under conditions of domestic scarcity when exchanges occur under long-term contracts, or (c) manipulate domestic power prices, as this could lead to the awkward situation of having to export even in scarcity conditions (under spot exchange arrangements). Most integration regulatory frameworks establish the *nondiscrimination principle*, under which every consumer must be treated equally without considerations of nationality. Therefore, in case of a supply disruption or power scarcity, the export country should not be allowed to cut the supply to consumers across the border just because they are not nationals. Accordingly, integration regulatory frameworks contain rules about how to cut supply in case of abrupt shortfalls; these rules generally obligate rationing based on the categories of consumers (for example, first industry, second commerce, then public buildings, and finally domestic consumers), but not by nationality.

Long-term contracts to sell electricity to consumers in other countries are usually based on the principle of "firm power," meaning that contracts are not interruptible or opportunistic, but predictable, secure, and reliable. Under these circumstances, the export country government cannot force the domestic power generator to relinquish its obligation or to use the allocated energy for another purpose. The regulatory framework or the supranational regulatory body (if one exists) should be strict enough to severely punish this kind of behavior.[11]

Prices are important for electricity, as with any commodity or traded good. Government manipulation of domestic prices (spot or retail) can cause severe distortions not only in the domestic market but also in trade. Suppose that two countries have wholesale (spot market) transactions—like Ecuador and Colombia—but country A puts price caps on spot prices to favor domestic consumers, while country B allows prices to reflect the actual costs of service. It may happen that, because of this artificially low price, demand in A may expand too much, creating scarcity and power shortfalls. But if both countries trade power based on their spot market price differential, country A may be left in the awkward position of having to export even in circumstances of scarcity, which is equivalent to an export subsidy.

Integration also entails renouncing some degree of sovereignty and giving power to supranational institutions (regulatory bodies and system operators). In the case of Central America, the regional electricity market has a supranational regulatory body (Comisión Regional de Interconexión Eléctrica—CRIE) and a regional system operator (*ente operador regional*—EOR) that have governing power over the regional transmission network and the international power trade. Finally, integration means that governments must postpone or abandon national plans to increase their domestic power supply and instead rely on trade for energy sufficiency purposes, based on least-cost alternatives under a regional or subregional perspective.

Domestic consumers in the export country could be opposed to export because domestic prices will increase, reflecting the additional demand coming from abroad. Therefore, export countries need to generate the mechanisms to compensate or alleviate the additional costs incurred by domestic consumers; otherwise, internal discontent may jeopardize the power integration efforts. Suppliers in import countries could have concerns that power trade will reduce their profits. In small importing markets with few participants, suppliers could exert pressure on politicians to limit power trade and avoid profit cutbacks.

Energy integration—and power integration in particular—is a complex process whose success will ultimately depend on four types of conditions:

- *Political.* Governments need to take bold actions to reduce their sovereign power to some degree (depending on the model of integration chosen) and to create the institutional safeguards to avoid relinquishing their commitments.
- *Institutional.* Strong institutions have to be put in place to manage the complexities of power trade, including coordinating national dispatches, operating the common infrastructure, solving commercial disputes, and overseeing competitive behavior.

- *Regulatory.* Regulatory frameworks need to be harmonized among all the participants or be created ad hoc to make the power transactions possible. This is a complex and difficult process, and regulations in each country have to compromise to facilitate international exchanges.
- *Physical.* There has to be enough actual generation and transmission capacity.

Power Integration in Central America: The SIEPAC Project

Central America is a region with a long tradition of integration.[12] Integration initiatives in the region are channeled through the Central American Integration System (Sistema de la Integración Centroamericana—SICA), created in 1991, which manages different organizations under it. In the energy sector, two regional organizations are part of SICA: the Central America Electrification Committee (Comité de Electrificación de América Central—CEAC) and the Central America Hydrocarbons Cooperation Committee (Comité de Cooperación de Hidrocarburos de América Central—CCHAC), which were organized more than 15 years ago. Since its creation, CEAC's prominence in the electrical integration of the region has progressively grown. It comprises representatives from the energy authorities of the different countries, and it has provided a forum for supporting initiatives such as the regional power market, the SIEPAC project, and the interconnections with Mexico and Colombia.

In 1996, the six Central American countries agreed to create MER, the regional electricity market. The Framework Treaty for the Central American Electricity Market was ratified by the governments in 1998. To support the MER, the treaty created the regional regulatory commission (CRIE), the regional system operator (EOR), and the company owner of the grid (*empresa propietaria de la red*—EPR). The SIEPAC project consists of two interdependent subprojects[13]:

- The development of a regional electricity market based on a standard set of trading rules at the regional (supranational) level. Part of the MER initiative is the creation of a regional institutional structure, including a regional regulator and a regional transmission operator.
- The development and completion of a new 1,800-kilometer international transmission line, running from Panama in the south to Guatemala in the north, that will expand transfer capacity at all borders in the region to 300 megawatts.[14]

The SIEPAC project is an initiative to create an integrated regional electricity market among the six Central American countries. The stated objectives are to (a) improve security of supply by widening reserve margins, (b) reduce the problem of electricity rationing in countries with capacity deficits, (c) improve operating efficiency and reduce fuel consumption, (d) introduce greater competition into the domestic markets, (e) lower end-user electricity costs, (f) attract foreign investment to the region's energy sector, and (g) contribute to the economic development of the region. The project costs approximately US$405 million, financed primarily by the Inter-American Development Bank (US$240 million), the Central American Bank for Economic Integration (US$100 million), and equity contributions from the nine shareholders of the EPR (US$50 million): the six Central American countries, ENDESA (Empresa Nacional de Electricidad) of Spain, ISA (Interconexión Eléctrica) of Colombia, and CFE (Comisión Federal de Electricidad) of Mexico.[15]

SIEPAC is part of a broader regional initiative under the Mesoamerica project (formerly known as Plan Puebla-Panama). The Mesoamerica project aims to develop and integrate energy, communications, and transport infrastructure across nine countries, including the six SIEPAC countries plus Mexico, Belize, and Colombia. The Plan Puebla-Panama was proposed in 2001 and formally institutionalized in 2004.

The Central America Power Sector in a Nutshell

The region generated around 38 terawatt-hours in 2007, equivalent to about 70 percent of the annual electricity supply of a medium-size country in Latin America, such as Chile or Colombia. Generation as a whole has grown at a rate of about 6 percent a year since 1990. Generation capacity is on the order of 9,700 megawatts, again similar to 70 percent in Colombia or Chile. The composition of installed capacity varies widely among countries (for example, 70 percent hydropower in Costa Rica and only 13 percent in Nicaragua), mainly as a result of institutional developments that took place in the middle and late 1990s. In those years, several countries implemented vertical unbundling, and only two (Costa Rica and Honduras) retained a vertically integrated state-owned monopoly. However, all countries allowed the entry of private sector enterprises to different degrees, either by selling assets or by purchasing power from new companies via the state-owned utility.

Restructuring of the Central American national power sectors has yielded differing sector structures. In the 1990s, the countries approved new laws and regulations that initiated restructuring processes in their power sectors. Those reforms aimed to promote private participation in a sector that had traditionally been controlled by fully integrated state-owned companies. Reforms in Costa Rica and Honduras were limited to opening the generation segment to private participation. However, significant reforms to liberalize electricity markets were implemented in Guatemala, El Salvador, Nicaragua, and Panama. These countries implemented vertical and horizontal unbundling of generation, transmission, and distribution activities, creating specialized companies in the electricity sector, as well as permitting retail competition for large consumers. In general, the role of the state was restricted—totally or partially—to the formulation of policies, the promotion of regulatory functions, and the administration of concessions. In all cases, economic dispatch was centralized and based on audited variable costs (except in El Salvador, where it was based on prices, but is now changing to variable costs).

The participation of new private generation enterprises has had both positive and negative consequences. Private investors installed thermal plants, which required less capital and could eventually be moved out of the country if necessary because of system size and lower perceived risk in comparison to renewables. Thermal power was also the least-cost option during the late 1990s due to the high efficiencies associated with heavy fuel oil and diesel plants and the prevalence of low oil prices. In fact, some of the initial investors (in Guatemala) chose to install mobile barge-mounted plants. Private sector investments provided much needed relief to former public sector companies with little access to capital. However, it also made the region increasingly dependent on oil products and on the volatility of the oil market, which resulted in extreme financial consequences in 2006–08, when the price of oil skyrocketed. The share of oil-based power generation grew from almost 0 in 1990 to more than 30 percent in 2007, and several countries have hydrocarbon shares in excess of 50 percent (see figure 5.2). Until 1990, Central American countries used their considerable hydrological resources to generate most of their electricity, and renewables represented 91 percent of the power generated. With demand for electricity growing rapidly, capacity grew from 4,009 megawatts in 1990 to 9,486 megawatts in 2007. However, over this period of almost 20 years, twice as much new generation capacity relying on fossil fuels was built than capacity derived from renewable resources.

Indicators point to difficulties associated with meeting the growing demand for electricity in Central America. The precarious balance of

Figure 5.2   Central American Power Generation, by Type of Power, 1985–2007

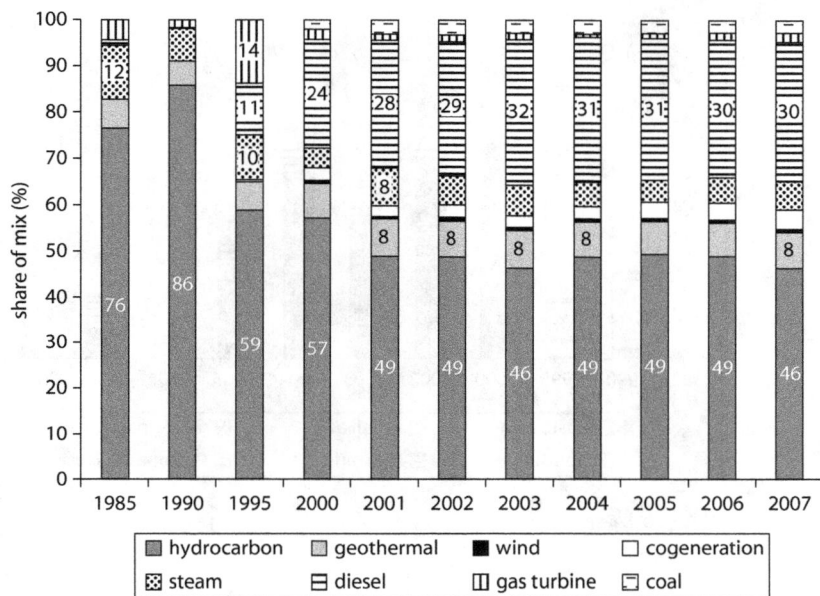

Source: ECLAC 2007.

supply and demand is a common threat to all nations in the subregion. Nicaragua experienced severe blackouts in 2006–07, and Costa Rica saw shortages in 2007. As a consequence of this deterioration, power trade among Central American countries has been declining over the past decade.

In the past, electricity trade in the Central America region was limited mostly to bilateral transactions in the spot market. As per the current MER regulations, all the contracts are "nonfirm" and must comply with the national legal and regulatory framework. Consequently, the regional market contracts are for import or export of electricity between agents represented by their respective national operators. The main objective of these transactions is to take advantage of energy surpluses and differences in marginal generation costs. As shown in figure 5.3, trade was active in the early 2000s, although restricted by the capacity of existing transmission links. However, trade has dwindled in recent years due mainly to a tight supply-demand balance as most of the countries in the region try first to meet their own internal supply-demand needs.

Figure 5.3   Electricity Exports, by Country, 1985–2008

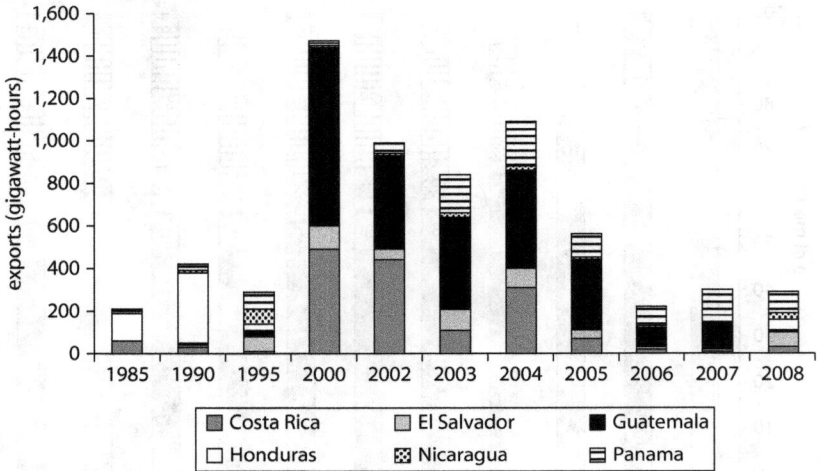

Source: ECLAC 2008.

Less than 300 gigawatt-hours of electricity is currently exported collectively between the six countries.

Currently, Central America faces a series of important challenges in the energy sector: (a) a tight balance between power supply and demand, which casts doubt on the security and reliability of the region's power sector and raises concern regarding the quality of supply; (b) significant exposure to oil price volatility and shocks due to the overdependence on oil imports, which have increased significantly for power generation purposes; (c) significant inefficiencies in the institutional and regulatory framework of several countries, which affect the financial sustainability of power utilities and their operations; and (d) relatively low levels of access in certain countries, in particular in rural areas.

The creation of an enlarged, well-functioning market would gradually help Central America to address some of the shortcomings of the electricity sector. Countries in the region are expected to benefit from increased security and reliability of electricity supply due to the enhanced interconnection. An improved investment environment that facilitates the financing of larger projects (for example, regional plants) is expected to flourish.[16] Savings from lower operating and investment costs will be realized in the medium to long term, as the regional market consolidates and eventually evolves into more advanced pool arrangements.

According to the regional organization CEAC, SIEPAC would produce savings in operational costs on the order of 4 percent and fuel savings of about 3 percent after 8–10 years based on indicative expansion planning exercises. In addition, preliminary estimates show that SIEPAC would result in 1 million tons of avoided carbon dioxide equivalent a year.

MER: An Independent Seventh Market

Signed in 1996 and ratified in 1998, the treaty creating MER is based on the principles of competition, gradualism, and reciprocity. The treaty establishes that the regional market will include a spot market, based on regional generation dispatch, and a medium- and long-term contract market and that the governments will establish adequate conditions for the future development of regional power plants. The treaty established a scheme of protocols for future adjustments and clarifications. The first protocol, agreed to in 1998, consisted of several clarifications of and corrections to the text of the treaty.

The regional electricity market established in the treaty and developed in the regulations is not an integrated regional electricity market, but a seventh market superimposed on the six national markets. As such, the MER was designed as a "loose pool" arrangement in which dispatch will be coordinated but not centralized as in more sophisticated pool designs (see note 7). The MER has its own rules and operates based on the following premises: (a) regional electricity trade can take place in a regional contract market and a spot market; (b) all MER agents with the exception of the transmission companies can purchase and sell electricity freely and have open access to the transmission system; (c) MER generation agents can install power plants in any of the member countries and sell energy at the regional level; (d) the MER is a market with its own rules, independent of the national markets, that makes energy transactions using the regional transmission grid and the national networks.

The second protocol, which was agreed to in 2007, includes the following relevant adjustments to the MER: (a) all agents of the national markets (that is, generation, transmission, distribution, and commercialization companies as well as large consumers) as ratified by the legislation of each country, are MER agents and can participate in regional electricity trading; if a country permits the existence of companies with integrated activities, they must separate their business units and employ independent accounting; (b) national interconnection systems and lines that make possible the regional energy transfers are part of the regional transmission grid, whose availability and use include charges that encompass variable transmission charges, the toll, and the complementary charge; and (c) the governments will carry out the necessary actions to harmonize the national with the regional regulations, permitting the normative coexistence of the regional and national markets.

Harmonization of national regulations is expected to happen gradually, allowing for firm energy interchanges in which the contracted energy will be prioritized to supply demand in the country where the buyer is located. Currently, the regulatory frameworks of all electricity markets foresee actions to guarantee local self-sufficiency in electricity supply (the bias toward national power sufficiency, mentioned above). One of the main agreements included in the second MER protocol refers to the gradual harmonization of regulations for the regional market. It is understood that this will allow energy trading by firms in the MER, which, in turn, will facilitate the financing of regional plants.

Obstacles to Integration of the Central American Power Sector

Political, institutional, regulatory, and physical obstacles exist to integration in the Central American power sector. This section deals with these in turn.

Political

Increasing prices of electricity in exporting countries and the availability of cheaper electricity in importing countries can spur opposition both from consumers in exporting countries and from existing generators in importing countries. If MER energy trading is included in the national economic dispatches, prices may be higher in electricity-exporting countries, while they would be lower in importing countries. This market rule is needed to guarantee nondiscrimination among the national markets (that is, agents in an exporting national market face the same spot price as for occasionally exported energy). However, this does not favor consumers in the exporting countries or generators in the importing countries. It is important for governments to hold strong positions against potential pressure from generators and consumer lobbies, while CRIE's role is to design appropriate and transparent mechanisms to address the effects of power interchanges in domestic markets, including the definition of congestion charges.[17]

Costa Rica is a key player in this integration agenda. Not only is it the richest country in the region, but it also has a strong power sector with few vulnerabilities as a result of having leveraged its renewable potential (primarily hydropower). However, at a political level Costa Rica lags the rest of the region: it is the only country that still has not ratified the second protocol (which has to be cleared at the congressional level). As it was not ratified before the end of 2009, the MER regulations will not enter into full application during 2010, and this may cause delays in the repayment of construction loans for the line.

Honduras, Nicaragua, and Panama are urged to modify the legal framework that gives priority to domestic demand in the supply of power. The failure to act may pose a definitive barrier to allowing long-term "firm power" contracts in the MER. *The main idea is quite simple: successful integration among the six small countries requires the development of scale-efficient regional plants; regional plants require long-term "firm power" contracts; and to have these kinds of contracts, Central America still has to remove several remaining obstacles.* These barriers include the priority given to domestic demand in some national regulations, the short tenure of transmission rights, the incomplete commercial framework, the weakness of the regulatory body, and the lack of a standardized power purchase agreement, among other issues.

Institutional

At present, there is still limited capacity and resources at CRIE (the regional regulator), which makes it vulnerable to national interests. Addressing the more substantial harmonization problems and preparing a strategy that takes into account national views and interests require additional analysis. However, there is a lack of technical staff and information technology resources in the CRIE, and the commissioners only meet about four times a year. Under these circumstances, the role of CRIE could become very weak and face the risk of allowing national interests to prevail over regional ones. The need to strengthen CRIE is urgent if it is to prepare an adequate foundation for the initial operations of MER.

Regulatory

Regulatory harmonization is needed to facilitate market operations and regional long-term firm power contracts between qualified agents. There is currently a lack of harmonization of national and regional regulations at the operational and commercial levels. This issue should be dealt with to implement the MER regulations (in substitution of the transitory regulations) and the appropriate interfaces so that MER regulations can work harmoniously with the corresponding regulations in each country.

To advance the harmonization agenda, CRIE will need to focus on two specific areas: (a) standardization of terms and clauses in long-term regional "firm energy" contracts and (b) institutionalization of regional competitive processes and mechanisms for the consolidation of regional coordinated contracts by multiple agents.

Asymmetry in the national markets can lead to a lack of reciprocity in the treatment of market agents, as is the case with the vertically integrated national electricity markets prevailing in two Central American countries (Costa Rica and Honduras) and the more open electricity markets already structured in the other four countries (Panama, Nicaragua, El Salvador, and Guatemala). The vertically integrated market structure would not allow regional generators (and national generators in the last four countries) to contract electricity directly, with potential distribution, commercialization, and large consumers in Honduras and Costa Rica, because every power operation in these two countries needs to pass through the state monopoly (National Electric Power Company [ENEE] and Costa Rican Electricity Institution [ICE], respectively). In addition, potential regional generators in these two countries would not have clear rules permitting them access to the national transmission grids. However, both ENEE and ICE will have the opportunity to sell to distribution and commercialization companies and large consumers in Panama, Nicaragua, El Salvador, and Guatemala. To correct this lack of reciprocity, significant time and resources (technical and financial) will be required to implement the necessary market reforms in Costa Rica and Honduras, which will have to develop clear rules for agents other than public utilities to participate in the MER.

In most countries, domestic demand is still prioritized in the case of power shortages, which creates an obstacle for firm contracts in the regional market. The regional market was designed to allow all SIEPAC members to benefit by using the surplus of one country to cover deficits in another country, a win-win situation. However, to ensure that all countries benefit equally from the regional interconnection, the priority given to national supply during power shortages will have to be eliminated.

Price controls lead to misallocation of resources and can imperil the success of a regional market. During the reform processes in the power sector, the stated objective was to achieve a situation where electricity would respond to market supply and demand signals, avoiding distortions in the wholesale price. Political considerations and influences, however, have affected regulatory decisions, for example, by setting ceilings for market prices. Avoiding the introduction of price controls in the supply of electricity to domestic markets is needed to support regional invest-ments based on true marginal costs. This issue can prove particularly problematic in interconnected spot markets during shortages: if prices in the spot market are not allowed to reflect such shortages, a country can be required to export electricity to a higher-cost neighbor in spite of hav-ing no surplus to export.

Lack of long-term transmission rights will hinder the signature of long-term contracts. Regional long-term firm energy contracts for the develop-ment of new regional power plants would have to be agreed for periods of 10 to 15 years. The EOR will forecast nodal prices periodically for only two-year horizons, while transmission planning is expected to be done for 10-year horizons. To support the regional long-term firm energy contracts associated with new regional power plants, the MER regulations will have to be adjusted to provide longer terms for transmission rights, and com-prehensive methodologies will have to be developed that allow for clear forecasts of transmission charges.

Physical

The precarious balance of supply and demand makes Central America vulnerable to an electricity crisis. In general, the system is not reliable due to insufficient generation capacity and insufficient transmission infrastructure. Operating costs are disproportionately high because individual country markets are small. With the sole exception of Costa Rica, which suffered some stress in the last few years but was able to invest in new infrastructure and return to a comfortable equilibrium, the other countries in Central America have important vulnerabilities and insufficient capacity to deal with a succesful integration agenda—at least in the short run:

- *El Salvador* adopted a comprehensive set of reforms in the 1990s, but the power sector is still extremely weak. The country is largely exposed to oil price volatility shocks because 50 percent of its capac-ity is based on fossil fuels–based generation. Moreover, the tight bal-ance between supply and demand in the recent past has compelled El Salvador to develop more diesel-based generation.
- *Guatemala*, the largest economy in Central America, made important reforms in the 1990s to modernize its power sector. However, there is a growing concern about the stability of the system, as power outages have become more frequent over the past three years. In addition, there have been problems meeting peak demand.

- *Honduras* has an immediate challenge in providing access to modern electricity services, in particular to the poorest population. National electricity coverage reached 71 percent in 2006, but only 44 percent in rural areas, where most of the poor are concentrated. However, inefficiency is very high: the state-owned ENEE had financial losses estimated at more than 2 percent of GDP in 2007, and these are continuing to rise.
- *Nicaragua* is the second poorest country in Latin America after Haiti; 46 percent of the population is living below the poverty line. Its power sector has several problems and weaknesses, such as high vulnerability to oil price shocks, large inefficiencies, unrealistic tariffs, poorly targeted subsidies, and the worst access index in the region.
- *Panama* has had problems attracting new investments into the power sector in recent years, which has produced a tight supply-demand balance that has put a lot of stress on the system and raised concerns about its reliability. In 2008–09, Panama had to contract emergency generation to meet its power needs.

In summary, of the four necessary conditions for success enumerated in this chapter, the Central American case has—under the current circumstances—the following assessment: decisive political actions still need to be taken; weak institutions need to be strengthened; the regulatory agenda is incomplete, with important obstacles still to be addressed; and the physical system is inadequate.

Reality or Mirage?

The backbone of SIEPAC transmission was completed in 2010 and should be ready to commission and initiate commercial operations by 2011. If one assumes that Costa Rica is able to obtain the congressional approval needed and that there are no technical impediments to transporting energy from one extreme of the backbone to the other, the key question becomes, will Central America experience a significant increase in the intraregional power trade? Our educated guess is no, at least in the short term.

First, there are no surpluses to export in any country. The tight balance between supply and demand that produced the dwindling trade of the last years has not changed significantly.[18] Second, ambiguities in the regulatory framework still need to be clarified, in particular, the transmission tariff. Participants and potential investors need to know how much they are going to be charged for using the SIEPAC grid. If the amount of energy to be transported through the line is small (as will probably be the case initially), then unit costs to other potential participants may be prohibitively high. Determining the tariffs for line use is fundamental, as are the potential complementary subsidies of the six countries necessary to cover revenue shortfalls from transported energy, because compensation payments will be due to line owners immediately after commissioning.

If—as we expect—the initial operation of the SIEPAC line does not translate into significant incremental power trade within the region and countries are simultaneously forced to pay fees to the owner of the line and to repay construction loans, the integration agenda may run into opposition. Given a pessimistic cost-benefit evaluation based on the short-term assessment only—benefits may be minuscule initially—this may discourage advances in the required reforms and completion of the regulatory framework that are necessary to attain the true benefits of the enhanced integrated market. If Central American authorities surrender to a negative sentiment of wastefulness and ineffectiveness because of a slow initial startup, failure in the integration process will be assured. On the contrary, Central America needs to renew its commitment to integration and to accelerate the integration process by completing the MER regulatory framework, strengthening their national markets, promoting investments in regional plants, and opening a new chapter for mutual cooperation, trust, and trade.

The major challenge faced by the regional market is to exploit the potential offered by the transmission line and the MER regulatory and institutional framework by attracting energy projects of a regional scale. Achieving this goal will be a clear test of the options for long-term success of the market. For this to happen, the regulatory framework and the regional institutions must demonstrate their credibility to investors.

As described above, several important barriers could impede the materialization of the full benefits from SIEPAC. These obstacles include weak national power markets reflected in tight supply-demand balances, regulatory and commercial barriers that hinder long-term contracting, and even political hurdles that will make reliable subregional power trade difficult to achieve (for example, the "national priority" issue). Addressing these obstacles should be an urgent priority for the Central American power authorities.

The interconnections between Mexico and Guatemala and between Colombia and Panama, if integrated with the regional transmission backbone, have the potential to provide enough power to address the precarious balance of supply and demand affecting all countries in the Central American region. A commonly agreed regional expansion strategy that takes into account potential imports from Mexico and Colombia (in the future) is urgently needed. This would also be a test of the rules of the regional market, which need to be flexible to accommodate an evolving reality and to benefit more fully from the opportunities offered by an enlarged market.

In summary, the integration process is a long and difficult road that countries need to transit with one eye on the national agenda (strengthening the domestic market in each country) and the other eye on the common integration agenda (strengthening the supranational institutions and removing the obstacles at both the regulatory and commercial levels). Doing so requires a massive and long-lasting dose of political will.

Conclusions

Power integration is much more than simply building transmission lines and interconnection facilities. Power integration is not a binary category, but rather a long process with different stages and degrees of complexity. Its success will depend on several conditions: political, institutional, regulatory, and physical. A hefty dose of political will is decisive because integrating means relinquishing some degree of sovereignty. Hence, integration is a two-sided coin, with enhanced trade on one side and more dependence and less sovereignty on the other.

Regional power integration makes a lot of sense in Central America, where the electric power market comprises six small markets. However, power integration is not a panacea, and the long path to this goal is fraught with technical and political hurdles. Energy efficiency, electricity access for the poor, optimal power pricing, efficient incentives, and the development of nontraditional renewable sources, among others, are clear examples of issues that will have to be dealt with at a national level, simultaneously with advancing in the integration agenda.

While Central America should pursue its power integration, this process is a long and difficult path. Each country needs to focus on strengthening its domestic market, while simultaneously working to strengthen the supranational institutions and remove obstacles, at both the regulatory and commercial levels. The consolidation of the regional regulatory and institutional framework and the creation of a strong regional power market will not succeed if they are based on weak, inefficient, and vulnerable national power sectors. *Achieving a strong integrated market based on weak national markets is a mirage.*

We do not foresee any significant change in the power trade after the commissioning of the SIEPAC line in 2011. First, there are no surpluses to trade. Second, there are still important issues to resolve in the regulatory and commercial framework. In the medium term, it is critical to promote the construction of regional power plants based on long-term firm power contracts. Central America needs to remove the remaining obstacles to making long-term contracts feasible. The conditions for this are not there yet.

A source of concern is, however, that modest initial impacts of the SIEPAC project may generate a negative sentiment toward the integration agenda and discourage the reforms and regulations that are necessary to attain the benefits of an enhanced integrated market. The Central American integration process could be in jeopardy if this happens. If, on the contrary, Central America accelerates the reform process and begins a new chapter of its development based on mutual cooperation, trust, and trade, SIEPAC may bring important benefits, as expected by its designers.

Notes

1. Once produced, electricity travels along the transmission grid according to Kirchhoff's law—that is, following the path of least resistance—and at the speed of light.

2. The exception is Chile, which reformed its electricity market in 1982, introducing competition in generation even before England's reform of 1990.

3. In many markets, the system operator is the same as the market administrator. However, some market regulations have preferred to separate both entities.

4. In a "radial" interconnection, the demand physically disconnects from its national system and is treated by the export country as if it were part of its own system. But there is no real interconnection of both systems at the same time.

5. In 2009, Brazil agreed to share electricity with Paraguay according to a fairer formula and allowed Paraguay to sell excess power directly to Brazilian companies instead of solely through Eletrobras.

6. These markets are known as "loose pools."

7. Sometimes power pools are divided into "tight pools," in which a centralized least-cost merit order dispatch is put in place, and "new pools," in which dispatching is not based on costs, but rather on the bid price of each generator (that is, on a competitive basis).

8. In Colombia, 80 percent of the congestion rents are destined for the Fondo de Energía Social, which finances rural electrification infrastructure, while the remaining 20 percent is used to alleviate the higher prices that Colombian consumers have to pay due to the electricity export.

9. The Peru-Ecuador interconnection was physically finished in 2004, and since then it has been used only in two instances, both in response to emergencies in Ecuador. The sharing of congestion rents has been the main obstacle to reaching commercial accords. Peru pushed for the same treatment as in the Colombian example (100 percent to the export country), while Ecuador insisted on the 50-50 scheme.

10. Wolak (2003) points out that the spread of wholesale forward contract markets throughout the United States during the early 1980s led to investments in new generation capacity.

11. The crisis between Chile and Argentina over natural gas exports is a clear example of how governments can intervene in private contracts and oblige domestic suppliers to relinquish their contracts in situations of growing scarcity. There was no clear regulation or safeguard for this kind of episode or any supranational body. This example highlights the difficulty associated with energy integration in South America because it shows that long-term firm contracts are difficult to enforce; future initiatives would need to have stricter rules of compliance and compensation.

12. This section is based on a World Bank study of the Central America regional electricity market (World Bank 2010).

13. See ECA (2009) for a complete overview of the SIEPAC project.

14. The SIEPAC line capacity is equivalent to only 3 percent of existing regional capacity and less than 5 percent of peak demand.

15. The remaining US$15 million is financed by loans from the Andean Development Corporation.

16. A generation project is considered regional when part of its generation is assigned to cover the demand of another country. A regional plant will have long-term contracts with neighboring countries. A merchant plant that operates exclusively in the spot market (without long-term contracts) eventually will be considered regional generation if the neighboring countries can rely on its supply to balance their supply-demand equation.

17. Incumbent generators in Guatemala have begun to exert opposition to the interconnection with Mexico, as cheaper imported electricity would affect their future profits.

18. However, the interconnection with Mexico could prove critical in overcoming the supply-demand imbalances in the region, because Mexico has a large idle generation capacity. Notwithstanding, the Mexico-Guatemala interconnection was possible due to a bilateral agreement, and it does not respond to a multilateral arrangement with SIEPAC or any subregional authority.

References

CIER (Comisión de Integración Energética Regional). 2010. *Informe Trimestral 1* (March). Montevideo.

ECA (Economic Consulting Associates). 2009. "Regional Power Sector Integration: SIEPAC Case Study." ECA, London.

ECLAC (Economic Commission for Latin America and the Caribbean). 2007. *Estadísticas subsector eléctrico: Statistical Yearbook 2007*. Santiago: ECLAC.

———. 2008. *Estadísticas Subsector Eléctrico: Statistical Yearbook 2008*. Santiago: ECLAC.

Hunt, Sally. 2002. *Making Competition Work in Electricity*. Hoboken, NJ: John Wiley and Sons.

Robinson, Peter. 2009. "International Power Integration: Early Findings from an ESMAP Regional Power Study." Report for the World Bank by Economic Consulting Associates, London.

USAID (U.S. Agency for International Development). 2008. "Sub-Saharan Africa's Power Pools: Development Framework." White Paper, USAID, Washington, DC.

Wolak, Frank. 2003. "Designing Competitive Electricity Markets for Latin America." Inter-American Development Bank, Washington, DC.

———. 2004. "Lessons from International Experience with Electricity Market Monitoring." Policy Research Working Paper 3692, World Bank, Washington, DC.

World Bank. 2001. "Regional Electricity Markets Interconnections—Phase I. Identification of Issues for the Development of Regional Power Markets in South America." Technical Paper, World Bank, Energy Sector Management Assistance Program, Washington, DC.

———. 2008. "Building Regional Power Pools: A Toolkit." World Bank, Washington, DC.

———. 2010. "Central America Regional Electricity Study." World Bank, Washington, DC.

CHAPTER 6

Supply Chain Analyses of Exports and Imports of Agricultural Products: Case Studies of Costa Rica, Honduras, and Nicaragua

Raquel Fernández, Santiago Flórez Gómez, Francisco Estrázulas de Souza, and Henry Vega

The signing and initial implementation of the Dominican Republic–Central America Free Trade Agreement (DR-CAFTA) represents an important step toward regional trade integration. However, for member countries to reap the potential benefits of DR-CAFTA, a complementary agenda is needed to establish a comprehensive mix of policy priorities that address key challenges of the region. Among these challenges is the weak logistics performance of Central American nations, which hinders their ability to integrate, not only with each other in the context of DR-CAFTA, but also with the rest of the global economy.

Studies on the impact of logistics costs on the final price of delivered goods reveal that (a) these costs represent a greater barrier to trade than import tariffs and (b) their impacts become increasingly relevant with the prevalence of free trade agreements such as DR-CAFTA (see Baier and Bergstrand 2001; Hummels 2001; Blyde, Moreira, and Volpe 2008). In fact, the World Bank has estimated that, on average, ad valorem tariffs for food imports declined in the Latin America and Caribbean region from 2005 to 2008 and currently range from 3 to 12 percent of product value (Schwartz, Guasch, and Wilmsmeir 2009; World Bank 2009). Transport and logistics costs, in contrast, measured in this case by the international maritime and road haulage components alone, can total about 20 percent of the free-on-board value of goods. By the time other costs, such as handling, storage, and distribution costs, are accounted for, logistics costs can add up to more than 50 percent of the final price of the good.

Quantifying these costs and understanding what factors affect logistics performance are crucial to pinpointing areas for potential policy action. This chapter is intended to address this need, particularly in the context of DR-CAFTA, by presenting the results of eight supply chain analyses pertaining to agricultural products moving within the Central American region: fresh tomato exports from Costa Rica to Nicaragua and wheat, rice, and corn imports from the United States to Nicaragua and Honduras.

The analyses performed in this study intend to shed light on the logistics bottlenecks affecting both *intraregional* and *extraregional* trade. In terms of intraregional trade, namely between Costa Rica and Nicaragua, the chapter's findings suggest that the biggest burdens are (a) high domestic transportation costs and (b) bottlenecks at the region's border crossings mostly attributed to customs delays, which are particularly relevant in the trade of perishable goods.

For extraregional trade—more precisely for grain imports from the United States—the supply chain analyses show that the most relevant logistics challenges are (a) high domestic transport costs, (b) bottlenecks at land border crossings that prevent countries from utilizing ports in neighboring countries and then bringing the product in by land, and (c) lack of harmonization of sanitary and phytosanitary standards within DR-CAFTA members.

The chapter is structured as follows. First, it explains the rationale for choosing tomato exports from Costa Rica to Nicaragua and wheat, rice, and corn imports from the United States to Nicaragua and Honduras and then presents the methodology of the standardized logistics survey (SLS) and the sources used for each of the products. Second, it presents the supply chain analyses, divided into the themes of road infrastructure, customs, sanitary and phytosanitary controls, and port use optimization and other port of entry issues. Third, this discussion is followed by specific cost breakdowns for each of the products. A final section concludes.

Case Studies of Agricultural Trade

This section explains the rationale for choosing to study tomato exports from Costa Rica into Nicaragua and wheat, rice, and corn imports from the United States into Nicaragua and Honduras.

Intraregional Trade: Fresh Tomatoes from Costa Rica to Nicaragua

While the United States is the region's major trade partner with respect to the trade of agricultural products, Central American countries themselves also represent increasingly important trade partners for the region. In 2008, agricultural exports from Central American countries totaled US$9.8 billion, out of which 35 percent were exported to the United States, 23 percent to the European Union, and 21 percent to Central American countries.[1]

Several facts are relevant to the decision to study trade between Costa Rica and Nicaragua: (a) Costa Rica is a high-performing country according to the 2010 logistics performance index (LPI); (b) out of all of Costa Rica's DR-CAFTA trade partners, the highest percentage of total exports goes to Nicaragua[2] due in great part to its geographic proximity; and (c) Nicaragua is the lowest-performing country, as ranked in the LPI. For these reasons, the supply chain analysis evaluates the logistics challenges faced by a higher-performing country exporting to a lower-performing country.

Furthermore, given that it is common for neighboring countries to trade agricultural goods throughout the year, the supply chain analysis takes tomatoes, the most important vegetable exported to Nicaragua in value terms, as the object of study. Moreover, since tomatoes are perishable goods, the exercise allows for an analysis of the critical bottlenecks faced in a supply chain requiring expedited and efficient delivery as well as transport in refrigerated containers.

International Trade: Rice, Wheat, and Corn from the United States into Nicaragua and Honduras

Rice, wheat, and corn are major agricultural commodities imported into DR-CAFTA member countries and represent important components of Central America's food basket. These commodities are imported mostly from the United States, through the port of New Orleans in Louisiana and into Puerto Corinto on the Pacific coast of Nicaragua and Puerto Cortés on the Atlantic coast of Honduras.

The 2009 World Integrated Trade Solution (WITS) trade data for Honduras and 2007 WITS data for Nicaragua show the following:

- 88 percent of the US$60 million of rice imported into Honduras and 97 percent of the US$58 million imported into Nicaragua come from the United States.
- 100 percent of the US$53 million of wheat imported into Honduras and 99.9 percent of the US$35 million come from the United States.
- 99 percent of the US$90 million of corn imported into Honduras and 98 percent of the US$29 million into Nicaragua come from the United States.

Methodology and Sources

For the supply chain analysis, we conducted a standardized logistics survey that collected cost data through primary interviews with several actors along the supply chain. These data were complemented by publicly available trade data compiled by government entities.

Standardized Logistics Survey (SLS)

The SLS was the primary tool used to collect data and was critical in ensuring the consistency and quality of data obtained and allowing us to compare the different supply chains described in this chapter. The SLS dictated the cost components to be compiled during field interviews, including farm gate prices, maritime and domestic transport costs, warehousing and storage costs, retail prices, and so forth. Other costs, such as milling costs for the grain supply chains as well as time costs for the fresh tomato supply chains, were exclusive to these particular products.

Information was collected through primary field interviews with key actors within the supply chains in Costa Rica and Nicaragua for tomato exports and the supply chains in Nicaragua and Honduras for rice, wheat, and corn imports. These interviews provided information that allowed us to identify the costs involved in the various steps of the supply chain, as well as qualitative information that allowed us to assess these countries' logistics challenges.[3] The interviews followed a conversation format and were guided by the SLS template.

Interviewees included independent producers and producer associations, exporters and importers, freight forwarders, customs agents and government agencies, retailers, and millers for the analysis of grain imports.[4] Producers provided data on farm prices and domestic shipping costs; exporters on shipping and handling, profit margins, and customs costs and procedures; importers on ocean shipping and port reception costs as well as profit margins; millers on operating costs and extraction losses; freight forwarders on transport and customs costs; customs agents on disaggregated customs costs; and retailers on final retail prices, profits, and distribution costs.

The SLS methodology allowed us to harmonize the data collected. By doing so, it enabled us to compare the supply chains of particular products. Furthermore, the methodology calls for a standard unit of measurement, in this case U.S. dollars per kilogram. However, while the SLS calls for the collection of data for similar logistics components (that is, shipping, handling, and customs costs), supply chain analyses for different products are not completely comparable due to their unique characteristics and the nature of their logistics requirements. It would be inaccurate, for example, to compare the costs involved in the movement of perishable tomatoes in refrigerated containers directly with the costs involved in the movement of grains transported in bulk via ocean shipping.

Aside from this challenge, the SLS also has limitations. Since the cost data are gathered primarily through conversational interviews, data points must be carefully understood and verified with as many reporters as possible. For example, in reviewing domestic transport costs for the tomato supply chain analysis, it was understood and confirmed that, as stated by both exporters and cargo carriers, these costs include fuel and labor costs, but do not include vehicle amortization or depreciation.

Finally, concerning the representativeness of the analyses presented in this chapter, it should be noted that the large tomato exporters and grain importers chosen for the study dominate their respective markets, so that the chains are representative of the logistics costs involved in the trade of these goods. The challenge lies in generalizing the conclusions to the rest of the Central American economies, as each country has its own market structures and areas of improvement in matters of logistics performance. Therefore, the supply chain analyses provide a snapshot of intraregional and extraregional trade for Costa Rica, Honduras, and Nicaragua, and an attempt is made to analyze how these results fit into country-level data provided by other efforts, like the Doing Business initiative from the World Bank, the *Global Competitiveness Report* from the World Economic Forum, and the logistics performance index from the World Bank.

Complementary Data and Information

In addition to data gathered during field visits in Costa Rica, Honduras, and Nicaragua, information was collected from complementary online data sources. These included trade statistics databases provided by the U.S. Department of Agriculture, the U.S. International Trade Commission, the World Integrated Trade Solutions, and national statistics institutes (in-country).

Supply Chain Analysis: Intraregional and Extraregional Trade

In the trade of fresh tomatoes from Costa Rica to Nicaragua, the small exporter receives the fresh product in 18-kilogram plastic boxes from a small producer in Cartago, located about 36 kilometers from San José, who transports it in a small, unrefrigerated truck to the exporter's distribution center located just 4 kilometers away from the farm gate. Once at the distribution center, the product is transferred to 23-kilogram cardboard boxes[5] and loaded into a 40-foot container, which then travels toward Peñas Blancas, the border town between Costa Rica and Nicaragua, located about 319 kilometers from the distribution center. The truck travels up the Pan-American Highway at a speed of 60 to 80 kilometers an hour and arrives in approximately seven hours, traveling nonstop. Once at the border, the shipment passes through Costa Rican and Nicaraguan customs and travels three to four hours from the border until it arrives at the Mercado Oriental, where the product is sold to both big wholesalers and retailers.

Overall, the large exporter's chain has a structure similar to that of the small exporter. The large exporter purchases products all year round from a large independent producer who controls market prices due to its overwhelming share of the country's tomato production. The large producer then transports the product in a 20-foot truck with a capacity of up to 700 boxes of 13 kilograms each to the large exporter's distribution center, located approximately 60 kilometers away. Once at the distribution center, the boxes are loaded into a 45-foot container that can carry up to approximately 1,200 boxes. After the container is fully loaded, the truck travels toward Peñas Blancas, crosses the border, and arrives at the distribution center in Managua, located 149 kilometers from the border. Finally, the product is consolidated with other goods at the distribution center and transported in refrigerated trucks that can carry up to 6,800 kilograms to different supermarket points in Managua.[6]

In the case of grain imports from the United States, the supply chains analyzed in this study assume that the grains originate at the farm gate in the states of North Dakota, Arkansas, and Minnesota, respectively. For all cases, the grain is loaded onto vessels at the port of New Orleans and transported into Puerto Corinto in Nicaragua and Puerto Cortés in Honduras. To reach the port of New Orleans, the grain travels by truck or rail, either directly to New Orleans or on barges. The maritime costs incurred for transportation to Puerto Cortés include freight and insurance for a three-day trip along the Atlantic Ocean, while ocean transportation to Puerto Corinto includes freight, insurance, and Panama Canal charges for a trip that takes 12 days and ends on Nicaragua's Pacific coast. Once in Honduras, the grain is transported via truck for about 40 to 100 kilometers to the mills in or around San Pedro Sula or to animal feed plants located throughout Honduras. In Nicaragua the grain is transported to mills in Managua or Granada or to animal feed plants in other areas, about 150 to 300 kilometers from Puerto Corinto.

Aside from maritime shipping costs, other costs in the analysis include customs clearance costs, which can be disaggregated into unloading expenses, sanitation costs, document processing—that is, customs broker charges—and inventory costs incurred in port or at the border. Milling costs can be disaggregated into extraction losses, unloading and loading, other fixed and variable costs, as well as the profits earned by the millers. The wholesale and retail costs are disaggregated into costs and profits.

Main Logistics Challenges

The information collected through the on-site interviews and secondary sources provides insight into four specific areas of concern in the countries studied: customs, road infrastructure, sanitary and phytosanitary controls, and optimization of port use and other port of entry issues.

Customs

According to the interviewees, specifically with respect to the trade of fresh tomatoes, time spent on the Costa Rican side of the border averages three hours for both large and small exporters, assuming that shipments have to go through customs, phytosanitary, and narcotics inspections. On the Nicaraguan side of the border, waiting time equals five hours for the same inspections.[7]

Apart from waiting times at the border, interviewees also cited the lack of technical skills of customs agents and customs personnel at the border as well as the lack of adequate physical infrastructure for carrying out inspections. With respect to the first challenge, interviewees mentioned that customs agents are often misinformed about customs procedures and the documentation required for both imports and exports, which can create delays in the processing of cargo movements. With respect to the lack of adequate physical infrastructure, tomato exporters highlighted the fact that when customs calls for a thorough inspection of shipments,[8] the cargo must be unloaded in open air areas that expose perishable products to warm temperatures and outside conditions.

Additionally, in the border crossing between Nicaragua and Costa Rica, inconsistencies in the working hours of customs agents and customs offices seem to be relevant in facilitating or deterring the trade of perishable products. Interviewees reported that customs agents often shut down operations after 5 p.m. and on weekends. Therefore, the paperwork and procedures related to shipments that arrive at the border on Saturday or Sunday get postponed to Monday, causing significant delays particularly on that day. Furthermore, a large importer on the Nicaraguan side said that if there are delays on the Costa Rican side of the border for shipments arriving in the afternoon, trucks must wait along the 1-kilometer road between Costa Rican customs and Nicaraguan customs because Nicaraguan customs has limited working hours. This implies extra fuel costs, as the containers must be kept refrigerated, extra hiring costs for the driver, delays in distributing the product to the retail point, underutilization of distribution trucks, associated costs for extra fleets, reduced shelf time for the product, and the exporter's loss of reputation, among others. Moreover, interviewees also mentioned that the electronic system, TICA, which was implemented at Peñas Blancas starting in 2006, shuts down constantly, causing significant delays at both the Costa Rican and Nicaraguan sides of the border. This is in great part due to deficiencies in telecommunications services.[9]

Another common challenge with respect to customs in Central American countries is corruption. Direct exporters, freight forwarders, and customs agents all said that bribes are a necessary evil to expedite the customs clearance of perishable products and that the cost of bribes is included in the cost of the services provided. Furthermore, bribes to transit police are particularly common during highly congested periods, when shippers pay extra to bypass the long lines of trucks that form at the border.

Road Infrastructure

Although not cited as frequently as bottlenecks at customs, several inter-viewees mentioned deficient road infrastructure at the country level. Most of these interviewees mentioned that, although the Pan-American Highway is in relatively good condition and trucks can travel at accept-able speeds of up to 80 kilometers an hour, secondary roads, especially those connecting farms to cities, are often unpaved.

These findings are consistent with empirical studies conducted at the country level. The World Bank has estimated that about 42 percent of Costa Rican firms, for example, have specifically identified road quality as a major or severe obstacle to growth (World Bank 2007). Additionally, the poor and worsening quality of the country's road net-work has been shown to cause direct losses from delays in shipments and breakage equal to 8 to 12 percent of the sales value of exported goods (World Bank 2006). In Nicaragua, 75 percent of the total road network was considered to be in poor condition in 2006, and nearly 50 percent of the network becomes unusable during the rainy season (see chapter 7 of this volume).

Sanitary and Phytosanitary Regulations

The findings of the research performed for this study suggest that sani-tary and phytosanitary regulations can restrict the free flow of trade of perishable as well as nonperishable agricultural goods. Perishable prod-ucts must undergo phytosanitary inspections at both the Costa Rican and the Nicaraguan sides of the border. As interviewees explained, on the Costa Rican side, the Ministry of Agriculture and Livestock obtains a sam-ple for each of the products being shipped and clears the cargo. On the Nicaraguan side, phytosanitary inspections are more thorough, as the products are being imported into the country. The Nicaraguan Ministry of Agriculture and Forestry (MAGFOR) obtains a laboratory sample for each of the imported products and sends it to the nearby town of Rivas, where the sample is analyzed.[10] For tomatoes specifically, the shipper does not have to wait for the laboratory results and can continue on its way to Managua. Should laboratory results confirm the existence of harmful agents in the product, MAGFOR sends personnel to track down the shipment and prevent importers from selling the product in the local market.

With respect to import procedures for nonperishable products such as grains, importers interviewed in Honduras and Nicaragua expressed dis-satisfaction with the way in which phytosanitary controls are managed in the region. They complained that even though the product has been sanitized and certified in the United States, OIRSA (Regional International Organization for Farming and Livestock Sanitation), an intergovernmental organization in charge of integrating sanitary regulations in the region, often does not accept U.S. certifications and forces importers to sanitize their products again. The sanitation process (fumigation) can take place on board the vessel, at the port, or at the mills and represents substantial additional costs, delays, and operational uncertainties. These additional costs include, for example, the purchase of the fumigant (US$11.25 per metric ton), delays in the unloading process and in the time that the vessel must remain in port,[11] and unpredictability in the timing of shipments, which may result in higher storage costs for the mills.[12]

Port Use Optimization and Other Port of Entry Issues

To understand bottlenecks at the port level, we examine the supply chain for wheat, rice, and corn being imported into Puerto Corinto on the Atlantic coast of Nicaragua and into Puerto Cortés on the Pacific coast of Honduras. Puerto Corinto, located 160 kilometers from Managua, handles all grain imports into Nicaragua. In 2008, it handled 1,919 metric tons of cargo, a significantly lower tonnage than that handled by other ports on the Pacific coast such as Balboa in Panama and Acajutla in El Salvador. Nevertheless, Puerto Cortés is the most important port in Honduras and the fourth busiest port in Central America in terms of volume handled.

Consistently throughout the interview process, Honduran grain importers indicated that the trip from New Orleans to Puerto Cortés takes an average of three days. The trip to Puerto Corinto in Nicaragua, which passes through the Panama Canal, can take up to 12 days.

Since grains are not highly perishable goods, extra days in transit do not add up to higher costs. Nevertheless, as the level of trade—for grains and other products alike—continues to rise with the implementation of DR-CAFTA, the potential exists for efficiency gains due to economies of scale and shorter transit times.

A possible solution to facilitate trade into Nicaragua would be to bring grains to Puerto Corinto and then transport them by land into Nicaragua through the border post known as El Guasaule. According to interviewees, some importers have used this route, but not very often. The experience of current importers of milled rice, who transport the product in bulk vessels through this path, sheds light on the numerous difficulties of the operation. The following are the most common complaints raised by milled rice importers:

- *Too much time needed for customs procedures.* Maritime companies take too long in delivering the bill of lading,[13] the document needed to initiate customs procedures in Nicaragua. Therefore, the product reaches El Guasaule within a period of three days, but importers cannot initiate the import authorization procedures with MAGFOR and the customs agency (Dirección General de Aduanas) because they do not have the bill of lading. Upon receipt of the bill of lading, clearance procedures take up to five working days.
- *Lack of influence by Nicaraguan customs brokers at Puerto Cortés.* Brokers are located in Managua, and completing the documentation and procedures required for imports can take between five and seven days. The current low volume of products imported through Cortés on their way to Nicaragua does not provide sufficiently strong incentives for brokers to open subsidiary offices in Puerto Cortés.
- *Lengthy phytosanitary controls at El Guasaule.* Upon arriving at El Guasaule, the grain samples have to be shipped to Managua to be inspected at the Universidad Centro-Americana and then sent back to El Guasaule, which results in a two-day delay of shipments at the border. The costs of having the product sit at El Guasaule average US$110 per day per truck.
- *Different documentation required at El Guasaule and Puerto Corinto.* More documents are needed to clear customs in El Guasaule than in Puerto Corinto.

The challenges faced by importers that move milled rice into Nicaragua via Honduras provide valuable insight into why countries are unable to take advantage of neighboring ports, such as Puerto Cortés, and create more efficient supply chains. Given that Nicaragua does not have a port with the capacity to handle bulk vessels on the Atlantic side, bulk shipments are forced to travel southbound and through the Panama Canal, incurring additional charges of US$3.59 per metric ton of product.[14] To reach Managua, the country's major consumption center located closer to the Pacific side, shipments do not travel through Nicaragua itself or through any other Central American country. In theory, if barriers to regional integration were eliminated, importers could use not only Puerto Cortés in Honduras, but also Puerto Limón in Costa Rica and then transport their shipments overland to Nicaragua.

If the challenges described in this chapter are illustrative of trade patterns not only between Honduras and Nicaragua, but also more broadly between Central American nations, countries are unable to take advantage of alternative routes partly because of logistics bottlenecks, including the lack of coordination of import processes and procedures between countries as well as inefficiencies and delays at border points.

Quantitative Results for the Fresh Tomatoes Supply Chain

The weight of logistics costs within a firm's cost structure has been shown to be sensitive to the size of the firm. In Latin America, total logistics costs are almost three times as high for the smallest firms in the sample, with a volume of less than US$5 million in sales, as for the largest firms, with more than US$500 million in yearly sales.

In an effort to explore the true drivers of the higher costs faced by smaller exporting firms, this section presents the quantitative results of two supply chain analyses of tomato exports from Costa Rica to Nicaragua, one for a small exporter and one for a large exporter.[15]

Price Breakdown

The cost breakdown for the price of tomatoes as they move from the farm gate until they arrive at the final retail point in Managua reveals differences between small and large exporters. As shown in figure 6.1, for the small exporter, the largest component of trade and logistics costs is transport (23 percent), followed by customs (11 percent) and duties (6 percent). Outside of trade and logistics costs, the farm gate price represents the largest component of costs as a percentage of the final price of tomatoes, sold at US$1.86 per kilo at the final retail point (see table 6.1).

The cost breakdown for the large exporter displays similar results, with customs (10 percent) and transport (6 percent) the two most important components of trade and logistics costs. The component "other" costs, which mostly refers to profits and margins and to administrative and other retail costs, occupies third place because (a) large supermarket chains have higher operational costs than an independent retailer with a stand at an open-air market, as in the small exporter's chain, and because (b) due to lower trade and logistics costs, mainly in transport, large supermarket chains make higher profits. Additionally, with respect to the farm gate link of the chain, the producer receives 24 percent of the final price of the good, 7 percent less than the small exporter receives (see figure 6.2 and table 6.2).

Figure 6.1 Breakdown of Costs for a Small Exporter of Tomatoes

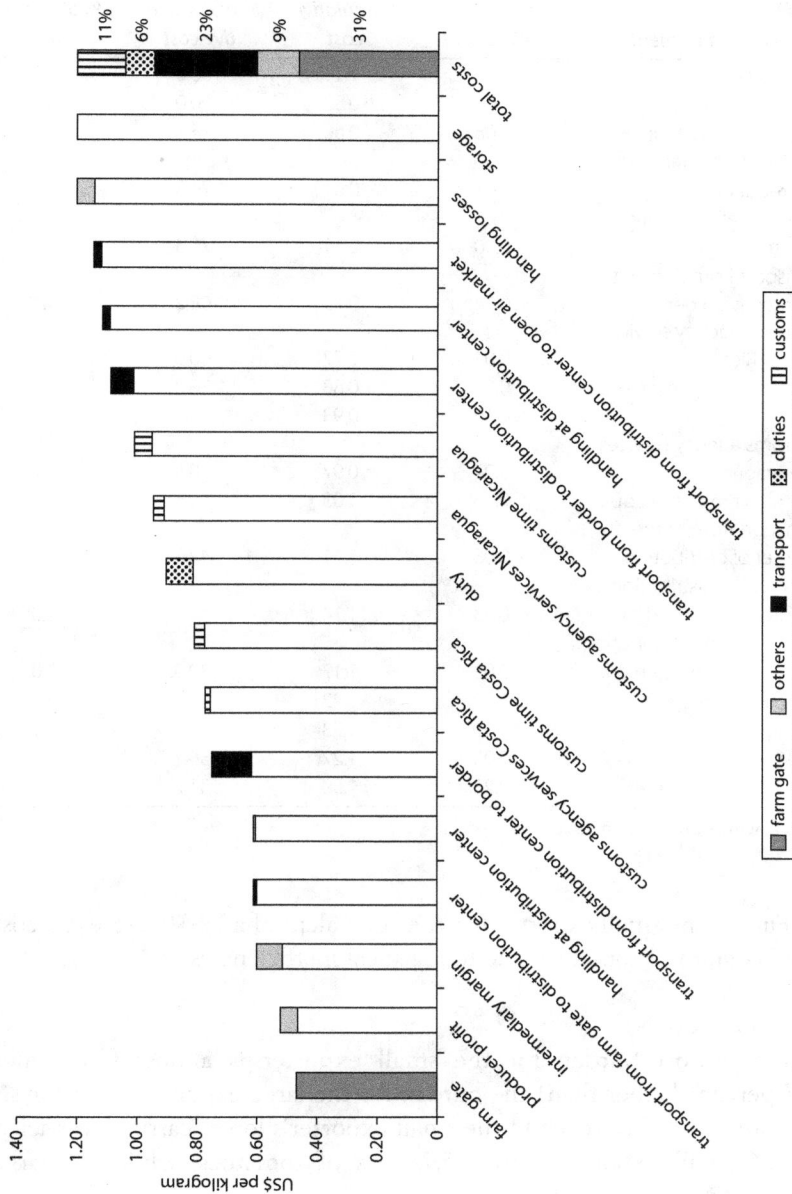

Source: Authors' calculations.
Note: The lines on each bar refer to the addition to costs from each category listed on the horizontal axis.

163

Table 6.1   Breakdown of Costs for a Small Exporter of Tomatoes

Supply chain element	Additional cost (US$ per kilogram)	Cumulative cost	Tomatoes as a % of cumula-tive cost	% of each element
Farm gate	0.47	n.a.	100.0	31.2
Producer profit	0.05	0.52	90.0	3.5
Intermediary margin	0.08	0.60	78.1	5.3
Transport from farm gate to distribution center	0.01	0.61	76.8	0.7
Handling at distribution center	0.00	0.61	76.3	0.3
Transport from distribution center to border	0.14	0.75	62.2	9.3
Customs agency services, Costa Rica	0.02	0.77	60.6	1.3
Customs time, Costa Rica	0.06	0.83	56.2	4.0
Duty	0.10	0.93	50.4	6.5
Customs agency services, Nicaragua	0.04	0.97	48.3	2.7
Customs time, Nicaragua	0.06	1.03	45.3	4.3
Transport from border to center of distribution	0.08	1.11	42.1	5.2
Handling at distribution center	0.03	1.14	41.0	2.0
Transport from distribution center to open-air market	0.03	1.17	39.9	2.0
Handling losses	0.05	1.23	38.2	3.6
Storage	0.00	1.23	38.1	0.1
Retail cost	0.05	1.27	36.7	3.2
Retail profit	0.23	1.50	31.2	15.0

Source: Authors' calculations based on interviews.
Note: n.a. = Not applicable.

Finally, the small exporter has the equivalent of a US$0.275 extra cost per kilogram of tomatoes due to logistical inefficiencies.

Transport Costs

The transport burden for the small exporter is almost four times (17 percent higher than) the burden for the large exporter. The analysis attributes this difference to the small exporter's lower carrying capacity, as the small exporter carries 5.7 tons of tomatoes, while the large exporter carries 15.6 tons.

Transport costs consist of two components: shipping and handling. Shipping costs refer to the service (fuel and salary costs) of moving a

Figure 6.2 Breakdown of Costs for a Large Exporter of Tomatoes

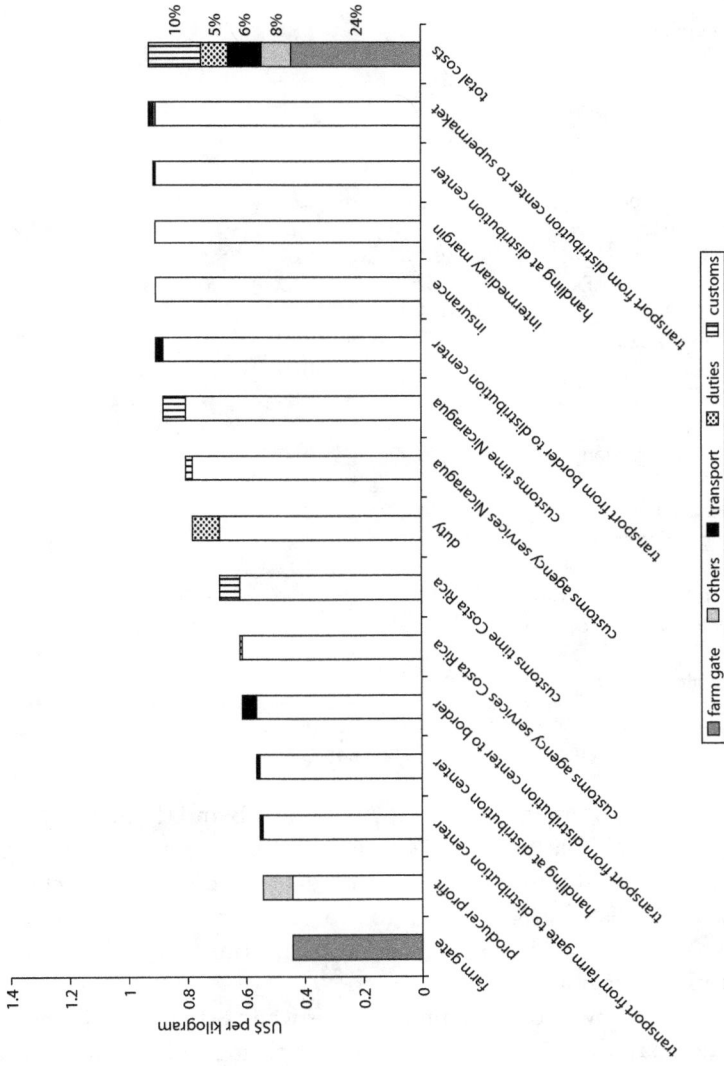

Source: Authors' calculations.

Note: The lines on each bar refer to the addition to costs from each category listed on the horizontal axis.

Table 6.2   Breakdown of Costs for a Large Exporter of Tomatoes

Supply chain element	Additional cost (US$ per kilogram)	Cumulative cost	Tomatoes as a % of cumulative cost	% of each element
Farm gate	0.44		100.0	24.3
Producer profit	0.10	0.54	4.7	5.5
Transport from farm gate to distribution center	0.01	0.55	4.6	0.6
Handling at distribution center	0.01	0.56	4.6	0.6
Transport from distribution center to border	0.05	0.61	4.2	2.6
Customs agency services, Costa Rica	0.01	0.62	4.1	0.6
Customs time, Costa Rica	0.07	0.69	3.7	3.7
Duty	0.09	0.78	3.3	5.0
Customs agency services, Nicaragua	0.02	0.80	3.2	1.2
Customs time, Nicaragua	0.08	0.88	2.9	4.2
Transport from border to center of distribution	0.03	0.90	2.8	1.4
Insurance	0.00	0.90	2.8	0.0
Intermediary margin	0.00	0.90	2.8	0.0
Handling at distribution center	0.01	0.91	2.8	0.4
Transport from distribution center to supermarket	0.02	0.92	2.8	0.8
Retail cost	0.60	1.52	1.7	33.0
Retail profit	0.31	1.83	1.4	17.1

Source: Authors' calculations based on interviews.

refrigerated container from point A to point B and do not include the truck's depreciation or amortization. Furthermore, transport costs are disaggregated into four stages: farm gate to distribution center in Costa Rica, distribution center to Costa Rican customs, Nicaraguan customs to distribution center, and distribution center to final sales point in Nicaragua.

The breakdown of shipping costs suggests that small and large exporters pay the same costs to transport their product from the farm gate to the distribution center, with both paying 1 percent of the final price of the good (see figure 6.3). The same holds for the costs of transporting the product from the distribution center in Nicaragua to the final retail point: costs for the small exporter represent 2 percent of the final

Figure 6.3   Breakdown of Transport Costs for Small and Large Exporters

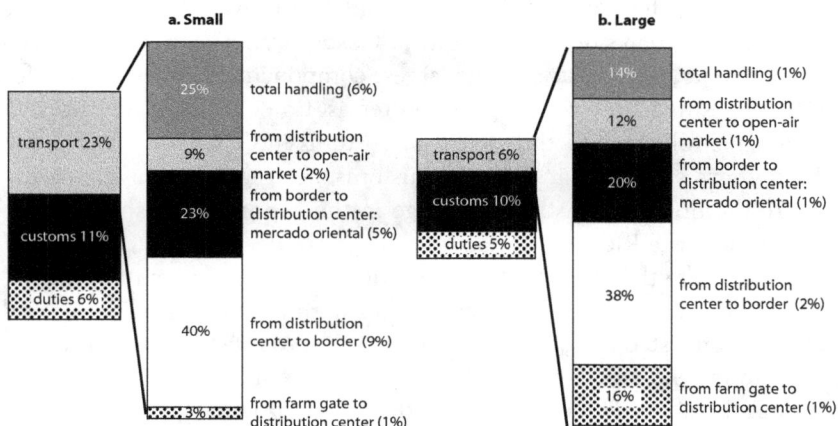

Source: Authors' calculations based on interviews.
Note: Data in parentheses are the share of the component in final price. Other percentages are the share of the component in total transport costs (right-hand bar) or the share of the component in total trade and logistics costs (left-hand bar).

price of the good, while costs for the large exporter equal only 1 percent. However, when looking at transport from the distribution center in Costa Rica to the distribution center in Managua, costs for the small exporter are higher. In fact, the transport costs from the distribution center in Costa Rica to the distribution center in Nicaragua are 14 percent of the final price of the good for the small exporter and only 3 percent for the large. These differences cannot be attributed to distance, as the difference is only 4 kilometers; rather, they are due to the small exporter's lower carrying capacity.

Additionally, handling costs are almost twice as high for the small exporter as for the large exporter. As a percentage of the final price of 1 kilogram of tomatoes, handling costs are six times as high for the small exporter. Moreover, just the handling costs for the small exporter are equal to the entire transport costs for the large exporter as a share of the final price of the tomatoes, both at 6 percent.

Customs Costs

Customs costs are the second most important trade and logistics cost for the small exporter (11 percent of the final price of a kilogram of tomatoes), but the most important cost for the large exporter, at 10 percent.

Customs costs are disaggregated into four components: customs agency service fees on the Costa Rican side, customs agency service fees on the Nicaraguan side, waiting time at Costa Rican customs, and waiting time at Nicaraguan customs. The largest component of customs costs for both the small and the large exporter is time spent in customs in Nicaragua, followed by time spent in customs in Costa Rica. Therefore, the findings suggest that delays at customs, not regulated payments per se, are the primary logistical challenge in the export of perishable products from Costa Rica to Nicaragua.

To illustrate the impact of delays on the cost of a kilogram of tomatoes, we calculate the cost difference between a normally congested period and a highly congested period assuming that the cargo must wait an entire day at customs (9.5 hours on the Costa Rican side and 14.5 hours on the Nicaraguan side). The results reveal that congestion delays at the border translate into an additional cost of US$0.22 per kilogram for the large exporter and US$0.20 per kilogram for the small exporter.

In summary, the findings show that a higher share of a small exporter's cost structure in the export of tomatoes from Costa Rica to Nicaragua can be attributed to logistics costs when compared to the cost structure for a large exporter. Trade and logistics costs, defined as transport (shipping and handling), customs, and duties for the small producer are approximately two times those of the large exporter (23 and 44 percent, respectively).

Quantitative Results: Wheat, Rice, and Corn Supply Chains

Understanding the logistics challenges involved in the importation of wheat, rice, and corn from the United States to Honduras and Nicaragua is important given these countries' overwhelming dependence on the U.S. market for these basic grains. For example, in value terms in 2009, 99 percent of yellow corn imports to Honduras originated in the United States, as did 89 percent of yellow corn imports to Nicaragua.

This section estimates the costs incurred in the process of transporting wheat from farms in Minnesota, paddy rice from Arkansas,[16] and yellow corn from Minnesota to wholesale markets in San Pedro Sula in Honduras and Managua in Nicaragua during December 2009 and January 2010.

The initial transport costs associated with these three supply chains are related to the truck and rail freight charges incurred from the originating farm to the port of New Orleans. Once the grains arrive at the port of New Orleans, costs include freight insurance and ocean shipping charges to transport the products to the seaport of Puerto Cortés on the Atlantic coast in the case of Honduras and the port of Puerto Corinto on the Pacific coast in the case of Nicaragua. Once at the port of destination, several steps account for additional costs.

For example, for wheat, shipping companies generally deliver the wheat free alongside ship (FAS), implying that costs are incurred in receiving the shipments and clearing customs. Next the wheat is loaded onto trucks and transported by road to the mill, where the grain is first stocked in silos and then milled. Once milled, it is packed in bags of 45 kilograms each and transported to bakeries in each country's capital city.

Similarly for rice, shipments are delivered in FAS terms and, once at the destination port, are loaded onto trucks and transported by road to rice mills, where the rice is turned into milled rice at an average conversion level of about 65 percent.[17] The milled rice is then packed into 100-pound bags and sold to local popular market retailers or supermarkets. In both Honduras and Nicaragua, large importers generally control most of the links of the chain taking place in-country and distribute the products directly to retailers and wholesalers, while smaller importers generally have to hire distributors or sell at the mill.

Finally, corn shipments are also delivered in FAS terms and, having undergone customs procedures, are loaded onto trucks and transported by road to the feed manufacturing plant where the grain is first stocked in silos and then crushed and milled. Once the corn has been crushed or milled, it is mixed with other ingredients in bags of 45.4 kilograms each, which are then transported to animal-raising plants.

Price Breakdown

Bearing in mind that all of the grain supply chains end at wholesale and thus are comparable, this section provides a cross-country and product analysis. In doing so, it pays close attention to the transport and logistics costs, shedding light on the logistics challenges facing Honduras and Nicaragua in the import of grains. Tables 6.3 and 6.4 show the breakdown of costs associated with wheat imports into Nicaragua and Honduras following the process described above.[18]

Figure 6.4 displays the aggregated cost components for each of the supply chains by product and country. Aside from the farm gate price,[19] the largest components for the wheat, rice, and corn chains are operating costs (see table 6.5 for a definition of costs) and transportation costs. The share of transportation costs in the final price of the good is the least significant for rice and the most significant for corn. However, total logistics

Table 6.3   Supply Chain Analysis and Cost Contributions to the Average Price of Wheat Flour Sold in San Pedro Sula, Honduras

Supply chain elements	Additional cost (US$ per kilogram)	Cumulative cost	Wheat as a % of cumulative cost	% of each element
Farm price in North Dakota	0.12	n.a.	100.00	13.71
Truck transport to rail terminal	0.01	0.13	91.91	1.21
Rail transport to port of New Orleans	0.06	0.19	61.05	7.54
Insurance, ocean freight, broker's profit	0.04	0.23	51.02	4.42
Reception at port and customs clearance and fumigation	0.06	0.29	40.51	6.97
Land transportation to mill	0.05	0.34	34.58	5.81
Silage and warehousing costs at mill	0.06	0.40	29.28	7.17
Losses during extraction	0.08	0.49	24.27	9.67
Milling additives	0.05	0.54	22.01	5.81
Sacking, packing, delivery to transportation vehicles	0.02	0.56	21.22	2.32
Other fixed variable costs	0.11	0.67	17.68	12.93
Mill's profit	0.05	0.72	16.45	5.81
Loading in trucks	0.00	0.72	16.40	0.23
Transportation to wholesalers	0.04	0.76	15.54	4.65
Wholesaler costs	0.08	0.84	14.13	8.83
Wholesaler profit	0.03	0.86	13.71	2.91

Sources: Authors' calculations, data from U.S. Department of Agriculture, interviews with millers, U.S. International Trade Commission statistics, Honduras's agricultural statistics, a prices survey.
Note: Wheat costs include local elevator costs. New Orleans port costs are estimates. n.a. = Not applicable.

costs (transportation plus other logistics costs) represent shares of the final price of the good at wholesale similar to those for wheat and rice, but almost four times larger than those for corn.

The similarity in the cost structure of the corn supply chain for Honduras and for Nicaragua is noteworthy. Fieldwork conducted for this study indicates that, in both countries, large poultry and pork producers control the whole supply chain, and competition among them is high, as their production systems are similar. This is reflected in relatively competitive markets for yellow corn, with similar cost structures in the two countries.[20] At first glance, it seems that the more competitive

Table 6.4   Supply Chain Analysis and Cost Contributions to the Average Price of Wheat Flour Sold in Managua

Supply chain elements	Additional cost (US$ per kilogram)	Cumulative cost	Wheat as a % of cumulative cost	% of each element
Farm price in North Dakota	0.17	n.a.	100.00	17.92
Truck transport to rail terminal	0.01	0.18	94.18	1.11
Rail transport to port of New Orleans	0.06	0.24	69.06	6.92
Insurance, ocean freight, broker's profit	0.04	0.29	58.54	4.66
Reception at port and customs clearance and fumigation	0.06	0.34	48.77	6.13
Land transportation to mill	0.06	0.40	41.79	6.13
Silage and warehousing costs at mill	0.04	0.45	37.66	4.70
Losses during extraction	0.10	0.54	30.84	10.53
Milling additives and costs	0.07	0.62	27.14	7.92
Sacking, packing, delivery to transportation vehicles	0.01	0.63	26.76	0.94
Other fixed and variable costs	0.13	0.75	22.30	13.40
Mill's profit	0.04	0.79	21.31	3.73
Loading in trucks	0.00	0. 79	21.28	0.11
Transport to wholesalers	0.05	0.84	20.11	4.91
Wholesaler costs	0.08	0.92	18.28	8.91
Wholesaler profit	0.02	0.94	17.92	1.96

Sources: Authors' calculations, data from U.S. Department of Agriculture, U.S. International Trade Commission statistics, interviews with millers, Nicaragua's agricultural statistics, prices survey.
Note: Wheat costs include local elevator costs. New Orleans port costs are estimates. n.a. = Not applicable.

the market is, the higher is the impact of transportation costs on the final price of the good.

Concerning profit margins, the analysis concludes that profit margins are greater along the Honduran supply chain for both wheat and rice. For wheat in particular, the mill's profit, for example, is estimated at US$50 per metric ton in Honduras and US$35 per metric ton in Nicaragua. Due to greater efficiency along the supply chain, Honduran millers seem to be enjoying larger profits.

While figure 6.4 displays the aggregation of all costs involved in each of the supply chains, figure 6.5 takes a closer look at the costs incurred

Figure 6.4   Cost Components as a Percentage of the Final Price of the Good, by Product and Country

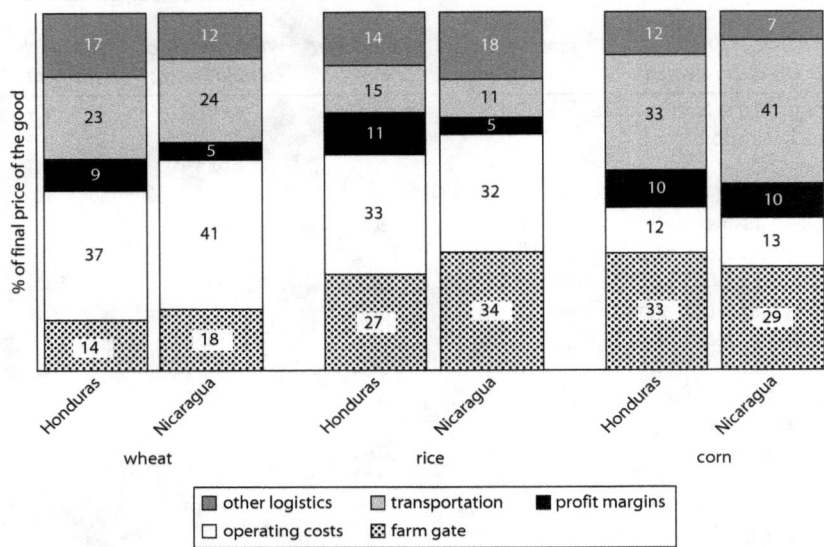

Source: Authors' calculations.

domestically once the products arrive in Central America (from reception at port and customs clearance up to the wholesaler). This approach indicates that, overall, controlling for distances, domestic costs are higher in Nicaragua than in Honduras, with the exception of the rice chain. These costs represent 6 percent more as a percentage of the final price of the good for wheat imports into Nicaragua than for wheat imports into Honduras. Likewise, for corn imports, domestic costs are 4 percent higher in Nicaragua. In contrast, when looking at rice imports, domestic costs are 8 percent higher in Honduras, making this the largest difference among the three products. Based on qualitative data obtained during the interview process, it appears that the market for rice imports is more vertically integrated in Nicaragua than in Honduras, allowing Nicaraguan importers to control more links along the supply chain. Such vertical integration, in which the same company controls the transport to mill, the milling process, and the packaging and distribution to wholesalers, avoids the double markup that takes place when distinct companies with sufficient market power at each step of the chain earn margins. These margins thus translate into a more costly supply chain in Honduras.

Table 6.5   Breakdown of Cost Components

Cost aggregates	Cost components
Transportation	U.S. transport costs (truck transport to rail terminal or barge, rail transport or barge to Port of New Orleans)
	Ocean shipping costs (ocean freight, insurance, broker's profit)
	Domestic transport costs (land transport to mill or feed manufacturer, land transport to wholesalers)
Other logistics	Reception at port and customs clearance and fumigation
	Silage and warehousing costs at mill
	Sacking, packing, delivery to transportation vehicles
	Loading in trucks
Total logistics	Transportation and other logistics
Operating costs	Losses during extraction
	Other milling losses and costs (for example, milling additives)
	Wholesaler costs
	Other fixed and variable costs (for example, administrative, marketing, and financial costs of the miller or manufacturing plant, price hedging against higher international price)
Profit margins	Mill's profit
	Wholesaler profit
	Retailer profit
Farm gate	Average farm price (North Dakota for wheat, Arkansas for rice, and Minnesota for corn)

Source: Authors' compilation.

Figure 6.5   Total In-Country Costs as a Percentage of the Final Price of the Good, by Product and Country

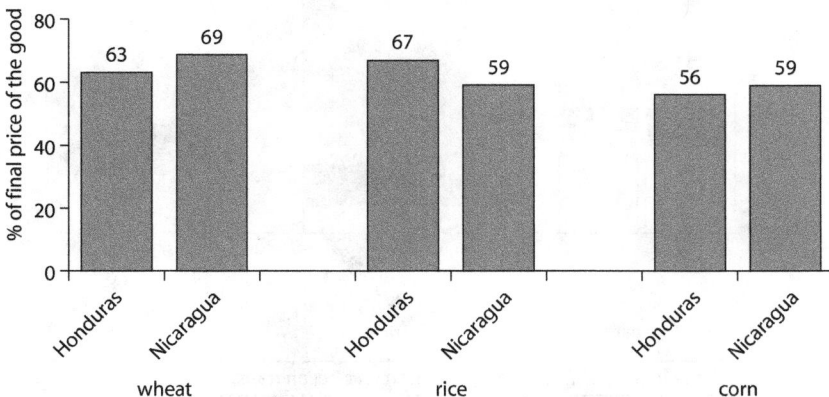

Source: Authors' calculations.

Transport and Logistics Costs

Figure 6.6 illustrates the share of logistics costs in each of the six grain chains. Results from the SLS suggest that logistics costs range from 36 to 40 percent of the final price of the good for wheat imports into Nicaragua and Honduras, are similar at about 29 percent for rice imports into both countries, and range from 45 to 48 percent for corn imports. For wheat and corn, these costs are higher than the producer's share; they are almost two to three times higher for wheat imports. In contrast, for the rice chain, the share of logistics costs is similar to the producer's share.

Within transport costs, the data show that, although the three grains are imported into Nicaragua through the Panama Canal, a journey that is four times as long as that for imports into Honduras, ocean transport costs are not significantly different between countries and products. For example, for corn, the share of ocean transport costs for both Nicaragua

Figure 6.6   Logistics Costs (Transport and Other Logistics Costs) as a Percentage of the Final Price of the Good, by Product and Country

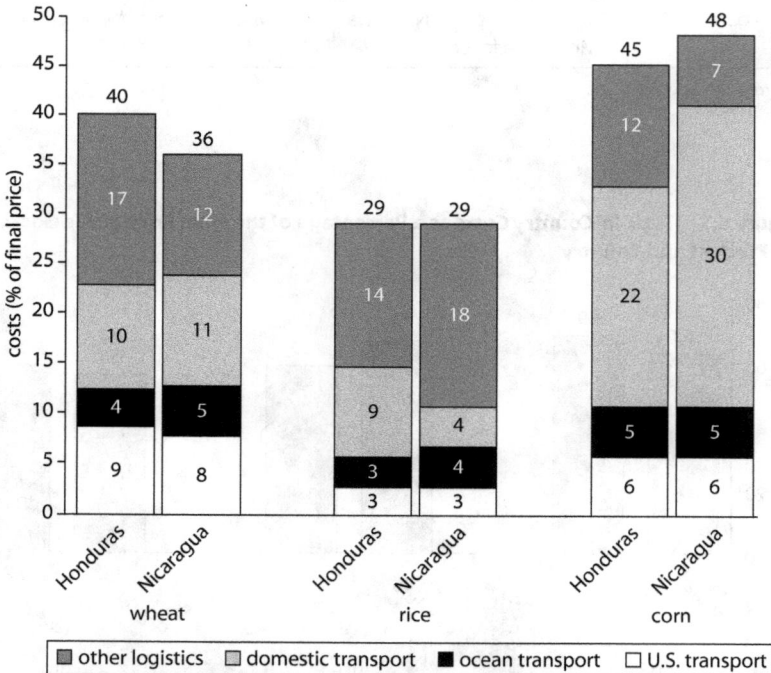

Source: Authors' calculations.

and Honduras is 5 percent of the final price of the good at wholesale. For rice, the share of ocean transport, at 4 percent, is only 1 percent higher for Nicaragua than for Honduras. As a percentage of total transportation costs, however, ocean transport costs for Nicaraguan rice importers are 12 percent higher than those for Honduran importers. For wheat and corn, ocean transport costs occupy similar shares within total transportation costs.

With regard to the other components of transportation—U.S. transport costs and domestic transport costs in-country—there is no significant difference between Honduras and Nicaragua for any of the products. However, domestic transport costs as a percentage of the final price of the goods at wholesale are 5 percent higher (twice as high) in Honduras for rice imports, but 8 percent higher in Nicaragua for corn imports. For wheat, the share of domestic transport costs is similar for both countries.

What is more important, however, is that, within transport costs, domestic costs occupy the largest share as a percentage of the final price of the goods. For the corn chain, specifically, domestic transport costs in Nicaragua are higher than the U.S. transport, ocean transport, and other logistics costs combined (30 and 18 percent, respectively). In Honduras, in contrast, domestic transport costs are similar to the other transport and logistics costs combined (22 and 23 percent, respectively).

As shown in figure 6.6, the corn supply chains are the only ones for which domestic transport costs are the highest both within transport costs and within total logistics costs. For the wheat and rice chains, although domestic costs occupy the largest share of transport costs, they are second to the "other logistics" component, consisting of reception at port and customs clearance and fumigation; silage and warehousing costs at mill; sacking, packing, and delivery to transportation vehicles or drayage; and loading in trucks at the mill or feed manufacturer.

Other Logistics Costs

A breakdown of the "other logistics" component for all three chains shows that significant costs are related to the reception of grains at the port of entry, including those related to the carrying out of phytosanitary and sanitary inspections (see figure 6.7). In fact, the port, customs clearance, and fumigation costs represent the most important subcomponent, next to silage and warehousing costs at the mill, for wheat imports into both Honduras and Nicaragua. Likewise, for corn imports into Honduras and Nicaragua, the costs of reception at port and customs clearance and fumigation occupy the largest percentage of the final price of corn at

Figure 6.7   Other Logistics Costs as a Percentage of the Final Price of the Good, by Product and Country

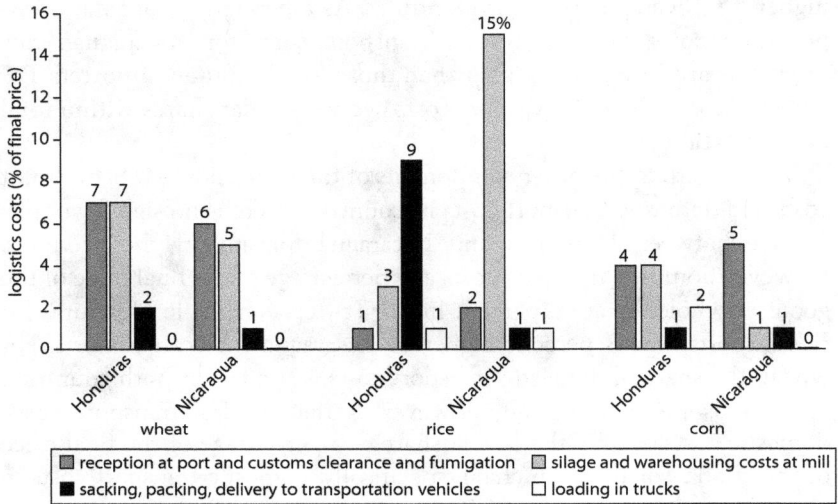

Source: Authors' calculations.

wholesale. The rice chains are interesting in that, for Honduras, reception at port and customs clearance and fumigation do not seem to be as important as the sacking, packing, and delivery of the product to transportation vehicles; for Nicaragua, silage and warehousing costs at mill are the most important component within "other logistics." This finding calls for a more in-depth analysis of logistics at the mill for both countries.

Conclusions

Logistics costs represent an important portion of the final price of delivered foods in Central America and are significant both for highly perishable goods, such as tomatoes, as well as for dry goods such as wheat, rice, and corn. These costs can range from 17 percent in the case of a small exporter of tomatoes in intraregional trade to 48 percent in the case of an importer of yellow corn from the United States to Nicaragua. Furthermore, logistics costs disproportionately affect smaller firms. In the case of fresh tomato exports from Costa Rica to Nicaragua, the weight of logistics costs for a small exporter is twice as high as for a large exporter.

Specifically, the study demonstrates that distance is not a central driver of transport costs, either for ocean transport or for domestic road transport. Even though grain imports into Nicaragua must travel longer distances in crossing the Panama Canal to Puerto Corinto in the Pacific than grain imports traveling into Honduras through Puerto Cortés, ocean transport costs as a share of the final price of the good are similar for all grain supply chains. For example, ocean transport costs represent 4 percent of the final price of the rice sold at wholesale in Managua, while they represent 3 percent of the final price of the rice sold in San Pedro Sula. Similarly, road transport costs, in the case of tomato exports, equal 17 percent of the final price of a kilogram of tomatoes for a small exporter, 3.4 times as much as for a large exporter, despite the fact that the small exporter travels 71 kilometers less, or 0.86 times what the large exporter travels.

Results from this study indicate that some of the drivers behind high logistics costs both for intraregional and for extraregional trade in DR-CAFTA countries can be addressed within four main policy areas: customs integration and reform, road transport development (increasing coverage and improving quality of the road network), harmonization of sanitary and phytosanitary regulations, and port use optimization. Bottlenecks in these areas represent particular challenges for Central America, and addressing them through DR-CAFTA's complementary agenda is crucial if the free trade agreement is to generate the most benefits for the region's economies.

Notes

1. Authors' calculations based on World Integrated Trade Solution (WITS).

2. Authors' calculations based on WITS. Excludes the United States.

3. Given the confidential nature of certain requested data, some of the figures were estimated using the results of previous supply chain analyses. See Schwartz, Guasch, and Wilmsmeir (2009).

4. Confidentiality was requested from the corporations and individuals interviewed for this study.

5. The exporter transfers the product to cardboard boxes, because transporting the product in plastic boxes would imply having to process the former as a temporary export, implying additional costs (approximately US$14.50 per trip per container and an extra US$61.80 for a *carta de política*).

6. Larger exporters with lower logistics costs usually sell directly to supermarket chains, while smaller and more expensive exporters sell to public markets.

7. This finding is interesting in itself, as one would think that the time spent at customs would be lower for the large exporter than for the small exporter. Given that the large exporter has continuous shipments and hires reliable and well-established customs agents to file customs documents that accurately reflect the volume, value, and other characteristics of their cargo, it is expected that the large exporter has developed a relationship of trust with customs authorities. For this particular study, however, the small exporters interviewed also expressed that they have developed good relationships with customs authorities. One small exporter did, however, emphasize that, at times, poorly skilled customs agents submit inaccurate information to customs, which, on inspection of the cargo, not only creates additional costs, but also jeopardizes the established relationship of trust. This suggests that, as long as this relationship of trust is maintained, waiting time at customs is similar for both large and small exporters. This logic also suggests that waiting time at customs as a result of thorough inspections is the longest for new market entrants.

8. The requirement for shipments to be fully inspected by customs is determined by a stoplight at the border. Once the customs declaration has been submitted, a stoplight determines whether the cargo is to be subjected to further inspections. If the light turns green, the cargo can be cleared, if yellow, customs documents must be reviewed thoroughly, and if red, customs must confirm that the documents submitted reflect the nature of the shipments through a detailed cargo inspection in addition to phytosanitary and narcotics inspections. If the light is red, the exporter himself must pay for approximately seven people to unload the cargo.

9. See "Furgones esperan ingreso en Costa Rica y Nicaragua: Nuevo control en Peñas Blancas crea presas de varios kilómetros," La Nación, Costa Rica, December 21, 2006, available at http://www.nacion.com/ln_ee/2006/diciembre/21/economia937007.html.

10. Previously, samples were sent to Managua, which implied longer waiting times at the border.

11. The regulations guiding charges during unloading at the ports differ in these two countries. In Puerto Corinto, Nicaragua, importers are rewarded US$5,000 a day if they manage to unload the vessel in less than three days. If they take longer, they are fined US$20,000 a day. In Honduras, there is no fine or reward system. Importers pay a flat fee of US$7,000 a day.

12. Importers may choose to buy storage space in advance to be able to fulfill fluctuations in demand.

13. The bill of lading is issued by the carrier, acknowledging that the goods have been received on board as cargo and are being transported to a specified place and recipient.

14. Panama Canal website, available at http://www.panacanal.com/eng/maritime/tolls.html.

15. For purposes of this study, the small exporter is defined as an independent exporter having his own transport infrastructure and traveling to Managua to sell his own product to private clients. The small exporter has a lower carrying capacity for tomatoes than does the large exporter, as he gathers four to five products on average, often from his own production, and consolidates the cargo. The large exporter has a year-round supply of product, purchased from well-established independent producers or producers associations, and makes at least two weekly trips from Costa Rica to Nicaragua.

16. Rough (or paddy) rice is the rice as it comes from the field. The rice kernels are still encased in an inedible, protective hull that, when separated from the kernel, can be burned as fuel for power plants and other industrial processes, be used as mulch, or become a component in abrasives and other products.

17. The conversion ratio is the percentage of final product—that is, white rice—recovered out of the total volume of paddy rice being milled. For modern mills such as the ones used in both Nicaragua and Honduras, the by-products of 100 kilograms of long-grain rough (paddy) rice are 62–68 percent milled rice, 4–5 percent rice bran, 25 percent rice husk, and 2–3 percent germ wastages. When the milled rice goes to supermarkets, the millers package the products in branded bags of various sizes (from 0.45 to 20 kilograms) at an additional cost. Retail prices are not included in the analysis performed for this study.

18. For more disaggregated information on cost regarding the supply chains for corn and rice, contact Raquel Fernández (rfernandez2@worldbank.org) or Santiago Gomez (sflorezgomez@worldbank.org).

19. Consistent with an analysis of free-on-board prices, the estimated farm price paid by Nicaraguan wheat and rice importers is 4 and 7 percent higher, respectively, as a share of the final price of the good when compared to that paid by Honduran importers. Due to larger volumes of imported wheat and exogenous factors such as the availability of better traders, Honduran importers may be better suited to import wheat at more competitive prices.

20. The authors calculate that the efficiency of Nicaragua's feed manufacturers is about 92 percent, while that of Honduran feed manufacturers is about 95 percent. These high and comparable efficiency levels can be attributed to the level of competition, which is high overall, and pressure from the animal-raising industry in both countries.

References

Baier, S. L., and J. H. Bergstrand. 2001. "The Growth of World Trade: Tariffs, Transport Costs, and Income Similarity." *Journal of International Economics* 53 (1): 1–27.

Blyde, J. S., M. Moreira, and M. Volpe. 2008. "Unclogging the Arteries: The Impact of Transport Costs on Latin American and Caribbean Trade." Inter-American Development Bank, Washington, DC; Harvard University, David Rockefeller Center for Latin American Studies, Cambridge, MA.

Hummels, D. 2001. "Time as a Trade Barrier." Unpublished manuscript, Purdue University, West Lafayette, IN.

Schwartz, J., J. L. Guasch, and G. Wilmsmeeir. 2009. "Logistics, Transport, and Food Prices in LAC: Policy Guidance for Improving Efficiency and Reducing Costs." World Bank and Inter-American Development Bank, Washington, DC.

World Bank. 2006. "Costa Rica Country Economic Memorandum: The Challenges for Sustained Growth." Report 36180-CR, World Bank, Washington, DC.

———. 2007. "Costa Rica Investment Climate Assessment." Report 35424-CR, World Bank, Washington, DC.

———. 2009. "Uruguay Trade and Logistics: An Opportunity." World Bank, Washington, DC.

World Economic Forum. 2009. *Global Enabling Trade Report.* Davos, Switzerland: World Economic Forum.

CHAPTER 7

Logistics Challenges in Central America

José A. Barbero

This chapter assesses the condition and performance of trade logistics and facilitation in Central America and the Dominican Republic to determine the region's ability to take advantage of the potential benefits of the Dominican Republic–Central America Free Trade Agreement (DR-CAFTA). After describing the main patterns of regional trade and the core factors influencing logistics performance, the chapter presents a set of policy priorities for strengthening the system's functioning.

The Relevance of Logistics as a Factor in Trade

The physical movement of goods is conditioned by numerous factors that can be organized in three major groups, which together constitute a country's logistics system: infrastructure and transport services, logistics business management by carriers and shippers, and trade facilitation procedures, including issues related to documentation, control, and provision of security for trade flows. Each major group encompasses components that are interrelated in a complex network. Infrastructure—the system's hardware—is critical to ensuring the efficient transportation and storage of goods. Business logistics include cargo owners and service providers; cargo owners are interested in improving the organization of the supply chain, while logistics providers are interested in improving and broadening the scope of their services by investing in new equipment and facilities. Trade facilitation initiatives (as well as other regulations related to the circulation of goods) are generally under the mandate of the public sector and—together with transport regulations—could be considered the system's "software." These have a large impact on the system's functioning, as they determine the processes and documents that users and service providers must understand and comply with if they wish to interact.

This basic definition of the factors involved in the flow of goods gives rise to two important conclusions. First, analyses and proposals should not be constrained to infrastructure bottlenecks (as they are most times), but should also consider relevant aspects in all of the system's components. Second, the performance of logistics systems depends on the coordinated efforts of stakeholders in both the public and the private sectors.

Logistics are directly related to the organization of productive activities among firms, most of them within the private sector, and have gained more relevance as the flow of goods has become more complex and pressures to reduce costs have increased. Until the 1980s, companies handled the transportation of inputs, distribution of products, and storage systems as separate functions, in a relatively independent manner. Subsequently, companies began to integrate them, considering logistics to cover the physical movements along the complete cycle of materials and the documentation and information from the purchase of inputs to the delivery of the final product, encompassing the functions of transport, storage, inventory management, and packaging of goods as well as the administration and control of these flows. Thus business logistics need to be analyzed from the broader perspective of supply chains, with the aim of boosting coordination among the links to improve efficiency and reduce costs.

The Impact of Logistics and Trade Facilitation on Trade Costs

As trade theory develops, the positive impacts of more efficient logistics and trade facilitation initiatives on the costs of trade are becoming increasingly explicit. The benefits of trade for general welfare have been widely researched (World Bank 2009); the analytical focus on the impacts associated with reducing the costs of trade by increasing logistics efficiency was developed in recent years. This type of analysis is needed to build a strong case for logistics-related reforms, as the findings would help define the benefits that can accrue from these initiatives. A recent World Bank document on border management presents a detailed review of the latest literature on the issue, which is summarized below:

- *Significance of trade costs versus tariffs.* The decline in tariff levels in the past 20 years has highlighted the existence of trade costs that are not related to traditional trade policy. Research by Anderson and van Wincoop (2004) is illustrative in this sense. The authors establish a broad definition of trade costs (including transport costs, tariff and nontariff costs, legal and regulatory costs, information costs, and so forth). Based on their findings, trade costs are large, and a significant part of them stems from economic policies not directly associated with trade, such as transport policy and related regulations. "Their estimate of the ad valorem tax equivalent of trade cost for industrialized countries is 170 percent, of which 21 percent falls under transportation costs . . ., 44 percent under border trade-related barriers, and 55 percent under retail and wholesale distribution costs. The authors assert that trade barriers in developing countries are higher than what is estimated for industrial countries" (World Bank 2009).

- *Time dimension of trade costs.* Trade barriers bring forward costs that are linked with time delays and uncertainty in moving goods across borders. Hummels (2001) was the first to explore this issue. He argues that each additional day spent on transport reduces by 1 to 1.5 percent the chances a country has of exporting to the U.S. market. Further research by Hummels and Schaur (2009) estimates the value of cross-border delays on the basis of average depreciation and inventory carrying costs: each day of delay is equivalent to additional costs of 0.8 percent of the value of freight.

- *Effectiveness of trade facilitation measures.* Research by Wilson, Mann, and Otsuki (2005) highlights potential gains from trade facilitation initiatives. The authors define trade facilitation in a broad manner, including port efficiency (port facilities, inland waterways, and airports), customs environment (hidden barriers to imports and bribes), regulatory environment (transparency of government policies and levels of corruption), and e-business infrastructure (speed and cost of Internet access). Based on data for 75 countries in 2000–01, the authors argue that improvements in the four areas have a positive impact on trade. More important, they highlight that, if the least-efficient countries could boost efficiency halfway to the sample's average, trade gains could amount to US$377 billion.

- *Infrastructure development and trade.* The links between trade and infrastructure development have been explored recently by Limao and Venables (2001). Their research shows that 40 percent of transport costs in coastal countries and up to 60 percent in landlocked countries result from infrastructure deficiencies. The authors estimate that if landlocked countries in the lower percentiles of infrastructure development would rise to the 75 percentile, they would be able to increase their volume of trade.

- *Trade and institutional quality.* Sadikov (2007) analyzes these issues by looking at specific measures that are under the control of customs and other regulatory authorities. His research analyzes the number of signatures required for exporting (considered a proxy for border barriers) and the number of procedures for registering a business (a proxy for behind-the-border barriers). Based on data for 126 countries, his findings show that reducing export signatures and registration procedures results in trade gains: each extra signature reduces aggregate exports by 4.2 percent. Finally, he points out that the impact of these measures is larger when products have a higher level of differentiation.

- *Impacts of trade costs at the firm level.* A series of studies conducted recently shows that exporting firms in a country are generally larger and more efficient than firms that do not export. The process of self-selection between the two groups is determined by the existence of cross-border trade costs: only firms that are productive enough to overcome the additional costs associated with expansion to larger new markets are able to export. Falling trade costs are thus linked with important decisions at the firm level: (a) entry and exit, (b) the decision to export, (c) the amount to export, (d) technology decisions, and (e) employment decisions (World Bank 2009). This strand of theory, represented by Melitz (2003), Bernard, Jensen, and Schott (2006), Yeaple (2005), and Bernard and others (2007), suggests that reduced trade costs push more firms to export and stimulate the growth of existing exporters, which, in turn, results in higher productivity.

Progress in the implementation of DR-CAFTA was expected to be positive for Central America for two main reasons. The first was that the agreement granted expanded access to the U.S. market, boosting trade volumes. Although the region already had certain privileges for access to the United States resulting from the Caribbean Basin Initiative, these were to deepen under DR-CAFTA. Other provisions that would foster trade included more flexible rules of origin for exports of apparel and textiles from *maquilas* (which would help to offset tough competition from Asian countries) and technical assistance to exporters of nontraditional agricultural products (which would help them to meet the sanitary and phytosanitary standards required for entry into the United States). The latter was expected to help diversify the region's base of exports. A second group of benefits for the region was given by the possibility of deepening integration among Central American countries. The fact that these agreed to make DR-CAFTA a treaty that would be applied multilaterally (instead of bilaterally between the United States and each Central American country individually) was a good starting point in this direction. The ability of Central American countries to pursue a complementary policy agenda in areas such as trade facilitation, regulatory reforms, transport policies, and innovation will determine to a great extent the magnitude of the benefits resulting from DR-CAFTA.

The financial crisis that hit the U.S. economy in mid-2008 had strong impacts on the region; however, the prospects of DR-CAFTA remain positive. The close trade ties between the United States and Central America strengthened when DR-CAFTA came into effect: between 2005 and 2008, Central American exports to the United States grew 10 percent, and in 2008, close to 30 regional exports went to the U.S. market (EIU 2009). Thus contraction in U.S. demand in the aftermath of the financial crisis had strong effects in the region, with export earnings falling 20 percent year on year as of January–March 2009 (EIU 2009). Uncertainties about the pace of U.S. recovery outline the need to develop new export markets. On the positive side, export diversification seems to be advancing, with nontraditional exports registering growth of close to 20 percent in 2008. In addition, integration among countries in the region has been strengthened: earnings from intraregional trade have expanded by an annual average of 12 percent since 2003, according to data from the Secretariat of Economic Integration in Central America (SIECA).[1] A regional policy agenda to address issues that are relevant from a trade perspective is also developing slowly, as noted below. Finally, in the short term, intraregional trade flows, together with the opening of new markets in Asia and Latin America for regional exports, will largely determine the volume of trade in the following years.

International Logistics Indicators

The logistics performance index (LPI) is a research initiative launched by a transport and trade facilitation alliance composed of several public and private international organizations, led by the World Bank. The LPI was estimated for the first time in 2007 based on a survey of international freight operators from 150 countries, who provided feedback on their perception of several logistics attributes of the countries in which they operate and with which they trade. The responses allow for the calculation of several subindexes, which together make up the LPI. The LPI is expressed through a score (from 1 to 5) and a ranking according to the position held by an individual country within the group. A second estimate was done in 2009, comprising 155 countries.

From a global perspective, the LPI shows that the region's logistics performance is relatively weak. The average regional rank (of the five Central American countries and the Dominican Republic) was 85 in 2007 and 79 in 2009, in a sample of 150 and 155 countries, respectively. The region is a clear example of the logistics gap that exists between the high-income countries (the top performers) and the middle- and low-income countries. Malaysia and Thailand,[2] which are relevant comparators in terms of income, ranked 29 and 35, respectively, in the 2009 survey. However, Central America's overall performance in the LPI improved significantly between 2007 and 2009. The scores of four of the six DR-CAFTA countries improved (Costa Rica, Dominican Republic, Honduras, and the Nicaragua), while those of El Salvador and Guatemala deteriorated somewhat (see figure 7.1).

On average, the region improved considerably the absolute value of logistics performance (from 2.48 to 2.73), which suggests that improvements in many logistics factors have been yielding results. If the average rank is analyzed to assess the relative—not the absolute—logistics performance, the region also shows some improvement, albeit more moderate (from 85 to 79). This suggests that other countries have also improved;[3] some of the Central American countries, however, show a significant decline in their relative position, even after achieving an absolute improvement in their logistics performance. For example, Guatemala and El Salvador had small gains in absolute terms, but declined from position 75 to 90 and from 66 to 86 in the LPI country rank.[4]

Analysis at the subindex level shows that the region has intermediate performance in customs administration efficiency and quality of transport and information technology infrastructure. Scores on these topics are only

Figure 7.1   LPI Rank of Central American and Comparator Countries, 2007 and 2009

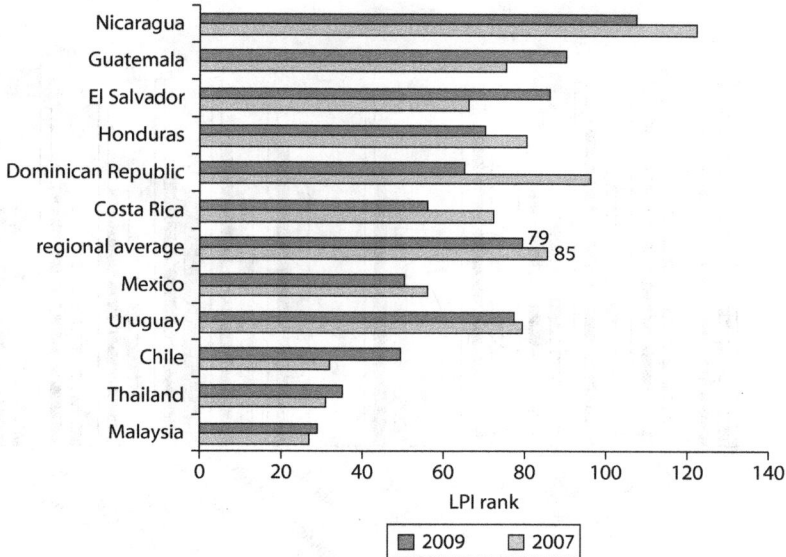

Source: 2007 and 2009 LPI surveys.

moderately lower than those of regional comparators such as Uruguay and Chile (the regional leader, whose performance decayed between 2007 and 2009).[5] The gap in Central American scores on infrastructure quality widens significantly when compared with that of Mexico, Thailand, and Malaysia, as shown in figure 7.2. Central America receives good scores for timeliness of shipments reaching their destination, in some cases scoring higher than Chile and Uruguay. However, regional performance is weaker in the rest of the topics covered by the survey: the ease and affordability of arranging international shipments are at an intermediate level when compared with Chile and Uruguay, with El Salvador and Guatemala bringing down the regional average. Tracking and tracing capabilities are much lower than in Chile, although Central America's average is higher than Uruguay's score. Scores for local logistics competence are also low, with the exception of Costa Rica. All Central American scores are well below those of Malaysia and Thailand, with differences close to one point in most cases, except for timeliness of shipments.

Figure 7.2   Performance on the LPI Subindexes of Central American and Comparator Countries

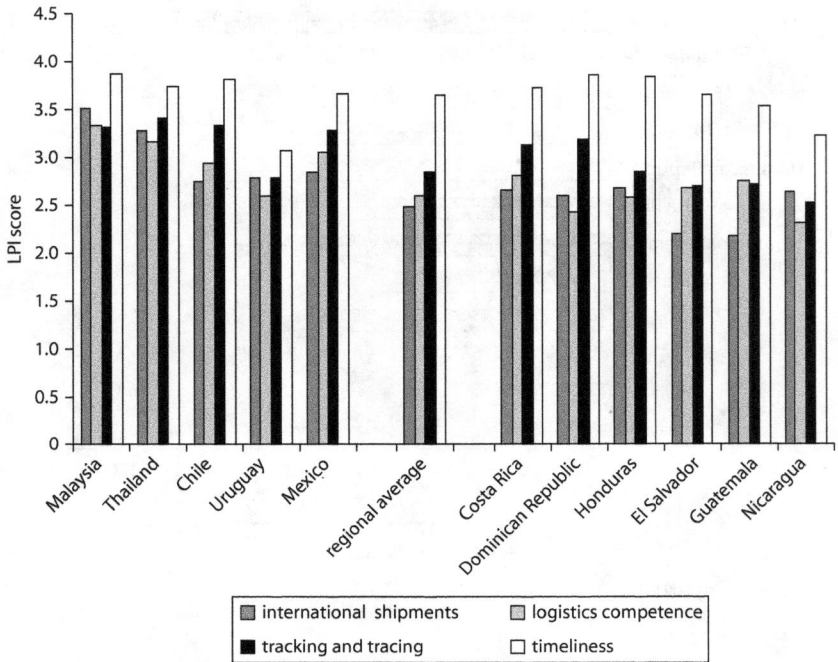

Source: 2009 LPI survey.

As stated, although overall performance appears to be relatively good in regional terms, the gap with high-income countries is wide. Nevertheless, good performers such as Costa Rica and El Salvador help to bring the regional average up in subindexes such as customs and infrastructure (see figure 7.3).

The Global Competitiveness Report and Trade Enabling Index

The results of the perception survey conducted by the World Economic Forum for the 2009 and 2010 editions of the *Global Competitiveness Report* (WEF 2009, 2010) provide additional information on the relative performance of Central American countries, although the results are not entirely consistent with those of the LPI. The overall condition of regional infrastructure has improved, but performance varies strongly among countries and sectors (see figure 7.4). The perceived quality of infrastructure is intermediate, with scores behind

Figure 7.3   Performance on Customs and Infrastructure of Central American and Comparator Countries, 2009

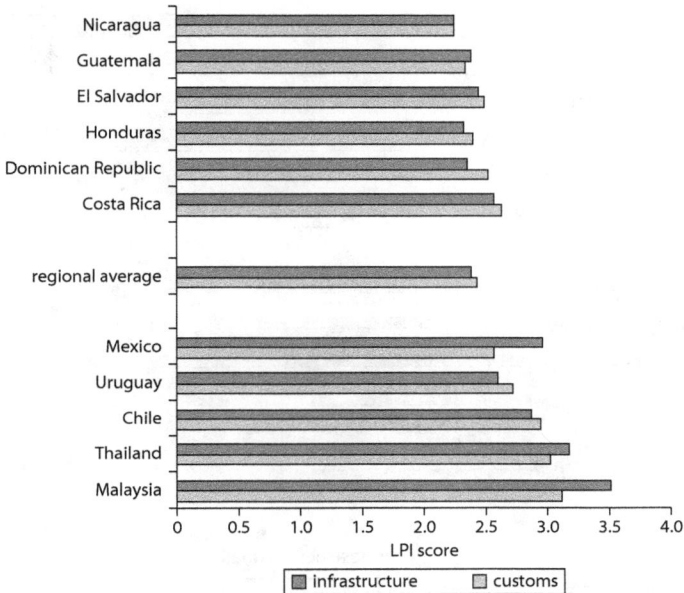

Source: 2009 LPI survey.

those of good performers such as Uruguay and Chile (the regional leader) and comparators in Southeast Asia. El Salvador and Guatemala are the region's strong performers; Honduras and the Dominican Republic are at an intermediate stage, while Nicaragua and Costa Rica lag behind (although the latter shows strong improvement in the 2010 survey).

Roads are the weakest sector, with regional averages well behind those of the comparator group. El Salvador is an exception, with quality at levels close to those of Chile, Malaysia, and Thailand. Nicaragua and Costa Rica register low scores, bringing down the regional average for road quality. The situation is similar regarding the perceived quality of ports, in which the regional average is far from the scores of comparator countries. However, most countries improved their scores on ports in the 2009 survey: Honduras is well positioned, reflecting the good performance of Puerto Cortés, while Nicaragua and Costa Rica are the weakest performers. The perception of the quality of railways is remarkably low, as a result of the limited development of this

Figure 7.4   Quality of Overall Infrastructure of Central American and Comparator Countries, 2008–10

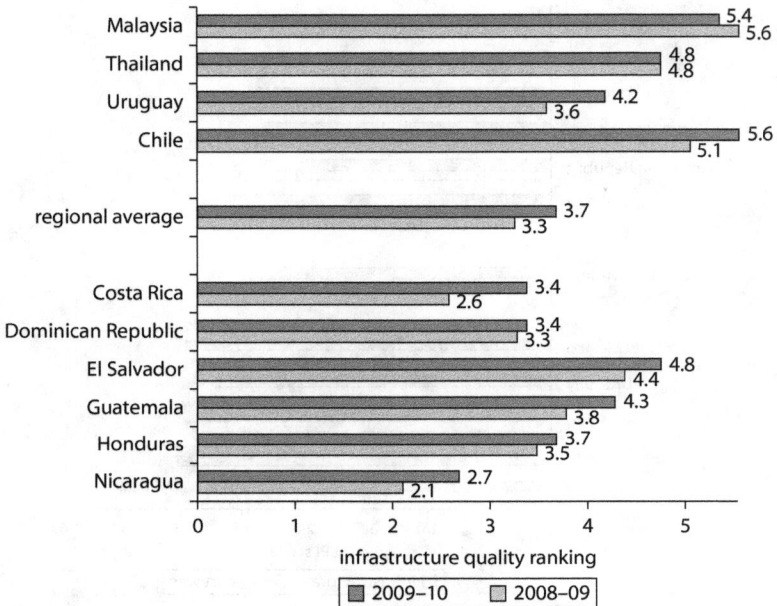

Source: WEF 2009, 2010.

subsector in the region. Finally, airports show a strong and balanced performance in the region, with average scores close to those of the comparator group.

Central America's performance on the global enabling trade index shows transport infrastructure and border administration at an intermediate level, close to Uruguay's scores and lagging behind those of Chile, Malaysia, and Thailand (see figure 7.5). Regional performance at the level of subindexes reflects the general scores, with some interesting points: the efficiency of import and export procedures is high in most countries, registering scores close to regional best practice as well as those of Thailand and Malaysia; transparency in border administration, particularly in the Dominican Republic, Honduras, and Guatemala, is rather low, and the efficiency of customs administration is poor in Nicaragua and Honduras. The availability of transport infrastructure is moderate from a regional perspective, but lags well behind the scores of Chile and countries in Southeast Asia. Finally, the availability and quality of transport services are quite weak in the region, except in Costa Rica and the Dominican Republic.

Figure 7.5   Performance on the Global Enabling Trade Index of Central American and Comparator Countries, 2009

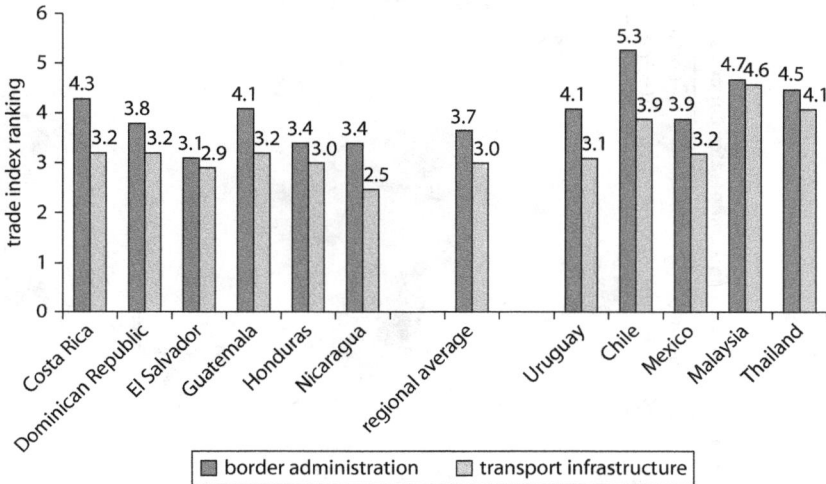

Source: WEF 2009.

Doing Business, Trading across Borders

The trading across borders indicator monitored by the World Bank's Doing Business database is a good tool for benchmarking transport costs and lead times for import and export processes. As shown in table 7.1, Central America's performance is at an intermediate level, well positioned in regional terms, but falling behind Malaysia, Thailand, and the Organisation for Economic Co-operation and Development (OECD) countries. The number of documents required for import and export operations is reasonable from a regional perspective, although performance is weaker for imports, with Central America's regional average of seven documents lagging behind the average for OECD and Thailand, at approximately four. Time to export and import measured in days also performs well (17 days) versus the comparator group but not the OECD countries (11 days). Nicaragua experiences the longest delays for imports and exports, with a lead time of 29 days in both cases. Finally, the costs associated with external trade are poor for the region. The small difference between Central American and OECD countries mostly results from the higher internal prices in OECD countries. The cost gap with other countries in the comparator group is much more significant: the cost to export or import a 20-foot container from a Central American

Table 7.1   Performance on Doing Business Indicators of Trading across Borders of Central American and Comparator Countries

Region or economy	Documents to export (number)	Time to export (days)	Cost to export (US$ per container)	Documents to import (number)	Time to import (days)	Cost to import (US$ per container)
Latin America and Caribbean (regional average)	7	19	1,244	7	21	1,481
OECD (regional average)	4	11	1,090	5	11	1,146
Chile	6	21	745	7	21	795
Uruguay	10	19	1,100	10	22	1,330
Mexico	5	14	1,472	5	17	2,050
Malaysia	7	18	450	7	14	450
Thailand	4	14	625	3	13	795
Central America (regional average)	7	17	1,112	8	17	1,179
Costa Rica	6	13	1,190	7	15	1,190
Dominican Republic	6	9	916	7	10	1,150
El Salvador	8	14	880	8	10	820
Guatemala	10	17	1,182	10	17	1,302
Honduras	7	20	1,163	10	23	1,190
Nicaragua	5	29	1,340	5	29	1,420

Source: World Bank, Doing Business database, 2009.

port is about US$1,100, more than twice the cost in Malaysia and considerably above the cost in Chile or Thailand. This factor is particularly relevant, as some developing countries have achieved high levels of efficiency in logistics and trade facilitation.

Country Logistics Review

In this section, we review specific logistics challenges and characteristics in the six countries that are signatories of the DR-CAFTA.

Costa Rica

Costa Rica's reliance on trade as an engine of growth highlights the need to improve logistics performance, which is currently hampering competitiveness. Based on the conclusions of recent World Bank assessments on sectors and topics associated with logistics (World Bank 2006b, 2007a, 2007b), infrastructure and transport services appear to be the main bottlenecks for increased efficiency of trade flows. Costa Rica has high levels of coverage in the road sector, but years of underinvestment have led to a marked deterioration of the network. Public investment in the sector fell from a peak of 2.1 percent of GDP in 1984 to below 0.6 percent on average in 1999–2005. In 2006, almost 35 percent of national roads were in poor condition. In 2006–07, the government undertook substantial investments to improve the state of roads, focusing on the links between the central plateau and the port of Limón-Moin on the Atlantic coast and Caldera on the Pacific coast, which are the high-volume corridors in the country. However, the fast-growing rates of motorization, together with increasing trade volumes, continue to put pressure on these corridors, generating congestion and deteriorating infrastructure. Ports and their associated services appear to be the weakest link. The port complex at Limón-Moin handles more than 80 percent of the volume of maritime freight, mostly in container traffic (more than 70 percent of total volume in 2007), followed by general cargo and liquid bulk. Inefficient management under the state-owned tool-port model has created serious challenges for operational efficiency in Limón-Moin: the cost per ton of moving cargo from Limón-Moin is estimated to be as much as twice as high as at most other ports in Central America (EIU 2008). The port of Caldera, in contrast, was concessioned recently, and since then container movement has nearly doubled. The government has plans to increase private participation in the sector by concessioning Limón-Moin and building a new mega-port in Limón through a public works concession.

Table 7.2   Freight Flows in Costa Rica, by Mode of Transport

Transport mode	Value US$ (millions)	Value % of value	Volume Tons (thousands)	Volume % of volume	Density (US$ per ton)	% originating in a free trade zone Value	% originating in a free trade zone Volume
Maritime	3,894	43	5,769	81	675	38	8
Air	3,720	41	52	1	71,537	91	35
Surface	1,476	16	1,300	18	1,136	13	2
Total	9,089	100	7,120	100	1,277	56	7

Source: Procomer (the agency responsible for the promotion of external trade in Costa Rica).

Costa Rica has two international airports, Juan Santamaría in northwest San José and Daniel Oduber near Liberia. Management of the former was transferred to the private sector, and efforts are under way to increase its operating capacity.

As shown in table 7.2, the three modes of transport participate actively in the country's export flows. Maritime transport takes the highest share freight in terms of volume, handling mostly dry bulk cargo of low value added per ton. The main challenges faced by this subsector are the lack of modern cargo-handling equipment and difficult access to the main port facilities. The development of air freight services is closely linked to the high-tech firms, which have brought efficiency to its operation. Thus air transport handles high value added goods and is heavily used by firms based in free trade zones. Urban congestion in the outskirts of San José generates some difficulties for cargo traveling toward the airport, increasing transit times. Finally, surface transport handles a low level of freight in terms of both volume and value, which reflects Costa Rica's relatively low participation in intraregional trade. Delays in the Peñas Blancas border crossing (which is the main link for trade with other Central American countries) are very significant and have a relevant economic impact, as the majority of companies using land transport for export of goods are small and medium enterprises (SMEs).

Dominican Republic

The provision and quality of infrastructure are regarded as relatively good in the Dominican Republic. The largest challenges for trade are mostly linked with regulatory issues and customs efficiency. Port infrastructure has improved significantly in the last five years, following the entrance of private operators. The port of Haina, located 20 kilometers west of Santo Domingo, handled the largest volume of general cargo and container traffic until 2004, followed by Puerto Plata. A privately financed state-of-the-art deepwater port at Caucedo was inaugurated in 2004 and has attracted most of Haina's existing business thanks to its large storage facilities and modern equipment. Caucedo is currently absorbing significant volumes of transshipment traffic in the Caribbean, and these are expected to grow as plans to expand existing facilities are implemented. Other important ports are Santo Domingo, which handles vehicle imports, and La Romana, which handles sugar exports. These two ports, together with Samana in the northeast of the country, are also the main destinations for cruise ships. The primary road network is in overall good condition as a result of a roads program implemented in the late 1990s, although current levels of maintenance are rather low. As the number of road concessions has grown, so have investments in the sector. The condition of the secondary and tertiary networks is not as good, which has a negative impact on access to ports. Airports perform well in the Dominican Republic, playing a key role in an economy that relies strongly on tourism and *maquilas*. Most airports were given in concession to the private sector during the 1990s, and the trend toward increasing private participation continues as new tourism centers develop.

However, many challenges persist with regard to logistics performance in the Dominican Republic. The most important of them is customs administration, which is considered rather inefficient, mostly due to the high degree of discretion of customs officials (particularly those in charge of collecting tariffs and fees). The rates of physical inspection of cargo are high, and documentation requirements are sometimes excessive and remain in paper rather than in electronic form. The development of logistics operators is also intermediate; however, increasing freight volumes in Caucedo are expected to attract international logistics operators to the Dominican market, pushing service quality closer to international standards. Finally, the trucking industry, which handles all of the internal flows of freight, is particularly fragmented and operates with very low levels of efficiency.

El Salvador

Throughout the 1990s, El Salvador made important improvements to enhance service provision in the transport sector: roads were rehabilitated, and the international airport and the main freight port (Acajutla) were developed. Despite these reforms, a comprehensive infrastructure assessment carried out in 2006 found that Salvadoran firms still consider transport infrastructure as the main bottleneck in their export supply chain, with associated costs representing between 15 and 22 percent of the total cost structure in the industries surveyed (the third-largest cost after labor and raw materials; World Bank 2006a).[6] The country's geography and foreign trade structure lead to intensive use of Guatemalan and Honduran ports, making the land-sea interface of paramount importance for foreign trade, emphasizing the importance of the primary network and trucking services. The road network faces important challenges: its condition is generally poor, and the country's two main highways (the Carretera Litoral, which runs along the Pacific coast, and the Pan-American Highway, which runs across the country's interior) are frequently affected by natural disasters. In addition, these major highways, which link the central region (where production and export activities are concentrated) with key trade nodes, require freight to pass through heavily congested urban areas. To address congestion around the city of El Salvador, a major ring is being built with support of a loan from the Inter-American Development Bank. Secondary and rural roads, particularly in the northern and eastern provinces, create additional challenges in terms of accessibility, as they become impassable during the rainy season.

In 2006, the government created a program to address these issues, devoting additional funds for rural roads development. However, based on the findings of the Recent Economic Development in Infrastructure (REDI), trucking services are considered to be highly inefficient and unreliable. Approximately 70 percent of freight trucks in the country are more than 15 years old. The market is extremely fragmented, and the lack of professionalism in service provision generates increasing levels of externalities. Congestion in the border crossings with Guatemala and Honduras also hampers the efficiency of surface transport in El Salvador. As regards waterborne trade, El Salvador's volume of containerized cargo is close to 600,000 20-foot equivalent units and is mostly shipped via ports in Honduras and Guatemala. Acajutla has been able to capture close to 20 percent of this volume, as a result of increased efficiency and reduced port fees. Still, port performance is considered average (particularly for container movement) due to the lack of freight-handling equipment. Vessels calling in at Acajutla are, in general, small carriers whose operation is inefficient and costly. The port of La Unión is currently under reconstruction with financing from the Japan Bank for International Cooperation. Plans to concession Acajutla and La Unión have suffered delays due to congressional objections to the bidding rules. Air transport generally performs well: the El Salvador International Airport is the main hub for TACA airlines, which has helped raise the quality of service.

Relatively competitive airport fees contribute to an increasingly competitive air freight service.

Guatemala

The Pan-American Highway and the Pacific and Atlantic Highway are the main corridors in the country. Although the network is being expanded (a new trunk road that crosses the Petén region is currently under construction) and upgraded, insufficient maintenance affects the state of roads. In 2000, 10 percent of the network was in bad condition, and this grew to 30 percent in 2008. Demand for transport continues to put pressure on the system as trade and motorization grow. The metropolitan region is congested, and trucks are not allowed to operate in the area for six hours a day. Only half of the road network is paved, which makes it vulnerable to natural disasters and hampers accessibility, particularly in rural areas. The main ports are Santo Tomás and Puerto Barrios on the Atlantic coast and Puerto Quetzal on the Pacific coast. Ports are mostly publicly owned and operated, with some exceptions. Although the quality of service is not bad, efficiency is low, and too few resources are devoted to investment. As a result, dredging is insufficient, and berths are unable to support modern cranes, so only feeder vessels are able to call in at Guatemalan ports. This has had a negative impact on maritime freight rates. Airports perform adequately with regard to air freight services. Customs administration has gone through an important modernization process; however, coordination among control agencies is still weak. The trucking industry encompasses a relatively old truck fleet, operating at low levels of efficiency. Trade is carried primarily by maritime transportation, although surface transportation is becoming more common. Trucks handle approximately 30 percent of exports and 20 percent of imports. The growing importance of surface transport highlights the need to improve the efficiency of customs administration, which tends to be lower in land border crossings.

Honduras

The country's two main corridors are the north-south highway, which connects Tegucigalpa with San Pedro Sula, and the Pan-American Highway, which runs alongside the Pacific coast and connects Honduras with Nicaragua and El Salvador. Although the condition of the road network has improved in recent years, the proportion of the national network in poor condition is still high, and it is even higher in the rural network, which is critical for agricultural activities. In addition, the low percentage of paved roads makes the network very vulnerable to natural disasters and increases vehicle operating costs. The trucking industry registers low levels of efficiency, with an extremely fragmented market and an aging fleet.

Additional challenges from the logistics perspective arise from long delays and smuggling in the main border crossings (particularly those with El Salvador and Nicaragua) and from poor cargo security, particularly around suburban areas. Puerto Cortés, on the northern coast of the country, is Honduras's main port and one of the most modern deepwater ports in Central America. It handles more than 50 percent of the country's exports as well as freight originated in or destined for El Salvador and Nicaragua. The levels of efficiency in its operation are considered high; however, the existing equipment is insufficient to handle increasing trade, thus generating delays. Honduras's four main airports (Tegucigalpa-Toncontin, San Pedro Sula, La Ceiba, and Roatan) are under concession to a national private operator. However, Toncontin was relocated recently to a military base after an accident in 2008. Approximately 20 percent of Honduran trade is transported by surface through the main border crossings: El Amatillo (on the border with El Salvador), El Guasaule (on the border with Nicaragua), and El Corinto (on the border with Guatemala).

Based on the results of the latest investment climate assessment carried out by the World Bank in Honduras (World Bank 2004), firms consider transport bottlenecks as one of the main constraints to efficient trade flows. Although overall quality of infrastructure is seen as moderate to regular, most firms consider air transport as the main bottleneck, followed by ports, particularly for large companies located in free trade zones. These companies are mostly large *maquilas*, which rely heavily on airports and ports to ship their products. In contrast, micro and small companies consider surface transport as the main bottleneck.

Losses resulting from spoilage and breakage constitute 1.8 percent of total sales; 36 percent of firms lose merchandise while in transit (compared with 26 percent in Nicaragua and 40 percent in Guatemala; World Bank 2004). The survey indicates that the time to clear customs is adequate for exports, but high for imports, registering marked peaks of up to 27 days. These delays affect particularly small firms.

Nicaragua

Nicaragua's performance in infrastructure services is among the lowest in Central America (EIU 2008). Given the limited development of ports, air transportation, and railways (which have ceased to exist), the largest bottlenecks to trade lie in the road sector (World Bank 2006c). The quality of Nicaragua's road infrastructure is the poorest in Central America: based on assessments carried out by the Ministry of Transportation and Infrastructure, more than 75 percent of the total road network was in poor condition in 2006. Nearly 50 percent of the network becomes unusable during the rainy season. In recent years, the primary network has been restored to good condition, but it represents less than 20 percent of the total network. Thus, the main challenge is associated with the quality of roads rather than their availability. The Pan-American Highway crosses the country from north to south and is the main road linking Nicaragua with other countries in Central America. It provides the country with access to seaports on the Atlantic coast of the isthmus, principally Puerto Cortés in Honduras and Puerto Limón in Costa Rica. Most of the country's agricultural exports must be shipped through these ports due to the lack of paved roads linking the Atlantic and the Pacific coasts. Approximately 400,000 tons of freight a year pass through the border crossings with Honduras and Costa Rica. Poor road quality affects rural development as well as competitiveness of agricultural products, which represent more than 80 percent of total exports. Transport services also perform poorly: more than 50 percent of the trucks are more than 10 years old and operate with extremely low levels of efficiency. The country has two ports on the Pacific coast, Puerto Sandino and Puerto Corinto. The latter has recently been rehabilitated, but it still cannot handle volumes sufficient to attract large vessels. Managua International Airport handles mostly air passengers, and the volume of air freight is very low.

Assessing Logistics Performance in Central America

Factors affecting logistics performance can be grouped as follows:

- Factors showing the most serious deficiencies in Central America are roads, ports, domestic and regional surface transportation (carried by the trucking industry), and the security of surface freight.
- Factors showing considerable problems, although less severe than the previous ones, are border management and border-crossing facilities.
- Factors in which problems exist, but to a lesser extent, are airports, international transport services (air and maritime), carriers' ability to manage their supply chain efficiently, and logistics operators and intermediaries.

The Most Critical Factor: Transport Infrastructure and Services

One of the weakest segments, highways have a role not just in freight logistics, but also in general mobility. Road coverage in Central America is relatively weak, with only about 15 percent of the network paved, and quality shows significant shortcomings, "failing to comply with the basic standards to ensure a smooth, safe, and effective regional traffic" (Sánchez and Wilmsmeier 2005). In addition, road infrastructure is vulnerable to frequent natural hazards (hurricanes, earthquakes, volcanic activity).

Countries need to overcome those structural deficits, while confronting two relevant needs. The first one is the need to increase capacity, as growing trade and motorization are pushing up demand for roads in key corridors and urban areas; bottlenecks are becoming more severe in large metropolitan regions (like San José), in the access to the main gateways (particularly ports), and in most important intercity highways passing through towns and villages. The second one is the need to ensure adequate maintenance, which requires additional resources as traffic increases. Private partnerships in highways are still rare in Central America. Poor road quality brings multiple challenges: first, it implies low levels of mobility for rural communities, hindering access to markets, health, and education among the poor. In addition, it affects the competitiveness of goods produced in rural areas; this is particularly relevant, as agriculture still represents more than 20 percent of regional GDP and employs close to 50 percent of the total workforce (SIECA 2009). Finally, the dynamism of intraregional trade, as well as growing flows to and from Mexico, which are largely shipped using surface transportation, outlines the need to improve the quality of roads to reduce costs.

Ports are key nodes for trade, particularly general cargo and container terminals. Central American countries are relatively small, generating a limited amount of freight, and most have access to two oceans; the historical trend has been for each country to develop its own facilities on each shore, causing the development of myriad terminals, each with limited scope.[7] As regards port organization, the tendency has been to keep the traditional state-owned tool-port model, without adopting (with a few exceptions) private participation under a landlord organization scheme, as has been done in other Latin American countries, with evident success (Mexico, Uruguay, or Chile).[8] Ports play a relevant role at the local level, and in many cases employees (current and retired) and municipalities try to extract as much rent as possible from them and block reform, disregarding the key role of ports as gateways for trade. The lack of strong and efficient regulators has also empowered public port operators, which are highly politicized institutions that tend to reduce the chances of implementing reforms. The combination of numerous small ports with small scale, organized under a low-efficiency operational model, clearly has a negative impact on the region's competitiveness (about two-thirds of Central American trade is waterborne). Low depth, inadequate berths, and lack of modern handling equipment constrain the type of vessel that shipping lines can deploy in the region.

Road freight transportation (truck transportation) is without question the most important domestic mode of transport in the region and has significant influence on logistics chains. Almost all surface transportation in Central America is carried by trucks, as railways are not operating (with a few exceptions). Trucks have increased their activity in regional trade, which is about one-fifth of total trade in Central America. Despite the importance and complexity of the sector, the lack of systematic data about road transportation is remarkable. Road transportation activities are performed almost entirely by the private sector, highlighting the importance of the regulatory framework. According to SIECA data, there are currently about 20,000 trucks in the region, with more than 100 companies providing international transport services. The remaining trucks are owned and operated mostly by individual owners. In accordance with the few studies available, the sector is inefficient. Typical average distances are 50,000 kilometers a year (which would be two to three times higher in an efficient operation). While truck productivity partially depends on the type of demand (type of product) and the time-space structure (directional imbalance, traffic seasonality), it is also a consequence of the organization of companies, which depends on the regulatory framework established by the state and the professionalism of the business sector. The impact of road transportation on a country's logistics is greater than what initial analyses may suggest. The improvements that may be achieved in price and service quality not only can reduce the costs and transit time faced by freight providers in the short run, but also can allow companies that produce goods to develop more efficient medium-term supply strategies (Dutz 2005).

Other modes of transport could potentially move the freight that is currently moved almost exclusively by truck, such as railways and maritime cabotage. Most railways in Central American countries have ceased to operate, and their infrastructure is antiquated. Although opportunity may exist to redevelop their activity, "investments needed to set up a new network with high technical standards would only be possible in corridors whose traffic density allows for a competitive participation" (Sánchez and Wilmsmeier 2005). Maritime cabotage—similar to the short sea shipping (SSS) developed in the European Union—is a long-standing project that seeks to use ocean routes for domestic and regional trade, without the complex regulations that control ocean trade. The implementation of efficient SSS services requires harmonized regulations and specific port infrastructure (Sánchez and Wilmsmeier 2005).

The stealing of freight from trucks is prevalent throughout the region. In Costa Rica, for example, cargo that used to be moved by truck is now being transported by air due to lack of security, at costs that are three times higher. Usually robbers target just the freight, but sometimes they also steal the truck (which is later dismantled and sold) and even kidnap the driver. Criminal activity involves products chosen by two criteria: the value of the merchandise and the ease of resale. Typical targets are food and drink, electronics, cigarettes, shoes and clothing, and medicine. This type of crime has multiple impacts: security costs and insurance premiums, satellite-positioning systems, guards, private surveillance posts, and other precautions that shippers and carriers need to take. It also undermines compliance with the client's requirements, harms the competitive position of the company responsible for the shipment, and diminishes the company's image and its products when cargo ends up being traded through clandestine channels without quality traceability. Another negative impact is felt in international traffic: in-transit freight is exempt from duties and border tariffs, but, if lost inside a territory, the customs office is obligated under the presumption of fraud to enforce the payment of warranties. In accordance with Central American regulations, the vehicle is the in-transit traffic warranty. Even if it is insufficient, the warranty facilitates the expansion of intraregional trade. However, customs agencies in the region have taken a negative attitude due to the frequency of robberies and the weakness of warranties, putting at risk a system that has facilitated trade and integration.

Border Management and Border-Crossing Facilities

Central American countries have gone through a process of modernizing customs, such as Guatemala's customs support for air express services, and the effort has helped to improve trade. But Central American countries, as most developing countries, need to expand the scope of intervention to facilitate trade, considering the entire border management process. Recent research conducted by the World Bank (2009) concludes that the necessary border reform is more than customs modernization:

> While improving the performance of customs administrations remains a high priority for many countries, it is only one of the agencies involved in border

processing, and evidence suggests it is often responsible for no more than a third of regulatory delays. . . . This highlights the need to focus attention on reforming and modernizing border management agencies other than customs (including health, agriculture, quarantine, police, immigration, standards, etc.).

There are several Central American initiatives in this regard, supported by SIECA and other multilateral institutions. DR-CAFTA includes obligations aimed at strengthening, improving, and modernizing the operation of customs to facilitate trade among signatory parties. Provisions seek to facilitate customs procedures and reduce room for discretion. The treaty includes rules of origin designed to be easier to administer. It also requires transparency, procedural certainty, and efficiency in administering customs procedures, including DR-CAFTA rules of origin. Central American countries have made a three-year commitment to accomplish goals such as the Internet publication of all norms and regulations, the automation of the clearance procedures, the electronic presentation of certificates of origin, and the implementation of management and risk evaluation systems. All signatories also have agreed to share information to combat the illegal transshipment of goods. A program of technical assistance was agreed to support Central American countries in carrying out their commitments in this area.

Similar to other developing countries, Central American countries have recognized the importance of addressing these issues and are looking for ways to harmonize, streamline, and simplify border management systems and procedures. This has led to several initiatives:

- Coordinated border management, which is based on approaches such as the co-location of facilities, close cooperation between agencies, delegation of administrative authority, cross-designation of officials, and effective information sharing
- One-stop border posts, which allow neighboring countries to coordinate import, export, and transit processes to ensure that traders are not required to duplicate regulatory formalities on both sides of the same border
- Single-window systems, which allow traders to submit all import, export, and transit information to regulators via a single electronic gateway instead of submitting the same information multiple times to different government entities.

The impact of trade facilitation and border management is evident. Specific measurement initiatives show that customs procedures and electronic commerce have an important impact on trade, although less so than port efficiency (Wilson, Mann, and Otsuki 2003). Their influence is generally measured as the rate of trade that a country loses due to inefficient performance and, therefore, as percentage points of GDP that a country loses. The subject has been analyzed in depth by several entities of the United Nations, both multilateral and bilateral, and they have formed an alliance to coordinate their efforts (Global Facilitation Partnership for Transportation and Trade).

A recent assessment carried out by the Inter-American Development Bank in the Pacific corridor concludes that border-crossing facilities—infrastructure and general layout—along this route are in very poor condition (IDB 2009).[9] The report finds that trade facilitation initiatives have resulted in improved lead times to cross the border (particularly among Guatemala, El Salvador, Honduras, and Nicaragua, members of the CA-4 agreement). However, the situation is more complex in the borders between Guatemala and Mexico and between Costa Rica and Panama, creating bottlenecks that are particularly costly in the case of the Mexican border, where trade flows have increased steadily in recent years. According to the assessment, important works should be carried out to improve border facilities (offices and adjacent platforms) and access roads, and a preliminary group of projects could be undertaken using a private participation scheme.[10]

Other Factors Affecting Logistics Performance

Airports have generally improved in Central American countries in the last few years, as they have in most Latin American countries. The increasing flow of passengers (due to growing tourism and increased economic activity) has created demand for improvements, which were made largely through public-private agreements. Latin America and the Caribbean is the region with the largest participation of the private sector in airports, both in number of facilities and in investment commitments; the preferred public-private partnership agreement is the concession, in most cases including runways and terminals (World Bank, Private Participation in Infrastructure Database). The improvement has been centered on the main airports, usually one or two per country; many secondary airports still constrain the efficient movement of freight. Although freight movements are generally not the driver of airport modernization, freight activities have benefited from it. Usually trade facilitation procedures are better organized and have faster responses in airports than in other gateways, particularly with regard to courier and express services. One of the key elements for moving freight is the existence of freight terminals in the airport (or close by), which helps organize and expedite the loading and unloading of freight. These needs become more relevant when perishable products are traded: diversification of exports toward nontraditional "specialty" products (such as tropical fruits, flowers, or fishing products) highlights the need for coordinated efforts among the public and the private sector.

Maritime transportation services basically include shipping lines with regular routes (whose freight is transported mostly in containers), bulk transportation (dry and liquid), and specialized services. Generally speaking, the first type of service is usually provided by regular lines, while the others are provided to satisfy specific demands. Markets for shipping services are habitually competitive, and shipping lines go where demands calls.[11] The regular service available for a country depends on the decisions that shipping lines make on how to organize the routes, defining ports of call, frequency, and type of vessel. Therefore, although the service is provided by international commercial companies, it is dependent— to a large extent—on decisions made by governments, particularly with regard to the organization of ports. In Central America the provision of maritime service is adequate, although uneven: Guatemala and the Dominican Republic are above the regional average in the liner shipping connectivity index (prepared by UNCTAD 2008),[12] while Nicaragua, Honduras, and El Salvador are below it; Costa Rica's rating fell after 2006, reflecting a decline in the operational performance of its Atlantic ports. This is mostly the result of the port policy adopted by the countries, the market size, and the existence of alternative ports (and their landside accessibility). There is also some cartelization of refrigerated freight in the shipping lines linking Central America and the Caribbean with the U.S. Gulf of Mexico.[13] Air freight transportation has few restrictions on commercial access and has more freedom than passenger transport services. A significant part of freight is transported in passenger planes, while the rest is transported in special freight planes. The main restrictions on the expansion of air freight transportation are centered on low demand, higher competitiveness of alternative modes (maritime and roads), and in some cases weak infrastructure at regional airports. A distinctive characteristic of air freight transportation is the need for fast processing during inspection and control procedures, to the point that customs (and other agencies) generally perform better at airports than at ports and border crossings.

Large companies (national or international) have usually optimized their supply chain, following the dominant trend, to reduce total logistics costs by optimizing (basically) inventory levels, transport costs, and quality of service. Small and medium enterprises tend to have much higher logistics costs than large companies, as a result not only of smaller scale, but also of limited capacity to organize the flow of materials throughout the procurement, production, and distribution processes. Partial studies in Latin America show that logistics costs tend to be two to three times higher for SMEs than for large companies. SMEs are important sources of employment, and their competitiveness is of great interest to countries and subnational entities. Support for the logistics development of SMEs can be linked to territorial policies, including the deployment of logistics platforms, which offer the possibility of sharing resources. In recent years, the development of areas for conducting logistics activity has exploded, and the impact has been particularly useful to SMEs. Public cold warehouses are a special case because Central American countries have very few public access facilities (Global Cold Chain Alliance 2009).

The organization of modern logistics practice, as summarized above, has led producing and trading firms to outsource several logistics functions, particularly distribution. Under this scheme, a specialized firm (the logistics operator) receives the products and distributes them according to the client's orders and the shipper's level of service request. The logistics operator has different functions than traditional transport firms or cargo agents, as they provide tailored services, usually under multiyear contracts, and maintain fluid communications with cargo owners. Many transportation firms have adopted this scheme and become logistics operators. This process can be viewed as one of modernization, generally led by market forces, but some agents have had difficulty adapting to the new needs, particularly small or individual trucking operators in remote areas. Logistics platforms could be implemented to enhance the efficiency of trade flows. These types of facilities play an important role in reducing the negative externalities that freight movements cause in densely populated areas. They also play a pivotal role in integrating SMEs to global supply chains by providing economies of scale in transport and inventory management. Efficiency gains are larger when these facilities are in periurban areas, near ports or airports, or in areas adjacent to high-traffic border crossings.

Current Initiatives

Several regional initiatives are in line with the logistics issues covered in this book. They can be grouped as infrastructure, trade facilitation, transport services, and analytical work.

In the area of infrastructure, the Mesoamerican project is an agreement that was signed in 2008 between Belize, Costa Rica, El Salvador, Guatemala, Honduras, Mexico, Nicaragua, Panama, and Colombia. It covers several areas, two of which are related to trade logistics: transport and trade facilitation. In transport, the project includes the construction of a regional highway network: the Red Internacional de Carreteras Mesoamericanas (RICAM).The first RICAM project is the Pacific corridor, a high-standard, 3,600-kilometer highway linking all signatory countries. The initiative goes beyond the construction, operation, and maintenance of the highway and includes the modernization of facilities and equipment in border crossings along the corridor. The initiative also addresses road safety, and technical studies are currently under way to identify critical sections and define the required improvements.

The Mesoamerican project includes a pillar to address challenges linked to trade facilitation, which is based on implementation of the Procedimiento Mesoamericano para el Tránsito Internacional de Mercancías (TIM), an improvement of the transit procedures aimed at reducing the time required for trucks to cross borders in transit. This project is being implemented with the support of SIECA, which is also involved in the Proyecto de Diseño y Aplicación de Políticas Comunes Centroamericanas (ADDAPCA) with support from the European Union. Initiatives under this project include regulatory harmonization of commercial policies and linked regulations (tariffs, customs procedures, and technical norms) among signatory countries.[14] Another relevant initiative in this area is implementation of the Paso Facil among the signatories of CA-4. Paso Facil is a mechanism for expediting procedures at the border. It encompasses initiatives to improve coordination and communications among border agencies in the different countries and to adopt standard documentation.

The Comité Técnico Regional Permanente de Transportes (COMI-TRANS), created under the framework of SIECA, comprises the heads of the roads directorates as well as sectoral experts. Its main objective is to reach agreement with a view to harmonizing transport policies in the region. Many relevant initiatives are under way under COMITRANS. First, the committee has recommended the creation of a regional training center for surface transportation companies, with the objective of raising the level of professionalization of firms in the sector. The center is intended to train drivers and other staff employed by transportation companies. COMITRANS has also undertaken the task of drafting regional manuals in sensitive areas of transport regulation. The first addresses the transportation of hazardous materials and waste, which includes actions to strengthen the capacity of public agencies with oversight of the sector. The second intends to harmonize regulations for vehicle inspections, with the ultimate goal of improving the state of the existing truck fleet and road safety conditions. Finally, a regional manual on road safety intends to foster coordination of national policies in this sensitive area.

The Comisión Centroamericana de Transporte Marítimo (COCA-TRAM) is leading several initiatives to strengthen harmonization of port policies in the region, such as the definition of a common port strategy and the simplification of maritime procedures. COCATRAM is also working to promote short-distance shipping services within the region.

Under the framework of the Mesoamerican project, the viability of increased railway transportation in the region is currently under study.

Policy Priorities to Enhance Trade Logistics

The analysis in this chapter suggests two main messages: first, logistics performance is relatively weak, and there is ample room for improvement; second, the diversity of factors influencing logistics performance calls for a broad range of coordinated activities by the public and private sectors.

Traditional trade patterns in Central America and recent trends resulting from implementation of the DR-CAFTA highlight the need for improved logistics. First, Central America's export base has traditionally relied heavily on agricultural commodities. Although its relevance has declined in recent years, agriculture continues to be a very relevant sector (encompassing 22 percent of regional GDP and employing 50 percent of the total workforce; SIECA 2009), particularly in Guatemala and Nicaragua. Given their low value added, transport costs (and logistics costs in general) constitute a large share of the total cost of commodities and are thus a key determinant of their competitiveness in international markets. As industry continues to develop in the region, countries have begun to reduce their reliance on agricultural commodities. However, competition from Asian countries (particularly after the expiration of the Multi-Fibre Agreement in 2005) brings to light inefficiencies in the local supply chains. Geographic proximity to the U.S. market has helped *maquilas* in Central America to offset some of these inefficiencies, but improvements are required if the region is to compete with Asia. The rapid growth of intraregional trade is a positive sign, as Central America's trade is highly concentrated in the U.S. market. But it also calls for enhanced road infrastructure and harmonized customs requirements, to ensure smoother flows. Finally, the expansion of nontraditional exports (such as tropical fruits or flowers) emphasizes the need to modernize logistics services to comply with the requirements of international customers, with a focus on improving air freight services and cold chain logistics. Based on these conclusions, the policies with the highest priorities pertain to surface transportation, border management, ports, and logistics software and institutions.

Surface Transportation

There is a need to increase private participation in the road sector. There are several ways to promote public-private partnerships, particularly on highways. Although most of the measures associated with increasing private participation in roads are under the oversight of national governments, measures can be undertaken at the regional level to achieve stronger synergies. Recommended actions are as follows:

- *Implement output-based contracts for rehabilitation and maintenance.* There are multiple examples in the region, like the contracts for rehabilitation and maintenance (CREMA) contracts in Brazil, Argentina, and Uruguay or the Prestación Privada de Servicios projects in Mexico. This modality helps to increase efficiency in the allocation of funds for the road sector and could have a substantial impact given the specific challenges this sector faces in Central America (particularly those linked with natural disasters).

- *Analyze the possibility of concessioning specific sections of the Pacific corridor.* Some sections of the corridor register sufficient levels of traffic to make concessioning attractive to private investors. Implementing this recommendation is especially feasible in Costa Rica and Guatemala, which have adequate frameworks for public-private partnerships.

- *Develop (or strengthen, depending on the country) public-private partnership frameworks at the national level.* This step encompasses not only the legal aspects of such partnerships, but also the institutional capacity required to design and implement them efficiently. Efforts to harmonize the public-private partnership frameworks in Central American countries would help to avoid competition among them and thus to attract private investors.

In addition, it is important to focus road investments on strategic points—urban bypasses and port access should be prioritized to improve highway circulation and relieve urban congestion—and to conduct research and collect data on the road sector and security. Informed decision making in infrastructure investment requires reliable data on the condition of roads. The development of a set of harmonized indicators at the regional level would be particularly helpful for managing the shared trade corridors more effectively. Additionally, a road freight security and protection program should be prepared by security forces. Firms may contribute by refining their personnel selection process, mapping the incidence of crime and sharing results with the authorities, loading trucks in ways less attractive to thieves, installing vehicle-monitoring devices, and improving channels of communication with the security authorities.

Also important would be undertaking a program to modernize the trucking industry. This effort would include reviewing current regulations, considering the inclusion of a unified register, and establishing a cargo document to be issued by carriers (a bill of lading, as is done in most countries). In addition, a program to renew the fleet, promoting the scratching of the oldest vehicles and providing incentives to incorporate new, more efficient, and clean trucks, would improve efficiency. It also would be important to implement a professionalization program, including mandatory training for workers (linked to the issuance of a professional driver's license) and entrepreneurs. Good examples are available from the Argentine and Uruguayan experiences.

Finally, it is important to harmonize regulations with key trading partners. As trade with Mexico increases, the lack of harmonization, forcing the loading and unloading of goods at the border, generates marked inefficiencies. The harmonization of standards, at least for the circulation of trailers (switching only tractor units at the border), may help to reduce logistics costs. The setup of logistics zones close to border crossings should be promoted.

Ports

New port legislation and institutional organization are needed. A new legal and regulatory framework would help enhance the performance of ports. Some of the key issues for the new legal framework, which should be consulted with the many relevant stakeholders, are creation of a centralized national policy and administrative organization, incentives to attract private investment in infrastructure, long-term planning, effective mechanisms for users' participation, and an adequate regulatory entity.

Border Management

The integration of border control functions is the main challenge to facilitating trade. For example, conducting joint inspections (customs, agriculture and food, narcotics, public health) would eliminate overlapping procedures, which are costly and time consuming. To improve intraregional trade flows, efforts could be made to improve the layout of infrastructure and the operational flow of the busiest or most strategic border crossings.

Logistics Software and Institutions

Efficient business logistics need the support of regulations and promotional policies. Two initiatives are proposed in this regard. The first is to facilitate access to warehousing, particularly for SMEs; logistics platforms are the most efficient way to do this. The second is to support the development of cold chain facilities. Guatemala has a very small capacity of refrigerated warehouses, and they are mostly private, with only 15 percent of the total capacity of refrigerated warehouses available for public use (Global Cold Chain Alliance 2009). In this context, the development of logistics centers would have a very positive effect on trade and help reduce the negative externalities produced by freight operations in densely populated areas. Various Latin American countries have designed networks of logistics platforms (Colombia, Peru); mapping the main value chains and analyzing their performance would help to identify the most appropriate locations and the type of functions that logistics centers should perform. Since logistics centers require the coordinated participation of several government entities, there would be a need to establish a coordination council—a national logistics council—at a high level of government, composed of representatives of the government areas involved (reflecting users and providers of logistics services) as well as representatives of the main private stakeholders. The council might be supported by a small technical office (a logistics observatory), responsible for generating key indicators of performance and knowledge with regard to trade logistics.

Notes

1. SIECA's Regional Trade Statistics are available at http://estadisticas.sieca.int/.
2. Malaysia is classified as an upper-middle-income country, while Thailand is considered a lower-middle-income one.

3. The 2009 LPI clearly shows that there has been a general improvement in logistics performance in the world.

4. The slight changes in the sample (several countries included in 2007 were no longer present in the 2009 LPI, and some new ones were incorporated) may have some effect when comparing ranks.

5. The LPI is based on perception surveys, which are subjective and, as such, highly sensitive to specific situations (positive or negative) affecting the interviewee. This can produce marked variations in the scores assigned.

6. Textiles, chemical products, and processed foodstuffs.

7. The region has 23 ports, 10 in the Caribbean and 13 along the Pacific coast (Sánchez and Wilmsmeier 2005).

8. The Caucedo container terminal, in the Dominican Republic, is the main exception.

9. The Pacific corridor starts in the City of Puebla, Mexico, and stretches along the Pacific coast to reach the City of Panama. It extends more than 3,000 kilometers and is the shorter link between Puebla and Panama, which makes it the most efficient corridor for integration in Mesoamerica.

10. The study proposes to focus on the Mexico-Guatemala border crossing (Ciudad Hidalgo-Tecun Uman) and the Costa Rica–Panama border. The large volume of trade that passes through these two crossings makes them attractive for private investors. The other two projects are a grouping of border facilities among CA-4 countries and along the border between Nicaragua and Costa Rica.

11. There is still some cartelization in the shipping services linking Caribbean ports with the U.S. Gulf of Mexico.

12. The index is calculated on the basis of five components: (1) the number of ships; (2) the container-carrying capacity of those ships; (3) the number of companies; (4) the number of services; and (5) the maximum ship size, always referring to the ships that are deployed to provide liner shipping services to a country's port(s) (UNCTAD 2008).

13. CADA (Central America Discussion Agreement) is an organization that works to obtain common decisions for most of the shipping lines covering this route, as conferences used to do in the past.

14. Costa Rica, El Salvador, Guatemala, Honduras, and Nicaragua. Panama will be included shortly.

References

Anderson, J. E., and E. van Wincoop. 2004. "Trade Costs." Working Paper on Economics 593, Boston College, Department of Economics, Boston, MA.

Bernard, A., J. B. Jensen, and P. K. Schott. 2006. "Trade Costs, Firms, and Productivity." *Journal of Monetary Economics* 53 (5): 917–37.

Bernard, A., J. B. Jensen, S. Redding, and P. K. Schott. 2007. "Firms in International Trade." *Journal of Economic Perspectives* 21 (3): 105–30.

Dutz, M. 2005. "Road Freight Logistics, Competition, and Innovation: Downstream Benefits and Policy Implications." Policy Research Working Paper 3768, World Bank, Washington, DC.

EIU (Economist Intelligence Unit). 2008. "Costa Rica Country Profile." EIU, London.

———. 2009. "Latin America Economy: DR-CAFTA's Progress amid Recession." EIU, London, November 26.

Hummels, D. L. 2001. "Time as a Trade Barrier." Purdue University, Department of Economics, Krannert School of Management, West Lafayette, IN.

Hummels, D. L., and G. Schaur. 2009. "Hedging Price Volatility Using Fast Transport." NBER Working Paper 15154, National Bureau of Economic Research, Cambridge, MA.

Global Cold Chain Alliance. 2009. *Global Cold Chain Logistics Report 2008–2009*. London: Global Cold Chain Alliance and Transport Intelligence. www.transportintelligence.com.

IDB (Inter-American Development Bank). 2009. "Proyecto Mesoamérica / Hojas Informativas." IDB Bank, Washington, DC. http://portal2.sre.gob.mx/mesoamer ica/dmdocuments/Hoja%20Informativa%20Transporte.pdf.

Limao, N., and A. J. Venables. 2001. "Infrastructure, Geographical Disadvantage, Transport Costs, and Trade." *World Bank Economic Review* 15 (3): 451–79.

Melitz, M. J. 2003. "The Impact of Trade on Intra-Industry Reallocations and Aggregate Industry Productivity." *Econometrica* 71 (6): 1695–725.

Private Participation in Infrastructure Database. World Bank, Washington, DC. http://ppi.worldbank.org.

Sadikov, A. M. 2007. "Border and Behind-the-Border Trade Barriers and Country Exports." IMF Working Paper wp/07/292, International Monetary Fund, Washington, DC.

Sánchez, R., and G. Wilmsmeier. 2005. "Bridging Infrastructural Gaps in Central America: Prospects and Potential for Maritime Transport." Economic Comission for Latin America and the Caribbean, Santiago.

SIECA (Secretaría de Integración Económica Centroamericana). 2009. *La integración económica centroamericana ante los efectos de la crisis económica internacional*. Guatemala. http://www.sieca.org.gt/site/VisorDocs.aspx?IDDOC= Cache/17990000003083/17990000003083.swf.

UNCTAD (United Nations Conference on Trade and Development). 2008. *Liner Connectivity Index*. Geneva.

WEF (World Economic Forum). 2009. *Global Enabling Trade Report*. Davos, Switzerland: WEF.

———. 2010. *Global Enabling Trade Report*. Davos, Switzerland: WEF.

Wilson, J. S., C. L. Mann, and T. Otsuki. 2003. "Trade Facilitation and Economic Development: Measuring the Impact." Policy Research Working Paper 2988, World Bank, Washington, DC.

———. 2005. "Assessing the Benefits of Trade Facilitation: A Global Perspective." *World Economy* 28 (6): 841–71.

World Bank. 2004. "Honduras Investment Climate Assessment." World Bank, Washington, DC.

———. 2006a. "Auditoria sobre facilitación del transporte y el comercio." Working Paper, World Bank, Washington, DC.

———. 2006b. "Costa Rica Country Economic Memorandum." World Bank, Washington, DC.

———. 2006c. "Project Appraisal Document: Nicaragua 4th Road Maintenance and Rehabilitation Project." World Bank, Washington, DC.

———. 2007a. "Investment Climate Assessment." World Bank, Washington, DC.

———. 2007b. "Public Expenditure Review." World Bank and Inter-American Development Bank, Washington, DC.

———. 2009. "Border Management Modernization: A Practical Guide for Reformers." World Bank, Washington, DC.

Yeaple, S. R. 2005. "A Simple Model of Firm Heterogeneity, International Trade, and Wages." *Journal of International Economics* 65 (1): 1–20.

CHAPTER 8

Access to Credit and Productivity in Central America

Inessa Love, Teresa Molina Millán, and Rashmi Shankar

As we have seen elsewhere in this volume, trade liberalization is an opportunity that calls for significant policy effort if countries are to realize the potential benefits. Complementary policies are examined in depth in various companion pieces to this chapter, with a view to understanding how the countries of Central America can become competitive enough to take advantage of the improved market access granted by the Dominican Republic–Central America Free Trade Agreement (DR-CAFTA). Productivity improvements are an important component of this enhanced competitiveness. Here we focus on the relationship between productivity improvements, access to finance, and likelihood of exporting.

A well-functioning financial system is an important component of economic growth and development. Numerous studies have found a strong and significant relationship between the level of financial development and long-run growth (Beck, Levine, and Loayza 2000; Calderón, Fajnzylber, and Loayza 2004, among others). Specifically, financial intermediaries and markets help to reallocate credit to its most productive uses and reduce transaction costs and information frictions (Levine 1997; Love 2003).

The international trade literature has traditionally focused on factor endowments, technology, and scale economies as sources of comparative advantage and used these as determinants of trade flows between countries. More recently, the role of finance has been named as another important influence on the pattern of international trade flows (Beck 2002). Thus, financial development may serve as a source of comparative advantage that might influence a country's trade patterns.

A growing literature has found evidence of the comparative advantage that financial development provides to exporters or firms entering foreign markets. In particular, some papers have argued that financially developed countries export relatively more in sectors that require more outside finance. For example, in a cross section of 56 countries and 36 industries, Beck (2002, 2003) and Svaleryd and Vlachos (2002, 2005) show that countries with better-developed financial systems have higher export shares and trade balances in industries that use more external finance. In another cross-sectional analysis for 1995, Becker and Greenberg (2005) reach a similar conclusion using different industry measures of fixed up-front costs. Similarly, Hur, Raj, and Riyanto (2004) show that a better financial environment is associated with a larger 1980–90 average share of exports in sectors with fewer internal funds and hard assets.

Manova (2008) presents further evidence on the causal influence of finance on trade by exploiting shocks to the level of local financial development. She uses incidences of stock market liberalizations and shows that liberalization increases exports disproportionately more in financially vulnerable sectors that require more outside finance or employ fewer collateralizable assets. Such evidence confirms that finance has a causal influence on trade; it does not simply follow trade and growth.

Another link between local financial development and trade is explored in Manova and Chor (2009), who show that tighter credit conditions, as measured by interbank lending rates, reduce a country's exports to the United States. This reduction is even more pronounced in industries that are likely to face more financing constraints (such as industries that require extensive external finance, have few collateralizable assets, or have limited access to trade credit). They argue that financially vulnerable industries are more sensitive to limited availability of finance and, further, that this sensitivity increased during the recent financial crises. In addition, they find that exports of countries with stronger pre-crisis fundamentals were less sensitive to a decline in trade that followed the crisis, suggesting that stronger financial markets may mitigate the otherwise damaging impact of a crisis.

These studies show that development of financial markets and intermediaries has a significant and causal impact on trade. There are many channels through which local financial development may influence trade. One channel is direct—the provision of trade finance to exporting or importing firms. Trade finance is a critical part of the institutions that countries need to take full advantage of trade-related opportunities. As some put it, trade finance "oils the wheels of trade," which is especially vital for countries with limited access to finance (World Bank 2003). The importance of trade finance is further underscored by the following quote (italics added) from Auboin (2007):

> Since more than 90 percent of trade transactions involve some form of credit, insurance, or guarantee, one can reasonably say that *trade finance is the lifeline of trade*. Producers and traders in developing or least-developed countries need to have access to affordable flows of trade financing and insurance to be able to import and export, and hence integrate in world trade. From that perspective, *an efficient financial system is one indispensable infrastructure to allow trade to happen.*

Another important channel through which financial development can affect trade is its impact on productivity, which allows firms to gain comparative advantage in global markets. Several models provide theoretical justification for the proposition that credit affects growth through its impact on productivity. In these models, the financial sector provides real services by alleviating information and transaction costs, in particular making the longer-gestation higher-return projects more attractive (see, for example, Levine 1991; Bencivenga, Smith, and Starr 1995). However, the existing empirical evidence on this channel is still limited.

At the macro level, Easterly and Levine (2001) show that total factor productivity (TFP) accounts for most of the cross-country variation in economic development and growth. They go as far as to claim that factor accumulation is not important for future growth, but productivity is. Levine and Zervos (1998) argue, "The major channel through which growth is linked to stock markets and banks is through productivity growth." Combining macro and micro data, Jeong and Townsend (2005) define a growth model with micro foundations and find that 73 percent of TFP growth in Thailand between 1976 and 1996 was the result of occupational shifts and financial deepening. However, rapid credit growth accompanied by resource misallocation could have an adverse impact on productivity. For example, Ghani and Suri (1999) argue that the rapid growth of bank credit was associated with negative growth of productivity in Malaysia because the allocation of credit was inefficient.

Among related papers, Bernstein and Nadiri (1993) estimate the effect of financial structure on productivity growth in U.S. manufacturing companies. Their focus is on estimating the impact of the agency cost of debt and the signaling benefits of dividends on productivity growth. Nickell and Nicholitsas (1999) find that financial pressure (defined as the ratio of interest payments to cash flow) has a positive effect on productivity. Using data from the United Kingdom and Italy, Schiantarelli and Sembenelli (1999) show that firms with a larger proportion of long-term debt in their capital structure have improved subsequent performance, measured as profitability, sales growth, and total factor productivity. Similar patterns are found in Schiantarelli and Jaramillo (1999) for Ecuador and Schiantarelli and Srivastava (1999) for India. However, due to data limitations, all these studies focus on the effect of leverage on productivity.

Several recent papers estimate the productivity impact of investment climate variables. Escribano and Guasch (2005) analyze the impact of different variables from investment climate assessments in Guatemala, Honduras, and Nicaragua. Among other results, they find that, by engaging in an external audit of their financial statements, firms could increase their productivity. Following their methodology, Fajnzylber, Guasch, and López (2008) conduct a similar study using investment climate assessment data, but their pooled database includes 16 Latin American countries. They also look at the productivity effect of indicators of governance, infrastructure, access to finance, and technology. However, they do not obtain consistent estimators of the productivity effect of access to credit indicators when they use their aggregate database, probably due to the heterogeneity among subregions in Latin America.

Numerous studies have also established a significant positive relationship between export expansion and economic growth via a productivity effect. The early literature on finance and growth established the robust relationship between the level of financial development and long-run growth (King and Levine 1993; Levine 2005). Once the link was established at the macro level, subsequent literature has aimed to understand the channels through which such a link may operate. Rajan and Zingales (1998), Demirgüç-Kunt and Maksimovic (1998), and Wurgler (2000) argue that finance may operate by allowing firms to invest in potentially profitable growth opportunities and thus support efficient allocation of capital. Love (2003) uses the Euler-equation approach and shows that financing constraints are more severe in countries with lower levels of financial development.

Productivity growth appears to be an important channel through which finance may affect overall economic development and growth. Gatti and Love (2006) use firm-level data and confirm a positive relationship between a firm's access to finance and its TFP. Ayyagari, Demirgüç-Kunt, and Maksimovic (2007) find that access to finance has a significant impact on the rate of innovation, which can also be linked to TFP and growth. Two mechanisms are hypothesized. First, the export-led growth theory suggests that exporting enhances productivity growth through a learning-by-doing process. Exporters improve productivity because they enter foreign markets, which increases the competitive pressures on them, while also enabling them to exploit economies of scale. Firms that enter the international market are also more likely to acquire new technology, which, in turn, contributes to productivity improvements (Almeida and Fernandes 2008).

However, an alternative theory highlights a self-selection process through which only competitive firms enter foreign markets. Firms that export incur additional costs, perhaps to modify domestic products for foreign consumption, for transportation, distribution, or marketing, or for skilled personnel to manage foreign networks. These costs are entry barriers that more productive firms are more likely to be able to overcome (Roberts and Tybout 1997; Bernard and Jensen 1999). Export markets are also likely to be more competitive than domestic markets, making it harder for less productive firms to enter. Firms might even be forward looking, with the desire to export leading them to improve productivity so as to become competitive in foreign markets (Wagner 2007).

Both mechanisms are plausible, but their importance is likely to vary across countries and industries. In fact, more evidence has found that, in the self-selection process, more efficient firms enter the export market and that this is the main reason why exporters are more productive than nonexporters (Yan, Chung, and Roberts 2000).

In this chapter we analyze the relationship between productivity, access to finance, and exports using a sample of manufacturing firms in Central America. Since we run a cross-sectional regression with one year of data, we are not able to infer causality. Rather, we present a plausible argument of how higher productivity may set off virtuous circles of opportunity and growth in Central America.

Productivity and Access to Financial Services in Central America

Assessing the role of financial services in determining productivity is particularly relevant in the context of regional integration in Central America. Although the region experienced high GDP growth during the years preceding the current financial crisis, productivity gains were limited and should be the focus of both public policy and private sector strategy. Figure 8.1 explores differences in TFP growth between the median country of Central America and other regions. This evidence suggests that Central America's TFP growth has not kept pace with that of other regions. In fact, except for the period from 1991 to 1995, Central America's TFP growth rates have been lower than those of most other regions. However, differences with Latin America's median country are not large. While Latin American TFP growth has improved in the past five years, both Latin America and Central America have been at the lower end of the sample since 1996. While East Asia and the Pacific, Central Asia, and South Asia experienced TFP growth of more than 1.5 percent between 2001 and 2005, TFP growth in Central America contracted slightly (–0.3 percent). From 1981 to 2005, Central America experienced average productivity growth of 0.34 percent a year, similar to Latin America and well below East and South Asia.

There is, however, significant country heterogeneity within the Central American region, as shown in figure 8.2, and variation across time for individual countries. Nicaragua and Honduras are well behind the rest

Figure 8.1   TFP Growth Rates, by Region, 1981–2005

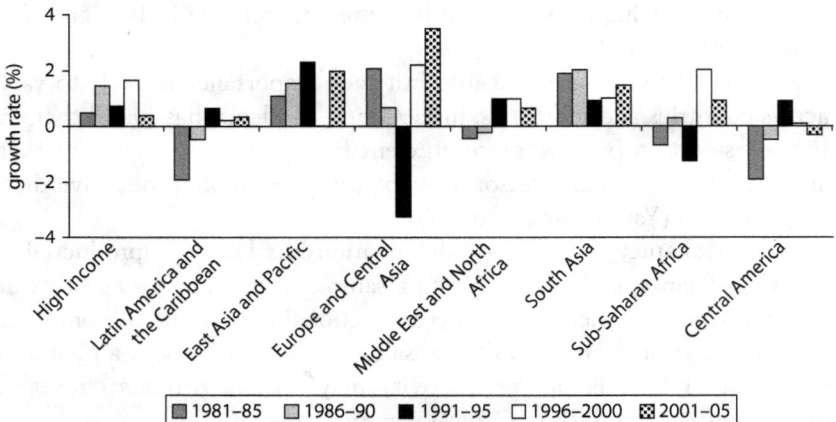

Legend: ■ 1981–85   ☐ 1986–90   ■ 1991–95   ☐ 1996–2000   ▨ 2001–05

Source: Auhtors' calculations.

Figure 8.2   TFP Growth Rates in Central America, by Country, 1981–2005

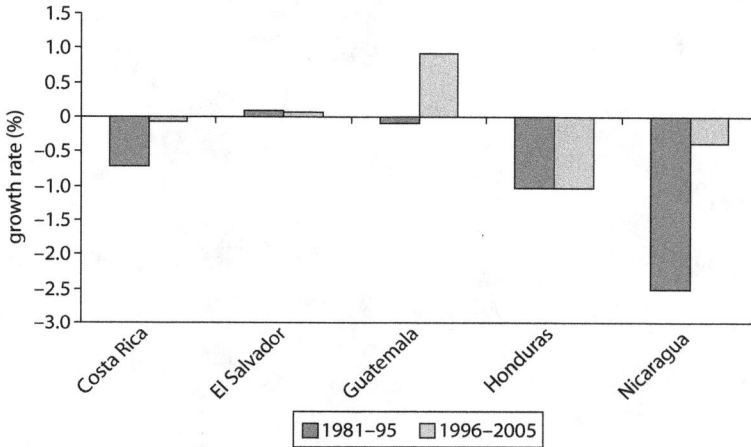

Source: Authors' calculations.

of the countries within the region. In the last decade Guatemala achieved the most improvement in productivity.

The financial sector in Central America grew substantially in the last decade. The average credit-to-GDP ratio rose from 29.41 percent in 1998 to 41.35 percent in 2008, while average M2 (measure of money supply) to GDP rose from 30.5 to 37.8 percent. Although financial depth varies significantly from one country to another (see figure 8.3), financial intermediation in Central America is above the average in Latin America. Another financial indicator that reflects the level of development of the region's financial system is the cost of banking services. The interest rate margins (the accounting value of a bank's net interest revenue as a share of its total earning assets) and overhead costs (the accounting value of a bank's overhead costs as share of its total assets) are taken as measures of the efficiency of the financial system. Central America's margins are similar to the average of Latin American countries, but larger than those of other developing countries. Within Central America, banks in Guatemala have the highest costs. Moreover, access to credit remains limited in Central America. The composite indicator developed by Beck, Demirgüç-Kunt, and Martínez Peria (2007) measures the percentage of the adult population with access to an account with a financial intermediary. The entire region is well behind the median of Latin America, especially Nicaragua. Although international comparative data on the extent to which firms and households use financial services remain limited, this index shows how far

Figure 8.3   Credit to the Private Sector and M2 as a Percentage of GDP in Central America, by Country, 2008

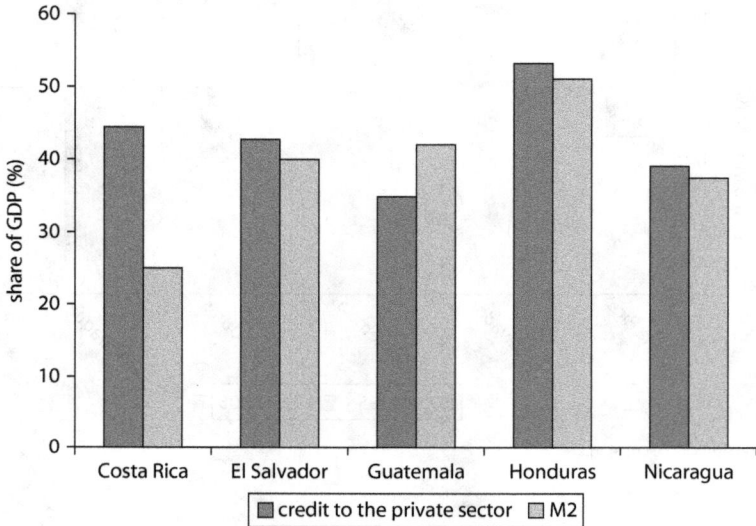

Source: Beck, Demirgüç-Kunt, and Levine 2000; World Bank, World Development Indicators.

Central America is from other Latin American countries in terms of financial breadth. Beck, Demirgüç-Kunt, and Martínez Peria (2007) also construct indicators of geographic barriers to accessing financial services. Table 8.1 reports the geographic and demographic penetration of bank branches and automated teller machines (ATMs) in the region. Costa Rica, El Salvador, and Guatemala are around the Latin American level of penetration, while Honduras and Nicaragua are well behind. These indicators are only crude proxies for geographic access, however, since branches and ATMs are never distributed equally across a country but are clustered in cities and some large towns.

Overall, even though the financial system has grown, access to finance remains a development issue for public policy, and productivity growth remains weak. Is there a link between lack of financial access and productivity for Central American firms? We next discuss the data used to address this question.

The Data

We use data from the 2005 and 2006 rounds of the World Bank enterprise survey for Central America. We construct a pooled sample with

Table 8.1   Geographic and Demographic Penetration of Branches and ATMs in Central America, by Country

Country and region	Branch		ATM	
	Geographic penetration	Demographic penetration	Geographic penetration	Demographic penetration
Costa Rica	7.52	9.59	10.07	12.83
El Salvador	14.58	4.62	34.89	11.07
Guatemala	11.49	10.12	22.93	20.20
Honduras	0.46	0.73	2.22	3.56
Nicaragua	1.29	2.85	1.18	2.61
Latin America and the Caribbean	4.94	7.50	10.61	12.51

Source: World Bank 2003.
Note: Geographic penetration refers to the number of branches or ATMs per 1,000 square kilometers. Demographic penetration refers to the number of branches or ATMs per 100,000 people.

Table 8.2   Distribution of Firms in Central America, by Country and Size of Firm

Country	Year	Number of firms	Size of firm[a]			
			Micro	Small	Medium	Large
Costa Rica	2005	343	170	111	27	35
El Salvador	2006	467	122	190	53	102
Guatemala	2006	328	90	136	37	65
Honduras	2006	263	96	93	31	43
Nicaragua	2006	365	160	156	30	19
Total		1,766	638	686	178	264

Source: Authors' calculations
a. Firm size is defined as follows: micro, less than 10 employees; small, from 11 to 50 employees; medium, from 51 to 100 employees; large, more than 100 employees.

information on more than 1,700 firms in the manufacturing sector from five countries in Central America. Table 8.2 reports the distribution of firms in our sample, by country and size. The sample is heavily dominated by micro and small firms, while medium and large firms constitute about a quarter of the sample. We follow the methodology in Gatti and Love (2006), who find credit to be positively and strongly associated with TFP using data from a cross section of Bulgarian firms.

The survey has several indicators of usage of financial products. Firms report whether they have a credit line or an overdraft facility. As one of our indicators of financial products usage, we use a variable (line) taking the

Table 8.3   Use of Financial Products in Central America, by Size of Firm
% of firms

Product	Micro	Small	Medium	Large	Total
Credit line	46	64	79	88	63
Checking account	74	92	95	95	86
Financial user	82	94	98	98	91
Financial obstacle	35	31	22	17	29

Source: Authors' calculations.

value of 1 if the firm has either overdraft or a credit line and 0 otherwise. We combine overdrafts and credit lines together, as both instruments represent easy access to immediate liquidity and both have short-term maturity. In addition, in some of the surveys (such as Costa Rica) the survey instrument does not allow us to separate lines of credit from overdraft usage. About 63 percent of firms in the sample have an overdraft facility, a line of credit, or both. Credit availability increases monotonically with firm size: 88 percent of large firms and only 46 percent of microenterprises have a credit line or overdraft facility. Table 8.3 reports the distribution of firms by their use of financial products and by size.

We also use an indicator for firms that use checking accounts. According to the literature, especially for microenterprises, the use of checking and savings products is equally or even more important than the use of credit products. About 86 percent of firms in the sample have a checking account. Among microenterprises, only 74 percent of all firms have a checking account, but among medium and large enterprises almost all firms have a checking account (95 percent in our sample). Although the use of checking accounts increases with size, the difference among size categories is smaller than in the use of credit products. This is likely because it is easier to open a checking account than obtain a line of credit or overdraft facility, especially for smaller firms.

Finally, we create an indicator variable for firms that use any financial product—that is, whether a checking account, overdraft facility, or line of credit. We call it financial user. This variable identifies firms that have any interaction with the formal financial sector and those that do not. Almost 91 percent of firms in the sample use at least one of these financial instruments. This again is monotonically related to size—82 percent of microenterprises, 94 percent of small firms, and 98 percent of medium and large firms use at least one financial instrument. Thus most firms in our sample use at least one financial product, and only a small percentage of firms are excluded (voluntarily or involuntarily) from the formal financial sector.

The survey also asks firms to rank various obstacles to doing business (rankings range from no obstacle to major obstacle). We create a dummy variable that equals 1 if the firm reports access to finance as a major or a severe obstacle and 0 otherwise. This measure of access is subjective in that it reports respondents' perceptions of the severity of the obstacle, whereas previously discussed measures capture a more objective dimension: actual use of financial products.

To summarize, we use one objective and three objective measures of the use of financial services: credit line, checking account, financial user, and financial obstacle. Descriptive statistics are presented in table 8.4.

Table 8.5 reports correlations among our four financial indicators. We observe a relatively low correlation between credit line and checking account use—about 23 percent. By construction, financial user is highly correlated with checking account or line of credit. The financial obstacle variable is not correlated with use of a checking account. This suggests again that checking account access is not perceived as a major or severe obstacle by firms in our sample. However, the financial obstacle variable is negatively correlated with credit line use. Thus, firms without access to a credit line are more likely to claim that financial access is a major or severe obstacle to operation of their business. When we tabulate the use of credit products against financial obstacle (not reported), we find that about 26 percent of firms with access to a credit line consider access to finance as a major or severe obstacle, compared to 35 percent of firms without access to a credit line. While the correlation is not large—only –10 percent—it is statistically significant at the 10 percent level.

The survey asks firms to report their share of domestic and external sales. We use this information to construct two variables used in our model to assess the relationship between productivity and exports. First, we construct a dummy that equals 1 if the firm exports at least 5 percent of its sales. We find that less than 15 percent of firms in our survey are exporters. We also use another proxy for export status, constructed as the share of domestic sales in total sales. The dummy variable measure has a more straightforward interpretation, and therefore we use it as the main measure in the regressions discussed below.

Table 8.4　Descriptive Statistics for Survey Variables

Variable	Minimum	25th percentile	50th percentile	75th percentile	Maximum	Mean	Standard deviation	Number
Log sales	4.52	10.30	11.69	13.41	19.82	11.92	2.26	1,667
Log value added	4.23	9.79	11.19	12.85	19.79	11.40	2.26	1,534
Log capital	3.13	8.41	9.98	11.62	18.43	10.11	2.41	1,333
Log labor	0.00	1.95	2.83	3.95	8.23	3.09	1.46	1,766
Log sales per worker	3.42	7.78	8.98	9.85	15.42	8.84	1.52	1,667
Log sales per capital	−4.32	0.92	1.85	2.89	9.30	1.96	1.60	1,312
TFP	−4.91	−0.63	−0.02	0.53	6.92	−0.01	1.06	1,312
TFP value added	−4.41	−0.63	−0.03	0.56	7.44	0.00	1.12	1,261
Log age	0.00	2.30	2.83	3.37	4.80	2.80	0.81	1,760
LLC	0.00	0.00	0.00	1.00	1.00	0.45	0.50	1,765
Credit line	0.00	0.00	1.00	1.00	1.00	0.63	0.48	1,764
Checking account	0.00	1.00	1.00	1.00	1.00	0.86	0.34	1,762
Financial user	0.00	1.00	1.00	1.00	1.00	0.91	0.29	1,763
Financial obstacle	0.00	0.00	0.00	1.00	1.00	0.29	0.46	1,742

Source: Authors' calculations.

Table 8.5   Correlations among Financial Indicators

	Checking account	Credit line	Financial user
Credit line	0.2371*	1	
Financial user	0.7912*	0.4094*	1
Financial obstacle	0.0024	−0.1004*	−0.0022

Source: Authors' calculations.
*$p < .10$.

Estimating Productivity

Firms also report the value of total sales and fixed assets as well as information on the number of employees, wages, and input costs. We use this information to obtain estimates of total factor productivity. TFP growth is often thought to be the result of product or production process innovations that increase the value produced using the same amount of factor inputs (that is, capital and labor). However, TFP also reflects unobserved improvements in the quality of factors of production related to human capital accumulation or the upgrading of physical infrastructure.

Recent years have seen a surge of interest in productivity analysis, and an extensive literature about different methodologies for estimating productivity has been developed. In this chapter we use a production function method that is based on the stochastic frontier approach and a parametric translog cost function to estimate the efficiency frontier. However, econometric issues arise when we estimate productivity as the difference between actual output and output estimated by a production function using actual quantities of inputs, as firm productivity can affect the choice of inputs. For example, firms that receive a productivity shock may alter their mix of inputs. This implies that the error and the regressors in our model might be correlated and that coefficient estimates obtained with ordinary least squares (OLS) might be biased. Various solutions have been proposed in the literature to overcome this problem. These include using country fixed effects that would deal with time-invariant individual effects and an instrumental variable strategy for choice of inputs. Although we are able to control for country and sector-specific effects, we do not have enough observations to build instrumental variables for input values.

As an alternative to fixed-effect regressions, Olley and Pakes (1996) develop a consistent semiparametric estimator, which solves the simultaneity problem by using a firm's investment choice to proxy unobserved productivity shocks. A strictly monotonous relationship between the proxy and output has to be met to obtain consistent estimates using this technique. This implies that any firm with no investment has to be dropped from the data, which reduces considerably the number of observations. Following this methodology, Levinsohn and Petrin (2000) argue that using information on choice of intermediate inputs such as demand for electricity—which tracks productivity shocks quite closely and cannot be stored—allows one to control effectively for productivity shocks and thus obtain consistent and unbiased estimates of capital and labor elasticity (see the discussion in Hallward-Driemeier, Iarossi, and Sokoloff 2002). However, we cannot follow either of these procedures since they do not fit the characteristics of our data set. The principal caveats that we face in our sample are the lack of information on the previous year's inputs and the reduced number of firms that report information on input proxies as expenditure on research and development or investment.

We use two measures of total factor productivity and one measure of labor productivity. The first measure is obtained as a residual from a regression with log sales as a dependent variable. The second measure is a residual from a regression with log value added as a dependent variable, and the third measure is the ratio of sales to number of employees.[1]

Table 8.6 presents production function estimates obtained using pooled OLS across countries. Labor is computed as the number of employees, while capital is the stock of fixed assets at the end of the previous fiscal year. We include country dummies to capture differences among countries. In an alternative specification, we add dummies for subsectors, but the results remain unchanged. The share of capital is estimated to be about 0.25, while the share of labor in output is close to 0.9. The sales regressions are estimated with an R^2 above 0.7. The second column reports a regression with value added as a dependent variable, which is used to obtain our main measure of TFP. The last column contains a regression of the determinants of labor productivity.

We find consistent results across three regressions. Among countries, firms from Costa Rica (the omitted category in all regressions) have the highest productivity, independent of the measure of productivity used, while firms from El Salvador have the lowest.

Our two measures of TFP are obtained as residuals from regressions in models 1 or 2, while our measure of labor productivity is the actual log of sales per worker (that is, the dependent variable in model 3).

Table 8.7 reports correlations among our three TFP measures. We find that both TFP measures obtained as residuals are highly correlated (correlation of nearly 90 percent), while labor productivity has a correlation of about 68 percent with each of the TFP measures.

Table 8.6   TFP Estimation

Variable	Log sales	Log value added	Log sales per worker
Log capital	0.253***	0.245***	
	(0.000)	(0.000)	
Log labor	0.976***	0.956***	
	(0.000)	(0.000)	
Log capital per worker			0.274***
			(0.000)
El Salvador	−1.597***	−1.446***	−1.376***
	(0.000)	(0.000)	(0.000)
Guatemala	−0.228**	−0.064	−0.219*
	(0.049)	(0.671)	(0.058)
Honduras	−0.266***	0.011	−0.277***
	(0.007)	(0.918)	(0.007)
Nicaragua	−0.559***	−0.271**	−0.522***
	(0.000)	(0.031)	(0.000)
Constant	7.055***	6.491***	7.488***
	(0.000)	(0.000)	(0.000)
Number of observations	1,312	1,261	1,312
R^2	0.723	0.67	0.327

Source: Authors' calculations.
Note: Robust p values are in parentheses.
* $p < .10$, ** $p < .05$, *** $p < .01$.

Table 8.7   Correlations among Estimated TFP and Observed Labor Productivity

	TFP	TFP value added	Labor productivity
TFP	1		
TFP value added	0.895***	1	
Labor productivity	0.764***	0.679***	1

Source: Authors' calculations.
*** $p < .01$.

TFP and Usage of Financial Products

We use estimated TFP to assess the relationship between the use of financial services and firms' productivity. Given the high correlation among the different estimates of TFP discussed in the previous section, we present the results using the TFP measure obtained from the value added regression and labor productivity.

We regress estimated TFP on country and firm characteristics described in the previous section.

To control for firms' characteristics with regard to productivity, we employ a rich set of control variables such as size, legal status, age, and landownership. In addition, we introduce country dummies to control for country fixed effects.

$$\text{TFP}_i = \alpha + \theta FI_t + \beta X_t + \gamma EXP_t + \varepsilon_t, \tag{8.1}$$

where TFP is the estimated residuals from equation 8.1;

$FI = (Checking_d; \ Credit \ line_d; \ Financial \ user_d; \ Financial \ Obstacle_d);$ and $X_t = \{log(age), \ LLC_d \ Land_d, \ Size_d \ Country_d\};$ and $EXP = Exports_d.$

Table 8.8 reports the basic results for our OLS model. We find that firms' age has no effect on productivity, probably because we are looking at a sample with a majority of old firms (firms' average age in our sample is about 17 years).

We do not find either a significant coefficient for the size dummy variables on TFP, partially because the sample is dominated by micro and small firms. However, we find that in terms of labor productivity, micro firms significantly below small firms, while small firms are significantly below medium and large firms (see table 8.9). This could be because of differences in education or labor skills, which are likely to be much lower in micro and small firms, due to the nature of their business.

We also control for other variables that could have an effect on productivity. We find that the legal status of the firm has an impact on the level of productivity. We define variable *LLC* as a dummy that equals 1 if the firm has limited liability (it includes publicly listed and privately held shareholding companies, limited liability companies, and limited partnerships) and 0 if the firm is a sole partnership or a partnership with unlimited liability. Limited liability companies seem to be more productive, and the effect is robust to different specifications. By contrast, landownership or belonging to a group of firms has no significant effect on the level of productivity of the company.

Productivity appears to be higher in exporting firms. We report the results with a dummy variable to account for the effect of being an exporter (dummy defined as 1 if the firm exports at least 5 percent of its sales). In an alternative specification, we use another proxy for export status (the reverse)—the share of domestic sales in total sales—and we obtain a significant and negative relationship. The OLS estimate suggests that being an exporter firm is associated with an increase in productivity

Table 8.8 Access to Credit and TFP value added

TFP value added

Variable	(1)	(2)	(3)	(4)	(5)	(6)
Checking account dummy		0.251*		0.192		
		(0.06)		(0.13)		
Line of credit dummy			0.194**	0.153*		
			(0.02)	(0.05)		
Financial user dummy					0.342**	
					(0.02)	
Financial obstacle						-0.046
						(0.57)
Micro dummy	0.057	0.075	0.114	0.117	0.076	0.056
	(0.65)	(0.55)	(0.38)	(0.36)	(0.55)	(0.66)
Small dummy	0.026	0.011	0.062	0.041	0.024	0.03
	(0.81)	(0.92)	(0.56)	(0.70)	(0.82)	(0.78)
Medium dummy	0.078	0.081	0.077	0.081	0.068	0.076
	(0.55)	(0.53)	(0.55)	(0.53)	(0.60)	(0.56)
Log of age	0.013	0.007	0.013	0.009	0.013	0.014
	(0.79)	(0.87)	(0.77)	(0.85)	(0.77)	(0.77)
LLC	0.278***	0.25**	0.275***	0.256**	0.248**	0.267***
	(0.01)	(0.01)	(0.00)	(0.01)	(0.01)	(0.01)
Direct exports dummy	0.184**	0.174*	0.174*	0.17*	0.172*	0.181*
	(0.05)	(0.06)	(0.05)	(0.06)	(0.06)	(0.05)
Landownership	-0.056	-0.065	-0.07	-0.074	-0.063	-0.055
	(0.55)	(0.48)	(0.45)	(0.42)	(0.48)	(0.57)
El Salvador	-0.116	-0.124	-0.181*	-0.173	-0.126	-0.12
	(0.28)	(0.24)	(0.09)	(0.11)	(0.23)	(0.27)

(continued next page)

Table 8.8 *(continued)*

Variable	(1)	(2)	(3)	(4)	(5)	(6)
Guatemala	0.193	0.208	0.134	0.159	0.205	0.186
	(0.12)	(0.10)	(0.26)	(0.19)	(0.10)	(0.13)
Honduras	0.244**	0.212*	0.197	0.179	0.235*	0.228*
	(0.05)	(0.09)	(0.11)	(0.15)	(0.06)	(0.07)
Nicaragua	0.142	0.188*	0.119	0.16	0.177	0.13
	(0.20)	(0.09)	(0.28)	(0.14)	(0.11)	(0.25)
Constant	-0.277	-0.472*	-0.389*	-0.513**	-0.582**	-0.252
	(0.23)	(0.06)	(0.09)	(0.04)	(0.03)	(0.29)
Number of observations	1,234	1,233	1,234	1,233	1,234	1,221
R^2	0.03	0.04	0.04	0.04	0.04	0.03

Source: Authors' calculations.

Note: Numbers in parentheses are robust p values.

* $p < .10$, ** $p < .05$, *** $p < .01$.

Table 8.9 Access to Credit and Labor Productivity

log sales per worker

Variable	(1)	(2)	(3)	(4)	(5)	(6)
Checking account dummy		0.627***		0.515***		
		(0.00)		(0.00)		
Line of credit dummy			0.426***	0.321***		
			(0.00)	(0.00)		
Financial user dummy					0.700***	
					(0.00)	
Financial obstacle						-0.143*
						(0.07)
Micro dummy	-0.72***	-0.653***	-0.586***	-0.564***	-0.672***	-0.705***
	(0.00)	(0.00)	(0.00)	(0.00)	(0.00)	(0.00)
Small dummy	-0.473***	-0.481***	-0.387***	-0.415***	-0.456***	-0.454***
	(0.00)	(0.00)	(0.01)	(0.00)	(0.00)	(0.00)
Medium dummy	-0.264	-0.271*	-0.233	-0.246	-0.274*	-0.238
	(0.10)	(0.08)	(0.15)	(0.12)	(0.08)	(0.17)
Log of age	-0.042	-0.034	-0.029	-0.025	-0.036	-0.037
	(0.43)	(0.53)	(0.56)	(0.62)	(0.50)	(0.50)
LLC	-0.1	-0.092	-0.145	-0.128	-0.116	-0.098
	(0.41)	(0.41)	(0.18)	(0.21)	(0.29)	(0.43)
Direct exports dummy	0.578	0.519	0.578	0.53***	0.542***	0.564***
	(0.00)***	(0.00)***	(0.00)***	(0.00)	(0.00)	(0.00)
Landownership	0.261**	0.235**	0.249**	0.231**	0.243**	0.265**
	(0.01)	(0.02)	(0.01)	(0.02)	(0.01)	(0.01)
El Salvador	-1.958***	-1.977***	-2.116***	-2.093***	-1.995***	-1.989***
	(0.00)	(0.00)	(0.00)	(0.00)	(0.00)	(0.00)

(continued next page)

Table 8.9 *(continued)*

Variable	*(1)*	*(2)*	*(3)*	*(4)*	*(5)*	*(6)*
Guatemala	-0.041	-0.012	-0.168	-0.113	-0.022	-0.065
	(0.75)	(0.92)	(0.16)	(0.35)	(0.86)	(0.61)
Honduras	0.015	-0.032	-0.093	-0.107	0.008	-0.012
	(0.91)	(0.80)	(0.49)	(0.41)	(0.95)	(0.93)
Nicaragua	-0.455**	-0.275*	-0.531***	-0.363**	-0.315**	-0.505**
	(0.03)	(0.08)	(0.01)	(0.01)	(0.03)	(0.02)
Constant	9.829***	9.241***	9.548***	9.135***	9.161***	9.869***
	(0.00)	(0.00)	(0.00)	(0.00)	(0.00)	(0.00)
Number of observations	1,630	1,628	1,630	1,628	1,629	1,608
R^2	0.44	0.46	0.46	0.48	0.46	0.44

Source: Authors' calculations.

Note: Numbers in parentheses are robust *p* values.

* $p < .10$, ** $p < .05$, *** $p < .01$.

of 0.17–0.18 points. Our OLS regressions cannot establish causality, as more productive firms may choose to become exporters or, once they become exporters, their productivity may increase because of competitive pressures.

We find that use of a credit line or an overdraft facility is positively and significantly associated with higher productivity (model 3). In addition, we find a positive and significant relationship between using a checking account and productivity (model 2). Having a checking account has a larger impact on TFP than having a line of credit. However, model 4 shows that, when included together, having a credit line remains significant, while having a checking account does not, indicating that the effect of having a checking account on value added productivity is not independent of having a credit line.

The combined measure of financial user has the largest impact in terms of magnitude, while our subjective measure of financial obstacle is negative, as expected (that is, higher obstacles, lower productivity), but it is not significant.

Next we assess whether our results are robust to using an alternative measure of productivity. Table 8.9 reports the results for labor productivity defined as the log of total sales per worker. Log of age remains negative, but not significant, while landownership, defined as a dummy variable taking the value of 1 when the company owns more than 50 percent of the land, is positive, but significant only in model 4.

As discussed, we find that micro and small firms are less productive than large firms; the difference in productivity between medium and large firms is not significant (partially because our sample of medium and large firms is quite small).

We find that credit line and checking account have the predicted and significant effect. In fact, the relationship between use of a checking account and productivity is more significant in regressions with log sales per worker than it is in regressions with a TFP measure. When both measures are included together, they both have significant coefficients (in model 4), while the magnitude of the checking account coefficient remains larger than the magnitude of the credit line coefficient. In addition, we find that the variable for financial obstacle now has a negative and significant relationship with labor productivity. The results we obtain are stronger with the measure of labor productivity for two reasons. First, the sample is larger because fewer data are required to estimate this regression (that is, we do not have to have values for fixed assets, which are often missing). Second, the TFP measure is an estimated variable (that is, a residual), while labor productivity is an actual value. Nevertheless, the fact that we obtain similar results using both measures strengthens the case that use of financial services is associated with higher productivity.

An important caveat is that our results are obtained from cross-sectional OLS regression, and thus we cannot claim causality. In other words, the association between use of financial services and productivity may stem from the fact that more productive firms are more likely to be able to use financial services or from a reverse relationship—that is, firms that use financial services are able to raise their productivity. Unfortunately, without time-series data or any suitable instruments (which are absent in current surveys), we cannot establish causality. Our results should not be treated as showing a definite positive impact of financial services on productivity.

Cross-Country Differences in the Relationship between TFP and Financial Products

To assess the differences among countries, we run the regressions by country and look at the differences in sample composition. Table 8.10 reports proportions of financial users, by country. Costa Rica has the lowest use of a credit line by firms (43.2 percent), while El Salvador and Honduras have the highest (75.8 and 72.1 percent, respectively). These patterns are replicated when we disaggregate by size of firm (see table 8.11). We find that firms in each size category in Costa Rica report less use of credit lines than similar size firms in other countries. Firms in Costa Rica also report higher financing obstacles than firms in other countries. Differences among countries are not so large when we look at the use of checking accounts.

Table 8.10   Use of Financial Instruments in Central America, by Country
% of firms

Country	Credit line	Checking
Costa Rica	43.2	92.7
El Salvador	75.8	92.1
Guatemala	68.6	84.5
Honduras	72.1	92.8
Nicaragua	52.5	70.0
Total	62.8	86.3

Source: Authors' calculations.

Table 8.11   Use of Financial Instruments, by Country and Size of Firm

% of firms

Country and instrument	Micro	Small	Medium	Large
Costa Rica				
Credit line	31	48	63	71
Checking	86	99	100	97
Finance obstacle	51	45	41	17
El Salvador				
Credit line	67	79	83	89
Checking	84	95	98	97
Finance obstacle	21	24	11	14
Guatemala				
Credit line	63	70	79	90
Checking	86	80	82	92
Finance obstacle	22	21	26	11
Honduras				
Credit line	51	77	100	99
Checking	84	98	99	97
Finance obstacle	32	33	6	19
Nicaragua				
Credit line	49	58	78	95
Checking	39	75	94	100
Finance obstacle	23	15	9	22

Source: Authors' calculations.

Tables 8.12 and 8.13 report the results by country for TFP and labor productivity, respectively, from the value added regression. In general, the results are in line with those reported for all countries estimated together, but significance is often lost because the sample size is much smaller for each country. While we find almost all positive coefficients on checking accounts and line of credit, they are not significant in all regressions. We find that having a checking account is more often significant in individual countries (three out of five in TFP regressions and four out of five in labor productivity regressions), while credit line is often not significant in individual-country regressions (only one out of five in TFP regressions is significant at the 5 percent level, while two out of five coefficients are significant in the labor productivity regressions). Because of the small sample size, these results should not be taken to imply that use of financial services is not important for these countries.

Table 8.12   OLS Regression: TFP, by Country
TFP value added

Variable	Costa Rica	El Salvador	Guatemala	Honduras	Nicaragua
Checking account dummy	0.454*	0.573**	0.694***	0.613	−0.219
	(0.091)	(0.025)	(0.004)	(0.129)	(0.293)
Line of credit dummy	0.241**	0.188	−0.183	0.061	0.16
	(0.024)	(0.298)	(0.402)	(0.770)	(0.382)
Micro dummy	0.049	0.054	−0.188	0.285	−0.366
	(0.794)	(0.890)	(0.469)	(0.279)	(0.267)
Small dummy	0.018	−0.159	−0.336	0.102	−0.366
	(0.926)	(0.319)	(0.102)	(0.668)	(0.256)
Medium dummy	−0.161	0.293	0.308	0.166	−0.204
	(0.559)	(0.137)	(0.196)	(0.470)	(0.578)
Log age	−0.002	0.25**	−0.085	0.214	−0.162
	(0.980)	(0.045)	(0.573)	(0.073)*	(0.172)
Constant	−0.524	−1.41**	0.028	−1.368**	0.789
	(0.167)	(0.018)	(0.951)	(0.031)	(0.147)
Number of observations	265	290	261	192	225
R^2	0.035	0.079	0.081	0.068	0.025

Source: Authors' calculations.
Note: Numbers in parentheses are robust p values.
* $p < .10$, ** $p < .05$, *** $p < .01$.

Exports and Productivity

In this section, we present additional evidence that exporting status of the firm is associated with higher productivity. Ideally, we would like to test whether firms become more productive after they become exporters (that is, learning by doing) or whether more productive firms self-select into exporting status. However, with only one year of data and no suitable instruments, we are not able to address this question. Here we simply present a partial correlation between exporting status and TFP, controlling for other firm characteristics associated with export status.

Our dependent variable is a dummy for exporting firm status, and we use TFP as one of the regressors. As table 8.14 shows, higher productivity is positively associated with higher likelihood of exporting status. As noted, our results do not provide any information about causality. The probability that a firm becomes an exporter also increases with size and differs significantly across countries. Costa Rica (which is the omitted category) and El Salvador seem to have the highest proportion of

Table 8.13   OLS Regression: Labor Productivity, by Country
log sales per worker

Variable	Costa Rica	El Salvador	Guatemala	Honduras	Nicaragua
Checking account dummy	0.684***	1.422***	0.502**	0.28	0.542**
	(0.000)	(0.000)	(0.012)	(0.267)	(0.017)
Line of credit dummy	0.089	0.569**	0.11	0.15	0.600***
	(0.339)	(0.019)	(0.563)	(0.425)	(0.001)
Micro dummy	−1.467***	−0.506**	−0.803***	−0.969***	−1.246***
	(0.000)	(0.030)	(0.001)	(0.000)	(0.000)
Small dummy	−0.885***	−0.24	−0.311	−0.772***	−1.444***
	(0.000)	(0.445)	(0.156)	(0.000)	(0.000)
Medium dummy	−0.577**	−0.192	−0.181	−0.197	−0.367
	(0.020)	(0.304)	(0.491)	(0.308)	(0.428)
Log age	−0.059	0.025	−0.068	0.043	−0.131
	(0.392)	(0.866)	(0.576)	(0.667)	(0.275)
Constant	10.214***	5.885***	9.522***	9.518***	9.776***
	(0.000)	(0.000)	(0.000)	(0.000)	(0.000)
Number of observations	314	439	305	235	327
R^2	0.298	0.199	0.14	0.125	0.29

Source: Authors' calculations.
Note: Numbers in parentheses are robust p values.
* $p < .10$, ** $p < .05$, *** $p < .01$.

exporters. In previous specifications, we introduced controls for foreign ownership, age, and other firms' characteristics, but they did not change our main results, which are fully consistent with those reported in chapter 3 of this book.

Conclusions

A growing body of empirical research strengthens the link between access to financial services and economic growth. Although the channels through which credit affects growth on the micro level are not entirely identified, we provide some evidence on the relationship between use of financial instruments and firm productivity in Central America. We also find a positive relationship between productivity and exports, even though we cannot distinguish between two hypotheses: self-selection of productive firms and learning by exporting firms. The results suggest that policy priorities should include further efforts to widen financial access and efforts to boost productivity.

Table 8.14   Probit: TFP and Exports
Y = 1 if firm exports

Variable	(1)	(2)	(3)
TFP	0.118**		
	(0.04)		
TFP value added		0.109*	
		(0.08)	
Labor productivity			0.140**
			(0.01)
Micro dummy	−0.948***	−0.98***	−1.055***
	(0.00)	(0.00)	(0.00)
Small dummy	−0.414***	−0.354**	−0.531***
	(0.01)	(0.02)	(0.01)
Firm group dummy	0.001	0.055	0.002
	(1.00)	(0.75)	(0.99)
El Salvador	−0.329**	−0.412**	−0.201
	(0.05)	(0.01)	(0.36)
Guatemala	−0.43*	−0.448*	−0.499**
	(0.08)	(0.07)	(0.03)
Honduras	−0.689***	−0.756***	−0.674***
	(0.00)	(0.00)	(0.00)
Nicaragua	−0.692***	−0.755***	−0.711***
	(0.00)	(0.00)	(0.00)
Constant	−0.129	−0.129	−1.41**
	(0.33)	(0.34)	(0.03)
Number of observations	1,284	1,235	1,633

Source: Authors' calculations.
Note: Numbers in parentheses are robust *p* values.
* $p < .10$, ** $p < .05$, *** $p < .01$.

Note

1. Productivity estimates can be obtained from a regression of the type $Y_i = A_i K_i^\alpha L_i^\beta$. Taking logs and rearranging equation 8.1, we derive a measure of labor productivity and two measures of TFP: (1) labor productivity: $\log(Y_i/L_i) = \alpha \log(K_i/L_i) + \varepsilon_i$ and (2) TFP productivity: $\log(Y_i) = \alpha \log(K_i) + \beta \log(L_i) + \varepsilon_i$.

   1. $TFP_i = \hat{\varepsilon}_i = \log(Y_i) - \log(\hat{Y}_i)$

   2. $TFP_i = \hat{\varepsilon}_i = \log(Y_i/L_i) - \log\left(\dfrac{\hat{Y}_i}{L_i}\right)$,

   where Y is firm's output, K and L are capital and labor, a and fl are capital and labor shares. We estimate the model by OLS.

References

Almeida, Rita, and Ana Margarida Fernandes. 2008. "Openness and Technological Innovations in Developing Countries: Evidence from Firm-Level Surveys." *Journal of Development Studies* 44 (5): 701–27.

Auboin, Mark. 2007. "Boosting Trade Finance in Developing Countries: What Link with the WTO?" Staff Working Paper ERSD-2007-04, World Trade Organization, Geneva.

Ayyagari, Meghana, Asli Demirgüç-Kunt, and Vojislav Maksimovic. 2007. "Firm Innovation in Emerging Markets." Policy Research Working Paper 4157, World Bank, Washington, DC.

Beck, Thorsten. 2002. "Financial Development and International Trade: Is There a Link?" *Journal of International Economics* 57 (1): 107–31.

———. 2003. "Financial Dependence and International Trade." *Review of International Economics* 11 (2): 296–316.

Beck, Thorsten, Asli Demirgüç-Kunt, and Ross Levine. 2000. "A New Database on Financial Development and Structure." *World Bank Economic Review* 14 (3): 597–605.

Beck, Thorsten, Asli Demirgüç-Kunt, and María Soledad Martínez Peria. 2007. "Reaching Out: Access to and Use of Banking Services across Countries." *Journal of Financial Economics* 85 (1): 234–66.

Beck, Thorsten, Ross Levine, and Norman Loayza. 2000. "Financial Intermediation and Growth: Causality and Causes." Policy Research Working Paper 2059, World Bank, Washington, DC.

Becker, Bo, and David Greenberg. 2005. "Financial Development and International Trade." Unpublished manuscript, University of Illinois at Urbana-Champaign.

Bencivenga, V. R., B. D. Smith, and R. M. Starr. 1995. "Transaction Costs, Technological Choice, and Endogenous Growth." *Journal of Economic Theory* 67 (1): 52–177.

Bernard, Andrew B., and Bradford Jensen. 1999. "Exporting and Productivity." NBER Working Paper 7135, National Bureau of Economic Research, Cambridge, MA.

Bernstein, J., and I. Nadiri. 1993. "Production, Financial Structure, and Productivity Growth in U.S. Manufacturing." Working Paper, New York University, New York.

Calderón, César, Norman Loayza, and Pablo Fajnzylber. 2004. "Economic Growth in Latin America and the Caribbean: Stylized Facts, Explanations, and Forecasts." Working Paper 265, Central Bank of Chile, Santiago.

Demirgüç-Kunt, Asli, and Vojislav Maksimovic. 1998. "Law, Finance, and Firm Growth." *Journal of Finance* 53 (6): 2107–37.

Easterly, W., and R. Levine. 2001. "It Is Not Factor Accumulation: Stylized Facts and Growth." *World Bank Economic Review* 15 (2): 177–219.

Escribano, A., and J. L. Guasch. 2005. "Assessing the Impact of the Investment Climate on Productivity Using Firm-Level Data." Policy Research Working Paper 3621, World Bank, Washington, DC.

Fajnzylber, Pablo, J. Luis Guasch, and J. Humberto López, eds. 2008. *Does the Investment Climate Matter? Microeconomic Foundations of Growth in Latin America.* Latin American Development Forum Series. Washington, DC: Inter-American Development Bank and World Bank; Santiago, Chile: Economic Commission on Latin America and the Caribbean, Santiago.

Gatti, Roberta, and Inessa Love. 2006. "Does Access to Credit Improve Productivity? Evidence from Bulgarian Firms." Policy Research Working Paper 3921, World Bank, Washington, DC.

Ghani, E., and V. Suri. 1999. "Productivity Growth, Capital Accumulation, and the Banking Sector: Some Lessons from Malaysia." Policy Research Working Paper 2252, World Bank, Washington, DC.

Hallward-Driemeir, M., G. Iarossi, and K. Sokoloff. 2002. "Exports and Manufacturing Productivity in East Asia: A Comparative Analysis with Firm-Level Data." NBER Working Paper 8894, National Bureau of Economic Research, Washington, DC.

Hur, Jung, Manoj Raj, and Yohanes E. Riyanto. 2004. "The Impact of Financial Development and Asset Tangibility on Export." Unpublished manuscript, National University of Singapore.

Jeong, Hyeok, and Robert M. Townsend. 2005. "Sources of TFP Growth: Occupational Choice and Financial Deepening." IEPR Working Paper 05.28, Stanford University, Institute of Economic Policy Research, Palo Alto, CA.

King, Robert G., and Ross Levine. 1993. "Finance and Growth: Schumpeter Might Be Right." *Quarterly Journal of Economics* 108 (3): 717–37.

Levine, Ross. 1991. "Stock Markets, Growth, and Tax Policy." *Journal of Finance* 46 (4): 1445–65.

———. 1997. "Financial Development and Economic Growth: Views and Agenda." *Journal of Economic Literature* 35 (2): 688–726.

———. 2005. "Law, Endowments, and Property Rights." *Journal of Economic Perspectives*, American Economic Association 19 (3): 61–88.

Levine, Ross, and Sara Zervos. 1998. "Stock Markets, Banks, and Economic Growth." *American Economic Review* 88 (3): 537–58.

Levinsohn, J., and A. Petrin. 2000. "Estimating Production Functions Using Inputs to Control for Unobservables." NBER Working Paper 7819, National Bureau of Economic Research, Cambridge, MA.

Love, Inessa. 2003. "Financial Development and Financing Constraints: International Evidence from the Structural Investment Model." *Review of Financial Studies* 16 (3): 765–91.

Manova, Kalina. 2008. "Credit Constraints, Equity Market Liberalizations, and International Trade." *Journal of International Economics* 76 (1): 33–47.

Manova, Kalina, and Davir Chor. 2009. "Off the Cliff and Back: Credit Conditions and International Trade during the Global Financial Crisis." Working Paper, Stanford University, Palo Alto, CA.

Nickell, S., and D. Nicholitsas. 1999. "How Does Financial Pressure Affect Firms?" *European Economic Review* 43 (8): 1435–56.

Olley, S., and A. Pakes. 1996. "The Dynamics of Productivity in the Telecommunications Equipment Industry." *Econometrica* 64 (6): 1263–97.

Rajan, Raghuram G., and Luigi Zingales. 1998. "Financial Dependence and Growth." *American Economic Review* 88 (3): 559–86.

Roberts, Mark, and James R. Tybout. 1997. "The Decision to Export in Colombia: An Empirical Model of Entry with Sunk Costs." *American Economic Review* 87 (4): 545–64.

Schiantarelli, Fabio, and Fidel Jaramillo. 1999. "Access to Long-Term Debt and Effects on Firms' Performance: Lessons from Ecuador." Policy Research Working Paper 1725, World Bank, Washington, DC.

Schiantarelli, Fabio, and Alessandro Sembenelli. 1999. "The Maturity Structure of Debt: Determinants and Effects on Firms' Performance: Evidence from the United Kingdom and Italy." Policy Research Working Paper 1699, World Bank, Washington, DC.

Schiantarelli, Fabio, and Vivek Srivastava. 1999. "Debt Maturity and Firm Performance: A Panel Study of Indian Companies." Policy Research Working Paper 1724, World Bank, Washington, DC.

Svaleryd, H., and J. Vlachos. 2002. "Markets for Risk and Openness to Trade: How Are They Related?" *Journal of International Economics* 57 (2): 369–95.

———. 2005. "Financial Markets, the Pattern of Specialization, and Comparative Advantage: Evidence from OECD Countries." *European Economic Review* 49 (1): 113–44.

Wagner, Joachim. 2007. "Exports and Productivity: A Survey of the Evidence from Firm-level Data." *World Economy* 30 (1): 60–82.

World Bank. 2003. "Trade Finance for Emerging Markets." International Finance Briefing Note 29, World Bank, Washington, DC.

Wurgler, Jeffrey. 2000. "Financial Markets and the Allocation of Capital." *Journal of Financial Economics* 58 (1–2): 187–214.

Yan, Aw B., Sukkyun Chung, and Mark J. Roberts. 2000. "Productivity and Turnover in the Export Market: Micro-level Evidence from the Republic of Korea and Taiwan (China)." *World Bank Economic Review* 14 (1): 65–90.

CHAPTER 9

Are Food Markets in Central America Integrated with International Markets? An Analysis of Food Price Transmission in Honduras and Nicaragua

Mario A. De Franco and Diego Arias

Central American countries have recently signed a free trade agreement with the United States—the Dominican Republic–Central America Free Trade Agreement (DR-CAFTA)—and are negotiating another one with the European Union and others. Food products, for the most part, are included in such agreements. This study seeks to shed light on whether the domestic markets of these food products are integrated with international markets by assessing the transmission of international prices to domestic prices of key agricultural commodities in Nicaragua and Honduras. In other words, we analyze to what degree (if any) a change in the international price of a given food product changes the domestic price

The authors would like to acknowledge the comments received from John Nash, Miguel Robles, Miguel Gómez, Dante Mossi, Daniel Lederman, J. Humberto López, Nabil Chaherli, Rashmi Shankar, Hector Peña, Martin Gurría, and Raquel Fernández.

of that same good, at the level of the consumer and producer as well as in different regions within each country.

This analysis provides important evidence of the price dynamics that guide recommendations for a complementary public policy agenda of agricultural trade liberalization in the region. Price transmission is a key indicator of the extent to which domestic food markets in Honduras and Nicaragua are integrated into international markets; however, the implications of this evidence for trade liberalization are limited because the price transmission indicator only measures the degree to which short-term movements in international food prices are translated into domestic food markets, not price levels. Trade liberalization may indeed lower food prices in the region, even if short-term price transmission continues to be low or sometimes nonexistent.

There are several ways to analyze the relationship between international and domestic prices. The first one (price wedge analysis) analyzes the difference between international and domestic prices. This involves analyzing data on prices, but also on transport costs and border protection (tariffs, fees, and others). This price wedge analysis was done for most of the same products and the same countries by Peña and Arias (2010), and the results are presented later in this chapter for comparison. The second methodological approach (price transmission analysis) analyzes the variation in percentages (growth) of international versus domestic prices. This is the approach taken in this chapter. The analysis presented here does not assess welfare, only price behavior.

Price behavior is important in a context of trade liberalization, as the reduction in border protection is supposed to translate into a reduction in prices for local consumers. With less border protection, farmers are expected to receive clearer market signals from international prices, enabling them to take advantage of export opportunities and higher international prices, as occurred during the 2007–08 global food crisis. Several related studies on the welfare effect of the DR-CAFTA (Bussolo and others 2010) assume a high elasticity of international price transmission to domestic prices. However, for these assumptions to hold, there needs to be a price transmission process that is perfect (or almost perfect) and timely (without much delay). If such transmission from international to domestic prices is not perfect or timely, it is difficult to imagine how food consumers and farmers could benefit from trade liberalization.

Evidence from previous analysis worldwide is mixed. Some countries and some products present high price transmission, while others present very little. A summary of the literature on price transmission of agricultural products in Latin America was prepared by the Food and Agriculture Organization (FAO 2006), and the different studies reach a consensus that analyses of price transmission processes must consider the entire supply chain (upstream and downstream) to understand the results.

Imperfect price transmission can be explained by several factors, but the two most basic explanations are (a) the existence of noncompetitive market structures in which one agent has sufficient market power to establish or influence a market price above the marginal cost and (b) the fact that, even in competitive market structures, price transmission is imperfect as long as there are costs to price adjustments at some point within the supply chain (Vavra and Goodwin 2005). These are important conclusions, as they point out that when trade liberalization is not accompanied by a review of domestic market structures or adjustment costs within a supply chain, it is unlikely to have the expected benefits for consumers and farmers.

However, even in a situation of complete free trade (no tariffs) in which the import market for a specific good is managed by a single importing firm (monopoly) or a group of colluded firms (cartel), the degree of price transmission will be determined by the degree to which consumers are able to substitute that good with another one. In other words, the degree to which the monopoly or cartel can arbitrarily set domestic prices will depend on the elasticity of substitution of the demand curve for that good. The same applies to a domestic food processor or exporter. The elasticity of substitution of crops being produced by farmers will determine the degree to which the buyer (monopoly) or colluded buyers (monopsony) are able to fix prices arbitrarily at the farm gate.

Adjustment costs can also play an important role even with strong domestic competitiveness and free trade. Domestic food prices can be "sticky" due to several market characteristics such as menu costs (the relabeling and reprinting of price lists); marketing costs (the negative impact on consumer demand of shifting prices); logistics costs (the larger volatility in inventory, storage, or transport costs from unexpected changes in demand generated by continuous price changes); and corporate image costs (the impact of staple food price volatility on the company's reputation). Furthermore, fluctuations in domestic food prices can undermine contract farming or result in the nonfulfillment of current contracts between farmers and buyers.

The food products studied here were selected based on their importance in the agriculture sector and rural economy of the country as well as their weight in the consumer basket, in particular of low-income households. A mix of import and export products was chosen to allow comparison and yield public policy recommendations. The seven products selected are highly tradable, in terms of exports and/or imports. Table 9.1 presents the weight of exports in overall production and the weight of imports in overall supply for Nicaragua. These seven food products represent 47.4 percent of the consumption basket of the lower income quintiles in Nicaragua and 74.7 percent of the consumption basket of households in extreme poverty in Honduras. Therefore, studying these products is to study a large part of the economy of these countries, in particular the rural economy.

To assess the price behavior of these products, the following questions were used to guide the econometrics analysis in both countries:

- Are changes in international prices transmitted throughout the domestic supply chain?
- What is the time lag of price transmission?
- Is price transmission asymmetric? In other words, do prices behave the same when they increase as when they decrease?
- Is price transmission homogeneous between geographic regions within the country?

The chapter begins by presenting a model and the results of the estimates of the price transmission process for the agricultural commodities

Table 9.1   Weight of Tradables of Select Food Products in Nicaragua, 2005

Product	% of total production	% of total supply
For export		
Sugar	45.7	—
Coffee	89.1	—
Meat (beef)	58.0	—
Beans	45.7	—
For import		
Maize (all)	n.a.	13.3
Rice (paddy)	n.a.	33.6
Vegetable oil	n.a.	33.9

Source: Central Bank of Nicaragua.
Note: — = Not available; n.a. = not applicable.

selected in Honduras and Nicaragua. It describes the industries of these products to characterize the functioning of these markets at a domestic and regional level and presents a simple model in which conditions are derived for an imperfect transmission of variations in international prices to domestic prices. The model is developed both for import and for export goods. The model assumes, as per the evidence presented, the existence of adjustment costs and a noncompetitive domestic market structure in which the elasticity of substitution of demand and supply plays a key role (following Dixit and Stiglitz 1977). This is followed by a section analyzing the results. A final section recommends some areas for public policy to complement agricultural trade liberalization in Honduras and Nicaragua.

Price Transmission of International to Domestic Prices of Food Products

This section explains the methodology used in this chapter and summarizes the results of the price transmission model.

The first step in determining the most convenient econometric process to follow is to determine the degree of integration of the study variables (as with all time-series analysis) to see whether they are stationary or nonstationary. To determine the degree of integration of the study variables, we use the unit root test Dickey-Fuller–generalized least squares (DF-GLS) with critical values of Eliott-Rothenberg-Stock, which is more powerful than tests such as augmented Dickey-Fuller (ADF), Phillips-Perron, and Kwiatkowski-Phillips-Schmidt-Shin (KPSS) tests according to Maddala and Kim (2004) and Dutoit, Hernández, and Urrutia (2009). This unit root test is applied to the natural log of prices through a general to particular method, as proposed by Enders (1995), which consists of proving initially the existence of unit root through a more complete model that includes the trend, constant, and lags.[1] Thus when the variables are nonstationary, we use cointegration techniques to avoid the spurious correlation problem. To determine the cointegration equation, we use the Johansen procedure after proving that the price variables have an order of integration larger than 0 but equal between them (Johansen and Juselius 1990). This cointegration technique consists of the formulation of an autoregressive vector of the variables in levels until the errors in each of the equations for each vector make up white noise. Subsequently, from this autoregressive vector a system is formed by the variables in first differences and a set of stationary combinations of the variables in levels.

To generate such combinations (known as cointegration vectors or long-term relations), we apply Johansen's maximum likelihood to the vector autoregression (VAR) model proposed. Finally, to determine whether the cointegration relations are significant, the trace and maximum value test is used.

The cointegration relations are estimated in pairs, between the international and the domestic price, at the producer level, at the consumer level, or by region. In other words, we do not estimate a VAR for the entire set because of the difficulties of controlling the large amount of information within a VAR and of generating a reasonable long-term relationship. Nevertheless, although the VAR allows us to generate individual models for domestic prices (for consumers, producers, and regions) with their respective cointegration relationships (when they exist), such VARs present three important limitations: (a) they are estimated using the econometric program E-views,[2] which does not present the option of considering international prices as super-exogenous variables, so such prices are considered in general terms as endogenous,[3] which is not correct; (b) they do not consider the existence of causality between domestic prices (the fact that consumer prices can affect producer prices and vice versa); and (c) they do not consider the possibility of different corrections when domestic prices are above the level suggested by the cointegration equation compared to the situation when they are below the level suggested by the long-term relationship.

Therefore, VAR is used only to determine the cointegration equation (or long-term relationship) between a domestic and an international price. The effective transmission of international prices to domestic prices is analyzed through a system of equations of the first logarithmic differences of domestic prices characterized by (a) the elimination of causality of domestic to international prices (considering the latter as strongly exogenous); (b) the statement of a possible causality between domestic prices (between consumer and producer prices and between regions); and (c) the possibility of asymmetries in the error correction of the cointegration equation. In this system, a convenient number of lags is introduced in the price variables, as in other variables such as salaries, exchange rates, input prices, and others. The final system is not necessarily estimated with an equal number of lags or of explanatory variables for the individual equations; thus the seemingly unrelated regressions method, as suggested by Enders (1995), is followed in search of efficiency in the estimation of parameters.

Consequently, to determine the existence of asymmetries in the error correction of the cointegration equation, a binary variable is included that is equal to 1 when the remainder of the cointegration relation is positive and equal to 0 when negative. Then the statistical significance of the parameter of this binary variable is tested through the t statistic that appears in the system of equations. When the order of integration of the price variables does not match, the variable for which the order of integration does not match the rest is excluded. When no cointegration relation is found between variables, we proceed in the same form, estimating the system of equations, but excluding the remainder of the long-term relationship, given that this does not exist.

Finally, when the domestic and international prices are determined to be stationary variables, a system of equations similar to the nonstationary case is estimated, but with three differences: (a) the variables are included not in first differences but in levels; (b) the lag remainder of one period of the cointegration equation is not excluded, given that this does not exist; and (c) the asymmetry of international price transmission is tested with dummies that take the value of 1 when international prices increase and 0 when they decrease.

Table 9.2 presents a summary of the results of the price transmission found in Nicaragua following the econometric methodology just

Table 9.2 Growth in Domestic Prices in Nicaragua Given a Permanent Increase of 10 Percent in the International Price

percent

Product	Average domestic producer price 1 month	Average domestic producer price Steady state[a]	Average domestic consumer price 1 month	Average domestic consumer price Steady state[a]	Managua consumer price growth 1 month	Managua consumer price growth Steady state[a]	Rest of the country consumer price growth 1 month	Rest of the country consumer price growth Steady state[a]
Vegetable oil	1.4	9.7	0.8	7.9	—	—	—	—
Rice	0.0	3.4	0.0	3.7	0.0	5.7	0.0	4.3
Sugar	0.0	0.1	0.0	0.2	0.0	0.3	0.0	0.1
Coffee	0.4	1.0	0.0	2.3	0.0	0.2	0.0	0.5
Meat (beef)	0.0	0.0	0.0	0.0	0.0	1.8	0.0	1.7
Maize	0.0	1.8	0.0	2.2	—	—	—	—
Beans	3.2	4.6	1.7	3.0	0.0	6.1	0.0	6.7

Source: Authors' calculations.
Note: — = Not available.
a. Increase after 45 months.

described. The first four columns show the growth of average domestic producer and consumer prices, and the last four columns show the growth in consumer prices in Managua and the rest of the country after one month and in the steady state as a result of a permanent variation of 10 percent in the international price of each product.[4] In the short run (one month), price transmission from international to domestic prices is low or nonexistent in all the food products studied in Nicaragua. Furthermore, not even in the long run (after 45 months) is price transmission complete,[5] with the exception of vegetable oil, where price transmission is almost 100 percent. In the case of beans, high price transmission is also observed in the long run.

In the case of Honduras, consumer prices in different regions of the country were obtained for the period January 2000 to June 2009. Table 9.3 presents a summary of the estimated changes in domestic consumer prices after one month and at the steady state (45 months) given a 10 percent change in international prices.

These results are backed by simple statistical tests of correlations between both variables. At first sight, these simple statistical tests also show the low correlation between international and domestic prices for the period studied.

To clarify the dynamics of price transmission, 12-month trajectories for each product are calculated given a 10 percent change in the international price of each product (see figures 9.1 and 9.2). For Nicaragua, both consumer and producer prices are available for all products, but regional price data are available only for rice, sugar, maize, and meat (the other products are not available), provided by the Ministry of Agriculture and Forestry; the same econometric methods are used as explained in the previous section. For Honduras, only consumer prices are available for the different regions of the country, with the exception of beans.

As shown in figures 9.1 and 9.2, in both countries the dynamics for coffee and rice are quite different. While rice presents very small price transmission estimates in both countries, even in the long term, coffee prices to farmers adjust fully after three months in Nicaragua. Table 9.4 presents the findings with respect to the transmission of consumer prices by region for both countries and with respect to consumer versus producer prices for Nicaragua.

For all cases, there is no evidence of price transmission asymmetries. The system of equations does not yield different results between a situation where the international price increases versus one where it

Table 9.3 Change of Consumer Prices in Honduras Given a Permanent Increase of 10 Percent in International Prices, by Region

percent

Product	Center (metropolitan)		Center (rest)		North (metropolitan)		North (rest)		West		East		South	
	1 month	Steady state	1 month	Steady state	1 month	Steady state	1 month	Steady state	1 month	Steady state	1 month	Steady state	1 month	Steady state
Rice	0.5	3.4	0.0	3.3	0.2	3.6	0.0	4.1	0.6	3.9	0.4	3.4	0.0	2.6
Sugar	0.1	-0.1	0.2	0.0	0.3	0.0	0.4	0.1	0.2	-0.1	0.2	-0.2	0.2	0.0
Coffee	0.5	3.0	0.7	3.6	0.3	2.1	0.4	2.2	0.3	1.7	0.5	2.6	0.4	2.6
Meat (beef)	0.0	5.4	0.0	6.0	0.0	5.6	0.0	6.9	0.0	5.1	0.0	6.8	0.0	5.0
Maize	0.0	4.8	0.0	3.8	0.0	4.3	0.0	3.1	0.0	3.6	0.0	4.5	0.0	4.8
Vegetable oil	0.0	7.3	0.0	6.9	0.0	5.3	0.0	6.0	0.0	4.4	0.0	6.8	0.0	5.3

Source: Authors' calculations.

Note: a. Increase after 45 months.

Figure 9.1   Transmission of Rice and Coffee Prices in Honduras[a]

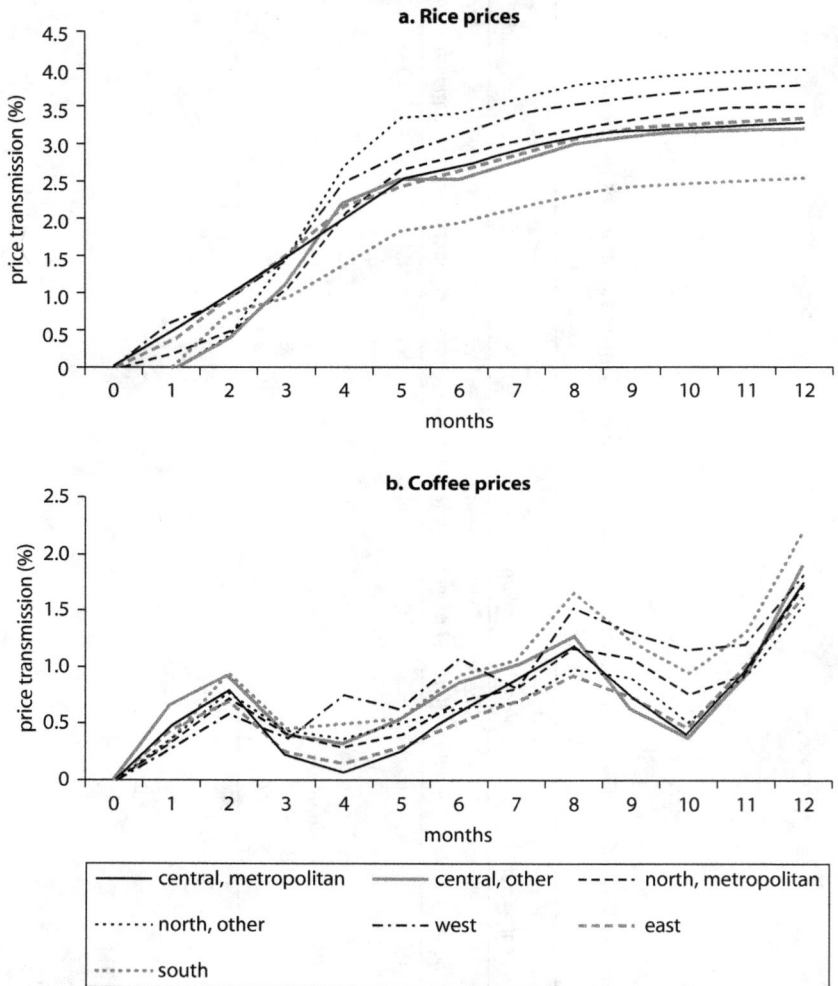

a. Rice prices

b. Coffee prices

Legend:
- central, metropolitan
- central, other
- north, metropolitan
- north, other
- west
- east
- south

Source: Authors' estimations.
a. Increase in local rice prices given a 10 percent increase in international prices.

decreases. In conclusion, for Nicaragua, coffee is the only product that presents high price transmission when looking at producer and consumer prices as well as at regional differences, although transmission is delayed a few months. For Honduras, consumer prices also show little reaction to international price changes within the first month. Even in the long term, most of the products present a price transmission that is less than

Figure 9.2   Transmission of Rice and Coffee Prices in Nicaragua[a]

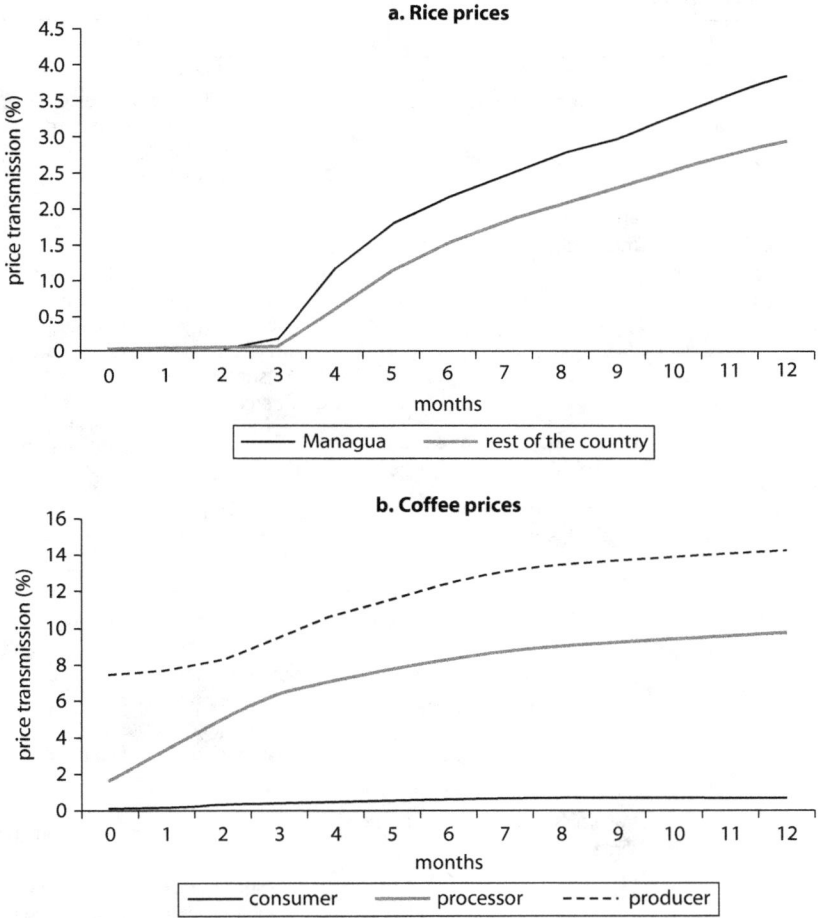

a. Rice prices

b. Coffee prices

Source: Authors' estimations.
a. Increase in local rice prices given a 10 percent increase in international prices.

50 percent. The only products with a price transmission more than 50 percent are meat and vegetable oil.

Understanding the Price Transmission Results

To understand the results, we present some basic characteristics of the agribusiness sectors involved in the production and commercialization of these food products and then propose a simple, general model for

Table 9.4   Findings of Estimates of Price Transmission Analysis of Select Food Products in Honduras and Nicaragua

Product	Honduras	Nicaragua
Vegetable oil	No or very little change is observed during the initial months, but after 12 months, prices change between 0.5 percent in the western region and 4.5 percent in the northern (nonmetropolitan) region.	After three months, consumer prices change only 2 percent and producer prices change 3 percent. After 12 months, prices change 6.0 and 5.1 percent, respectively.
Rice (paddy and processed)	After the first month, there is almost no change, and after 12 months, consumer prices change between 2.5 and 4.0 percent, with the northern region presenting the highest transmission and the southern region the lowest.	After one month, producer prices do not change and consumer prices change only 0.5 percent. After six months, producer and consumer prices change less than 3 percent. However, after three months, prices seem to change more in Managua than in the rest of the country.
Sugar	No or very little change is observed.	No significant change is found through the entire first 12 months. Regional price differences are minimal.
Coffee	During the first month, a change between 0.25 and 0.75 percent is observed; after 12 months consumer prices change between 1.50 and 2.25 percent, with the northern region presenting the lowest transmission and the southern region the highest.	Consumer prices (for ground coffee) do not change significantly during the first 12 months, but producer prices for green bean coffee change more than 6 percent during the first three months and 10 percent during the first 12 months; producer prices for ground coffee change 10 percent after the first three months. Consumer prices for ground coffee change more in Managua than in the rest of the country.
Maize (white)	No change is observed during the first month, but in the second month, price changes range from 2.5 percent in the southern region to 0 percent in the eastern region. After 12 months, changes vary from 2.5 percent in the northern (nonmetropolitan) region to 6.0 percent in the southern and eastern regions.	During the first eight months, there are no significant changes in domestic consumer or producer prices or by regions.

(continued next page)

Table 9.4   *(continued)*

Product	Honduras	Nicaragua
Meat (beef)	No or very little change is observed during the first month; after 12 months, consumer prices change 1.50 percent in the northern region and –0.25 percent in the southern and central (nonmetropolitan) regions.	There is no transmission of international prices into domestic prices.
Beans	Data are not available.	During the first month, producer and consumer prices change 3.2 and 1.7 percent, respectively. After 12 months, they change 3.1 and 3.9 percent, respectively.

Source: Authors' calculations.

imperfect international price transmission. At the end of the section, we compare the findings with the results on price wedges presented by Peña and Arias (2010).

Agribusiness Industry Structure
Information on the number, market share, and type of agribusinesses in Nicaragua and Honduras has been difficult to obtain; however, some evidence is presented in tables 9.5 and 9.6 for Nicaragua.

With the exception of beans and to some extent dairy products, the domestic market structure concentrates market power (market share) in a small number of trading and processing companies. This situation indicates a potential for reduced competition in these agribusiness markets, which could explain some of the low price transmission estimates presented in the previous section.

Modeling Imperfect International Price Transmission
The model produced in this study has a simple, general structure. Its purpose is to derive, in a consistent manner and with reasonable assumptions, the conditions in which international price transmissions are reflected in a perfect or imperfect fashion in domestic markets. By finding these conditions, we can then derive public policy and program recommendations to complement trade liberalization and improve consumer and producer welfare.

The model assumes that demand for a product composed of import and local inputs, Q, with respect to the total final goods of the economy,

Table 9.5   Number and Market Share of Large Agribusiness Companies in Nicaragua, 2005

Product	Number of large companies	Market share (% of total supply)
Sugar	2	90
Meat (beef)	3	70
Vegetable oil	3	90
Poultry	2	75
Wheat (flour)	3	100
Rice	1	70

Source: Central Bank of Nicaragua.

Table 9.6   Number and Export Share of Large Exporters in Nicaragua, 2005

Product	Number of producers	Number of large export (import) companies	Export (import) market share (% of total exports)
Sugar	—	2	90
Meat (beef)	> 35,000	4	90
Coffee	35,000	2	60
Dairy products	—	1	40
Beans	—	3	30
Rice (imports)	—	1	84 and 45[a]

Source: Customs Division, Managua, Nicaragua.
Note: — = Not available.
a. 84 percent within quota and 45 percent over quota imports.

Q_G, is simply a function of its own price, P, with respect to the general price index of the economy, P_G, elevated to the elasticity of substitution, σ, defined as

$$\frac{Q}{Q_G} = \left(\frac{P}{P_G} \right)^{-\sigma}. \tag{9.1}$$

Assuming that, in line with the evidence presented previously, there is only one seller (or a group of colluded sellers) of the good; to supply this good, the seller(s) acts as the only buyer for the local producers (farmers), who, in turn, sell the product at price P_p and quantity Q_p. Moreover, because of storage, package, and financial market imperfections and difficulties, the seller(s) is the only importer of the good, Q_m, of similar quality at price P_m. These assumptions, although extreme, are not far from reality in the countries and products being studied.

Ignoring other costs for simplification purposes, the seller(s) of the good maximizes its profits, Π, in a traditional fashion:

$$\Pi = PQ - P_m Q_m - P_p Q_p. \tag{9.2}$$

Nevertheless, the supply of farmers with respect to the set of final goods responds to producer prices with respect to the general price index of the economy, given a certain (low) elasticity of substitution of production, γ, by other goods:

$$\frac{Q_p}{Q_G} = \left(\frac{P_p}{P_G} \right)^{\gamma}.$$
(9.3)

Given that the total imports of this good are not greater than the total quantity minus the purchases made to local farmers,

$$Q_m = Q - Q_p.$$
(9.4)

Substituting equations 9.3 and 9.4 in the profit equation, we obtain

$$\Pi = \frac{PQ_G P^{1-\sigma}}{P_G^{-\sigma}} - \frac{P_m Q_G P^{-\sigma}}{P_G^{-\sigma}} + \frac{P_m Q_G P_p^{\gamma}}{P_G^{\gamma}} - \frac{Q_G P_p^{1+\gamma}}{P_G^{\gamma}}.$$
(9.5)

For the monopolist or cartel described above, the chosen variables are the price to be paid to local farmers (P_p) and the sale price (P). Deriving equation 9.5 with respect to P, equaling 0 and solving for P, we obtain the results of the model based on the elasticity of substitution assumption of Dixit and Stiglitz (1977):

$$P = \frac{\sigma}{\sigma - 1} P_m.$$
(9.6)

Equation 9.6 says that the price at which the monopolist (or cartel) can sell is determined by the elasticity of substitution of the international price. Following an equivalent process with respect to producers, we arrive at a purchasing price fixed by the monopolist that is a function of the elasticity of supply given international prices:

$$P_p = \frac{\gamma}{1+\gamma} P_m.$$
(9.7)

If σ or γ tend toward large values—in other words, if the elasticities are high—consumer and producer prices will tend to be equal to international prices; when the elasticities are low, the opposite occurs. The results in equations 9.6 and 9.7 correspond to situations where adjustment costs do not exist; their role in this theoretical model is for reference, given the fact that they are used later on as the base scenario to compare the evolution of domestic prices with respect to a change in international prices.

In determining the variation in domestic prices with respect to the variation in international prices (elasticity of domestic prices with respect to international prices), one needs to include not only the elasticity of substitution and elasticity of production of that good, but also the adjustment costs that occur with a price change. To complete the model, we express it in growth rates. Noting each initial price with the subscript 0, growth rates are expressed in the following fashion:

$$P_{m0} \to P_{m0}(1+m), \tag{9.8}$$

$$P_0 \to P_0(1+\varepsilon_c), \text{ and} \tag{9.9}$$

$$P_{p0} \to P_{p0}(1+\varepsilon_p), \tag{9.10}$$

where m, ε_c, and ε_p are the growth rates of import, consumer, and producer prices, respectively. Using these three definitions of price, we can rewrite the profit function expressed in equation 9.5 in terms of growth rates of consumer, producer, and import prices:

$$\Pi(\varepsilon_c, \varepsilon_p, m) = \frac{Q_G}{P_G^{-\sigma}} \left[P_o(1+\varepsilon_c) \right]^{1-\sigma} - P_{m0}(1+m) \frac{Q_G}{P_G^{-\sigma}} \left[P_o(1+\varepsilon_c) \right]^{-\sigma}$$

$$+ P_{m0}(1+m) \frac{Q_G}{P_G^{\gamma}} \left[P_o(1+\varepsilon_p) \right]^{\gamma} - \frac{Q_G}{P_G^{\gamma}} \left[P_o(1+\varepsilon_p) \right]^{1+\gamma} \tag{9.11}$$

$$- A_1 \varepsilon_c^2 - A_2 \varepsilon_p^2.$$

This structure allows us to include the two new terms on the right-hand side of equation 9.11, A_1 and A_2, which represent the adjustment costs to the firm from changing consumer and producer prices, respectively. As in similar models, the quadratic form is used to derive the model, rather than just to represent the empirical behavior of these costs, given that the simplified form includes the existence of adjustment costs, because prices both increase and decrease with respect to the baseline.

Deriving equation 9.11 with respect to ε_c and ε_p, equaling to 0, and simplifying, we obtain the following first-order conditions to maximize profits:

$$\left[\frac{Q_G}{P_G^{-\sigma}} P_0^{-\sigma} \right] \left[(1-\sigma)(1+\varepsilon_c)^{-\sigma} P_0 + \sigma P_{m0}(1+m)(1+\varepsilon_c)^{-\sigma-1} \right] = 2A_1 \varepsilon_c. \tag{9.12}$$

$$\left[\frac{Q_G}{P_G^{\gamma}} P_{p0}^{\gamma} \right] \left[\gamma P_{m0}(1+m)(1+\varepsilon_p)^{\gamma-1} - (1+\gamma)P_{p0}(1+\varepsilon_p)^{\gamma} \right] = 2A_2 \varepsilon_p. \tag{9.13}$$

Given the above, consumer price elasticity with respect to international prices, η_c, and producer price elasticity with respect to international prices, η_p, can be calculated by taking the total difference of equations 9.12 and 9.13 with respect to ε_c, ε_p, and m and assuming that we start from an initial situation where growth rates are 0, so that the results established in equations 9.6 and 9.7 hold true.[6] In this context, the price transmission elasticities are defined as follows: $\eta_c = \partial\varepsilon_c/\partial m$, $\eta_p = \partial\varepsilon_p/\partial m$.

After several manipulations we obtain equations 9.14 and 9.15, which express the key variables that determine the transmission of international prices to consumer and producer prices, respectively:

$$\frac{\partial\varepsilon_c}{\partial m} = \frac{\sigma P_{m0}\dfrac{Q_G}{P_G^{-\sigma}}P_0^{-\sigma}}{2A_1+\sigma P_{m0}\dfrac{Q_G}{P_G^{-\sigma}}P_0^{-\sigma}}. \tag{9.14}$$

$$\frac{\partial\varepsilon_p}{\partial m} = \frac{\gamma P_{m0}\dfrac{Q_G}{P_G^{\gamma}}P_0^{\gamma}}{2A_2+\gamma P_{m0}\dfrac{Q_G}{P_G^{\gamma}}P_0^{\gamma}}. \tag{9.15}$$

If in equation 9.14 the elasticity of substitution of consumption goods is low, we conclude that, if $A_1 > 0$, the international price transmission into domestic (consumer) prices is less than 1—in other words, the transmission is imperfect. However, independent of the elasticity of substitution of demand, if $A_1 = 0$, we conclude that the transmission elasticity equals 1—the transmission is perfect.

Finally, if in equation 9.15 the elasticity of supply is low, we conclude that, if $A_2 > 0$, the transmission of a change in international prices into domestic (producer) prices is less than 1—in other words, the transmission is imperfect. However, independent of the elasticity of substitution of supply, if $A_2 = 0$, the transmission elasticity of international prices is equal to 1—the transmission is perfect.

Similar conclusions are obtained when considering exportables (goods that are produced in the domestic market and exported) and when the firm has domestic market power given that it is the only one that sells in the domestic market. In fact, if we assume that one firm buys an amount of inputs Q_P domestically at price P_p and then transforms them to produce a good to be sold in the domestic market (quantity Q) at price P and exported (quantity Q_x) at price P_x, then the profit function is as follows:

$$\Pi = P_x Q_x + PQ - P_p Q_p.$$ (9.16)

However, assuming that the supply of domestic inputs follows equation 9.17, where Q_G is a quantum measure of the rest of the goods in the economy and P_G is the producer price index for the rest of the goods in the economy, we then have the following:

$$\frac{Q_p}{Q_G} = \left(\frac{P_p}{P_G}\right)^\gamma,$$ (9.17)

where γ is the elasticity of transformation of input Q_p with respect to the rest of the goods in the economy. There also exists demand for the good sold by the monopoly in the domestic market, which presents an elasticity of substitution $-\sigma$:

$$\frac{Q}{Q_G} = \left(\frac{P}{P_G}\right)^{-\sigma}.$$ (9.18)

Given equations 9.16, 9.17, and 9.18 and assuming in the meantime the absence of adjustment costs, then the producer (farmer) establishes the sale price of the good in the domestic market and the purchase price of inputs in the domestic market according to the following relationships:

$$P_p = \frac{\gamma}{1+\gamma} P_x$$

$$P = \frac{\sigma}{\sigma-1} P_x.$$ (9.19)

The prices in equation 9.19 are used as reference to analyze the variations in domestic prices when export prices change in light of the adjustment costs of price changes.

Using a procedure similar to the case of imports, we obtain a profit equation that includes adjustment costs and looks as follows:

$$\Pi = P_x(1+x)\frac{Q_G}{P_G^\gamma}\left[P_p(1+\varepsilon_p)\right]^\gamma - P_x(1+x)\frac{Q_G}{P_G^{-\sigma}}\left[P(1+\varepsilon_d)\right]^{-\sigma}$$
$$+ \left[P(1+\varepsilon_d)\right]^{1-\sigma}\frac{Q_G}{P_G^{-\sigma}} - \left[P_p(1+\varepsilon_p)\right]^{1+\gamma}\frac{Q_G}{P_G^\gamma} - A\varepsilon_d^2 - B\varepsilon_p^2,$$ (9.20)

where A and B are the adjustment cost coefficients of price variations, ε_d and ε_p represent the percentage change in domestic prices (consumers and input suppliers, respectively) with respect to the baseline, and x represents the change in export prices with respect to the baseline. Finally, if the same procedure is used for the case of imports, we obtain the following sensitivities of domestic prices to export prices:

$$\frac{\partial \varepsilon_d}{\partial x} = \frac{\sigma P_{x0} \frac{Q_G}{P_G^{-\sigma}} P_{d0}^{-\sigma}}{2A + \sigma P_{x0} \frac{Q_G}{P_G^{-\sigma}} P_{d0}^{-\sigma}}$$

$$\frac{\partial \varepsilon_p}{\partial x} = \frac{\gamma P_{x0} \frac{Q_G}{P_G^{\gamma}} P_{p0}^{\gamma}}{2B + \gamma P_{x0} \frac{Q_G}{P_G^{\gamma}} P_{p0}^{\gamma}}.$$

(9.21)

Similar to the case of importables, the existence of small adjustment costs of domestic prices (even if A and B are slightly above 0) is enough for the elasticity of substitution and transformation of equations 9.17 and 9.18 to play a significant role in the degree of international price transmission to domestic prices.

The model shows that the transmission elasticity between international and domestic prices is a function of the elasticity of substitution of demand and supply and the adjustment costs. Therefore, the low price transmission found in the analysis must necessarily be explained by one or several of the following factors: (a) low elasticity of substitution of supply, (b) low elasticity of substitution of demand, or (c) high price adjustment costs.

It is no surprise that the elasticity of substitution of supply of food products is low. Changes in agricultural production in general are costly and have time lags of several months, and sometimes more than a year, to switch from one crop to another. The main factor that could enable (constrain) faster changes in agricultural production in response to price changes is technology (or the inefficiency in the adoption of improved technologies). Technological advantage could produce plant varieties with shorter life cycles, or better soil conditioning for switching crops (or livestock) could increase the elasticity of supply for food products by allowing shorter time periods and reducing the costs of substituting the production of one product by the production of another. Other factors that influence the elasticity of supply of agricultural products could be the amount of spare capacity, either in the form of human or physical capital (idle land) and the amount of stock of the good in question. Unfortunately, we were unable to find information to estimate the elasticity of supply for these products in Nicaragua and Honduras.

With respect to the elasticity of the substitution of demand, we were also unable to find time-series information that could capture the significance of the elasticity of substitution of demand for determining the low price transmission for each food product. However, cross-sectional information is available through the Living Standards Measurement Survey (LSMS),[7] so an analysis is undertaken to assess the importance of the elasticity of substitution of demand in determining domestic prices across regions. The analysis is based on a model assuming that the elasticity of substitution of demand is an endogenous variable that depends on other factors such as income per capita, education, demographic factors, and spatial factors.[8]

The results for Nicaragua show the following:

1. The baseline category (or reference category), which is a household in the fifth income quintile, with a woman head of household over 54 years of age, with no education, and residing in urban Managua, has a significant impact on the elasticity of substitution of demand for all food products, except powdered milk. This category also presents higher values for elasticity of substitution of demand for vegetable oil and meat (beef) than for beans, eggs, maize, and rice.
2. The education of the head of household increases significantly the elasticity of substitution of demand for rice, plantains, beans, and eggs.
3. The elasticity of substitution of demand for coffee, chicken meat, beef, and powdered milk does not change with geographic location.
4. The presence of a male head of household increases the elasticity of substitution of demand for vegetable oil, sugar, beans, maize, bread, and tortillas, but has no effect on other products.
5. The presence of younger members in the household with respect to older (above 54 years old) has a statistical significance in reducing the elasticity of substitution of demand for eggs and tortillas, but has the opposite effect for powdered milk. For the rest of the food products, age composition of the household does not seem to play a role.
6. Households in the central rural region have elasticities of substitution of demand that are higher for eight food products (sugar, coffee, chicken, meat, powdered milk, milk, maize, and tortillas); however, those in urban Managua have the lowest in the country, with the exception of vegetable oil, beef, and bread.

7. Following table 9.7, consumers in the lower income quintiles have in general higher elasticities of substitution than those in higher income quintiles. This could be explained in part by the fact that the food products selected make up more than 80 percent of the consumption basket of the lowest income quintile, so that a change in food prices immediately forces households in this income segment to adjust to their budget restriction. However, in some special cases the changes in elasticity could be explained by the greater practical difficulty that consumers in different quintiles have in substituting these products.

For Honduras, the estimates show similar results:

1. When the head of household is a man, the elasticity of substitution of demand decreases for rice, sugar, beans, eggs, milk, maize, plantains, and tortillas. For vegetable oil and beef, the opposite occurs.
2. With respect to regional differences, there is no systemic finding, with the exception of rice, sugar, and plantains, for which the elasticity of substitution of demand increases when going from the central urban region to the eastern rural region. However, for coffee it is the opposite (elasticity of substitution of demand decreases).
3. The regions with the highest elasticity of substitution of demand are the eastern rural region for rice, sugar, and beans and the central urban

Table 9.7 Elasticity of Substitution of Demand for Select Food Products in Nicaragua, by Quintile

Product	1	2	3	4	5
Vegetable oil	−0.20	−0.38	−0.57	−0.84	−1.34
Rice (grains)	−1.45	−0.95	−0.75	−0.35	0.31
Sugar	−1.40	−0.89	−0.63	−0.29	0.20
Coffee (ground and beans)	−0.99	−1.03	−0.94	−0.90	−0.77
Chicken	−0.96	−0.87	−0.78	−0.79	−0.96
Beef	−1.00	−0.94	−1.02	−1.04	−1.27
Beans (grains)	−1.37	−0.92	−0.52	0.05	0.82
Eggs	−1.19	−1.10	−1.01	−0.93	−0.75
Powdered	−1.04	−1.03	−0.99	−0.96	−0.92
Milk	−0.96	−0.85	−0.69	−0.48	−0.10
Maize (grains)	−0.74	−0.42	−0.15	0.12	0.47
Bread	−0.79	−0.81	−0.82	−0.79	−0.62
Green bananas, plantains, or banana squares	−1.02	−0.93	−0.86	−0.79	−0.58
Tortillas	−1.00	−0.90	−0.79	−0.67	−0.47

Source: Authors' calculations based on regression analysis.

region for coffee and beef. The lowest elasticity of substitution of demand is in the central urban region for rice, sugar, and beans and in the eastern rural region for coffee and beef (inverse results for these two regions for the same food products).

4. A higher percentage of children in the household between birth and four years old with respect to members 54 years of age and older produces higher elasticity of substitution of demand for eggs, milk, plantains, and tortillas. However, for chicken, it is the opposite. In contrast, the higher percentage of 15–54 year olds with respect to members 54 years of age and older produces lower elasticity of substitution of demand for rice, sugar, beans, and maize. However, for chicken, it is the opposite.

5. When the level of poverty of the household increases, the elasticity of substitution of demand for rice, sugar, beans, maize, plantains, and tortillas increases (see table 9.8). This is because these products constitute a relatively larger portion of the consumption basket of low-income households.

6. For the other food products, the change in the elasticity of substitution of demand moves in the opposite direction; however, these other food products make up a smaller portion of the lower-income household's consumption basket.

To grasp the extent to which the elasticity of substitution of demand for the food products studied here explains domestic price

Table 9.8   Elasticity of Substitution of Demand for Select Food Products in Honduras, by Level of Poverty

Product	Extreme poverty	No extreme poverty	No poverty
Vegetable oil	0.22	−0.78	−0.70
Rice	−1.62	−0.87	−0.11
Sugar	−1.58	−0.89	−0.13
Coffee	−0.26	−0.62	−1.12
Chicken	0.76	−0.12	−0.93
Beef	−0.59	−1.21	−1.74
Beans	−0.99	−0.90	−0.06
Eggs	−0.09	−0.57	−0.63
Milk	−0.64	−0.71	−0.81
Maize	−1.32	−0.87	−0.37
Bread	0.38	−0.38	−0.67
Plantains	−1.32	−1.06	−0.71
Tortillas	−1.85	−1.60	−0.67

Source: Authors' calculations based on regression analysis results.

differences, we construct an indicator of consumer price deviations with respect to their average and analyze, through regressions, several supply and demand factors for their impact.[9] The main results show that for Nicaragua a decrease in the elasticity of substitution of demand for rice, sugar, coffee, beans, eggs, milk, bread, and plantains is accompanied by an increase in the price of the food product with respect to the average price in the economy. This could be evidence that, in regions or income segments of the population where the elasticity of substitution of demand is low, firms with significant market share (monopolists or cartels) can increase market prices, which reduces the degree of international price transmission.

To assess the importance of demand factors in explaining domestic price variations, we compare the R^2 of regressions with and without demand factors. As table 9.9 shows, demand factors in Nicaragua explain more than 20 percent of the deviations of household prices for vegetable oil, coffee, rice, chicken, milk, and plantains, while in Honduras the list includes vegetable oil, coffee, eggs, maize, bread, and plantains.

Finally, the third factor that has an influence over international price transmission is the price adjustment cost. As mentioned in the introduction, such costs can be due to several factors, but for agricultural and food products they are likely due mainly to logistics costs, which refer to larger volatility in inventory, storage, or transport costs due to unexpected

Table 9.9   Importance of Demand Factors in Explaining Domestic Food Price Deviations in Nicaragua and Honduras

% of impact

Product	Honduras	Nicaragua
Vegetable oil	39.4	80.5
Rice	9.3	34.7
Sugar	1.9	13.5
Coffee (ground and beans)	27.7	23.1
Chicken	9.6	24.0
Beef	11.8	16.2
Beans (grains)	4.6	9.8
Eggs	28.4	8.1
Milk	8.8	32.6
Maize	49.2	15.6
Bread	43.0	8.6
Green bananas, plantains, or banana squares	38.8	59.9
Tortillas	2.5	9.8
Global average	22.9	25.9

Source: Authors' calculations based on regression analysis results.

changes in demand generated by continuous price changes. Other costs such as menu costs, marketing costs, or corporate image costs are likely to play a smaller role in international price transmission, especially for basic staple foods.

Unfortunately, no systemic time series for the logistics costs of these products exists for Nicaragua and Honduras, but a recent logistics costs study (Fernández and others 2010) presents interesting results that point to the importance of such costs in the supply chain for wheat and rice in these countries. The results show that producer prices are less than 25 percent of the price paid by the consumer of that same product, while most of these margins (often more than 75 percent) are related to the logistics costs of taking the product from the farm gate to the consumer's hands. It is no surprise that adjustment costs play an important role in the degree to which international prices are transmitted into domestic prices.

Price Transmission versus Price Wedges

The Organisation for Economic Co-operation and Development (OECD) methodology for measuring the market price support (MPS) of agricultural products is useful for understanding the extent to which domestic food prices in Honduras and Nicaragua are composed of price supports.[10] The methodology takes the international price of a given agricultural product and, by adding known transport costs, calculates the farm gate international price, which is the price that the producer or consumer would pay if there were no border protection or market distortions (law of one price).

The difference between the international price (at farm gate) and the producer (or consumer) price is known as the price wedge (or MPS in the OECD methodology nomenclature). Tables 9.10 and 9.11 present the results obtained by Peña and Arias (2010) for select food products in 2006 and 2007 for Nicaragua and Honduras. In this analysis, price wedges are explained by policy-based price interventions (border measures, such as tariffs and export taxes) and "other" factors. These "other" factors may be the same factors that produce low elasticities of international price transmission, and this is shown by the fact that beans seem to present the most competitive market structure, with a relatively larger portion of the price wedge (MPS) than other products, explained by border protection. This is the same result obtained in the price transmission analysis for Nicaragua, where beans present a relatively higher international price transmission estimate than the rest of the products.

Table 9.10   Price Wedges for Select Agricultural Products for Honduras, 2006 and 2007

L per ton, unless otherwise noted

Year and product	International price at farm gate level	Domestic price at producer level	Difference	% attributed to tariff rates	% attributed to other factors
2006					
Rice	3,694.40	7,887.00	4,192.60	17.0	83.0
Beans	9,382.00	11,089.80	1,707.80	77.9	22.1
Maize	3,239.40	6,116.00	2,876.60	7.2	92.8
Pork	27,937.80	22,355.10	−5,582.70	—	100.0
2007					
Rice	4,136.50	9,372.00	5,235.50	0.0	100.0
Beans	11,343.80	24,805.00	13,461.20	12.0	88.0
Maize	4,240.30	9,174.00	4,933.70	9.8	90.2
Pork	41,736.70	22,556.50	−19,180.20	—	100.0

Source: Peña and Arias 2010.
Note: The Honduran currency is the lempira. The applied rate corresponds to a weighted customs rate that takes into account the actual imports in and out quota with corresponding tariff rates. — = Not available.

Table 9.11   Price Wedges for Select Agricultural Products in Nicaragua, 2006 and 2007

C$ per ton, unless otherwise noted

Year and product	International price at farm gate level	Domestic price at producer level	Difference	% attributed to tariff rates	% attributed to other factors
2006					
Maize	2,832.60	2,970.80	138.20	0.0	100.0
Rice	4,609.80	4,328.70	−281.10	—	100.0
Beans	6,957.40	9,170.40	2,213.00	91.6	8.4
Soy	4,424.40	4,918.60	494.20	0.0	100.0
Beef	32,304.40	54,491.10	22,186.70	0.0	100.0
Pork	38,561.20	41,377.60	2,816.40	0.0	100.0
2007					
Maize	3,827.70	4,887.20	1,059.50	0.0	100.0
Rice	5,215.90	4,483.20	−732.70	—	100.0
Beans	10,605.70	16,476.40	5,870.70	53.2	46.8
Soy	6,185.10	4,766.70	−1,418.40	0.0	100.0
Beef	33,835.10	54,037.90	20,202.80	0.0	100.0
Pork	42,001.10	53,028.80	11,027.70	0.0	100.0

Source: Peña and Arias 2010.
Note: The Nicaraguan currency is the córdoba. The applied rate corresponds to a weighted customs rate that takes into account the actual imports in and out quota with corresponding tariff rates. — = Not available.

Main Conclusions and Policy Implications

This study's findings indicate that a complementary agenda should accompany agricultural trade liberalization so that consumers and farmers in Honduras and Nicaragua may fully benefit from international price signals and market opportunities. Given that the transmission of international to domestic prices for the agricultural products studied here is largely imperfect, a careful assessment of welfare should be done in the context of future trade liberalization, since food consumers and farmers are receiving very low and delayed transmission of price signals. These results are confirmed by testing for regional differences, for consumers, and for farmers in an aggregated and disaggregated fashion. They also are confirmed by assessing estimates of a recent agriculture price wedge analysis for these countries. When fluctuations in international prices are transmitted only slowly and imperfectly to domestic markets, consumers and producers at any point in time may be making decisions based on prices that do not represent the real social costs and benefits of their actions, implying losses in the economic welfare of society.

While logistical costs play an important role in the price wedge differential, they may not be an important determinant of price transmission. But the cost of price adjustment may affect the latter. It is important to distinguish between price wedges and price transmission when discussing the welfare effects of trade liberalization. Price wedge analysis is a static assessment of the average difference at the farm gate between domestic and international prices, while price transmission is a dynamic analysis of changes in the relation between international and domestic prices, which is one indicator of the degree of market integration. The level of transaction costs may not necessarily be the only culprit in the low or incomplete transmission of price signals between international and domestic agriculture markets.

Evidence from Nicaragua suggests that, for most of the agriculture supply chains studied here (except for beans), there is little competition in the country's domestic market structure. A few Nicaraguan companies own the majority share of the market, both to purchase and export agricultural products and to import and sell food domestically. Further assessment is required of other countries and food products to identify whether a lack of competition is the main cause of imperfect transmission of international agricultural prices into domestic markets.

Obtaining information about the structure of domestic agriculture and food markets could shed light on country-specific impediments to increasing agricultural growth, reducing poverty, and improving rural competitiveness. Information on domestic market structure was difficult to obtain for this study, particularly for Honduras. But, as this chapter points out, even in a context where the domestic market structure concentrates purchasing and selling power in a few agribusiness companies, price transmission could be high. The drivers of imperfect price transmission in a context of a monopsony or cartel are a low elasticity of substitution of demand, low elasticity of substitution of supply, or high costs of price adjustment. Thus, even with a concentrated market structure in the agribusiness sector, public policy could increase the degree to which market signals reach domestic farmers by improving the capacity for and lowering the costs of switching from producing one food product to producing another (elasticity of substitution of supply), as well as lowering the costs for agribusinesses (traders and processors) to adjust the prices they pay farmers.

Price transmission dynamics vary among products and countries. Honduras and Nicaragua display similarities and differences in commodities, economies, and cultures. This suggests that distinct public policies should be developed for the Central American countries, to support their transition to free trade. For example, public policies respecting highly internationally traded agricultural commodities such as coffee and vegetable oil should address international price volatility as a key source of risk for farmer and consumer income. For other products with low price transmission estimates, such as meat and sugar, public policy could focus more on managing domestic market risks, such as market power, productivity, product quality, and local food availability. That said, coffee consumers in Honduras seem more responsive to international prices than consumers in Nicaragua, given the higher price transmission coefficients. Public policies to expand domestic demand for coffee in Honduras should address international price volatility, while in Nicaragua they could focus solely on domestic constraints.

These are but a few examples of the differences among countries and products. Without complementary and differentiated public policies to improve international price transmission, domestic consumers and farmers in Honduras and Nicaragua will continue to lag in their response to international market signals in agricultural trade.

Notes

1. The number of lags is determined by the information criteria of Schwarz (1978), with a maximum of 36 lags.

2. All econometric estimations are done with this program.

3. The most one can do is to consider that international prices are weakly exogenous; in other words, that these prices do not suffer corrections when deviations from the cointegration relation exist.

4. No significant differences are found in the behavior of domestic prices as a result of positive or negative changes in international prices.

5. The value of prices after 45 months is irrelevant from a public policy point of view, but not from a theoretical one.

6. This is done to simplify the results.

7. Encuesta de Medición Nacional de Vida in Spanish.

8. The equation is as follows: $Q/Q_G = (P/P_G)^{-\sigma}$, where Q is the quantity of a given product composed of imported and local inputs, Q_G is the total quantity of final goods in the economy, P is the price of the same product, P_G is the general price index of the economy, and σ is the elasticity of substitution of demand for that product.

9. For each food product, an average price paid by all households in the LSMS is estimated. Then the price that each household has to pay for each food product is divided by the average of each product for the entire set. This coefficient is a measure of the deviation of the price that the household must pay for a given food product with respect to the average price of that same product in the economy.

10. See the OECD methodology for details: http://www.oecd.org/dataoecd/33/48/32361345.pdf.

References

Bussolo, Maurizio, Samuel Frieje-Rodríguez, Calvin Djiofack, and Melissa Rodríguez. 2010. "Trade Shocks and Welfare Distribution in DR-CAFTA Countries." World Bank, Washington, DC.

Dixit, Avinash K., and Joseph E. Stiglitz. 1977. "Monopolistic Competition and Optimum Product Diversity." *American Economic Review* 67 (3, June): 297–308.

Dutoit, Laure C., Karla Hernández, and Cristóbal Urrutia. 2009. "Transmisión de precios para los mercados del maíz y arroz en América Latina." The Selected Works of Laure C. Dutoit. http://works.bepress.com/laure_dutoit/6/.

Enders, W. 1995. *Applied Econometric Time Series.* New York: Wiley.

FAO (Food and Agriculture Organization). 2006. *Agriculture Price Transmission in Latin America and the Caribbean in the Context of Trade Liberalization.* Santiago, Chile: FAO. www.rlc.fao.org/prior/desrural/fao-bid/.

Fernández, Raquel, Henry Vega, Santiago Flores, and Francisco Estrazulas. 2010. "Logistics Analysis of Selected Food Products in Nicaragua, Honduras, and Costa Rica." World Bank, Washington, DC.

Johansen, Soren, and Katarina Juselius. 1990. "Maximum Likelihood Estimation and Inference on Cointegration." *Oxford Bulletin of Economics and Statistics* 52 (2): 169–210.

Maddala, G. S., and In-Moo Kim. 2004. *Unit Roots, Cointegration, and Structural Change*. Cambridge, U.K.: Cambridge University Press.

Peña, Hector, and Diego Arias. 2010. "An Assessment of Price Wedges in Central America." World Bank, Washington, DC.

Schwarz, G. 1978. "Estimating the Dimension of a Model." *Annals of Statistics* 6 (2): 461–64.

Vavra, Pavel, and Barry Goodwin. 2005. "Analysis of Price Transmission along the Food Chain." Food, Agriculture, and Fisheries Working Paper 3, OECD, Paris.

CHAPTER 10

Intellectual Property Rights and Foreign Direct Investment: Lessons for Central America

Walter G. Park

This chapter discusses the effects of intellectual property rights (IPRs) on foreign direct investment (FDI) and the role that regional economic integration may play in determining those effects. The discussion is applied to the Dominican Republic–Central America Free Trade Agreement (DR-CAFTA) region. In terms of GDP and population, the DR-CAFTA region is a relatively small market with geographic advantages related to its proximity to the U.S. market. The region accounts for a small share of U.S. outward FDI. Most U.S. FDI in the region is concentrated in the wholesale trade and manufacturing industries, such as textiles. Other FDI from Asia occurs in agriculture and fishing. Given the characteristics of the DR-CAFTA market and its potential growth, the aim of this chapter is to analyze how strengthening IPRs in the context of economic integration will influence the incentives of U.S. and other foreign firms to acquire or establish subsidiaries in this region.

Chapter 15 of the DR-CAFTA lays out a comprehensive set of provisions to raise intellectual property standards and enforcement mechanisms in the region. The agreement calls for the ratification of or accession to the Copyright Treaty of the World Intellectual Property Office, Patent

Cooperation Treaty, Trademark Law Treaty, Madrid Agreement Concerning the Registration of Trademarks, and other global treaties. The agreement calls for national treatment, strengthens protection for digital products, and contains provisions for technological protection measures (such as prohibitions on circumvention devices). Enforcement levels and resources for IPRs are to be commensurate with the enforcement of laws in general. The agreement also protects pharmaceutical and agricultural chemical data that are submitted to regulators for purposes of evaluating safety and efficacy, the public disclosure of which may enable unfair commercial use of the data. The agreement has provisions to extend the terms of pharmaceutical patents if delays in marketing approval result in an unreasonable curtailment of the effective patent term. The question is, how influential are these and other intellectual property provisions for FDI into the region?

Regional economic integration (via a free trade agreement) can affect foreign direct investment, as can intellectual property rights in general. But intellectual property reforms induced by a free trade agreement may have particular characteristics and effects on FDI. For example, a strengthening of IPRs will influence FDI in combination with a change in market size and market access. Furthermore, IPRs may matter differently depending on the nature of the FDI—that is, whether it is for production, research, sales, or distribution.

This chapter is organized as follows. It begins by reviewing some descriptive statistics on intellectual property regimes and foreign direct investment within the DR-CAFTA region. Three measures of IPRs are examined: an index of patent protection based on statutory and case laws, an index of IPRs based on surveys of business executives, and rates of software piracy. Two sources of FDI data are examined: United Nations Conference on Trade and Development (UNCTAD) data and U.S. Bureau of Economic Analysis (BEA) data on U.S. outward FDI in the region. It then reviews some theoretical and empirical studies on the relationship between FDI and regional economic integration, followed by a review of some theoretical and empirical studies on the relationship between FDI and IPRs, of which there are two types of studies. One type focuses just on FDI, and the other examines FDI alongside other modes of technology transfer. The chapter then builds on the literature reviewed to analyze the effects of IPRs on FDI within the context of an economic region such as DR-CAFTA. A final section provides some concluding remarks.

Trends in IPRs and FDI in the DR-CAFTA Region

It would be useful to start with a review of some trends in intellectual property rights as well as some trends in inward and outward foreign direct investment in the DR-CAFTA region. For perspective, these trends are compared to a reference group of countries in Latin America. These descriptive statistics are provided in tables 10.1–10.6. First, since the early 1990s, intellectual property laws have evolved in the DR-CAFTA region. In particular, patent rights have expanded. Table 10.1 shows an index of patent rights (from Park 2008). Although intellectual property protection encompasses many kinds of rights—patents, copyrights, trademarks, geographical indications, industrial designs, and so forth—patent rights are likely to be the most relevant type of IPR for businesses that engage in inventive activity and for technological transfers that involve new inventions. The index of patent rights ranges from 0 (weakest) to 5 (strongest). The value of the index is obtained by aggregating the following five components: extent of coverage, membership in international treaties, duration of protection, absence of restrictions on rights, and statutory enforcement provisions.[1]

As table 10.1 shows, El Salvador has the strongest patent system in Central America. The Dominican Republic has the weakest. All six DR-CAFTA countries have adopted stronger patent law provisions since the

Table 10.1   Strength of Patent Protection in DR-CAFTA Countries and Comparison Groups, 1990–2005

Country or region	1990	1995	2000	2005
Argentina	1.71	2.73	3.98	3.98
Brazil	1.28	1.48	3.59	3.59
Chile	2.26	3.91	4.28	4.28
Colombia	1.13	2.74	3.59	3.72
Mexico	1.36	3.14	3.68	3.88
Costa Rica	1.16	1.56	2.89	2.89
Dominican Republic	2.12	2.32	2.45	2.82
El Salvador	1.71	3.23	3.36	3.48
Guatemala	0.88	1.08	1.28	3.15
Honduras	1.25	1.9	2.86	2.98
Nicaragua	0.92	1.12	2.16	2.97
Latin America				
Mean	1.35	2.28	3.18	3.42
Standard deviation	0.44	0.77	0.73	0.42

Source: Park 2008.

Trade-Related Aspects of Intellectual Property Rights (TRIPS) agreement came into force in 1995. Five of the six DR-CAFTA countries are below the average strength of patent protection in Latin America. Only El Salvador is above the mean during 2000–05. As of 2005, the patent protection levels of the DR-CAFTA countries are all below those of the five largest Latin American economies: Argentina, Brazil, Chile, Colombia, and Mexico.

Table 10.2 provides an idea of the sources of the recent strengthening of IPRs in the DR-CAFTA region. All six member states are signatories to the TRIPS agreement, to the Paris Convention for the Protection of Industrial Property, and to the Berne Convention for the Protection of Literary and Artistic Works. However, none is a member of the Madrid agreement. Only Nicaragua thus far is a member of the International Union for the Protection of New Varieties of Plants. However, patent protection for pharmaceuticals and chemicals in Nicaragua remains an issue. Otherwise, the other five countries have expanded the subject matter of

Table 10.2   Intellectual Property Provisions in DR-CAFTA Countries, 2005–07

Provision	Costa Rica	Dominican Republic	El Salvador	Guatemala	Honduras	Nicaragua
TRIPS agreement	1	1	1	1	1	1
Paris convention	1	1	1	1	1	1
Berne convention	1	1	1	1	1	1
Patent Cooperation Treaty	1	0	0	0	0	1
Madrid agreement	0	0	0	0	0	0
Patentability of chemicals	1	1	1	1	1	0
Patentability of pharmaceuticals	1	1	1	1	1	0
Patentability of software	0	1	0	0	0	0
Utility model protection	1	0	1	1	1	0
Plant and variety protection	0	0	0	0	0	1
Pretrial injunctions	1	1	1	1	1	1
Compulsory licensing for not working	0	1	0	0	0	1

Sources: Sinnott, Sinnott, and Cotreau 2008; Park 2008.
Note: 1 = Signatory or available; 0 = Not a signatory or not available.

patenting to include chemicals and drugs. The patentability of software remains an issue, except in the Dominican Republic. Four countries allow for utility model protection (that is, for adaptive and minor inventions, such as tools). All six countries allow for preliminary injunctions against an accused infringer while a patent case is pending. This is a useful mechanism for enforcing patent rights. Still, four of these countries issue compulsory licensing for patented inventions that are, from the authorities' perspective, inadequately exploited (either by local production or by importation).

An alternative perspective on IPRs is provided by a survey of business executives conducted by the World Economic Forum (WEF). One of the survey questions in the WEF's *Global Competitiveness Report* asks respondents in each country to rate, on a scale from 1 (lowest) to 7 (highest), whether intellectual property rights are well protected. The responses in each country are then averaged.[2] A shortcoming of the IPR part of the survey is that a single question (or response to it) lacks nuance. The question the survey poses is very broad, since IPRs include patents, copyrights, trademarks, geographical indications, trade secrets, industrial designs, and so forth. Other drawbacks are that the survey responses are subjective or based on perceptions, not on actual rulings or prevailing legal conditions. The overall rating for a country may also not be fully comparable to the ratings of other countries since a different sample of respondents rates each country. For example, it is hard to compare a score of 3.5 for Costa Rica and a score of 3.0 for the Dominican Republic. Had the same group of people scored both countries, at least the scores could be comparable in an ordinal sense. Notwithstanding these limitations, the surveys provide useful information on the actual experiences of firms with IPR protection in their countries. The statutes may, for example, provide for preliminary injunctions, but in practice obtaining one may be a time-consuming and bureaucratic process. Furthermore, what may drive business behavior is the firm's *perception* of the adequacy of IPRs rather than the stated provisions in the legal statutes.

Business perceptions of IPR adequacy fell in 2005 but rose thereafter to reach a peak in 2006. The signing of the United States and DR-CAFTA free trade legislation by the White House in August 2005 may have contributed to the spike in perception (but a more formal statistical test would better explain the temporal patterns). After 2006, perceptions appear to fall toward levels that may be more consistent with the levels of IPRs prevailing in these countries. In terms of the relative perception of the adequacy of IPR protection across countries, Costa Rica, the

Dominican Republic, and Honduras are above the Latin American mean, while El Salvador, Nicaragua, and Guatemala are below.

Another perspective on the IPR regimes in DR-CAFTA can be gleaned from statistics on software piracy rates in the region. The Business Software Alliance estimates the rate of piracy as the ratio of the level of piracy to total sales (that is, the sum of legitimate sales and illegitimate sales). The level of piracy is the difference between total installations of software and legal shipments of software. Since the TRIPS agreement was enacted, piracy rates have fallen significantly in the region. In 1995, rates were in the 90–98 percent range. In 2008 they were between 60 and 80 percent. However, those rates are still relatively very high. Only Costa Rica's rate of piracy is below the mean rate of piracy in Latin America. The other five DR-CAFTA countries have piracy rates in the high 70 percent range. This may be why business perceptions of IPR adequacy remain low. To the extent that the software industry is representative, IPR enforcement remains an issue. More effective deterrents and resources for intellectual property agencies are needed.

Table 10.3 shows that the three measures of the state of IPRs are correlated in the Latin American region. Business perceptions of IPR adequacy are generally high in countries that have strong patent systems. Piracy rates have an inverse correlation with patent strength and business perceptions of IPRs; that is, they are lower if patent rights are stronger and if IPRs are more adequately enforced. As these are simply correlations, causality cannot be established without a more formal statistical analysis. For example, IPR issues and reforms may take on greater importance in regions that have high levels of piracy, imitation, and infringement. Thus IPR laws may respond to piracy and perceptions, as well as vice versa.

Table 10.3   Correlations among Intellectual Property Measures

	Patent law index	Piracy rate	Intellectual property perception
Patent law index	1		
Piracy rate	−0.46	1	
Intellectual property perception	0.42	−0.71	1

Sources: The patent law index is from Park (2008), the piracy rate is from the Business Software Alliance's estimates of software piracy, and the intellectual property perception is from the World Economic Forum's survey of business managers.

Note: Sample size is 18 Latin American countries (for 2005): Argentina, Bolivia, Brazil, Chile, Colombia, Costa Rica, the Dominican Republic, Ecuador, El Salvador, Guatemala, Honduras, Mexico, Nicaragua, Paraguay, Peru, Trinidad and Tobago, Uruguay, and República Bolivariana de Venezuela.

To reveal some trends in FDI in the DR-CAFTA region, table 10.4 presents statistics on inward and outward FDI *flows* in the region, while table 10.5 shows the same for *stocks*. The flows and stocks are in nominal U.S. dollars. As such, the growth rates of FDI activity are downplayed, since the figures are not in real terms. Some important and interesting cross-sectional observations can nonetheless be made. First, there are far more inward FDI flows into DR-CAFTA countries than outward FDI flows from them. DR-CAFTA countries are not a major source of global capital. The inward flows of capital are important to DR-CAFTA countries insofar as they represent a fairly significant percentage of gross fixed capital formation. In 2007, foreign capital inflows equaled almost half of domestic investment in El Salvador (see table 10.4) and about a third in Costa Rica. However, in Guatemala, FDI inflows are just 10 percent of domestic fixed investment. For Latin America as a whole, FDI inflows account for about a fifth of gross fixed capital formation. Over time, for all six countries, the ratio of FDI inflows to gross fixed capital formation has increased, indicating greater exposure to global supplies of capital and some trend expansion in inward FDI flows.

FDI flows into and out of DR-CAFTA pale in comparison to those of the world or even of Latin America as a whole. The inward and outward stocks of FDI in DR-CAFTA tell a similar story (see table 10.5). As a percentage of GDP, the inward stock of FDI in 2007 was 55 percent for Nicaragua, about 20 percent for the Dominican Republic, almost 14 percent for Guatemala, and about 30 percent for the other countries in the group. Again, the stock of FDI in DR-CAFTA is a small percentage of the stock of FDI capital in Latin America and the world as a whole. Again, while the stock of FDI is in nominal rather than real dollars, the ratio of FDI stock to GDP suggests that it has expanded relative to market size, measured by GDP.

Table 10.6 presents data on U.S. outward FDI to the DR-CAFTA region. The United States is, of course, an important player in the DR-CAFTA and has been a significant source of inward FDI for the region. In 2008, the United States accounted for about a fifth of the stock of inward FDI in Costa Rica and about half of the stock in El Salvador. Altogether, about 47 percent of the stock of inward FDI in Latin America (and other Western Hemisphere) countries is due to the United States.[3]

Table 10.7 shows the industry composition of U.S. FDI in DR-CAFTA, along with the composition in some reference groups. The figures here are an average of 2004 and 2008. Most of U.S. FDI occurs in

Table 10.4 Flows of Foreign Direct Investment in DR-CAFTA Countries and Comparison Groups, 1980–2008

Country or group and mode	1980	1990	1995	2000	2005	2006	2007	2008
Costa Rica								
Inward flow	52.7	162.4	336.9	408.6	861.0	1,469.1	1,896.1	2,021.0
Inward flow as % of GrossCap	4.0	11.1	15.1	14.4	22.7	32.6	33.4	
Outward flow	4.5	2.1	5.5	8.5	−43.0	98.1	262.5	5.9
Outward flow as % of GrossCap	0.3	0.1	0.2	0.3	−1.1	2.2	4.6	
Dominican Republic								
Inward flow	92.7	132.8	414.3	952.9	1,122.7	1,528.3	1,578.9	2,884.7
Inward flow as % of GrossCap	5.5	8.0	16.4	19.7	20.5	23.5	20.5	
Outward flow	0.0	0.0	14.6	61.0	20.8	−61.3	−16.8	−19.1
Outward flow as % of GrossCap	0.0	0.0	0.6	1.3	0.4	−0.9	−0.2	
El Salvador								
Inward flow	5.9	1.9	38.0	173.4	511.1	241.1	1,508.5	784.2
Inward flow as % of GrossCap	1.1	0.3	2.1	7.8	19.6	8.0	46.0	
Outward flow	0.0	0.0	−2.3	−5.0	112.9	−26.4	100.3	65.4
Outward flow as % of GrossCap	0.0	0.0	−0.1	−0.2	4.3	−0.9	3.1	
Guatemala								
Inward flow	110.7	59.3	75.3	229.6	508.3	591.6	745.1	837.8
Inward flow as % of GrossCap	8.1	5.7	3.4	7.0	10.2	9.7	10.8	
Outward flow	2.0	0.0	−19.1	40.1	38.2	40.0	25.4	16.3
Outward flow as % of GrossCap	0.1	0.0	−0.8	1.2	0.8	0.7	0.4	

Honduras								
Inward flow	5.8	43.5	69.4	381.7	599.8	669.1	815.9	877.0
Inward flow as % of GrossCap	0.8	6.0	6.2	20.6	24.7	22.3	21.8	
Outward flow	1.0	−1.0	−2.0	6.5	1.0	0.6	1.0	1.8
Outward flow as % of GrossCap	0.1	−0.1	−0.2	0.4	0.0	0.0	0.0	
Nicaragua								
Inward flow	12.5	0.7	75.4	266.5	241.1	286.8	381.7	626.1
Inward flow as % of GrossCap	4.6	0.1	11.7	23.6	17.4	19.3	22.5	
Outward flow	0.0	0.0	0.4	8.0	18.1	21.0	9.2	16.1
Outward flow as % of GrossCap	0.0	0.0	0.1	0.7	1.3	1.4	0.5	
Latin America and the Caribbean								
Inward flow	6,415.8	8,926.1	29,513.0	98,354.6	77,069.7	93,303.2	127,491.4	144,377.1
Inward flow as % of GrossCap	3.3	4.0	8.8	25.8	16.2	15.9	17.8	
Outward flow	898.8	299.7	7,459.2	49,579.0	35,967.2	63,619.4	51,741.1	63,207.0
Outward flow as % of GrossCap	0.5	0.1	2.2	13.0	7.6	10.9	7.2	
World								
Inward flow	54,076.4	207,273.3	341,144.3	1,381,675.2	973,329.1	1,461,074.1	1,978,837.9	1,697,353.2
Inward flow as % of GrossCap	2.1	4.1	5.3	20.0	10.0	13.6	16.2	12.3
Outward flow	51,549.8	239,111.1	361,679.3	1,213,794.8	878,987.7	1,396,915.5	2,146,521.6	1,857,734.0
Outward flow as % of GrossCap	2.1	5.0	5.6	17.6	9.0	13.0	17.5	13.5

Source: UNCTAD 2009.

Note: Figures are in millions of current U.S. dollars. The % of GrossCap denotes percentage of gross fixed capital formation.

Table 10.5   Stocks of Foreign Direct Investment in DR-CAFTA Countries and Comparison Groups, 1980–2008

current US$, millions, unless otherwise noted

Country or group and mode	1980	1990	1995	2000	2005	2006	2007	2008
Costa Rica								
Inward stock	497.1	1,323.7	409.1	2,709.1	5,416.9	6,780.5	8,802.8	10,818.0
Inward stock as % of GDP	8.1	18.2	3.5	17.0	27.1	30.5	34.0	36.8
Outward stock	7.2	44.1	66.3	86.1	153.6	262.9	525.8	531.6
Outward stock as % of GDP	0.1	0.6	0.6	0.5	0.8	1.2	2.0	1.8
Dominican Republic								
Inward stock	238.7	571.5	–1,835.0	1,672.8	5,276.0	6,960.6	8,523.3	11,408.0
Inward stock as % of GDP	2.9	6.1	7.1	7.1	15.7	19.5	20.8	24.8
Outward stock	0.0	0.0	0.0	0.0	0.0	0.0	0.0	0.0
Outward stock as % of GDP	0.0	0.0	0.0	0.0	0.0	0.0	0.0	0.0
El Salvador								
Inward stock	154.3	212.1	293.0	1,973.1	4,166.5	4,407.8	5,916.3	6,701.4
Inward stock as % of GDP	4.1	4.4	3.1	15.0	24.4	23.6	29.0	30.3
Outward stock		56.1	53.3	74.0	310.1	283.7	384.0	449.4
Outward stock as % of GDP		1.2	0.6	0.6	1.8	1.5	1.9	2.0
Guatemala								
Inward stock	701.0	1,734.2	2201.6	3,419.9	3,319.2	3,897.8	4,617.6	5,455.4
Inward stock as % of GDP	10.0	25.4	16.9	19.9	12.2	12.9	13.8	14.3
Outward stock			23.7	92.8	250.3	293.4	315.6	331.9
Outward stock as % of GDP			0.2	0.5	0.9	1.0	0.9	0.9

Honduras

Inward stock	5.8	292.9	555.6	1,391.6	2,708.3	3,333.9	4,223.8	5,112.2
Inward stock as % of GDP	0.2	8.1	11.8	19.4	27.8	30.8	34.3	36.3
Outward stock	0.0	0.0	0.0	0.0	23.5	24.6	26.1	24.6
Outward stock as % of GDP	0.0	0.0	0.0	0.0	0.2	0.2	0.2	0.2

Nicaragua

Inward stock	121.4	144.8	384.2	1,414.5	2,461.0	2,747.8	3,129.5	3,755.6
Inward stock as % of GDP	5.8	5.3	12.1	35.9	50.7	51.8	55.1	59.3
Outward stock			0.4	22.4	93.9	114.9	124.1	140.2
Outward stock as % of GDP			0.0	0.6	1.9	2.2	2.2	2.2

Latin America and the Caribbean

Inward stock	40,959.5	110,546.8	185,122.7	502,487.2	817,560.1	933,610.3	1,125,109.4	1,181,615.7
Inward stock as % of GDP	5.3	9.5	10.3	24.4	31.5	30.9	32.0	25.7
Outward stock	47,518.1	57,642.9	87,892.1	204,387.9	335,424.2	430,344.6	500,548.1	561,432.9
Outward stock as % of GDP	6.2	5.0	4.9	9.9	12.9	14.2	14.2	8.3

World

Inward stock	705,211.4	1,942,207.2	2,915,311.4	5,757,359.9	10,050,885.0	12,404,439.0	15,660,498.0	14,909,289.0
Inward stock as % of GDP	6.5	8.8	9.8	18.0	22.3	25.4	28.7	24.4
Outward stock	548,932.5	1,785,583.9	2,941,724.2	6,069,881.8	10,603,662.0	12,953,546.0	16,226,586.0	16,205,663.0
Outward stock as % of GDP	5.3	8.4	9.9	19.0	23.5	26.6	29.7	26.4

Source: UNCTAD 2009.

Table 10.6   Amount of U.S. Foreign Direct Investment in DR-CAFTA Countries and Comparison Groups, Historical Cost Basis, 2004–08
current US$, millions

Country or group	2004	2005	2006	2007	2008
All countries	2,160,844	2,241,656	2,477,268	2,916,930	3,162,021
Latin America and other Western Hemisphere countries	351,709	379,582	418,429	508,711	563,809
Costa Rica	2,687	1,598	2,105	2,265	2,525
Dominican Republic	1,028	815	789	766	960
El Salvador	851	934	626	1,559	3,215
Guatemala	410	386	436	614	915
Honduras	755	821	864	640	700
Nicaragua	131	163		237	162

Source: U.S. Bureau of Economic Analysis, http://www.bea.gov/international/di1fdibal.htm.

the manufacturing sector of DR-CAFTA. About half of U.S. FDI is in the manufacturing sector of the Dominican Republic. The exception is Nicaragua, where about 43 percent of U.S. FDI is in wholesale trade. Within manufacturing, the food and beverages sector in Guatemala is a major recipient of U.S. FDI. The food and electrical equipment sectors receive a significant share of U.S. FDI in Costa Rica. The sectoral distribution of U.S. FDI is somewhat more distinct in DR-CAFTA than in Latin America as a whole, where about a third of U.S. FDI is in finance and insurance and almost 40 percent is in holding companies. This reflects U.S. FDI across the world as a whole. Less than a fifth of U.S. global outward FDI is in manufacturing, a little more than a fifth is in finance, and a little more than a third is in holding companies. Wholesale trade accounts for just over 5 percent of U.S. global outward FDI. Thus, in comparison to these reference groups—that is, Latin America and the world as a whole—U.S. FDI in DR-CAFTA exhibits a difference in specialization or motivation. For example, manufacturing production (due to lower labor costs) and wholesale trade (due to geographic location between North and South America) appear to be the key areas of focus in the DR-CAFTA region.

Regional Integration and FDI

This section briefly reviews previous studies on the relationship between regional integration and FDI. There is a large literature on this, so this chapter defers to studies cited in this section, which provide a more thorough

Table 10.7 U.S. Foreign Direct Investment in DR-CAFTA Countries and Comparison Groups, by Industry, 2004–08 Average
share of total industries (%)

Industry	All countries	Other Western Hemisphere countries	Costa Rica	Dominican Republic	El Salvador	Guatemala	Honduras	Nicaragua
Mining	4.8	5.4	0.0	0.0	0.5	0.0	0.0	−18.0
Manufacturing	17.7	11.7	37.8	52.0	14.3	33.9	22.2	0.0
Food	1.3	1.2	5.9	2.7	0.0	13.5	0.4	0.0
Chemicals	4.1	2.6	3.8	5.9	0.0	0.0	1.1	0.0
Metals	1.0	1.0	1.5	2.6	−1.0	0.1	0.5	0.0
Machinery	1.1	0.6	0.0	0.0	0.0	0.2	0.0	0.0
Computers and electronics	2.4	0.1	0.0	−1.0	0.0	0.0	0.0	0.0
Electrical equipment and related	0.7	0.3	4.6	0.0	0.0	0.0	0.0	0.0
Transportation	2.1	1.5	0.0	0.0	0.0	0.0	−0.6	−1.5
Other manufacturing	5.1	4.4	0.0	39.5	0.0	0.0	0.0	0.0
Wholesale trade	5.7	4.0	4.8	13.5	0.0	11.6	9.2	43.3
Information	3.2	1.7	0.3	0.0	0.3	0.6	0.0	−0.7
Depository institutions	3.7	0.3	0.0	0.0	0.0	0.0	0.0	13.3
Finance and insurance	20.1	33.3	0.0	0.1	1.6	19.2	7.7	0.0
Professional, scientific, technical services	2.5	0.4	3.3	0.1	0.0	0.2	0.0	3.5
Holding companies	35.5	38.5	0.0	−0.1	0.0	−1.1	−0.1	0.0
Other industries	6.8	4.8	−4.7	5.8	31.1	19.3	0.0	−1.2

Source: U.S. Bureau of Economic Analysis, http//www.bea.gov/international/di1fdibal.htm.

background. As of yet, there are limited, if any, empirical economic studies on DR-CAFTA, since this is a new agreement. Most of the evidence is based, therefore, on other experiences with regional integration; for example, the European Community (EC), the Southern Cone Common Market (Mercosur), the North American Free Trade Agreement (NAFTA), the Association of South East Asian Nations (ASEAN), and the United States–Canada Free Trade Agreement. In a review of previous empirical studies, it would, of course, be useful to examine which prior cases best approximate DR-CAFTA. It would be especially useful to understand the basic principles or mechanisms by which regional integration influences FDI. It then becomes an empirical issue as to which mechanisms are most applicable to or observed in the DR-CAFTA region.

Regional economic integration typically leads to a reduction in within-region trade barriers and investment restrictions. Studies on the relationship between integration and foreign direct investment focus mostly on the impact on inward, rather than outward, FDI. Theoretically, on the one hand, the easing of investment restrictions should enhance inward FDI. On the other hand, the easing of trade barriers may reduce FDI to the extent that the main motivation for FDI is to evade tariffs (that is, tariff-jumping motivation) or defuse tariffs by setting up a subsidiary that employs and produces locally. Another important motivation for FDI is to exploit intangible assets, such as a firm's intellectual property assets (trademarks, copyrights, patents, or trade secrets) or marketing expertise. Another channel by which regional economic integration should affect FDI is through market size. In addition to providing a source of greater demand for a multinational firm's products (which may be served more efficiently through local production rather than through exports), the larger common market enables a firm to spread the fixed costs of affiliate investments. To the extent that freer trade and investment stimulate economic growth, regional economic integration also produces dynamic effects: increased growth enhances the future profitability of the common market, thereby attracting more FDI. The larger and faster-growing market may, in turn, feed the incentives of multinational firms to innovate—to create new products or improve the quality of existing products. This should stimulate the research and development (R&D) of parent firms and augment the stock of intangible assets.[4]

Empirical studies on the effects of regional economic integration on foreign direct investment are based either on descriptive statistical analyses or on formal econometric modeling. Examples of the former include Mirus and Scholnick (1998), a study that focuses on U.S. FDI into Canada after the bilateral trade agreement between the United States and Canada. The data analysis here suggests a positive response of U.S. FDI to the agreement. The authors argue that this evidence dispels the notion that U.S. FDI was motivated by tariff jumping (since FDI continued and intensified after Canadian tariffs were lowered). They also dispel the notion that U.S. FDI occurred to take advantage of Canada's natural resources (such as oil and timber). The evidence indicates that U.S. FDI increased in the manufacturing sectors, not in resource extraction. Lastly, the study finds evidence of agglomeration effects—that is, economies enjoyed by firms from clustering. One source of these effects may be knowledge spillovers and improved opportunities to learn about new technologies and markets; another may be the availability of more supporting industries (producers of components and services) that would not otherwise be available in less dense markets. Mirus and Scholnick (1998) find that FDI is greater in those sectors where U.S. firms were already present in Canada.

Blomstrom, Globerman, and Kokko (2000), however, do not detect any significant cross-border affiliate activity between Canada and the United States after the free trade agreement. They argue that the United States–Canada Free Trade Agreement constituted a minor environmental change in the business climate. The two countries had already engaged in much cross-border investment such that increased regional economic integration had a marginal effect. Instead they find that regional economic integration has larger effects on FDI if the integration involves a northern country and a southern country (as in the case of NAFTA) or a southern country and another southern country (as in the case of Mercosur), rather than a northern country and another northern country (as in the case of the United States–Canada Free Trade Agreement). Blomstrom, Globerman, and Kokko (2000) identify two critical factors that determine the extent to which regional economic integration boosts FDI. The first is the existence of sufficient trade and investment liberalization. The second is the presence of good locational advantages in the regions concerned. For example, post-NAFTA, Mexico received a larger influx of FDI, not so much from U.S. and Canadian firms, but from firms outside NAFTA. Mexico has a locational advantage: proximity to the United States. Along with cheaper Mexican labor, foreign firms would find easier supply routes into the United States and thus have an incentive to invest in Mexican subsidiaries. Moreover, NAFTA occurred alongside other reforms in Mexico, such as investment and regulatory reforms, that may have been the more significant drivers of inward flows of FDI.

FDI in the Mercosur region also increased substantially, but was not evenly distributed within the region. Inward FDI increased especially in the larger markets of Argentina and Brazil, but not significantly in the smaller markets of Paraguay and Uruguay. Of course, other factors were involved (in addition to regional economic integration); namely, macroeconomic stability in the larger member countries, which helped to reduce investor risk and uncertainty. Where the southern region can serve as an export platform for the products of foreign multinational firms, regional economic integration can attract vertical FDI in particular. In this case, different regions can contribute to the different stages of a product's value added. A free trade and liberalized investment region can allow different multinational affiliates to specialize more efficiently according to their location-specific advantages, whether they are resources or local know-how and skills.

Balasubramanyam and Greenaway (1993) also study a regional economic integration case involving a northern country and a group of northern countries, namely, Japan and the European Community. In this case, the European common market had a significant influence on Japanese FDI into the EC. For Japan, the EC represented an important environmental shift, since prior Japanese affiliate activity in the EC was limited. However, Balasubramanyam and Greenaway (1993) argue that Japanese FDI was driven more by protection-defusing motives. There was concern that a "Fortress Europe" would block imports from Japan—hence the motivation for establishing Japanese branches within Europe. However, because the EC common market had tremendous growth potential, Japanese FDI continued to expand into the EC. Ultimately, the longer-run driver of Japanese FDI was the desire to serve consumers in the EC.

The studies cited above have rested on descriptive statistical analysis. More recent work has used econometric analysis to disentangle the effects of regional economic integration on FDI from other potential determinants. Cuevas, Messmacher, and Werner (2005) use cross-country data to find a positive association between regional economic integration and FDI flows, controlling for the increase in worldwide FDI flows. The results are applied to the case of Mexico under NAFTA. The authors estimate that Mexican inward FDI was 60 percent greater than it would have been in the absence of NAFTA.

Another econometric study is by Antras and Foley (2011), which looks at the case of South-South economic integration, namely, the ASEAN agreement of 1992 involving Brunei Darussalam, Indonesia, Malaysia, the Philippines, Singapore, and Thailand.[5] This study provides comprehensive evidence from firm-level data. The focus of attention is U.S. outward FDI to the ASEAN countries before and after the agreement. The United States accounts for about a fifth of the inward FDI of this region. The key finding is that there is a statistically significant increase in U.S. affiliate activity after the agreement. There is an increase in the extensive margin (that is, growth in the number of U.S. affiliates in the ASEAN region) and in the intensive margin (that is, expansion in affiliate activity per affiliate, such as sales, capital investment, and asset growth). U.S. affiliates grew faster and larger in ASEAN countries than in other Asian countries. Hence there appears to be an effect associated with ASEAN membership. Overall, this study finds evidence to support the view that regional economic integration among smaller countries can attract FDI. The ASEAN experience offers probably the closest test case for DR-CAFTA, given that the DR-CAFTA region also consists of small developing economies, although the ASEAN countries are more populous. Antras and Foley (2011) identify lower trade costs within the ASEAN as an important factor driving the growth of inward FDI into the ASEAN countries. The lower trade costs make the establishment of a subsidiary plant within the ASEAN especially attractive as a platform for exporting goods to other countries in the region.

Intellectual Property Rights and FDI

This section discusses theoretical and empirical work on the relationship between FDI and IPRs. In theory, firms engage in FDI to maximize profits or value. Thus their FDI is influenced by the strength of IPRs to the extent that intellectual property protection affects the ability of firms to capture rents and returns on their investments.

The North-South theoretical literature has some relevance here since it studies the effects of IPRs in developing countries on FDI into the developing world. However, the predictions in this literature regarding the effects of stronger IPRs on FDI are mixed. For example, Lai (1998) develops a model in which northern firms innovate, while southern firms imitate. If and when a southern firm successfully copies a northern innovation, it becomes the producer and exporter of the good due to its factor cost advantage, thereby displacing the northern firm that was the original innovator of the good. Northern firms, however, have the option to produce in the South—that is, to be a multinational firm. Wages are lower in the South, but imitation risks are higher. Thus, stronger IPRs in the South reduce the risks of imitation and increase the expected returns to being a multinational firm. As a result, more production is transferred from the North to the South. In this model, stronger IPRs are associated with higher rates of foreign direct investment.

In Glass and Saggi (2002), imitative activity in the South is assumed not to be a costless activity. Imitators incur fixed costs to imitate successfully. Imitators in the South target the goods of both northern and multinational firms for imitation. An increase in the strength of IPRs reduces the incentives to imitate but raises the total resources devoted to imitative activities. Southern imitators expend greater resources to invent around foreign goods (that is, resource absorption effect). Thus, stronger intellectual property protection in the South results in greater resource scarcity. Less FDI would occur due to the higher costs of production. This model predicts a decline in FDI due to stronger IPRs.

One shortcoming of these North-South models is that they examine only one form of technology transfer, in this case, FDI. The models ignore the composition of technology transfer, among, say, exporting, FDI, and licensing. The strength of IPRs in the host country can affect not only the volume of technology, but also the mode of entry. For example, stronger IPRs may appear to reduce inward FDI but actually increase technology transfers overall if another mode of entry is expanded (say, licensing).

However, a shortcoming of studies that examine the composition of technology transfers is that they are either partial-equilibrium analyses or single-country analyses; they do not model the reaction of agents in the home country. Nonetheless, by using a choice-theoretic framework, they provide useful insights into the ways in which the intellectual property regime in a host country affects the decision making of foreign investors.

First, IPRs have ambiguous effects a priori on the overall volume of technology transfers. Maskus and Penubarti (1995) and Yang and Maskus (2001) identify two opposing effects of stronger IPRs on technology transfers: *a market expansion effect* and *a market power effect*. Consider a firm in country A that transfers IP-sensitive commodities to country B, and suppose that country B strengthens its IPRs. On the one hand, the firm perceives an expansion in its market due to a reduction in imitation by local firms. The demand curve it faces in country B shifts out. On the other hand, stronger IPRs in country B increase the firm's market power, reducing the elasticity of the demand it faces. The market expansion effect is likely to dominate in countries where the market environment is competitive, and the market power effect is likely to dominate in regions where local competitors pose a weak threat of imitation.

Next, the composition of technology transfers depends on a variety of factors. These factors can be organized conceptually using the ownership, location, and internalization (OLI) framework of Dunning (1980). The *ownership* factor influences a firm's decision to enter a foreign market. A firm selling a good abroad has a disadvantage competing with producers who know the local market better. To compensate, the firm needs to have some advantages, such as ownership of a superior technology. The *location* factor influences a firm's decision to enter via exports or FDI. For example, exporting may involve lower agency or setup costs than locating a subsidiary abroad. To compensate, the foreign market needs to provide some locational advantage, such as lower factor costs. The *internalization* factor affects a firm's decision to produce the good through its subsidiary or to license the production to another party (affiliated or unaffiliated). The firm chooses to internalize production if there are advantages to controlling the production process, such as the avoidance of transaction costs.

Stronger IPRs in the host country can affect each of these factors—the ownership value of technology, the attractiveness of locating production abroad, and the incentive to deal with agents external to the firm. First, the possession or ownership of a valuable intangible asset helps a firm to overcome the costs of setting up a subsidiary abroad (versus exporting), as its product would be in demand and be profitable. To the extent that stronger intellectual property protection in the host country stimulates a multinational firm's incentive to innovate, the multinational firm would make greater investments in R&D that yield more valuable intangible assets. These assets, in turn, would become the basis for future FDI or other technology transfers. Second, the strength of intellectual property protection in a host country, along with other institutional factors, makes up part of the local business investment climate. Hence, the strength of IPRs provides a locational advantage for firms to establish a presence in the host country. Third, IPRs can affect the choice between FDI and licensing at the margin. If intellectual property rights are strong and very secure, firms that own valuable intangible assets are more likely (and more willing) to license the production and distribution of the product to arm's length parties. The advantage of licensing to other parties is that firms can tap into the sales and distribution capabilities of other agents. Few plants or affiliates of a multinational parent firm may have the capacity to satisfy local demand on their own, particularly if the local market is large—hence the desirability of licensing to a third party. However, if IPRs are not sufficiently strong, firms are more likely to internalize the value of the asset by producing the good in-house (within a local plant or a subsidiary) or by licensing it to a close affiliate.

Thus, IPRs may have a nonmonotonic relationship with FDI. That is, FDI may rise as IPR levels strengthen. The volume of FDI rises as local markets appear more profitable due to the increased protection of intellectual property rights. The volume of FDI also rises as firms shift from exporting to setting up subsidiaries abroad. But as the level of IPR increases further, the volume of FDI may remain stable or even decline as firms shift toward licensing as a means of marketing their products. This nonlinear relationship may help to explain why some empirical studies find a negative effect of IPRs on FDI (particularly if the studies do not control for the mode of entry of foreign firms).

Industry differences may also affect how intellectual property protection affects FDI through these OLI channels (see Vishwasrao 1994; Nicholson 2007). In particular, industries vary by complexity of technology and therefore by the setup costs of plants. These setup costs tend to be very high for technologies that are quite complex. Indeed, such costs can act as a natural barrier against imitation. For industries in which technologies are relatively hard to replicate, firms may choose or switch to licensing at relatively lower levels of intellectual property protection. In contrast, for technologies that are relatively easy to replicate, the threshold strength of intellectual property that would induce licensing would be much higher. Thus, the internalization motive for conducting FDI (and keeping production within a local subsidiary) is greater for technologies that are easy to replicate and for industries characterized by such technologies (chemicals, software).

Such theoretical discussions have abstracted from the type of technology transferred. A firm that transfers technology can choose not just the mode of transfer, but also the vintage of the technology to be transferred (see Taylor 1994; Fosfuri 2000). For example, if intellectual property protection is weak and risks of imitation are consequently high, the firm may transfer an older version of the technology or not transfer its best-practice research technology.

In summary, the theoretical literature is divided as to whether developing countries would attract increased technology transfers by strengthening their intellectual property rights. On the one hand, stronger IPRs could increase developed-country incentives to increase technology transfers to the South (by reducing imitation risks and contractual costs). On the other hand, developed-country firms could enjoy increased market power as stronger IPRs in the South raise the cost of imitation or erect barriers to inventing. Thus the effect of IPRs on FDI, particularly in developing countries, is an empirical issue.

The empirical evidence on the effects of IPRs on FDI can be divided into two kinds: the first focuses on FDI as the dependent variable of interest; the second examines FDI jointly with other modes of foreign entry, such as exports and licensing. Both kinds of evidence are discussed below.

FDI as the Sole Dependent Variable

Most empirical studies employ U.S. data (that is, the outward FDI of U.S. multinational firms).[6] This section first discusses studies using U.S. data and then turns to studies using non-U.S. data or global panel data. Evidence using data prior to the TRIPS agreement is mixed. Primo Braga and Fink (1998), for example, examine the stocks of outward U.S. foreign direct investment in 42 countries in 1992 and find that they weakly correlate with the strength of patent protection, controlling for other factors. In contrast, Lee and Mansfield (1996) examine a panel of 14 developing countries around the same period and find that the strength of IPRs (as perceived by managers in the survey of Mansfield 1994) is a significant determinant of the volume of U.S. outward FDI flows. Lee and Mansfield (1996) also find that weaker IPRs can affect the composition of FDI, causing firms to invest in nonmanufacturing and non-R&D activities, like sales and distribution outlets.

More recent studies have used up-to-date U.S. data. Nunnenkamp and Spatz (2004) find that patent rights are a significant determinant of U.S. outward FDI stocks, particularly in developing countries. A reason that IPRs may matter more for FDI in less developed countries is that IPR strength is generally low in developing regions, so that a given change in IPRs represents a relatively major development. In larger countries, the environment for FDI is conducive for other reasons, such as market size, strong contract enforcement, quality of infrastructure, labor skills, and so forth, so that IPRs may matter relatively less. Moreover, a further strengthening of IPRs results in firms considering other options, such as licensing instead of expanding their subsidiaries.

Branstetter and others (2007) examine the activities of U.S. multinational firms in 16 countries during the period 1982–99. They examine multiple dependent variables associated with FDI activity, such as local affiliate sales, employment, capital stock, R&D, and industry output. The reason for examining a comprehensive set of variables is to ensure that IPR reforms did not merely increase firms' market power but led to "quantity" effects, such as increased production, employment, and investment in capital and technology. Their results indicate that an IPR reform is followed by an expansion in multinational sales, employment, investment, production, and technology transfer and that these expansions are especially prominent if the parent firms are heavy users of the patent system. Thus, more recent evidence (which includes some post-TRIPS years) suggests a positive effect of IPRs on FDI by U.S. multinational firms, particularly in developing countries.

As for studies using non-U.S. data, Mayer and Pfister (2001) examine data on French multinational firms and find that stronger patent rights have a negative influence on the locational decisions of multinational firms. When they split their sample into developed and developing host countries, they find that the strength of a developing country's patent laws has a statistically insignificant influence on the probability that a French multinational firm will locate in the developing country. The strength of a developed country's patent laws has a quadratic (inverse-U) effect on the firm's probability of locating in the developed country; that is, increasing the probability and then decreasing it after some critical level of patent law strength is reached.

It is important to note that Mayer and Pfister (2001) study locational decisions, not FDI flows or stocks. For firms already located in a country, the intensity of technology transfer in response to changes in patent laws is not captured in the location data alone. A difficulty with interpreting their results is that they can be consistent with both the market power and market expansion hypotheses of IPRs. If firms are exercising greater market power, they would reduce the flow of new branches or affiliates being opened up so as to enjoy greater rents from existing outlets. Otherwise, if firms are taking advantage of expanded markets, they may be exploiting alternative modes of marketing their goods and services, such as licensing or joint ventures. Thus, a key limitation of focusing on single modes like this is that it is difficult to draw decisive conclusions about whether stronger IPRs enhance or reduce technology transfer.

Using firm-level data for Eastern Europe and the former Soviet Union states, Smarzynska Javorcik (2004) finds that stronger patent rights have a positive and statistically significant effect on the probability of foreign investment in high-technology sectors and an insignificant effect in other sectors. Moreover, foreign investors are more likely to invest in sales and distribution outlets than in manufacturing or R&D facilities when patent protection is weaker. This propensity is found in all sectors, not just in high-technology ones. These findings conflict with those of Mayer and Pfister (2001), but are consistent with those of Lee and Mansfield (1996).

Using Japanese firm-level data, Belderbos, Fukao, and Kwon (2006) study the R&D investment decisions of 605 Japanese multinational firms in 42 countries. Their survey data allow for a rough separation of R&D investments into research-related investments (R) and development-related (D) investments. Both R and D abroad are found to be positively influenced by the strength of a host country's patent laws.[7] This supports Smarzynska Javorcik's (2004) conclusions as well.

Thus, the non-U.S. evidence on the effects of IPRs on FDI is varied. However, the breakdown of FDI by function and by sector is valuable in indicating that the effects of IPRs on FDI depend on whether FDI is largely for purposes of sales and distribution or for production and R&D or whether the investment is in technology-intensive industries.

Again, many of these studies employ data that are not very recent— either the sample period is before TRIPS or ends shortly thereafter. Park and Lippoldt (2008) assemble a panel data set of more than 90 countries from 1990 to 2005 using UNCTAD data. In their regression model, the real stock of inward FDI is a function of different IPRs (patent rights, copyrights, trademark rights, and perceptions of IPR enforcement) and a measure of openness (namely, an index of freedom to trade internationally), among other variables. The study finds that, individually, patent rights, copyrights, and trademark rights are statistically significant determinants of inward FDI. However, when all three measures are entered together, only the patent rights variable remains strongly significant. This suggests that, when the index of copyrights or trademark rights is examined alone (along with the control variables), it tends to pick up the effects of patent rights. If so, inward FDI that helps establish plants or subsidiaries is largely sensitive to the protection of inventive output rather than business names, symbols, or artistic creations. But in some sectors, copyrights and trademark rights may be more important if they are the only legal means of protecting an intellectual property asset; for example, software may only be copyrightable, not patentable.

Of course, some of this FDI could be for the establishment of plants whose main purpose is sales and distribution or manufacturing rather than research. The fact that the investments of multinational firms are sensitive to patent rights, holding other factors constant, suggests that valuable intangible assets are at stake, whether they are for production, research, or sales.

Park and Lippoldt (2008) also find that IPRs are more effective when economies are more open to trade (particularly in developing economies). This is relevant for intellectual property reform that is part of a regional economic integration agreement. Furthermore, they find that business executives' perceptions of IPR strength are also a significant determinant of inward FDI. The positive relationship between IPRs and inward FDI is picked up for both developed- and developing-country samples. However, the quantitative relationship does vary by level of development. The impact is larger among developed countries. This may be due to the existence of complementary factors in the North that make FDI more profitable in developed-country markets.

An interesting finding is that business perceptions of a stronger intellectual property regime have a weak or negative effect on inward FDI in the least developed countries. There are a couple of possible reasons. What matters in least developed countries is not just the perception of strength but actual legislative changes and statutory rights that give a clear signal to agents as to what their intellectual property rights are and what means of enforcement exist. Also, the survey of business perceptions reflects not just patent strength but also intellectual property rights in general, including copyrights and trademark rights. A negative effect may then reflect the possibility that strong, comprehensive intellectual property enforcement exerts some market power effects. Firms that enjoy increased market power have an incentive to reduce the stock of inward FDI and accordingly reduce the output of plants.

FDI in Conjunction with Other Modes of Entry

The studies cited above focus on FDI in isolation from other modes of entry. But firms typically have a menu of choices for breaking into a foreign market. Recent empirical work has explored both the volume and the composition of technology transfers and how each mode varies relative to another in response to stronger IPRs. The results are often conditional on the presence of other factors. Using U.S. aggregate data, Smith (2001) finds that stronger patent rights expand the scale of all technology transfer activities considered (exports, FDI, and licensing), but in favor of licensing and FDI. This appears to support the OLI framework where strong intellectual property rights enhance locational advantages and alter internalization considerations. The effects depend, though, on the imitative capacity of the host country (measured by whether there are sufficient R&D scientists and engineers per million people). Weak imitative capacity itself provides de facto protection against imitation so that patent protection matters less when the threat of imitation is weak.

Nicholson (2007) works with count data on the number of U.S. firms engaged in FDI or licensing in 1995 by industry. The count data help provide a perspective on the quantity effects of IPR changes, but obviously leave out information on the value of the transactions. As discussed earlier, firms in capital-intensive industries are likely to enjoy de facto protection from imitation due to their complex, hard-to-replicate inputs. This is reflected in the empirical results: in countries where capital costs are high and patent protection is strong, firms prefer licensing to FDI. But where capital costs are high and patent protection is weak, firms prefer to internalize production in their affiliated subsidiaries. Thus, how IPRs influence the choice of mode is conditional on the capital intensity of firms. For destinations other than the Organisation for Economic Co-operation and Development (OECD), this study finds patent protection to have no significant influence on FDI or licensing counts, regardless of the capital intensity of an industry. This could suggest that much of the positive effects on technology transfer (especially licensing) in developing countries may be price effects, not quantity.

The above studies use data from U.S. multinationals. Fosfuri (2004) examines plant-level data for the global chemical industry. The data set tracks the technology transfer investments of 153 firms (for example, U.S., Japanese, and European firms). The investments refer to the costs of establishing a wholly owned subsidiary, a joint venture, and a licensing deal. The finding here is that patent protection plays no role in any of the three technology transfer investments. There is one qualification: if patent protection is interacted with a variable representing imitative capacity (that is, average years of schooling), stronger patent rights are found to reduce investments in licensing in countries where imitative capacity is weak. These results, however, are partly attributable to the fact that the sample of chemical plants largely consists of firms with process innovations. For such innovations, patents may not be the most effective mechanism for appropriating the returns to innovation. The results therefore do not preclude the importance of other kinds of IPRs, such as trade secrecy.

These empirical studies do not explicitly treat North-South issues.[8] For different country income groups, Park and Lippoldt (2003) study the relationship between IPRs and the various modes of technology transfer (such as trade, FDI, and affiliated and unaffiliated licensing) using both aggregate and U.S. firm-level data. They also consider various kinds of IPRs—patent protection, copyright laws, and trademark protection. Consistent with other studies, they find that stronger patent rights increase FDI or licensing relative to exports in both developed and developing countries. The response of FDI to stronger patent rights is larger in developing countries (where IPR regimes are relatively weaker) than in developed countries (where IPR regimes are relatively stronger). Thus, patent rights appear to have a positive, but diminishing association with FDI as the strength of patent rights increases, controlling for other factors. The diminishing association is consistent with findings that firms prefer licensing in countries where IPRs are relatively much stronger, namely, in the relatively richer countries.

Some evidence from international patenting may provide insight into the types of technology transferred to developing countries. Allred and Park (2007), for example, find that patent rights in developing countries have a statistically insignificant influence on foreign patenting in developing countries. Yet some studies find that stronger patent protection increases inward FDI in developing countries. Thus, it is odd that stronger patent protection in developing countries attracts FDI but not foreign patents. The explanation might be that the technologies being transferred to the South are relatively older or that FDI is geared largely toward sales and distribution rather than R&D and production. Transferring older vintages obviates the need to file foreign patent applications, since the technologies are "prior knowledge" (and thus do not qualify for a new patent). To the extent that developing countries receive transfers of older vintages or not-best-practice research technologies, foreign patenting is less sensitive to variations in patent rights in developing countries.

Indeed, Contractor (1981) provides evidence that U.S. firms tend to transfer older technologies to unaffiliated parties in developing countries than they transfer to agents in industrial economies. The commercial age of a technology is defined as the time from commercial introduction to the inception of a technology transfer agreement. In Mansfield (1994), chemical and manufacturing firms reported that they would not transfer new technologies to countries with weak intellectual property laws. More recently, Nunnenkamp and Spatz (2004) find that weaker IPRs are associated with lower-quality FDI, as judged by the small increases in local R&D, employment, and value added.

Implications for DR-CAFTA

As mentioned in the previous section, IPRs have both market expansion and market power effects on technology transfers. Controlling for other factors, a strengthening of IPRs is likely to enhance FDI if the market expansion effects of IPRs dominate the market power effects. Intellectual property reforms combined with regional economic integration should help to tilt the balance in favor of market expansion effects. An agreement that opens up markets and creates competitive pressures can act as a check on the exercise of market power. In the case of DR-CAFTA, significant trade liberalization has occurred in the region. According to the index of the freedom to trade internationally,[9] since the mid-1980s, the trade regimes of DR-CAFTA countries have become freer. By 2007, these countries had index values in the range of 7–8. For comparison, the United States and the United Kingdom had scores of 7.6 that same year.

Another factor that determines the relative importance of market power effects is the capacity of local agents to imitate protected technologies. As work by Smith (2001) has shown, in countries where the threat of imitation is weak, stronger IPRs are more likely to enhance the market power of intellectual property owners since the absence of imitative threats acts as a de facto form of protection against copying. But if the data on piracy are any indication, the capacity to make copies is not weak in the DR-CAFTA area.

Furthermore, the IPR provisions of DR-CAFTA are quite comprehensive, covering not just patent rights, but also trademarks, copyrights, geographical indications, and trade secrets. These comprehensive provisions should be applicable to a wide variety of business activities: technology markets, cultural and creative industries, and the food and agriculture sector. DR-CAFTA countries are starting from initially low levels of IPR strength. Thus intellectual property reform in this region is not likely to push DR-CAFTA into zones of excessive protection. Moreover, to the extent that stronger IPRs stimulate incentives for innovation by local agents and foreign affiliates in the region, they generate dynamic competition, which could mitigate the market power effects of IPRs. That is, innovation results in the creation of new products that can compete with existing technological (intellectual property–protected) goods. Often, long before IPRs expire, intellectual property–protected goods may become obsolete or displaced as a result of technological innovations by rivals. This creates incentives on the part of the incumbent owners of intellectual property–protected goods to continue to innovate and compete, rather than to exploit monopoly power. The main point here is that the market expansion effects of IPR reform in DR-CAFTA should offset the market power effects of stronger IPRs.

However, a question to consider is, how big is the change in market size due to an expansion of IPRs in DR-CAFTA? An examination of the real GDP of the DR-CAFTA countries suggests that together they represent a very small share of the world market. The sum of the GDP of the DR-CAFTA countries is just over 6 percent of the GDP of Latin America and the Caribbean. Holding other factors constant, a change in IPRs may not expand GDP significantly enough to alter the size of the DR-CAFTA market. Furthermore, the change in IPRs is likely to affect GDP with a lag. Typically, IPRs are assumed to affect inventive and creative activity. These, in turn, affect the stock of knowledge (which helps to generate future innovations) and the productivity of existing resources. The latter, in turn, affects incomes and eventually market size (GDP). However, each step involves a lag (of uncertain length), and the elasticities are likely to be modest, though there is no solid consensus on the estimates of those elasticities (that is, the percentage change in innovation due to a given percentage change in IPRs, the percentage change in productivity due to a percentage change in the stock of innovations, and so forth). Thus, it is likely that, in the short run, market size will not change radically as a consequence of intellectual property reform. Of course, internally, the DR-CAFTA market is more liberalized as a result of economic integration. The reduced barriers to intraregional trade work to expand market *access* from that perspective. However, it is moot whether the IPR reforms will significantly expand the *size* of the DR-CAFTA market in the short run.

Increased economic integration, freer trade, and FDI (resulting from regional economic integration) should provide *growth* benefits so that market size expands in the longer run. There may be some positive feedback effects, in which larger market size attracts FDI and increased FDI boosts the marginal productivity of other resources, local production potential, income growth, and future market size.

As discussed earlier, there are several determinants of FDI. Market size is one of them. But other factors should not be neglected. The DR-CAFTA region has certain locational advantages, such as its geography, natural resources, and factor costs. As the region experiences increased economic growth and inward FDI, factor costs are likely to increase. A substantial increase in wage costs—without a compensating increase in the skill level of labor—could offset the benefits of increased market size in attracting foreign capital. Other factors that could offset the gains from economic integration and IPRs are onerous business regulations. Thus predictions on FDI are conditional on what happens to these other factors.[10]

Given that FDI is one of several other modes of entry for foreign multinationals, as intellectual property protection and enforcement are strengthened, inward FDI may actually decline if stronger IPRs encourage foreign firms to engage in licensing. DR-CAFTA still benefits from an inflow of technologies. However, it will occur through a mechanism other than foreign direct investment. Being aware of this possibility will help researchers to avoid drawing the conclusion that IPRs have negative effects on technology transfers if FDI declines. In other words, it is important to control for the other modes of technological transfer, such as licensing, joint ventures, and imports. Whether or not foreign firms will increase their licensing to local agents in DR-CAFTA will depend not just on the IPR regime, but also on whether local agents have sufficient manufacturing and distribution capacity. Presently, according to BEA data, U.S. foreign affiliates in the DR-CAFTA region conduct very few licensing transactions as a percentage of net income or sales, and what little they do is with other affiliates and the parent firm.[11] Thus, in the short to medium term it is not likely that licensing will displace FDI much, if at all, in the region.

The discussion in this chapter has dealt with potential variations in the level of inward FDI due to IPR reforms combined with economic integration. Another important perspective is the *function* of FDI. What will the purpose of expanded FDI be in the DR-CAFTA region: sales, distribution, production, or research? Economic integration in this region should enable multinational firms to use the region as a platform for exports, particularly for exports to the United States and other neighboring markets. But would DR-CAFTA be involved in high value added production or assembly as an export-processing zone? This might be where IPRs could play an important role. More secure protection for IPRs could give foreign firms an incentive to transfer higher-value technologies to their affiliates or subsidiaries and direct some higher value added phases of the production process to this region. Presently, levels of R&D performed by foreign affiliates and local agents are relatively low. R&D in the DR-CAFTA region is less than 1 percent of GDP. The highest rate of R&D is in Costa Rica, where R&D expenditures equal 0.37 percent of GDP a year on average (from 2000 to 2008). The R&D conducted in other countries over the same period is less than 0.01 percent of GDP. These are all well below the average rate of R&D in Latin America, which is about 0.6 percent of GDP. It is not likely that IPR reforms will transform this region into multinational R&D centers, as levels of IPR are still relatively low compared to levels in OECD countries and since complementary factors are still lacking, such as a supply of trained scientists and engineers, university-industry collaboration, and state-of-the-art technological facilities. Thus, inward FDI will likely be in sales and distribution outlets and manufacturing facilities. However, there is scope for economic integration and stronger IPRs to attract FDI for purposes of sourcing higher value added manufacturing in this region.

In summary, this section has discussed how economic integration can interact with IPRs to affect inward FDI. Economic integration and more openness should help moderate the market power effects of IPRs and enable the market expansion effects of IPRs to dominate. However, there are some reservations about how significantly the intellectual property reforms will affect market size (although market access has widened). But to the extent that economic integration and stronger IPRs stimulate productivity and income growth, FDI could in the longer run respond more significantly to changes in market size. Another potential effect to look for is whether the IPR reforms in DR-CAFTA shift the nature of inward FDI away from low-wage manufacturing, sales, and distribution to higher value added production activities. Finally, any anticipated effects on FDI must control for other variables (factor costs, regulations) and other modes of technology transfer (that is, whether firms switch from FDI to licensing).

Concluding Remarks

What steps might the DR-CAFTA take if it seeks to use intellectual property rights to influence inward foreign direct investment?

The first step concerns factors that complement IPR policies. As Maskus (1998) points out, IPRs are one important element of a broader policy for attracting inward FDI and for promoting dynamic competition. Complementary policies include flexible labor markets, market liberalization, forward-looking regulatory regimes, and competition policy. Park and Lippoldt (2008) echo the point that technology transfers are facilitated by factors complementary to IPRs, such as absorptive capacity, quality of infrastructure, government policies, and regulations. For example, regional economic integration provides scope for agglomeration effects, which help to attract FDI. But for agglomeration effects to occur, adequate infrastructure and facilities for trade and communication must be available. One area to explore further is whether the business environment and public goods support FDI, production, and innovation.

A second step concerns the quality of FDI. How can DR-CAFTA countries design foreign investment and IPR policies to attract state-of-the-art technology or new-vintage capital? This may require tailoring IPR policies to reward specific high-value technologies or inputs relevant to sectors in which DR-CAFTA has a competitive advantage or structuring complementary policies, such as tax-subsidy incentives.

Finally, while the DR-CAFTA represents a comprehensive move to expand and strengthen IPR standards in the region, enforcement in practice has lagged the agenda to strengthen IPRs, according to reports filed by firms with the U.S. Trade Representative.[12] Piracy is still a serious issue in Costa Rica and Guatemala. Costa Rica and the Dominican Republic have established a special prosecutor's office within the Office of the Attorney General to deal with IPR violations. However, due to under-funding, IPR violators are not prosecuted fully, conviction rates are low, and delays in prosecution have arisen. Honduras and Nicaragua lack personnel and resources, and cases are still pending in the court system. Thus, an important priority for the DR-CAFTA countries is to ensure that IPR laws are carried out effectively and to address the shortage of resources for enforcement, prosecution, and other IPR-related matters, such as the training of intellectual property specialists, judges, and other personnel.

Notes

1. Coverage refers to the subject material (type of invention) that can be protected; duration refers to the length of protection; restrictions refer to the less than exclusive use of those rights; membership in international treaties indicates the adoption into national law of certain substantive and procedural laws of those international agreements. The enforcement component consists of mechanisms that aid in enforcing one's patent rights (such as preliminary injunctions against infringers). Each of these components is scored on a scale from 0 to 1 (reflecting the fraction of legal features that are available). The overall value of the patent rights index is the unweighted sum of the component scores.

2. The WEF uses a *moving average* approach to calculate the score for a particular year—that is, a weighted average of this year's score and last year's score, where the weights are such that the more recent period gets a weight of 0.6 plus its share of the sample size. Taking a moving average of scores reduces the sensitivity of the responses to a specific time period when the survey is undertaken. Furthermore, the approach is more likely to capture the overall perception of IPRs during a whole year. Since the survey is conducted at a specific point during the year, a weighted average of this year's and last year's responses provides a better measure for the year as a whole.

3. This figure is arrived at by comparing data in table 10.6 to data in table 10.5.

4. The question is whether the feedback effect will be that significant from a relatively small market area, such as DR-CAFTA.

5. Four additional countries later joined: Vietnam in 1995, the Lao People's Democratic Republic and Myanmar in 1997, and Cambodia in 1999.

6. The source of data is typically the BEA.

7. Further evidence on the responses of Japanese multinational firms to IPRs can be found in Nagaoka (2009) and Wakasugi and Ito (2009). These studies find technology transfers to be positively associated with the patent strength of host countries.

8. Nicholson (2007) examines non-OECD countries, but for one period only. Moreover, among non-OECD countries, there exist countries of different income classifications.

9. This index is from the Fraser Institute (http://www.freetheworld.com). The index takes into account five factors: impediments to trade due to taxes and tariffs; impediments to trade due to regulations; size of the trade sector; international capital controls; and black market exchange rates. The index ranges from 0 to 10. The higher the index value, the freer is the ability of agents to engage in international trade.

10. Political strife, such as the recent political turmoil in Honduras, the temporary closing of borders in Honduras (affecting trucking, among other things), and high crime rates in El Salvador and Guatemala, are also factors important to FDI.

11. See Bureau of Economic Analysis, "U.S. Direct Investment Abroad 2004 Final Benchmark Data," table III.J1. http://www.bea.gov/international/pdf/usdia_2004f/Table%20III%20Group/IIItables-j1_j10.pdf.

12. See U.S. Trade Representative (2009). Of course, the complaints of firms may largely reflect their perceptions of how the IPR regime works rather than the actual carrying out of IPR laws.

References

Allred, Brent, and Walter G. Park. 2007. "Patent Rights and Innovative Activities: Evidence from National and Firm-Level Data." *Journal of International Business Studies* 38 (5): 878–900.

Antras, Pol, and C. Fritz Foley. 2011. "Regional Trade Integration and Multinational Firm Strategies." In *Costs and Benefits of Regional Economic Integration*, ed. Robert Barro and Jong-Wha Lee. New York: Oxford University Press, January.

Balasubramanyam, V. N., and David Greenaway. 1993. "Regional Integration Agreements and Foreign Direct Investment." In *Regional Integration and the Global Trading System*, ed. Kym Anderson and Richard Blackhurst, 147–66. New York: Harvester Wheatsheaf.

Belderbos, Rene, Kyoji Fukao, and Hyeog Kwon. 2006. "Intellectual Property Rights Protection and the Location of R&D Activities by Multinational Firms." Working Paper, Catholic University of Leuven, Leuven, Belgium.

Blomstrom, Magnus, Steven Globerman, and Ari Kokko. 2000. "Regional Integration and Foreign Direct Investment: Some General Issues." In *Regions,*

Globalization, and the Knowledge-Based Economy, ed. John Dunning, 109–30. New York: Oxford University Press.

Branstetter, Lee, Raymond Fisman, C. Fritz Foley, and Kamal Saggi. 2007. "Intellectual Property Rights, Imitation, and Foreign Direct Investment: Theory and Evidence." NBER Working Paper 13033, National Bureau of Economic Research, Cambridge, MA.

Contractor, Farok. 1981. *International Technology Licensing.* Lexington, MA: D. C. Heath.

Cuevas, Alfredo, Miguel Messmacher, and Alejandro Werner. 2005. "Foreign Direct Investment in Mexico since the Approval of NAFTA." *World Bank Economic Review* 19 (3): 473–88.

Dunning, John. 1980. "Towards an Eclectic Theory of International Production: Some Empirical Tests." *Journal of International Business Studies* 11 (1): 9–31.

Fosfuri, Andrea. 2000. "Patent Protection, Imitation, and the Mode of Technology Transfer." *International Journal of Industrial Organization* 18 (7): 1129–49.

———. 2004. "Determinants of International Activity: Evidence from the Chemical Processing Industry." *Research Policy* 33 (10): 1500–614.

Glass, Amy, and Kamal Saggi. 2002. "Intellectual Property Rights and Foreign Direct Investment." *Journal of International Economics* 56 (March): 387–410.

Lai, Edwin. 1998. "International Intellectual Property Rights Protection and the Rate of Product Innovation." *Journal of Development Economics* 55 (1): 133–53.

Lee, Jeong-Yeon, and Edwin Mansfield. 1996. "Intellectual Property Protection and U.S. Foreign Direct Investment." *Review of Economics and Statistics* 78 (2): 181–86.

Mansfield, Edwin. 1994. "Intellectual Property Protection, Foreign Direct Investment, and Technology Transfer." IFC Discussion Paper 19, World Bank, Washington, DC.

Maskus, Keith E. 1998. "The Role of Intellectual Property Rights in Encouraging Foreign Direct Investment and Technology Transfer." *Duke Journal of Comparative and International Law* 9 (1): 109–61.

Maskus, Keith, and Mohan Penubarti. 1995. "How Trade-Related Are Intellectual Property Rights?" *Journal of International Economics* 39 (3–4): 227–48.

Mayer, Thierry, and Etienne Pfister. 2001. "Do Stronger Patent Rights Attract Foreign Direct Investment? Evidence from French Multinationals' Location." *Région et Développement* 13: 99–122.

Mirus, Rolf, and Barry Scholnick. 1998. "U.S. Foreign Direct Investment into Canada after the Free Trade Agreement." Bulletin 15, Joint Series of Competitiveness, University of Alberta, Alberta School of Business, Edmonton.

Nagaoka, Sadao. 2009. "Does Strong Patent Protection Facilitate International Technology Transfer? Some Evidence from Licensing Contracts of Japanese Firms?" *Journal of Technology Transfer* 34 (2): 128–44.

Nicholson, Michael. 2007. "The Impact of Industry Characteristics and IPR Policy on Foreign Direct Investment." *Review of World Economics* 143 (1): 27–54.

Nunnenkamp, Peter, and Julius Spatz. 2004. "Intellectual Property Rights and Foreign Direct Investment: A Disaggregated Analysis." *Review of World Economics* 140 (3): 393–414.

Park, Walter G. 2008. "International Patent Protection: 1960–2005." *Research Policy* 37 (4): 761–66.

Park, Walter G., and Douglas Lippoldt. 2003. "The Impact of Trade-Related Intellectual Property Rights on Trade and Foreign Direct Investment in Developing Countries." *OECD Papers: Special Issue on Trade Policy* 4 (294): n.p.

————. 2008. "Technology Transfer and the Economic Implications of the Strengthening of Intellectual Property Rights in Developing Countries." Trade Policy Working Paper 62, OECD, Paris.

Primo Braga, Carlos A., and Carsten Fink. 1998. "The Relationship between Intellectual Property Rights and Foreign Direct Investment." *Duke Journal of Comparative and International Law* 9 (1): 163–88.

Sinnott, Jessica, John Sinnott, and William J. Cotreau. 2008. *World Patent Law and Practice*. Vol. 1, 2A-P. New York: Matthew Bender.

Smarzynska Javorcik, Beata. 2004. "The Composition of Foreign Direct Investment and Protection of Intellectual Property Rights: Evidence from Transition Economies." *European Economic Review* 48 (1): 39–62.

Smith, Pamela. 2001. "How Do Foreign Patent Rights Affect U.S. Exports, Affiliate Sales, and Licenses?" *Journal of International Economics* 55 (2): 411–39.

Taylor, M. Scott. 1994. "Trips, Trade, and Growth." *International Economic Review* 35 (2): 361–81.

UNCTAD (United Nations Conference on Trade and Development). 2009. *World Investment Report*. Geneva: UNCTAD. www.unctad.org/fdistatistics.

U.S. Trade Representative. 2009. *National Trade Estimate Report on Foreign Trade Barriers*. Washington, DC: Government Printing Office.

Vishwasrao, Sharmila. 1994. "Intellectual Property Rights and the Mode of Technology Transfer." *Journal of Development Economics* 44 (2): 381–402.

Wakasugi, Ryuhei, and Banri Ito. 2009. "The Effects of Stronger Intellectual Property Rights on Technology Transfer: Evidence from Japanese Firm-Level Data." *Journal of Technology Transfer* 34 (2): 145–58.

World Economic Forum. Various issues. *Global Competitiveness Report*. Oxford: Oxford University Press.

Yang, Guifang, and Keith E. Maskus. 2001. "Intellectual Property Rights and Licensing: An Econometric Investigation." *Weltwirtschaftliches Archiv* 137 (1): 58–79.

CHAPTER 11

Trade Openness and Labor Gender Gaps

Maurizio Bussolo, Samuel Freije, Calvin Z. Djiofack, and Melissa Rodríguez

Gender disparities are an important component of overall inequality. Ample evidence shows that, in spite of recent improvements, large gender disparities still exist in Central America and elsewhere in the developing world. For example, across the developing world, females account for 56 percent of all (male and female) adults with no formal education, whereas they represent just 46 percent of those with completed secondary or higher education. Due to social norms and discrimination outside as well as inside the household, women and men differ not only in their level of education but also in their access to labor markets, remuneration, sectoral employment, control over resources, and role within the household. Because of these disparities, men and women cannot uniformly take advantage of the opportunities created by trade liberalization. Furthermore, these gender-specific disparities are exacerbated for poorer households (Lipton 1983; Marcoux 1998; Filmer 1999).

This chapter assesses the relationship between gender disparities and trade for the Dominican Republic–Central America Free Trade Agreement (DR-CAFTA) region and, more specifically, answers the following two questions: Does trade expansion increase women's employment opportunities relative to men's? What are the effects of trade on gender earnings gaps?[1]

Given that the countries in this region have all recently engaged in a major trade agreement with the United States, a further objective of the chapter is to identify possible complementary economic policy measures that may enhance the favorable effects and compensate the unfavorable outcomes of trade on gender disparities and ultimately on household welfare.

There are various ways of addressing these questions, but we have adopted an approach based on microeconomic household data. Cross-country regressions can identify strong correlations between gender inequality and poverty and even between gender inequality and growth (Morrison, Raju, and Sinha 2007), but, as in the case of the cross-country analyses on trade and growth, strong correlation does not mean causation. Additionally, the policy relevance of this literature is very weak.

As a result of this analysis, we identify both equalizing and disequalizing effects of trade openness on the gender wage gap for the countries in the region. Liberalization of own tariffs may induce a larger gender wage gap if not compensated by reciprocal reductions in faced tariffs (in this case, tariffs in the United States) and actual market integration (as proxied, for example, by increasing shares of imports to GDP). Equally relevant is the absence of a statistically significant association between trade liberalization and labor market participation or job reallocation (for both males and females or differential across gender). This absence is surprising given employment shifts observed for the region since the passage of DR-CAFTA, and it deserves further investigation. These two main findings call for different policy recommendations for dealing with the adverse effects of trade liberalization.

The chapter is organized as follows. After reviewing the main findings of the recent literature on trade and gender, it provides a brief description of the main indicators of trade openness for the DR-CAFTA countries during the past decade. It then describes the recent evolution of the main indicators of gender gaps, explains the methodology applied to estimate the impact of trade openness on changes in family welfare as well as the available data sources, and explains the results. A final section concludes.

Literature Review

Interest in the gender effects of trade policies has been growing.[2] Since 1994, when the first comprehensive review of empirical evidence in this area was published (Joekes and Weston 1994), several new initiatives have been promoted, in the form of lobbying, awareness campaigns, training, the activity of several women's nongovernmental organizations (such as the London-based One World Action and the Washington, D.C.–based Women's EDGE and Center of Concern), the creation of worldwide networks (such as www.genderandtrade.com), workshops, and new research.

Much of what has been written, however, is either quite theoretical or mainly anecdotal. Reviews of existing literature abound (to name a few, Beneria and Lind 1995; Fontana, Joekes, and Masika 1998; Cagatay 2001; Gammage, Jorgensen, and McGill 2002, Tran-Nguyen and Beviglia-Zampetti 2004) and vary in emphasis and tone. Despite an intense debate, sound empirical evidence is sparse (see, for example, Bussolo and De Hoyos 2009). Analyses are still limited by the absence of gender-differentiated data in many areas and the difficulty of disentangling the effects of trade liberalization from those of other simultaneous changes.

Trade liberalization alters the distribution of income between different social groups and between women and men. It operates mainly through changes in the relative prices of goods. These changes, by modifying incentives, may induce the reallocation of factors of production among sectors that use women and men with different intensities and therefore may induce changes in their employment or remuneration. The same variations in relative prices bring about changes in real incomes that affect groups differently due to differences in their consumption patterns. Trade liberalization is also likely to reduce tariff revenues, and this, in turn, may have group-specific effects on the size and composition of government expenditure.

The effects of trade liberalization on gender inequalities in a country may be either negative or positive. Many things mediate the effects and are important in determining the final outcomes. They include resource endowments, labor market institutions, systems of property rights, access to markets and information, and other socioeconomic characteristics.

This brief review of the literature is organized around two main questions: Does trade expansion increase women's employment opportunities relative to men's? What are the effects of trade on gender gaps in earnings? Another important question asked in the literature on trade and gender is whether trade alters the intrahousehold allocation of resources, time, and tasks, but this chapter does not consider this theme and so does not review this literature.

Women's participation in paid employment has risen in most countries in recent decades (Gammage and Mehra 1999). While this trend has had causes other than trade, the increased openness of individual countries has contributed to it, although its effects on women's employment vary by sector and region (Standing 1999).

Women gain employment the most in countries that are abundant in unskilled labor and have a comparative advantage in the production of basic manufactures. This is because women are disproportionately represented among unskilled workers and because prevailing norms make their entitlement to the rewards from their own labor stronger than those from any other factor of production. These forces are also likely to have contributed to the weak supply response of African agriculture to export opportunities. Darity (2007) formalizes some of these aspects in a model of an archetype gender-segregated, low-income economy.

Weak marketing structures and lack of the technical expertise required to comply with regulations and output standards are other important factors preventing women small producers from enjoying the new opportunities created by trade liberalization (Carr 2004; Tran-Nguyen and Beviglia-Zampetti 2004).

Another constraint that prevents women from seizing new opportunities, both in agriculture and in wage employment, is the heavy burden of household responsibilities, which falls disproportionately upon them. Studies from settings as different as the cut flower industry in Ecuador (Newman 2001), export-processing zones in Malaysia (Kusago 2000), the off-farm informal sector in Guatemala (Katz 1995), and nontraditional agricultural exports in Kenya (McCulloch and Ota 2002) all point to the presence of other female members in the household as a determinant of women's participation in new opportunities created by trade.

Several studies (Gammage and Mehra 1999; Tzannatos 1999; United Nations 1999) find little decline in employment segregation by gender over the past two decades. Female workers have remained confined to female jobs, with little opportunity to enter previously male-dominated sectors and occupations. Women continue to be employed in low-skill and low-pay jobs.

Evidence on changes in female and male wages associated with trade liberalization is even sparser than the evidence on employment. Trade liberalization might affect wages by altering the relative demand for various types of workers or by influencing discriminatory practices. Most of the studies available investigate this latter aspect and can be grouped in one of two schools of thought. Following Becker (1959), some researchers assert that globalization is likely to create competitive pressures that will reduce the scope for employers to discriminate, including against women.

By contrast, others argue that increased competition might reduce the bargaining power of wage workers, especially female workers, if they are disproportionately employed in sectors competing internationally on the basis of "cheap" labor. Oostendorp (2004) finds a negative association between openness and the size of the gender wage gap. In Taiwan, China, Berik (2000) finds that, after controlling for employment segregation by gender and other industry characteristics, greater export orientation is associated with smaller wage differentials between women and men. This result is due to the fact that export orientation has a larger adverse impact on men's wages than on women's wages. In Mexico, Artecona and Cunningham (2002) find that the residual gender wage gap (after accounting for differences in human capital characteristics) declined more in concentrated industries that were exposed to competing imports than in industries that were not concentrated over the period 1987–93. In Bangladesh, trends in female-male wage differentials in garments indicate a narrowing of the gap from 1983 to 1990, but a widening from 1990 to 1997. This change is attributed to a higher proportion of men taking up high-skilled jobs and an increase in the number of temporary workers among women (Zohir 1998; Paul-Majumder and Begum 2000). A similar trend toward widening of the gender wage gap is predicted in Madagascar for similar reasons (Nicita and Razzaz 2003).

A few studies of East Asian countries explain pay discrimination as a result of the employer's effort to maintain export competitiveness, predicting and finding that greater openness widens the gender wage gap. For example, Seguino (2000) argues that divergent trends in the unadjusted gender wage ratio in Taiwan, China, and in the Republic of Korea during 1981–92 are related to differences in the nature of foreign direct investment flows in the two countries. Berik, van der Meulen Rodgers, and Zveglich (2004) find that increases in international competition in concentrated industries in both Taiwan, China, and Korea during 1981–99 are associated with widening wage gaps between men and women.

Recent Trade Patterns in DR-CAFTA Countries

Trade openness has increased considerably in the region, as illustrated by the upsurge in the ratio of trade to GDP. In fact, for all countries but the Dominican Republic, these ratios have increased by 15 to 20 percentage points from the average for the 1990s to that for the 2000s; in Honduras the ratio has increased almost 40 points. In contrast, the Dominican Republic has recorded a slight decrease in trade openness.

These general trends, however, may be different when looking at specific countries and specific trade partners such as the United States. The share of imports from the United States within total manufacturing output has declined in all countries but Costa Rica, whereas the share of imports from the United States within total agricultural output has increased in all countries for the period under study. These trends have been accompanied by a more recent (that is, during the decade of the 2000s) reduction in tariff rates in the partner countries of the DR-CAFTA group. In other words, this group had already reduced its own tariffs to the United States. Most DR-CAFTA countries already had fairly open access to the U.S. market, and—compared to the reduction in their own tariffs—the increase in market access did not represent a major change in trade policy. The recent evolution of the export orientation of the Dominican Republic and Central American countries shows that the ratio of exports to the United States to GDP has remained fairly stable or increased slightly among agricultural products and, with the exception of Nicaragua, manufacturing exports have declined. Intraregional exports are quite important for El Salvador and Nicaragua, whereas they represent a small fraction of total exports for Costa Rica and the Dominican Republic.

In conclusion, the previous decade for the DR-CAFTA countries was characterized by a further decline in already low tariffs with the United States. This liberalizing trend was accompanied by diverse patterns in import penetration and export orientation toward the United States during a period of growing trade openness with the world.

Labor Gender Gaps in DR-CAFTA Countries

Previous studies have focused on identifying and assessing the magnitude of the channels through which changes in trade policy and increased exposure to international trade affect gender gaps. The main difficulty in this endeavor is the attribution of changes in these gaps to trade, since economies rarely, if ever, experience a pure trade shock and no other change. Without attempting any attribution, which is carried out in the next two sections, this section simply outlines the main stylized facts about recent changes in gender gaps, participation rates, unemployment, sector specialization (segregation), and labor earnings. These stylized facts are determined by analyzing micro (that is, individual-level) data from all household and labor surveys available for the countries in the region from the early 1990s to the end of the 2000s.

These data sets have been harmonized by a joint team from Universidad de La Plata in Argentina and the World Bank to produce a database of comparable surveys for Latin American countries.[3] A list of the surveys used in this study is presented in table 11.1.

Gender Gaps in Participation Rates

During the period under investigation, the gender gap in participation rates has narrowed for all countries, confirming a tendency observed at the global level. This narrowing is mainly due to the increasing participation of women. With some variation across countries, men's participation has remained more or less stable: for the Dominican Republic, El Salvador, and Costa Rica, in the range of 75 to 80 percent and for Honduras, Nicaragua, and Guatemala, in the range of 82 to almost 90 percent. Conversely, women have increased their participation from initial rates in the low 30 to 40 percent to final rates of about 45 to 50 percent.

These trends have helped to close participation gaps. At the beginning of the period, differences in participation rates between women and men were in the range of 40–50 percentage points, while more recent data show differences that have shrunk, on average, about 6 percentage points. As shown in figure 11.1, gender gaps in labor market participation have fallen in Costa Rica, the Dominican Republic, El Salvador, and Honduras. The same trend is evident, but not statistically significant, in Guatemala and Nicaragua.

Table 11.1   Sources of Data Used

Country	Survey	Periodicity	Years available[a]
Costa Rica	EPHPM\	Annual	1997, 2000–07
Dominican Republic	Encuesta Nacional de Fuerza de Trabajo	Biannual[a]	1997, 2000–07
El Salvador	EPHPM	Annual	1998, 2000–07
Guatemala	Encuesta Nacional de Empleo e Ingresos (ENEI)	Annual	2000, 2002–06
Honduras	Encuesta Permanente de Hogares de Propósitos Múltiples (EPHPM)	Biannual[a]	1997, 1999, 2001, 2003
	EPHPM	Annual	2004–06
Nicaragua	Encuesta Nacional de Hogares sobre Medición de Niveles de Vida (EMNV)	Annual	1998, 2001, 2005

Source: Authors' compilation.
a. Second semester only.

Figure 11.1   Gender Gaps in Labor Participation Rates (Women's Minus Men's) in DR-CAFTA Countries, 1990–2007

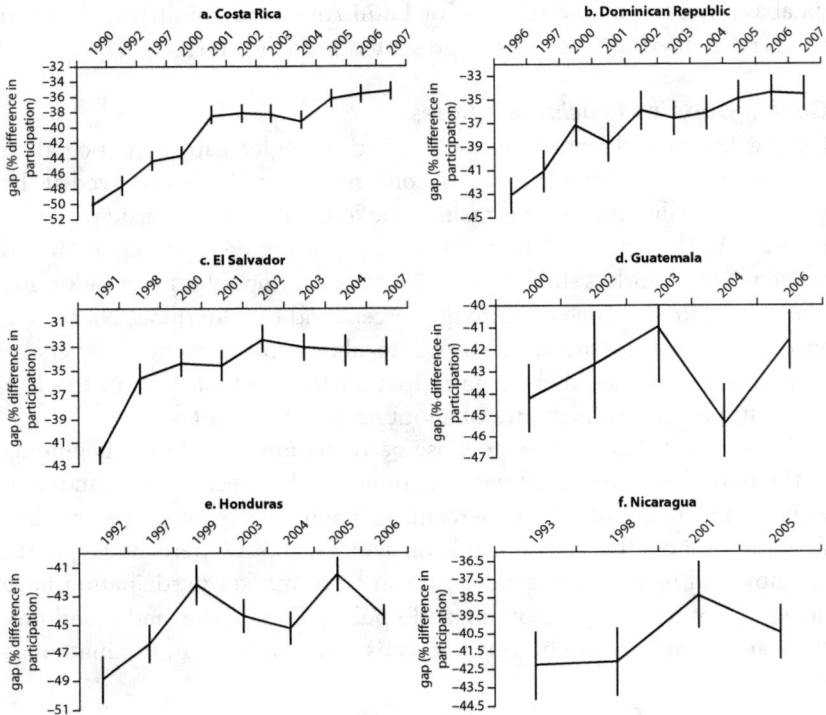

Source: Authors' calculations using household surveys from respective countries.

These changes in participation gaps are similar when different types of workers are considered. Gender differences of participation between skilled and unskilled individuals have fallen by very similar amounts: 5.3 percentage points for skilled people and 5.9 for unskilled. Given the higher initial gaps for unskilled individuals, the reduction of 5 percentage points counts relatively less for unskilled individuals than for skilled ones. On average in the region, the difference in participation is 52 percentage points between unskilled women and men versus 28 points between skilled women and men, thus the 5 percentage point reduction translates into a 17 percent reduction in the gap for skilled workers and a 9 percent reduction for unskilled workers.

Similar observations apply to rural versus urban and old versus young groups of men and women. Compared to urban and young women, rural and old women tend to have initially higher gaps vis-à-vis their male counterparts, but the absolute reductions are similar. However and perhaps not surprisingly, rural females experience the largest initial gaps in participation—on average in the region, a woman is 56 percentage points less likely to participate in the labor market than a man—and older women enjoy the largest absolute reduction in their participation gap: 7.6 percentage points. This underlines the importance of demographics in explaining the change in participation rates between men and women.

Gender Gaps in Unemployment

Before examining the situation and trends of employment in the region, it is useful to consider the evolution of unemployment. At the outset, it should be noted that unemployment rates measured by the surveys do not seem fully comparable. For example, Guatemala reports very low unemployment rates of about 1.9–1.7 percent for women and men.[4] The main stylized facts deducted from analyzing these micro data sets are as follows. First, for each country, unemployment rates, for both men and women, are relatively stable, with a tendency toward slight improvements toward the end of the period under study. Second, Nicaragua, with a significant reduction in unemployment throughout the period, seems to represent an exception to this general trend. Third, gender gaps in unemployment between men and women do not change much (see figure 11.2). The gender gap in unemployment rates appears to have increased in Costa Rica (from about 1.5 percentage points to about 3.5 percentage points) and to have declined in El Salvador (from about –0.1 percentage point to –0.6 percentage points), whereas it is not statistically different over time for the other countries.[5]

Gender Gaps in Sector Specialization Rates

Trade shocks tend to affect sectors in different ways. They create opportunities in certain sectors and result in new and better jobs, whereas in other sectors they represent challenges and result in output and job losses. Before considering whether shifts in employment by sector are different for men and women, it may be useful to consider the initial employment situation and the overall—that is, irrespective of gender—evolution of employment for countries in the region. Two questions are addressed here. How has the employment structure changed between the 1990s and the 2000s by sector and by formal and informal character of work? Has this structure changed differently for men and women?

In terms of the initial employment structure, Costa Rica and the Dominican Republic have a high concentration of employment in their tertiary sectors, and about two-thirds or more of total workers are employed

Figure 11.2   Gender Gaps in Unemployment Rates (Women's Minus Men's) in DR-CAFTA Countries, 1990–2007

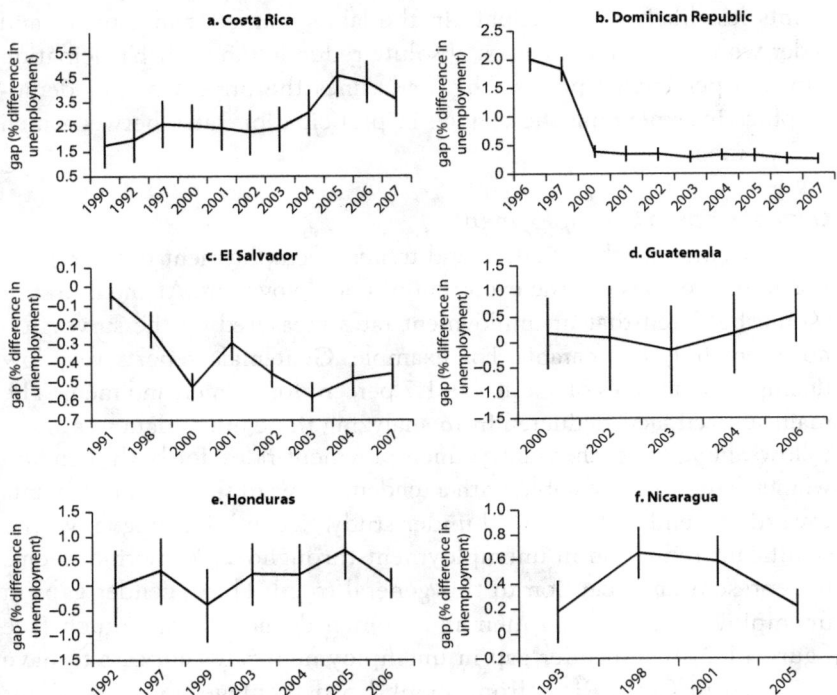

Source: Authors' calculations using household surveys from respective countries.

in service activities. These activities also employ close to 55 percent of workers in El Salvador and Nicaragua, but are less important in Guatemala and Honduras. At the beginning of the period under consideration, agriculture was still employing more than a third of all workers in Guatemala, Honduras, and Nicaragua and relatively less in Costa Rica, the Dominican Republic, and El Salvador. Finally, manufacturing employs about a fifth of workers across all countries with the exception of Nicaragua and Guatemala, where this sector uses only 10 and 14 percent of the workforce.

Employment shares have decreased in agriculture, remained more or less stable in manufacturing, and increased in services. The size and, in some cases, even the sign of these general trends differ from country to country. There is thus quite a bit of heterogeneity in the share of employment by gender across sectors and countries and, even at this aggregate level and considering just the changes in gross employment, it seems that there has been a high degree of job churning in these economies. Consider these two examples. Agricultural employment has collapsed 8 percentage points in El Salvador, from 27 percent to 18 percent, and service employment has soared 10 percentage points in Honduras, from 47 percent to 57 percent.

The "quality" (formal or informal character) of the jobs does not show the same degree of churning, and shares of informality have remained more or less constant during the period we are considering. Costa Rica is the only country that recorded a slight reduction in informality, which decreased 2 percentage points from 43 percent to 41 percent. The other countries increased the share of informal employment by about 1 to 2 percentage points; Honduras is the exception, having experienced a large increase in informality (see figure 11.3).

How have men and women fared against these general trends? One way of looking at the evolution of employment shares for men and women is to consider how the gender employment gap has changed. The employment gap is the difference between the percentage distribution of women and men in the agriculture, manufacturing, and service sectors. For example, on

Figure 11.3   Employment Shares, by Informal and Formal Status in DR-CAFTA Countries, ca. 1990–2007

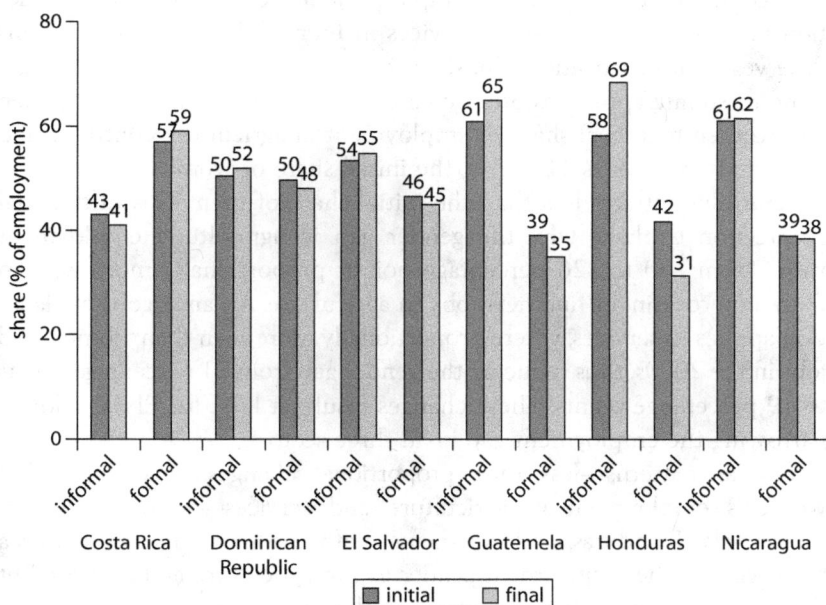

Source: Authors' calculations using household surveys from respective countries.

average during the 1990s, the comparison between 100 Costa Rican women and 100 men is as follows: 1 percent of working women were working in agriculture versus 9 percent of men; 19 percent of women were in manufacturing versus 15 percent of men; and 80 percent of women were in services versus 76 percent of men.[6] The corresponding gender gaps, as shown in figure 11.4, are –8 percentage points in agriculture, 3 percentage points in manufacturing, and 4 percentage points in services; in other words, the percentage share of men was leading that of women by 8 points in agriculture, but lagging by 3 and 4 percentage points in manufacturing and services, respectively.

Figure 11.4 reveals that (a) for all countries, the employment of women is less concentrated in primary activities; (b) for most countries, women tend to find proportionally more jobs in services; and (c) although with lower initial gaps, women are also more intensively working in manufacturing.

In terms of the evolution of the gaps, we find that the general trend of a reduction of employment in agriculture and an increase in services, which is observed for all workers irrespective of gender, is somewhat muted for female workers. In fact, the overall reduction of employment in agriculture tends to be less strong for women, who experience a general reduction in their (negative) gap in agriculture and, similarly, a reduction in their (positive) gap in services in four of the six countries. This deserves some clarification. Consider the case of El Salvador, although the same reasoning applies to other countries. In El Salvador, the total (men and women together) share of employment in agriculture contracts, and it expands in services. However, the initial share of women employed in agriculture contracts less than the initial share of men. This differential contraction explains why the gender gap in agricultural employment varies from –30 to –26 percentage points: proportionally more women than men remain, or find new jobs, in agriculture. An analogous explanation applies to services, where proportionally more men than women find jobs in the 2000s, thus reducing the gender gap from 21 percentage points to 19 percentage points. These changes result, at least for El Salvador, in narrowing the employment gap in all three sectors.

Similar patterns—less than proportional changes in the share of women's employment in agriculture and services—are observed for Guatemala, Honduras, and Nicaragua, with the same final outcome: a narrowing of the employment gender gap in agriculture and services. But there are also quite a few exceptions, with some sectors using one gender more intensively than the other, thus widening the employment gender

Figure 11.4 Gender Gaps in Employment Shares (Women's Minus Men's Shares) in DR-CAFTA Countries, by Sector, ca. 1990–2007

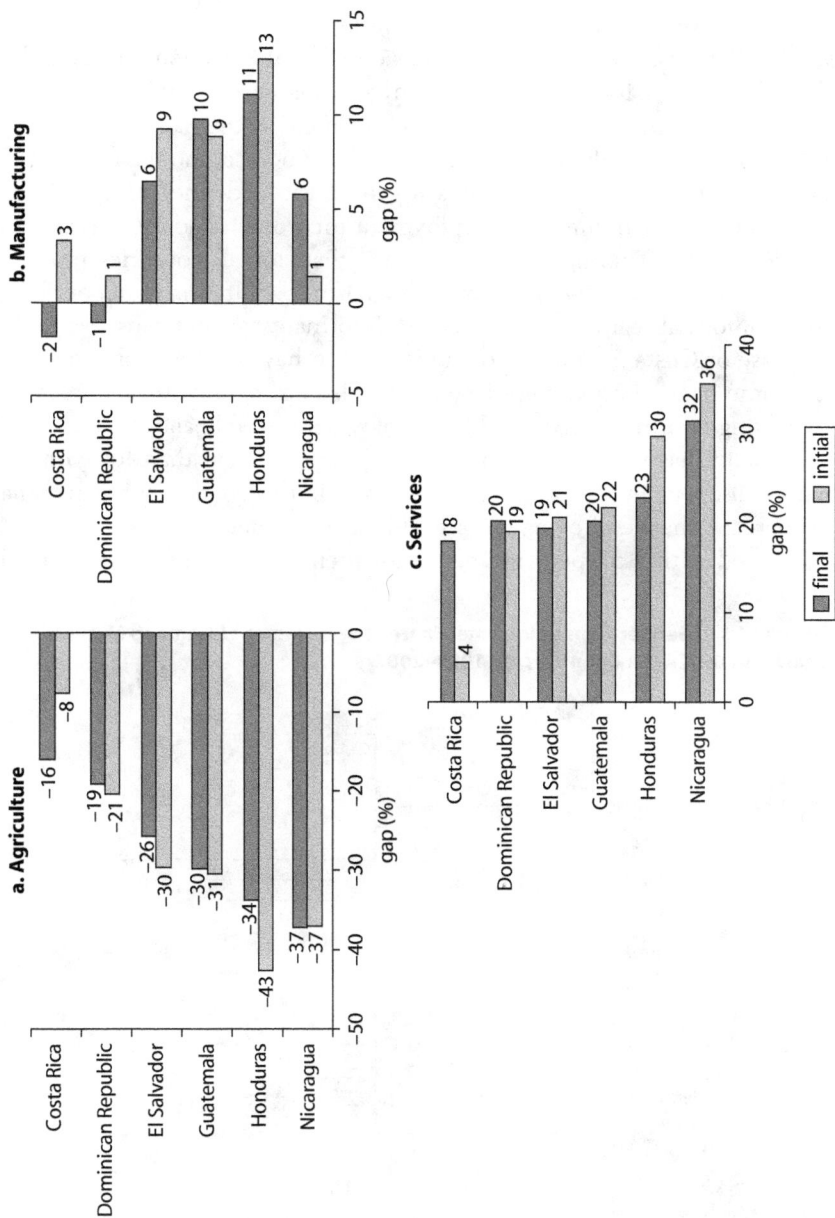

a. Agriculture

Country	final	initial
Costa Rica	−16	−8
Dominican Republic	−19	−21
El Salvador	−26	−30
Guatemala	−30	−31
Honduras	−43	−34
Nicaragua	−37	−37

b. Manufacturing

Country	final	initial
Costa Rica	−2	3
Dominican Republic	−1	1
El Salvador	6	9
Guatemala	10	9
Honduras	11	13
Nicaragua	6	1

c. Services

Country	final	initial
Costa Rica	18	4
Dominican Republic	20	19
El Salvador	19	21
Guatemala	20	22
Honduras	23	30
Nicaragua	32	36

gap (%)

■ final ▫ initial

Source: Authors' calculations using household surveys from respective countries.

321

gap. In Nicaragua, manufacturing specializes in employing women; in Costa Rica, employment in agriculture becomes much more male oriented, whereas women's proportional concentration in services increases.

The last set of questions to be considered in this section concerns the formal or informal character of employment. Is there a difference in the degree of informality between men and women? Is the pace of change in informality uniformly slow for men and women, as noted for overall employment? As in previous cases, a gender gap is defined as the difference in the share of informal employment for women and men, as shown in figure 11.5. This figure clearly shows that, for all countries but the Dominican Republic, women have a higher probability than men of being in the informal segment of the market. Informality gender gaps, except in the case of Costa Rica and Honduras, tend to have declined or remained the same in the period considered here. This contrasts with the trend of increasing informality recorded for employment overall, and it means that informality has increased proportionally more for men than for women. This is also true in the Dominican Republic: In this country, women had a 46 percent chance of being employed in the informal sector in the 1990s compared with a 52 percent chance for men, thus resulting in an initial

Figure 11.5   Gender Gaps in Informal Share of Employment (Women's Minus Men's Shares) in DR-CAFTA Countries, ca. 1990–2007

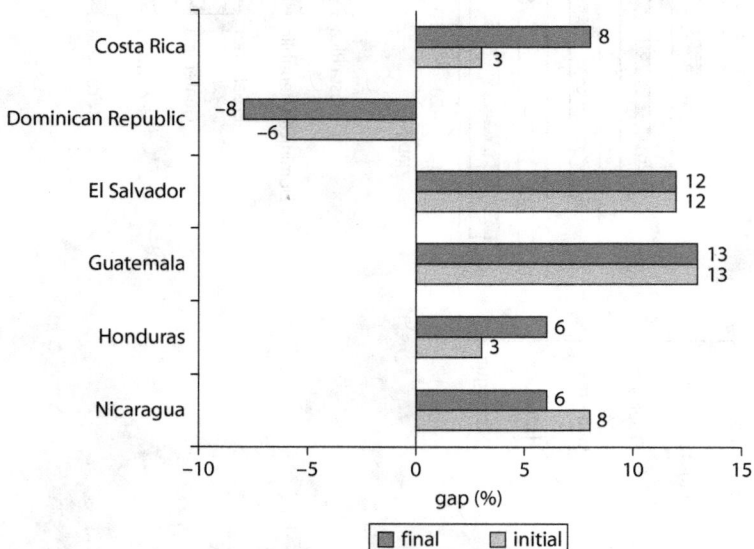

Source: Authors' calculations using household surveys from respective countries.

gap of –6 percentage points. Because of an increase in men's probability of informal employment and an unchanged probability for women, this gap increased to –8 percentage points in the 2000s. In Costa Rica, the only country experiencing an overall reduction in informality, the gap increased because new formal jobs were taken by men, leaving women's share of informal employment constant at 46 percent throughout the period.

Figure 11.6, by considering country, gender, sector, time periods, and informality, attempts to sum up all the information on employment structure and its evolution in this region. Employment structure changed significantly in the period under investigation, and, notwithstanding quite a bit of heterogeneity across countries, the following general trends are

Figure 11.6   Informal Share of Employment in DR-CAFTA Countries, by Gender and Sector, ca. 1990–2007

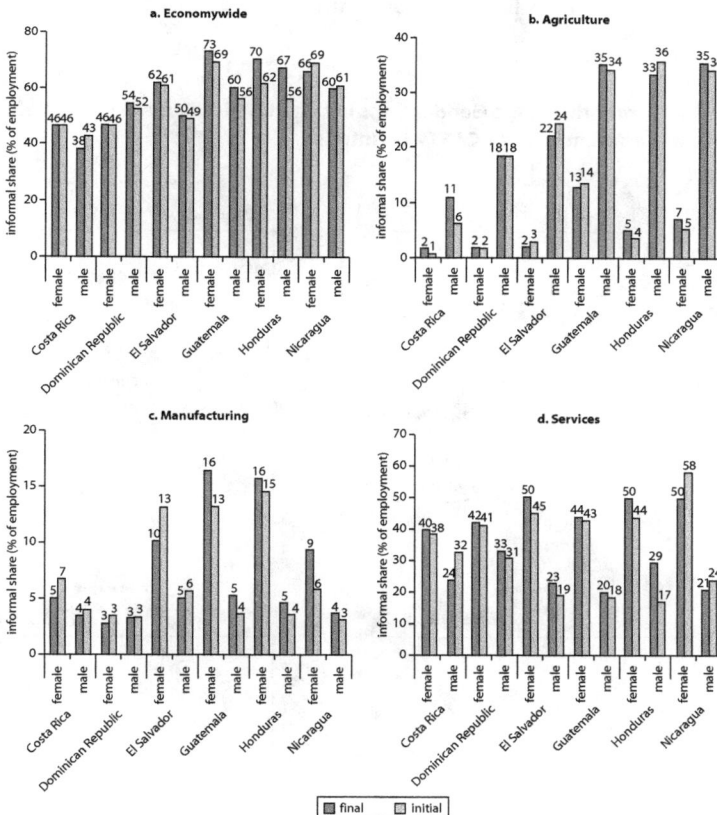

Source: Authors' calculations using household surveys from respective countries.

highlighted: (a) informality did not change much, and women—initially more likely than men to work informally—tended to close their informality gap; (b) during the 1990s–2000s period, women, proportionally less intensively than men, found new jobs in services, somewhat decreasing their specialization in this sector; however, (c) women also reduced their employment gap in agriculture, a sector that is still employing predominantly men. Although women are still far from having employment opportunities across sectors similar to men, the movement appears to be toward equalization in the region.

Gender Gaps in Wages

The "quantity" churning described in the previous subsections is complemented here by considering the evolution of labor income earned by men and women. This percentage difference is reported on the vertical axis of figures 11.7 and 11.8 for urban and rural areas, respectively.

Figure 11.7   Monthly Wage Gender Gaps in Urban Areas (Female Minus Male Percentage Difference) in DR-CAFTA Countries

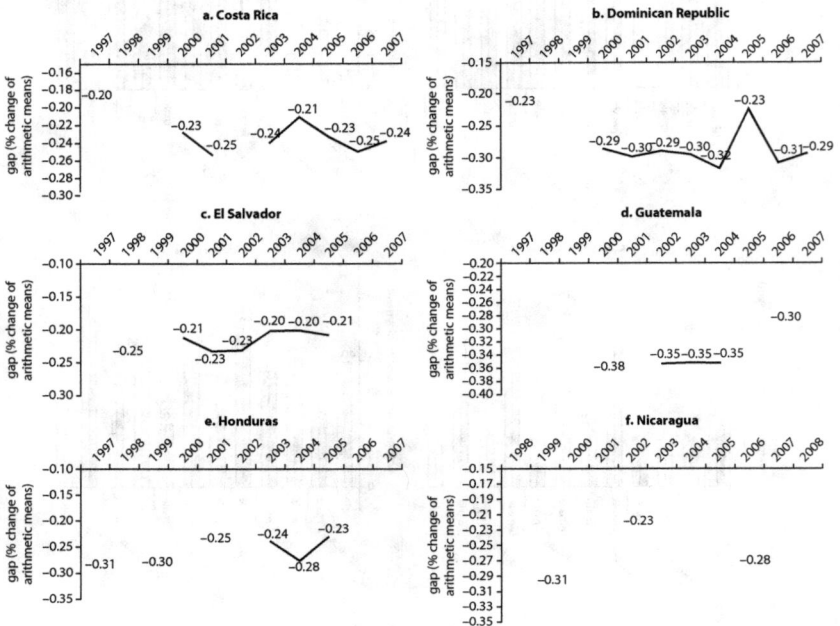

Source: Authors' calculations using household surveys from respective countries.
Note: Broken lines mean that correct information is not available for the intervening years.

Figure 11.8   Monthly Wage Gender Gaps in Rural Areas (Female Minus Male Percentage Difference) in DR-CAFTA Countries

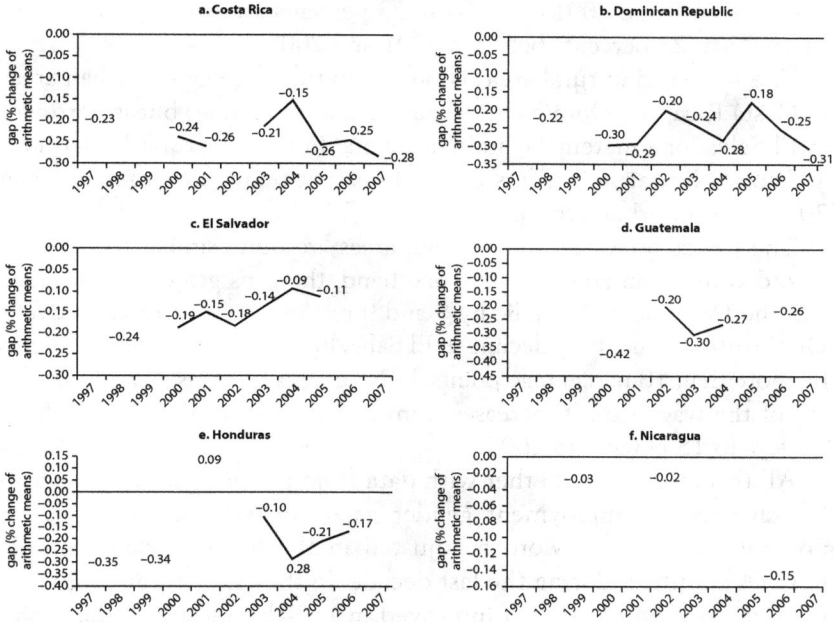

Source: Authors' calculations using household surveys from respective countries.
Note: Broken lines mean that correct information is not available for the intervening years.

Countries in the DR-CAFTA region are quite heterogeneous in their initial gender income differentials and their evolution through time. In urban areas, the wage gap is smaller in Costa Rica, where it oscillates between 20 and 25 percent, and is larger in Guatemala, where it stays above the 30 percent mark for the entire period under study. The gender wage gap in the Dominican Republic and El Salvador usually stays between 25 and 30 percent. Finally, the wage gap ranges between 20 and 30 percent for Honduras and between 25 and 35 percent for Nicaragua.

In terms of trends, Costa Rica and the Dominican Republic show a slight increase in the wage differential (the wage gap increased about 4 percentage points in Costa Rica and 6 percentage points in the Dominican Republic, between 1997 and 2007). In contrast, the wage gaps declined in El Salvador, Guatemala, and Honduras (4 percentage points for the former and 8 percentage points for the other two) for the respective periods with available data. The case of Nicaragua stands alone, with an inverted-U trend that first shows a decline in the gap between 1998 and 2001 (from 31 to 23 percent) followed by an increase (from 23 to 28 percent) between 2001 and 2008.

The wage gap in rural areas is similar to the wage gap in urban areas in Costa Rica, the Dominican Republic, and Honduras, but is narrower in El Salvador, Guatemala, and Nicaragua. In fact, for rural El Salvador and rural Nicaragua it is less than 20 percent (compared to more than 20 percent in urban areas).

The trends for wage gaps in rural areas are quite similar to the ones recorded in urban areas. On the one hand, the gaps grow in Costa Rica and the Dominican Republic by 5 and 9 percentage points, respectively. On the other hand, they decline in El Salvador, Guatemala, and Honduras by more than 10 percentage points. In Nicaragua, there is a large worsening of the wage gap: It increases from 2–3 percent in the first available surveys to 15 percent in 2005.

All this evidence, together with data from previous sections regarding changes in employment gender gaps, suggests that the relative position of men and women adjusted in the labor markets of DR-CAFTA countries during the last decade. In the case of wage gaps, the relative position of women improved in El Salvador, Guatemala, and Honduras and deteriorated in Costa Rica, the Dominican Republic, and Nicaragua.

Methodology

To identify whether gender gaps are associated with trade, we use a version of a two-stage procedure adopted in the recent literature (see, for instance, Ferreira, Leite, and Wai-Poi 2007; Pavcnik and others 2004). This procedure consists of, first, estimating wage and employment equations and obtaining industry and skill wage premiums and employment propensities. Then, in a second stage, these wage premiums and employment propensities—which have been estimated separately for male and female workers—are regressed against trade-related variables to measure how much changes in trade openness explain the overall change in the gender gaps.

This two-stage methodology differs from a single-stage estimation procedure, which normally uses changes in local prices, after a trade shock, as the variable explaining changes in employment and wages.

This single-stage approach relies on the estimation of a pass-through model that links trade shocks to local prices. Instead, the method used here does not use a pass-through model and therefore allows trade to affect labor markets through several channels (for example, import penetration, tariff reductions, and so forth), which may or may not directly affect local prices.

In the *first stage*, labor market participation and earnings regressions are estimated separately for males and females. A multinomial logit model has been used for estimating labor market participation. The following participation decisions are included in the model: unemployed/inactive, informal in agriculture, formal in agriculture, informal in manufacturing, formal in manufacturing, informal in services, and formal in services. In the case of the earnings equations, selection correction methods are used and the dependent variable is the logarithm of monthly labor earnings (ln W) in the principal occupation. The main explanatory variables include age, skill level, firm-size, sector of activity, and interaction of skill and sector.

The *second stage* aims at explaining the impact of trade liberalization on employment and wages. A linear model (using ordinary least squares, OLS, method) that has one of the coefficients from either the participation or the earnings models as dependent variable and trade–related variables as explanatory variables is specified as follows:

$$\mu_m = D'\lambda_m^D + T'\lambda_m^T + \lambda_m^G G + (T * G)'\lambda_m^{TG} \tag{11.1}$$

where D stands for a vector of controls for year, gender, country, and region; T stands for a vector of trade-related variables (own tariffs, faced tariffs, import penetration, export shares, real exchange rates); and G stands for a gender. The dependent variable μ and its subindex m represent one of the relevant coefficients from the participation or earnings equations. In fact, five specific coefficients from the first stage participation and the earnings models are separately used as dependent variables in the specification of equation (11.1). These are, from the participation equation, (i) the intercept, and, from the earning equation, (ii) the intercept (β_0), (iii) the sector premia (β_{ind}), (iv) the skill premia (β_{skill}), and (v) the skill premia associated to each sector (β_{skind}). Because all trade variables in equation (11.1) are interacted with gender, we can identify whether the impact of trade differs between males and females.

Formally, earnings (ln W) are affected by trade via the above five variables of interest as follows:[7]

$$\frac{\partial \ln W}{\partial T} = \frac{\partial \ln W}{\partial \beta_0}\frac{\partial \beta_0}{\partial T} + \frac{\partial \ln W}{\partial \beta_{educ}}\frac{\partial \beta_{educ}}{\partial T} + \frac{\partial \ln W}{\partial \beta_{Ind}}\frac{\partial \beta_{Ind}}{\partial T}$$

$$+ \frac{\partial \ln W}{\partial \beta_{skInd}}\frac{\partial \beta_{skInd}}{\partial T} = (\lambda_0^T + G'\lambda_0^{TG}) + Skill \qquad , \qquad (11.2)$$

$$\times (\lambda_{Skill}^T + G'\lambda_{Skill}^{TG}) + Ind \times (\lambda_{Ind}^T + G'\lambda_{Ind}^{TG})$$

$$+ Skill \; x \; Ind \times (\lambda_{skInd}^T + G'\lambda_{skInd}^{TG})$$

which indicates that the impact depends on whether the individual is skilled or not, working in tradeables or nontradeables industries, and on the gender of the worker. This formula, then, defines the impact of trade openness on eight groups:

	Nontradable	Tradable
Nonskilled female	λ_0^T	$\lambda_0^T + \lambda_{Ind}^T$
Nonskilled male	$\lambda_0^T + \lambda_0^{TG}$	$\lambda_0^T + \lambda_0^{TG} + \lambda_{Ind}^T + \lambda_{Ind}^{TG}$
Skilled female	$\lambda_0^T + \lambda_S^T$	$\lambda_0^T + \lambda_S^T + \lambda_{Ind}^T + \lambda_{Indsk}^T$
Skilled male	$\lambda_0^T + \lambda_0^{TG} + \lambda_S^T + \lambda_S^{TG}$	$\lambda_0^T + \lambda_0^{TG} + \lambda_S^T + \lambda_S^{TG} + \lambda_{Ind}^T + \lambda_{Ind}^{TG} + \lambda_{Indsk}^T + \lambda_{Indsk}^{TG}$

It also defines changes in the gender wage gap through the following terms:

	Nontradable	Tradable
Nonskilled	λ_0^{TG}	$\lambda_0^{TG} + \lambda_{Ind}^{TG}$
Skilled	$\lambda_0^{TG} + \lambda_S^{TG}$	$\lambda_0^{TG} + \lambda_S^{TG} + \lambda_{Ind}^{TG} + \lambda_{Indsk}^{TG}$

Results

This section presents the results of the analysis. The first-stage model, for occupational choice and earning equations, assesses the significance and quantitative strength of various factors affecting the individual's occupational choice. The second-stage model estimates trading equations. In this multinomial model, the coefficients for skill premiums and the intercepts are, in turn, regressed against several trade-related variables with the aim of assessing the relationship between trade and occupational choice. The findings of the two models are described in the following subsections.

First-Stage Models: Occupational Choice and Earning Equations

The following intuitive stylized facts emerge by inspecting the results of estimating this multinomial model. Being a skilled worker increases the likelihood of working in formal services in all countries for both males and females and in formal manufacturing in some countries. For both males and females in all countries, these two categories of employment have statistically significant odds ratios, most of the time well above unity, with odds ratios for formal services above those for formal manufacturing. Skilled workers are conversely less likely to work in the informal sector, in whatever activity (the exception being informal manufacturing in the Dominican Republic). This shows that skilled workers have a clear advantage when it comes to participating in the formal sector, particularly in the nontradable sector. The odds ratio for working in the formal services sector has increased for urban females in all countries, but declined for males in all but two countries (El Salvador and the Dominican Republic). A similar pattern is evident in the odds ratio associated with skill for rural workers. Again, skilled workers are more likely to work in formal services in rural areas, and this propensity has increased over time for most countries in the study (the exceptions being Nicaragua and El Salvador).[8]

The second model in our methodology estimates how labor earnings are determined using a familiar Mincerian-type approach. As for the multinomial model, several factors affect earnings, but here we focus on returns to skills and economic activity premiums. These variables are those most likely affected by trade-related factors, as shown in the trade models described below. The results from the earnings models are quite stable over time and across countries, and some interesting patterns can be identified. We concentrate on the four coefficients of interest: returns to unskilled and skilled labor, economic sector premiums, and returns to skills in a specific sector.[9]

The returns to skilled labor are, as expected, positive and statistically significant for both males and females in every country and every year in the sample. For El Salvador and Nicaragua, formal education matters but generates wage premiums that are lower than those recorded in the other countries. With the exceptions of El Salvador and Nicaragua, the returns to skilled labor are higher for females than for males in every country, in both urban and rural areas. The premiums for skilled workers range from a minimum of about 4 percent for rural workers in El Salvador to a maximum of 89 percent for rural females in Honduras, but most coefficients hover around 30–40 percent.

No clear time evolution can be observed for the returns to skilled labor. Plotting all the coefficients shows that skill premiums have an upward trend for urban males in Honduras and El Salvador, for urban females in Nicaragua, and for rural males in the Dominican Republic. The other cases display either a flat or a downward trend. This indicates that the returns to skill show no apparent trend over the period under study and no clear pattern that could be associated with the recent widening of trade openness in these economies.

The specification of the earnings models includes an interaction term between skills and sector of employment; therefore, skilled workers would have an additional wage premium when employed in agriculture or in manufacturing (services is the reference sector). These coefficients show no regularity across countries, and few stylized facts can be derived from them. Returns to skilled labor are statistically lower in agriculture than in services for several years in rural Costa Rica, El Salvador, and Honduras. However, returns to skilled labor are statistically lower in manufacturing than in services in urban El Salvador and the Dominican Republic (only among women) and are statistically higher in urban Guatemala.

The wage premiums associated with work in tradable sectors (that is, agriculture or manufacturing) show a remarkable regularity: coefficients for agriculture are negative and statistically significant for almost every country, region, and gender. In other words, after controlling for other characteristics such as age, skill, firm size, geographic locality, and so forth, workers in agriculture earn less than workers in the services sector. Namely, equally qualified workers earn lower wages in agriculture than in services. In the other countries or areas, the coefficients show no regular statistical significance, which means that the average wage is the same for equally qualified workers in manufacturing and in services.

The coefficients for agriculture range between –0.16 to –0.90, which means that ceteris paribus, a worker in agriculture earns approximately 16 to 90 percent less than a worker in services. If we focus on rural workers, where agricultural employment is concentrated, the size of the disparity is relatively lower in the Dominican Republic than in the other countries. The wage premiums in agriculture for males and females show an upward trend (which means a reduction in the wage discount experienced by agricultural workers) for rural males in El Salvador and Honduras and for rural females in Costa Rica. The rest of the countries show either a flat or a downward trend. With few exceptions, no clear improvement in the relative wages of agricultural workers can be identified for the decade under study.[10]

Regarding the wage premiums in manufacturing, no uniform pattern can be found across countries, regions, or gender. The coefficients are negative, in a range between –0.05 and –0.20, for almost every year and country among urban males. These coefficients are not significant for all the cases, implying that at times average wages in manufacturing do not differ statistically from average wages in services. When statistically significant (for instance, in El Salvador), manufacturing premiums are negative and produce wages statistically different by 20 percent. In the case of urban females, manufacturing workers in the Dominican Republic show a positive coefficient, which has been statistically significant for some years, representing a wage difference of up to 24 percent (with respect to comparable women working in services) in 2006. For the other countries the wage differential is negative most of the time and is sometimes statistically significant, involving wage differentials of up to 20 percent (for instance, 13 percent in Guatemala and 17 percent in El Salvador in 2004). As in the case of wage premiums for agricultural workers, very few upward trends can be identified. Only El Salvador shows a positive trend in the wage premiums for manufacturing, with abrupt increases in the two most recent surveys.

In sum, wage premiums associated with workers in tradable sectors (agriculture and manufacturing) show no upward trends but for a few cases. For an already quite open region, this indicates that the recent period of trade liberalization has not had an apparent effect on the wages of workers in tradable sectors. However, this last claim needs to be tested in a multivariate regression setting, given that returns to skills and sector premiums can be affected by factors not related to trade. A multivariate analysis is used to address this in the following subsection.

Second-Stage Models: Trade Equations

In the case of occupational choice, the econometric results show no association between trade and labor market participation in the six categories under study. Columns 1 and 2 of table 11.2 present the results from these employment models. In most cases, trade variables are either not significant or, when statistically significant, not robust to changes in specification. After attempting to use several trade-related variables, with different trading partners, no statistically significant association between trade and employment choices is found. Hence, the observed changes in the gender distribution of the labor force between formal and informal sectors and among economic activities show no statistical association with trade variables.

Conversely, in the case of earnings equations, the econometric results show some link between trade openness and the wage premiums, especially for skilled workers and for workers employed in tradable sectors. In the case of the intercept of the Mincerian equations—which represents

Table 11.2 Regressions of Coefficients on Trade Variables in the Labor Market Models

Variable	Employment models		Earnings equations			
	Intercept	Coefficient on skilled labor	Intercept	Coefficient on skilled labor	Coefficient on skilled labor in tradable sector	Coefficient on employment in tradable sector
Dummy of gender (1 for male and 0 for female)	106	59.32	0.333	0.0625	−0.0985	0.125*
	(158.50)	(91.53)	(0.43)	(0.04)	(−0.0953)	(0.07)
Weighted real exchange rate on imports	−4.043	−2.438	0.00433	1.49E-05	0.00266	−0.00107
	(42.20)	(24.43)	(0.01)	(0.00)	(−0.00279)	(0.00)
Own weighted tariffs, applied to U.S. products	16.5	9.468	0.275	−0.108*	−0.0935	−0.113
	(13.25)	(7.69)	(0.59)	(0.06)	(−0.134)	(0.10)
Import penetration of trade from the United States	110.8	61.16	0.0215	0.0144***	0.00525	−0.0148*
	(271.30)	(160.70)	(0.05)	(0.01)	(−0.011)	(0.01)
Weighted tariffs faced in U.S. market	6.279	4.85	0.0284	−0.0113**	−0.0124	0.00379
	(17.23)	(10.31)	(0.05)	(0.00)	(−0.0101)	(0.01)
GDP share of exports to United States	−61.44	−43.59	−0.177	0.0891	0.0749	0.05
	(171.80)	(104.40)	(0.56)	(0.06)	(−0.127)	(0.09)
Standard deviation of tariffs faced in U.S. market	−2.363	−1.56	−0.00656	0.00380***	0.00203	−0.00356*
	(3.58)	(2.14)	(0.01)	(0.00)	(−0.00255)	(0.00)

Multiplicative variable of faced tariffs in United States and gender dummy	-2.96	-1.849	0.00371	0.00395	0.00499	0.0101*
	(13.46)	(7.80)	(0.03)	(0.00)	(-0.00779)	(0.01)
Multiplicative variable of own tariffs applied to U.S. products and gender dummy	0.483	-0.505	-0.03	-0.0161***	0.012	-0.0280***
	(12.94)	(7.48)	(0.05)	(0.00)	(-0.0101)	(0.01)
Multiplicative variable of import penetration of products from United States and gender	-81.14	-39.85	-0.951**	-0.036	0.0604	-0.0128
	(255.80)	(147.60)	(0.38)	(0.04)	(-0.084)	(0.06)
Constant	-261.8	-127.4	6.574***	0.0986	-0.384	0.206
	(246.20)	(172.50)	(1.46)	(0.15)	(-0.328)	(0.24)
Number of observations	359	353	172	172	323	331
R^2	0.056	0.052	0.818	0.732	0.165	0.528

Source: Authors' calculations using labor and household surveys from respective countries.

Note: Standard errors are in parentheses. Coefficients from OLS regressions of coefficients on school level from multinomial logits. The estimation also includes year, country, area (urban or rural), and economic activity (agriculture or manufacturing). Real exchange rates, import penetration, and GDP share of exports are lagged two periods.

$*p < .10, **p < .05, ***p < .01.$

the average wage for unskilled workers in nontradable sectors[11]—almost no trade variable is found to be statistically significant, with the exception of the interaction term between gender and the share of imports from the United States (see column 3 of table 11.2). This can be interpreted as follows: a reduction of 1 percentage point in the share of imports to GDP increases male wages for all groups of workers (assuming that all other variables remain constant) by approximately 0.95 percent. In the case of returns to skilled workers, there is a statistically significant difference between males and females from changes in own tariffs, favoring the former, so that a 1 percent reduction in own tariffs increases the gender wage gap among skilled workers by approximately 1.6 percent (see column 4 of table 11.2). Faced tariffs and import penetration also have statistically significant impacts on the wages of both skilled males and females. A 1 percent reduction in the former increases wages by approximately 1.13 percent, whereas a 1 percent increase in the latter decreases wages by about 0.11 percent. Hence, this exercise provides some evidence that trade liberalization, as measured by a reduction in own tariffs, does affect gender wage gaps via changes in male-female wage skill premiums.

A further exploration of the impact of trade on gender wage differentials through skills is reported in column 5 of table 11.2. In this case, there is no evidence of statistically significant and robust effects of trade variables on the wage advantages of skilled workers in tradable sectors (that is, agriculture and manufacturing). Trade does not appear to affect skilled males and females working in tradable sectors differently.

Another plausible channel of the trade effects on wages is through wage differentials according to sector of employment. Workers in tradable sectors, controlling for other productive characteristics, face international competition as a consequence of trade openness, and this can affect their employment opportunities and their labor productivity. We find some evidence of this link. In the last column of table 11.2, own and faced tariffs have an effect on wages in tradable sectors. A reduction of own tariffs increases wages among males and females, but does so faster among the former (approximately 2.8 percent) than the latter (1.48 percent), thus increasing the gender wage gap. However, a reduction in faced tariffs reduces the gender wage gap by approximately 1 percent.

In summary, these estimates show some, albeit small, impact of changes in trade openness on gender wage gaps in DR-CAFTA countries. Table 11.3 summarizes the impacts from our preferred specifications. First, own and faced tariffs have statistically significant effects through skill and sector

Table 11.3 Summary of Results on the Impact of Trade Variables in Wage Models

| | Individual coefficient | | | | Combined effect[a] | | | |
| | Unskilled | | Skilled | | Unskilled | | Skilled | |
Variable	Female	Male	Female	Male	Female	Male	Female	Male
Not tradable								
Weighted real exchange rate on imports								
Import penetration of trade from the United States		-0.9510	-0.108			-0.9510	-0.1080	-1.0590
GDP share of exports to United States								
Own weighted tariffs, applied to U.S. products			0.0144	-0.0161			0.0144	-0.0017
Weighted tariffs faced in U.S. market			-0.0113				-0.0113	-0.0113
Standard deviation of tariffs faced in U.S. market			0.0038				0.0038	0.0038
Tradable								
Weighted real exchange rate on imports								
Import penetration of trade from the United States						-0.9510	-0.1080	-1.0590
GDP share of exports to United States								
Own weighted tariffs, applied to U.S. products	-0.0148	-0.0280			-0.0148	-0.0428	-0.0004	-0.0445
Weighted tariffs faced in U.S. market		0.0101				0.0101	-0.0113	-0.0012
Standard deviation of tariffs faced in U.S. market	-0.0036				-0.0036	-0.0036	0.0002	0.0002

Source: Authors' calculations.

Note: Coefficients are significant with 90 percent or more confidence intervals.

a. The combined effect shows the impact of each trade variable on all eight groups.

premiums. Additionally, import penetration has a statistically significant effect on all workers. No impact of export shares and real exchange rates is found for any of the groups under consideration. The right panel of table 11.3 shows the impact of each trade variable on the eight main groups. These combined effects show that tariffs affect wages for skilled workers in both nontradable and tradable sectors and also affect skilled and unskilled workers in the tradable sector. These combined coefficients, if multiplied by a 1 percent change in the corresponding trade variable, render the elasticity of wages to changes in trade variables. Table 11.4 summarizes these elasticities and shows that trade liberalization through a reduction of own tariffs increases the wages of all workers in the trade sector. The rise ranges from 0.04 percent for skilled women to 4.45 percent for skilled men. This, however, increases the wages of men more than women, and it widens the gender wage gap by 2.69 percentage points for the unskilled and 4.22 percentage points for the skilled. A reduction of faced tariffs also increases the wages of workers in the tradable sector, but in this case favors women more than men. Skilled females earn 1.13 percent more, whereas skilled men earn only 0.12 percent more (and unskilled men earn 1.01 percent less). This combined effect reduces the gender wage gap by about 1 percentage point for both skilled and unskilled workers.

These results indicate that trade liberalization through tariff reductions has diverse effects. A reduction in own tariffs (that is, cheaper imported goods) increases wages for all workers in the tradable sector, but also increases the gender wage gap. A reduction in faced tariffs (that is, easier access to the U.S. market) favors the wages of skilled women and reduces the gender wage gap.

However, an increase in trade openness through a higher ratio of imports to GDP is associated with lower wages in both tradable and nontradable sectors. These reductions are small (below 1 percent) and affect men more than women. This brings about a reduction of nearly 1 percentage point in the gender wage gap.

The impacts described above are ceteris paribus. That is, they assume that all the other explanatory variables—related to trade and not related to trade—are held constant. They also assume that all countries experience the same change in trade variables (the 1 percentage point change assumed here). However, the observed pattern of trade liberalization significantly varies across countries. Thus, even if the regression coefficients of our trade model were the same for all countries, the final trade-related impact on labor market variables would be different for each country. As shown in table 11.5, DR-CAFTA countries have different combinations

Table 11.4 Simulated Impact of Trade Liberalization through Different Indicators

| Variable | Trade shock | Total effect (elasticity) | | | | Change in gender wage gap | |
| | | Unskilled | | Skilled | | Unskilled | Skilled |
		Female	Male	Female	Male		
Not tradable							
Weighted real exchange rate on imports	Plus 1 percentage point	0.00	0.00	0.00	0.00	0.00	0.00
Import penetration of trade from the United States	Plus 1 percentage point	0.00	−0.95	−0.11	−1.06	−0.96	−0.96
GDP share of exports to United States	Plus 1 percentage point	0.00	0.00	0.00	0.00	0.00	0.00
Own weighted tariffs, applied to U.S. product	Minus 1 percentage point	0.00	0.00	−1.44	0.17	0.00	1.61
Weighted tariffs faced in U.S. market	Minus 1 percentage point	0.00	0.00	1.13	1.13	0.00	0.00
Standard deviation of tariffs faced in U.S. market	Minus 1 percentage point	0.00	0.00	−0.38	−0.38	0.00	0.00
Tradable							
Weighted real exchange rate on imports	Plus 1 percentage point	0.00	0.00	0.00	0.00	0.00	0.00
Import penetration of trade from the United States	Plus 1 percentage point	0.00	−0.95	−0.11	−1.06	−0.96	−0.96
GDP share of exports to United States	Plus 1 percentage point	0.00	0.00	0.00	0.00	0.00	0.00
Own weighted tariffs, applied to U.S. product	Minus 1 percentage point	1.48	4.28	0.04	4.45	2.69	4.22
Weighted tariffs faced in U.S. market	Minus 1 percentage point	0.00	−1.01	1.13	0.12	−1.02	−1.01
Standard deviation of tariffs faced in U.S. market	Minus 1 percentage point	0.36	0.36	−0.02	−0.02	0.00	0.00

Source: Authors' calculations.
Note: The gender wage gap is defined as the ratio of female to male wages. A negative sign implies a reduction of such ratio in percentage points.

Table 11.5 Change in Explanatory Variables in DR-CAFTA Countries, by Sector

Sector and country	Time period		Real exchange rate	Changes in			
	Initial	Final		Share of imports from United States to sector GDP	Weighted own tariffs	Weighted faced tariffs	Standard deviation of faced tariffs
Manufacturing							
Costa Rica	1997	2007	-0.49	0.06	-2.96	-6.70	-7.39
Dominican Republic	1996	2007	0.21	-0.04	-6.77	-7.74	-7.08
El Salvador	1998	2004	-2.85	-0.05	0.50	-2.31	-1.32
Guatemala	2000	2006	0.17	-0.20	-1.01	-1.30	-0.49
Honduras	2001	2005	-0.07	-0.07	-2.26	-1.16	-0.91
Nicaragua	1998	2005	1.00	0.00	-0.16	-3.06	-1.42
Agriculture							
Costa Rica	1997	2007	-0.49	0.09	-1.68	-0.41	-4.43
Dominican Republic	1996	2007	0.21	0.10	-5.48	-1.19	-5.93
El Salvador	1998	2004	-2.85	-0.02	-0.40	-0.17	-5.04
Guatemala	2000	2006	0.17	0.06	-3.53	-0.53	6.92
Honduras	2001	2005	-0.07	0.03	-2.99	-0.80	-5.84
Nicaragua	1998	2005	1.00	0.02	-0.99	-7.88	-8.67

Source: Authors' calculations.

of factors that narrow the gender gap (larger shares of imports to GDP and lower faced tariffs) and factors that widen the gender gap (lower own tariffs), and these may be different for different sectors, particularly for agriculture and manufacturing. For instance, in Guatemala, import shares declined in manufacturing and increased in agriculture, while own tariffs fell in both agriculture and manufacturing. The trend in own tariffs is the same in all countries (except in manufacturing in El Salvador). In the Dominican Republic, own and faced tariffs declined, but import shares either remained constant or fell. This means that sometimes it is difficult to identify a clear direction in the change of trade openness.

Because of the multiple channels of transmission and the varied changes in trade variables, it is difficult to draw general lessons applicable across all the countries. In Nicaragua, trade explains 54 percent of the fall in the wage gap, mainly through reductions in gender differences among skilled workers. In Costa Rica and the Dominican Republic, the evidence clearly favors the hypothesis that trade openness reduces the gender wage gap, although each country experienced a different set of trade changes in the recent decade. In the case of Nicaragua, the evidence is also favorable, but the size of the influence is smaller. Guatemala, El Salvador, and Honduras show an adverse impact of trade openness, which is somehow more than compensated by other factors not related to trade.

Conclusions

The most important findings of this analysis consist of identifying (a) an equalizing effect of trade openness as measured by import shares and tariffs faced in the United States on the gender wage gap, (b) a wage gap–widening effect of trade openness as measured by own tariffs (imposed against U.S. imports), and (c) no statistically significant link between trade openness and gender differentials in labor market participation and job reallocation. The latter is somewhat surprising given the evidence of large job churning recorded for the region.

Trade affects gender differentials by affecting skill, sector, and combined skill-sector premiums. Lower tariffs faced in the United States (that is, increased market access and potentially increased export orientation) reduce the gender wage gap because they modify returns to employment in the tradable sector. A similar effect, but with an opposite sign, is found for own tariffs. A reduction in own tariffs imposed on exports to the

United States increases the gender wage gap among skilled workers (in all sectors) and among workers in tradable sectors (skilled and unskilled). A 1 percentage point change in own tariffs brings about changes in the wage gap that range between 1.6 and 4.4 percentage points, whereas a 1 percentage point change in faced tariffs results in changes of 1.0 point. In sectors producing tradables, exposure to external competition (import shares from the United States) brings a reduction in wages that is relatively larger for men than for women. Therefore, an increase of 1 percentage point in the share of imports results in a fall in the gender wage gap of about 1 percentage point. In the end, the final impact of trade openness is an empirical matter that depends on the relative changes of both faced and own tariffs and trends in import shares, which may end up canceling or reinforcing each other.

According to our simulations, the impact of trade openness can be relatively large in some countries, but its full impact is sometimes more than compensated by other factors. These other factors may be associated with, but not restricted to, changes in labor market participation and job reallocations as well as changes in institutions and regulations that affect wages and participation in occupations. Changes in capital intensity of the exporting firms, and of the economy in general, demographic changes, and other economic or institutional changes may also affect the gender gap. The natural question then is, what prevents the equalizing effect of trade from taking place? What forces compensate or reinforce this effect?

The evidence presented here hints at two main problems. Given the lack of significant statistical association between trade and employment, the first problem is that trade does not seem to induce a reallocation of factors of production that would normally lead to economic and welfare gains. Excessive informalization of the labor market and lack of employment creation in trade-related activities are signs of a labor market that is not responding to the incentives of trade. In countries of this region, these may be associated with a lack of flexibility in the labor market, lack of mobility from one activity to another, lack of retraining, and so forth.

This calls for implementing a series of actions that allow for reallocation and flexibility in times of economic change. A process of further economic trade openness like DR-CAFTA may lead to changes in employment patterns and in returns to human capital, and those who may be affected by such a process need to be able to rely on some mechanisms that allow them to find a place in the labor market. In this regard, training and reallocation programs may be a fundamental part of a complementary agenda.

The second problem lies in the evidence that trade may produce wider gender wage gaps. This seems to indicate that trade exposure may affect the relative wages of men and women, particularly in the tradable sector. Reducing own tariffs induces wage increases for skilled and unskilled workers in the tradable sector. But it does so more among males than females, particularly those who are skilled, hence increasing the gender wage gap. These impacts can be partly offset by reductions in faced tariffs from the United States, which increases the wages of skilled women and reduces the gender gap among workers in the tradable sector. These differential impacts call for both policies that enhance female participation in the tradable sector, the acquisition of skills (through schooling and training), and perhaps institutional measures that prevent discrimination in the workplace.

An increased exposure to trade, as measured through import shares, is shown to have a negative effect on wages, although the effect is stronger for men than for women, so it is accompanied by a reduction in the wage gap. These effects are particularly associated with import penetration and hence may be associated with job losses or other competitive pressures on the labor market of workers in the tradable sector. In this case, remedial policies should include, on the one hand, mechanisms to facilitate reallocation from declining sectors unable to face external competition and, on the other, incentives to accumulate capital (both human and financial) to support the expansion of areas that can compete in the new liberalized markets. In this regard, training particularly in areas associated with tradables seems necessary. Several countries inside and outside the region have had to retrain their labor force in the event of new competitive forces from international markets. Finally, compensation mechanisms for workers who lose their employment due to external competition can also be devised. These mechanisms should be put in place as a temporary alleviation of trade shock, but they may also spur a recomposition of the labor force and the labor market in general.

Notes

1. A companion paper by Bussolo and others (2010) assesses the effects of trade on poverty, taking into account the gender channel. See chapter 12 of this volume.

2. This section relies heavily on Bussolo and De Hoyos (2009, ch. 2).

3. The data sets are harmonized such that income definitions and several other variables relevant for socioeconomic analysis are comparable over time and across countries. More information about the Socio-Economic Database for Latin America and the Caribbean (SEDLAC) is available at www.cedlas.org.

4. The same rates for the Dominican Republic are about 30 percent.

5. Furthermore, for the Dominican case, there are probably some changes in the definitions: unemployment was recorded at 30 percent in 1997 and dropped to 7 percent in 2000.

6. For the whole economy, the total number of employed men is larger than the total number of employed women.

7. For simplicity here we do not include the changes of trade on the intercept of the participation model.

8. The complete set of the multinomial model results is available from the authors on request.

9. Full econometric results from the selection correction earnings models are available from the authors on request.

10. Figures and statistical results are available from the authors on request.

11. Recall that the Mincerian equations include dummies representing sector of occupation and skill levels and that these dummies have "unskilled" workers in "nontradable" sectors as reference categories. Therefore, when these dummies are at their 0 value, the intercept represents the average wage for unskilled workers in nontradables. When this intercept increases due to a trade-related impact, the average wage for unskilled workers in nontradables increases, but this increase affects everybody else as well.

References

Artecona, R., and W. Cunningham. 2002. "Effects of Trade Liberalization on the Gender Wage Gap in Mexico." Gender and Development Working Paper 21, World Bank, Washington, DC.

Becker, G. S. 1959. *The Economics of Discrimination*. Chicago: University of Chicago Press.

Beneria, L., and K. Lind. 1995. "Engendering International Trade: Concepts, Policy, and Action." Gender and Sustainable Development (GSD) Working Paper 5, Cornell University, Ithaca, NY.

Berik, G. 2000. "Mature Export-Led Growth and Gender Wage Inequality in Taiwan." *Feminist Economics* 6 (3):1–26.

Berik, G., Y. van der Meulen Rodgers, and J. E. Zveglich. 2004. "International Trade and Gender Wage Discrimination: Evidence from East Asia." *Review of Development Economics* 8 (2): 237–54.

Bussolo, M., and R. E. De Hoyos, eds. 2009. *Gender Aspects of the Trade and Poverty Nexus: A Macro-Micro Approach.* Washington, DC: World Bank; Basingstoke, U.K.: Palgrave Macmillan.

Bussolo, M., S. Freije., C. Djiofack, and M. Rodríguez. 2010. "Trade Openness and Welfare Distribution in DR-CAFTA Countries." World Bank, Washington, DC.

Carr, M., ed. 2004. *Chains of Fortune: Linking Women Producers and Workers with Global Markets.* London: Commonwealth Secretariat.

Cagatay, N. 2001. *Trade, Gender, and Poverty.* New York: United Nations Development Programme.

Darity, W. 2007. "The Formal Structure of a Gender-Segregated Low-Income Economy." In *Feminist Economics of Trade,* ed. D. Elson, C. Grown, I. Steveren, and N. Catagay, 78–90. London: Routledge.

Ferreira, F. H. G., P. G. Leite, and M. Wai-Poi. 2007. "Trade Liberalization, Employment Flows, and Wage Inequality in Brazil." Policy Research Working Paper wp-4108, World Bank, Washington, DC.

Filmer, D. 1999. "The Structure of Social Disparities in Education: Gender and Wealth." Background paper for World Bank, Engendering Development, Washington, DC. www.worldbank.org/prr/filmer.pdf.

Fontana, M., S. Joekes, and R. Masika. 1998. *Global Trade Expansion and Liberalisation: Gender Issues and Impacts.* BRIDGE Report 42. Brighton, U.K.: Institute of Development Studies.

Gammage, S., H. Jorgensen, and E. McGill. 2002. "Framework for Gender Assessments of Trade and Investment Agreements." Women's Edge, Washington, DC.

Gammage, S., and R. Mehra. 1999. "Trends, Countertrends, and Gaps in Women's Employment." *World Development* 27 (3): 533–50.

Joekes, S., and A. Weston. 1994. *Women and the New Trade Agenda.* New York: United Nations Development Fund for Women.

Katz, E. 1995. "Gender and Trade within the Household: Observations from Rural Guatemala." *World Development* 23 (2): 327–42.

Kusago, T. 2000. "Why Did Rural Households Permit Their Daughters to Be Urban Factory Workers? A Case from Rural Malay Villages." *Labour and Management in Development Journal* 1 (2): 1–24.

Lipton, M. 1983. "Demography and Poverty." World Bank Staff Working Paper 623, World Bank, Washington, DC.

Marcoux, A. 1998. "The Feminization of Poverty: Claims, Facts, and Data Needs." *Population and Development Review* 24 (1): 131–39.

McCulloch, N., and M. Ota. 2002. "Export Horticulture and Poverty in Kenya." IDS Working Paper 174, Institute of Development Studies, Brighton, U.K.

Morrison, A., D. Raju, and N. Sinha. 2007. "Gender Equality, Poverty, and Economic Growth." Policy Research Working Paper 4349, World Bank, Washington, DC.

Newman, C. 2001. "Gender, Time Use, and Change: Impacts of Agricultural Export Employment in Ecuador." Gender and Development Working Paper 18, World Bank, Washington, DC.

Nicita, A., and S. Razzaz. 2003. "Who Benefits and How Much? How Gender Affects Welfare Impacts of a Booming Textile Industry." Policy Research Working Paper 3029, World Bank, Washington, DC.

Oostendorp, R. 2004. "Globalization and the Gender Wage Gap." Policy Research Working Paper 3256, World Bank, Washington, DC.

Paul-Majumder, P., and A. Begum. 2000. "The Gender Imbalances in the Export-Oriented Garment Industry in Bangladesh." Policy Research Report on Gender and Development Working Paper 12, World Bank, Washington, DC.

Pavcnik, N., A. Blom, P. Goldberg, and N. Schady. 2004. "Trade Policy and Industry Wage Structure: Evidence from Brazil." *World Bank Economic Review* 18 (3): 319–44.

Seguino, S. 2000. "The Effects of Structural Change and Economic Liberalization on Gender Wage Differentials in South Korea and Taiwan." *Cambridge Journal of Economics* 24 (4): 437–59.

Standing, G. 1999. "Globalization through Flexible Labor: A Theme Revisited." *World Development* 27 (3): 583–602.

Tran-Nguyen, A., and A. Beviglia-Zampetti, eds. 2004. *Trade and Gender: Opportunities and Challenges for Developing Countries.* Geneva: United Nations Conference on Trade and Development.

Tzannatos, Z. 1999. "Women and Labour Market Changes in the Global Economy: Growth Helps, Inequalities Hurt, and Public Policy Matters." *World Development* 27 (3): 551–69.

United Nations. 1999. *1999 World Survey on the Role of Women in Development: Globalization, Gender, and Work.* New York: United Nations.

Zohir, S. C. 1998. *Gender Implications of Industrial Reforms and Adjustment in the Manufacturing Sector of Bangladesh.* Ph.D. dissertation, University of Manchester, Department of Economics and Social Studies.

CHAPTER 12

Trade Liberalization and Welfare Distribution in Central America

Maurizio Bussolo, Samuel Freije, Calvin Z. Djiofack, and Melissa Rodríguez

The effects of trade openness on poverty or welfare distribution are difficult to track because the relationship between these two variables may take multiple paths. In a synthesizing effort, Winters (2003) identifies four main institutional channels through which trade policy affects poverty: (1) goods and services markets, (2) households, (3) factor markets, and (4) government. First, the channels of retail and wholesale distribution that exist in a country affect the transformation of international prices into local prices. In this regard, market structures as well as storage and transportation channels affect the final impact of trade liberalization on local prices and hence on families' welfare. Second, the effect of trade openness on households depends on the net position of households in the supply of each of the final goods and services whose prices are affected by trade openness—that is, if families are sellers (or buyers) of a product whose prices have been affected by trade openness. Third, trade policy can affect first the price and allocation of factors of production (both labor and capital) in several ways and then the sources of income for households and governments. Finally, taxes, subsidies, and public expenditures can be affected by trade agreements that curtail some forms of tax-subsidy policy and industry promotion. In a more general way, some studies (for instance, Bardhan, Bowles, and Wallerstein 2006) highlight the existence of multiple social and political agreements that foster or hinder the opening of an economy and the redistributive mechanisms, via social insurance or social assistance, that governments adopt to manage its distributive impacts.

A small economy takes international prices of tradable goods (p_i) as given. These international prices are turned into local prices (p_l) after the operation of two mechanisms: trade policy and output markets. Trade policy implies changes in import or export tariffs (t), quotas (q), and exchange rates (xr). Output markets involve transportation costs (r) and markups (m) associated with market structures and geographic dispersion. Therefore, changes in trade policy—that is, changes in tariffs (Δt), quotas (Δq), and exchange rates (Δxr)—imply changes in local prices (Δp_l) via a process known as "pass-through." Changes in local prices affect consumption patterns (Δc) and sources of labor income $(\Delta w, \Delta E)$. Finally, taxes (t) collected from or subsidies (s) allocated to international markets (import and export taxes), output markets (sales and value added taxes), and factor markets (income and payroll taxes) are affected by changes in trade policy and local prices. In this regard, public sector interventions that address problems in output and factor markets such as building infrastructure or pro-competition regulation could enhance the benefits of trade reform. Similarly, public investment in programs for human capital accumulation may improve the productive characteristics of household members and their ability to reap the benefits of an internationally competitive labor market. Finally, social programs may serve as a safety net for households that are unfavorably affected by trade reforms.

This chapter concentrates on the impact of trade liberalization policy on household consumption and labor income distribution—namely, channels 1 and 3 according to Winters (2003). Furthermore, based on this analysis we hint at the main issues of a complementary agenda (public policies through channel 4) that may be pursued to enhance the favorable welfare results and compensate the unfavorable outcomes of a trade liberalization policy like the Dominican Republic–Central America Free Trade Agreement (DR-CAFTA).

In particular, the chapter aims to answer the following question: Does trade liberalization affect household welfare and its distribution in DR-CAFTA countries? It quantifies the impact on welfare through the channels of consumption prices and labor markets. In that respect, the chapter aims to understand how welfare distribution is affected by changes in consumer prices and labor earnings of households due to trade openness in DR-CAFTA countries.

Since DR-CAFTA has only recently started operating, its economic impacts may still be developing, and there may be important data constraints on the effort to analyze them. Hence, this study considers the general relationship between trade shocks and changes in goods and labor markets in the countries of this region. An attempt to identify the precise effects of the DR-CAFTA shock is not explored here.[1]

This study proceeds with a review of the main findings of the recent literature studying the relationship between trade openness and welfare distribution in Latin American countries. It then describes the recent evolution of the main indicators of poverty and inequality in DR-CAFTA countries, explains the methodology applied to estimate the impact of trade openness on changes in the distribution of family welfare, and describes the data sources available. The next section explains the results, and a final section concludes with the implications of these results for the adoption of a complementary agenda to the DR-CAFTA.

Literature Review

The literature on the impact of trade on welfare in general, and on poverty in particular, is vast. Winters, McCulloch, and McKay (2004) review the international evidence on whether poverty has declined or increased due to trade liberalization policies adopted in developing countries. The evidence they collect shows that outcomes vary from country to country. According to these authors, the final outcome depends on many factors, such as the starting point of the economy, the specific trade reform, and the characteristics of the poor and how they sustain themselves. That is to say, it is very difficult to reach an a priori general conclusion about the relationship between trade liberalization and poverty.

Empirical evidence supports the theoretical view that trade liberalization alleviates poverty both on average and in the long run. However, according to Winters, McCulloch, and McKay (2004), this argument does not mean that trade policy is one of the most important mechanisms for decreasing poverty or that liberalization effects are always positive for the poor. The empirical literature that they survey shows that there is strong evidence for the beneficial impact of trade liberalization on productivity. However, the links between trade and growth are ambiguous. The authors argue that concerns over adverse effects on the employment and wages of poor people or on government spending on the poor due to falling fiscal revenues are not well founded, despite the fact that specific cases of each of these two problems can be identified.

Winters, McCulloch, and McKay (2004) also indicate that there are many gaps in our knowledge about trade liberalization and poverty and many important questions for further research. Little is known about the transitional unemployment that results from liberalization, the effects of trade liberalization on poverty dynamics at the household level, and how households respond to adverse shocks or potential opportunities. There is little information about the way in which border price changes are transmitted to local levels and how this transmission may differ for the poor and nonpoor.

In a more recent study, Goldberg and Pavcnik (2007) summarize empirical evidence about the exposure to globalization and the evolution of inequality in many developing countries during the 1980s and 1990s. The authors analyze several channels through which trade openness could affect inequality, discuss empirical evidence, and investigate the possibility of establishing a causal relation between the increase in inequality and globalization. They single out several specific labor market factors such as wage premiums and transitional unemployment, among others. Moreover, a non–labor market impact is the effect of trade on home production and consumption. Each of these factors merits some discussion.

Regarding the effect of trade on the skill wage premium, the authors comment that theoretical trade models seem inconsistent, in some way, with the empirical evidence. Conventional trade theory predicts labor reallocation that favors employment in low-skilled sectors and a reduction of the skill wage premium. However, many empirical studies in developing countries do not find evidence of labor reallocation. Additional evidence seems to indicate an increase in the proportion of skilled workers within most industries in developing countries, which could be seen as evidence in favor of skill-biased technological change. Outsourcing, increased foreign investment, and complementarity between capital and skilled labor are all additional reasons that could explain an increase in the skill wage premium, which worsens earnings distribution.

Another channel that Goldberg and Pavcnik (2007) analyze regarding the link between inequality and trade is transitional unemployment. The authors comment that it is believed that trade openness leads to transitional unemployment, which affects the poor, and then has consequences for income inequality. However, international trade models usually assume full employment, so limited discussion exists about this topic. Another way globalization can affect inequality is by "inducing noncompliance of firms with labor market standards and by increasing the proportion of workers in the informal sector of the economy" (Goldberg and Pavcnik 2007, 73), which could contribute to an increase in inequality. With a reduction in tariffs, firms are exposed to foreign competition and then are forced to lower their costs. Once again, there is not enough evidence about the relationship between informality and trade reform, and the few analyses have mixed results. Unfortunately, the authors affirm that the lack of empirical evidence relating trade liberalization with wage uncertainty in developing countries makes it difficult to reach a conclusion on this issue.

Finally, globalization can affect inequality through household consumption. According to Goldberg and Pavcnik (2007, 76), "To the extent that household consumption depends on the relative position of households in the welfare distribution, globalization induces price changes that may affect inequality through consumption. Furthermore, the increased availability and lower prices of traded goods may shift demand away from nontradable services (for example, household services, such as housekeeping, cooking, and so forth) toward tradable goods (washing machines, dryers, microwaves, etc.), further depressing the earning prospects of the poor." The authors comment that the consumption analysis has not been included in empirical work and that Porto (2006) is the only study they know that takes into account how trade policy affects welfare distribution through consumption.[2] Porto finds that the impact of trade liberalization on inequality through the consumption channel is smaller in degree than its impact via the labor income channel.

Establishing a causal relation between globalization and inequality has proved to be challenging due to the various channels through which this relation may operate. Evidence shows that it depends on many factors that are country specific. In the following paragraphs we summarize the findings from the most recent studies for Latin American countries.

Argentina

There are two recent studies on the impact of trade on welfare in Argentina, and they show different results, largely as a result of differences in the methods and data used.

Porto (2006) estimates the impact of trade policies on the prices of traded goods, nontraded goods, and wages and how they affect households across the entire distribution of income. He finds that the impact of trade reform on tradable and nontradable goods is regressive (that is, welfare losses for the poorer and welfare gains for the richer), whereas the impact on wages is progressive (that is, welfare gains for the poorer and welfare losses for the richer). Given that the labor gains are larger (in absolute terms) than the welfare losses, the total effect is progressive.

Galiani and Sanguinetti (2003) concentrate on the impact of trade liberalization in the 1990s on the skill premium for Argentine manufacturing firms. They find evidence of a higher skill premium among those activities that show increasing import penetration. However, they also argue that the impact attributable to trade represents only 16 percent of the total increase in the skill premium for the period. Therefore, the authors argue that the increase in skill premiums, as a main driver for increasing inequality, cannot be fully attributed to trade opening.

Brazil

Ferreira, Leite, and Wai-Poi (2007) analyze changes in the wage distribution in Brazil during trade liberalization (1988–95) by studying the impacts of trade on industry wage premiums, industry and economywide skill premiums, and employment flows. The authors find that trade liberalization played a significant role in decreasing wage inequality in the Brazilian economy (overall, not just in the manufacturing sector) through employment flows across sectors, industries, and categories of formality and not through changes in industry-specific (wage or skill) premiums. They also find that the returns to education fell over the period, which contributed to a decrease in inequality.

Colombia

Attanasio, Goldberg, and Pavcnik (2004) analyze the effects of trade liberalization on wage inequality in Colombia. They investigate the relation between tariff reductions in the 1980s and 1990s and wage distribution. They find that wage distribution was affected by an increase in returns to education, changes in industry wages, and changes in the labor force toward the informal sector. However, they conclude that the increase in wage inequality observed over that period cannot be fully explained by these factors. According to the authors, "Changes in the skill premiums are roughly the same across industries and cannot be related to changes in tariffs across sectors" (Attanasio, Goldberg, and Pavcnik 2004, 333). They also find that the shares of industry employment stay constant over the period and that the small changes they find cannot be linked to trade liberalization, so there is no evidence of labor reallocation across sectors. Another finding is the increase in the proportion of skilled workers in every indus-try, which is consistent with the hypothesis of skill-biased technological change. The increase in the proportion of skilled workers is larger in sec-tors that are exposed to larger tariff reductions. The authors conclude that trade reforms in Colombia affected the wage distribution—through the impact on skill-biased technological change, industry wage premiums, and informality—and therefore, at least in part, an increase in inequality.

Mexico
Nicita (2004) analyzes the effects of trade liberalization in Mexico between 1989 and 2000. His study is an ex post analysis, which takes into account regional differences in the Mexican economy. He estimates the effects of trade liberalization on changes in regional prices and wages and the effect on households' welfare. The author finds that trade liberaliza-tion affects domestic prices and labor income in different ways across income groups and across regions of the country. Trade liberalization low-ered relative prices of most agricultural products. It increased the wages of skilled workers, but decreased the wages of unskilled workers in many regions. The states that are closer to the U.S. border gained threefold more relative to the states in the south. Therefore, trade liberalization was ben-eficial, but contributed to an increase in inequality between the south and the north, urban and rural areas, and skilled and unskilled labor. It reduced poverty by about 3 percent and benefited all income groups, although richer households benefited more, in absolute and percentage terms, than poorer households.

In a more recent study, Chiquiar (2008) finds that indicators of trade openness in Mexico such as foreign direct investment and share of man-ufacturing within GDP are associated with reductions in the skill pre-mium, whereas other variables such as import penetration are not. The author argues that there is a regional divide that favors regions closer to the United States (the main trading partner), which receive the largest share of foreign investment. Therefore, unskilled workers in the north improved their wages more than unskilled workers in the south, despite a reduction in the skill premium in the country as a whole. These results are generally consistent, despite the use of a different methodology and database, to those of Nicita (2004).

Central American Countries
There are few studies on the impact of trade openness for Central American countries. Jaramillo and Lederman (2005) report that Central

American countries had hardly noticeable changes in their Gini coefficient between 1990 and 2000, a period of intense trade liberalization, whether measured by average tariffs (which declined from 14.1 percent to 7.1 percent) or by trade openness (which grew from 0.47 to 0.76).[3] The same volume reports the results of a study by Bussolo and Niimi (2005), who estimate the probable impact of the DR-CAFTA on Nicaraguan welfare distribution. Making use of predicted prices and wages from a computable general equilibrium, the authors simulate the distribution of changes in household welfare. They find that the agreement produces an income gain of nearly 1 percentage point (0.91), but with a larger gain for urban households (1.05) than for rural households (0.55). A full distributional analysis, however, shows that gains are higher for urban than for rural households across the income distribution, but that gains are higher for those in the bottom 5 percent of the distribution than for the rest. The study also identifies the winners and losers from the agreement, making clear that average gains may hide important differences among specific households. In particular, the authors take advantage of the full heterogeneity of household information to identify who gains and who loses from the trade agreement. In their simulations, they find that up to 33 percent of poor households in rural areas and 14 percent of poor households in urban areas suffer welfare losses of 1.83 and 1.90 percent, respectively. Finally, the authors identify that welfare gains and losses are due to changes in factor prices (basically wages) more than output prices. Hence they conclude that complementary policies ought to concentrate on human capital and other asset accumulation rather than on food subsidies or other transfer policies.

Evolution of Poverty and Inequality in DR-CAFTA Countries

Usually, poverty and inequality are considered indicators or proxies of social welfare. In a reduced form, poverty and inequality indicators are considered fundamental parameters of most social welfare functions. Usually, if these indicators move in different directions, the total effect on social welfare is ambiguous and depends on the society's preference for or aversion to inequality.[4] Given that the trade-off between inequality and efficiency is a matter of preferences, a priori evaluations of social welfare using poverty and inequality require that both indexes move in the same direction or that one moves and the other remains constant. In most cases, a reduction of either one or both of the poverty and inequality indexes is considered welfare increasing, whereas an increase in any of them (keeping the other constant) is welfare reducing. A review of the general trends in these indicators provides a rough profile of welfare changes in a society.

Central American countries, with the exception of Costa Rica, have high levels of poverty and inequality. Their performance in poverty reduction has been similar in a general way. Large declines in poverty were achieved at the end of the 1980s and in the 1990s, but this trend has slowed down or even reversed since the end of the 1990s in some countries. The Dominican Republic experienced an increase in poverty during the last decade mainly due to a financial crisis in 2003–04. Costa Rica has experienced very slow poverty reduction since the late 1990s and even a reversal since 2007. El Salvador, Honduras, and Nicaragua continued to experience poverty reduction during the last decade, although with some setbacks (as reported for El Salvador) toward the final years of the decade.

Regarding inequality, the performance of these countries is also mixed. Inequality (as measured by the Gini coefficient) has increased in Costa Rica and Honduras, remained stable in the Dominican Republic, and decreased in El Salvador, Guatemala, and Nicaragua.

Given these general trends, and a reduced social welfare function that is assumed to be nondecreasing in any of these indicators, we can say that El Salvador, Guatemala, and Nicaragua have had unambiguous welfare improvements in the period under study. Costa Rica and Honduras, due to their conflicting trends in poverty and inequality, have had no clear change in welfare. The Dominican Republic, given the rise in poverty and relative stability of inequality, could have experienced a reduction in welfare for the period under study. This section provides a more detailed description of the trends in poverty and inequality based on recent World Bank reports for these countries.

Costa Rica

According to the World Bank (2007), the recent evolution of poverty rates in Costa Rica can be explained by a reduction in growth and the exclusion of poor households from the benefits of growth. These factors have contributed to a decrease in the real income of poor and near-poor households in Costa Rica. "These shifts in how the fruits of growth are distributed reflect broader changes in the Costa Rican and world economies that have led to a decline in the relative demand for less skilled workers at the same time that the relative supply of low-skilled workers has increased" (World Bank 2007, xii). The study also comments that some education problems, such as the decrease in labor force participation of high school graduates and the increase in dropouts at this educational level, have resulted in growing inequality, higher unemployment, or more part-time work among the poor and low-skilled workers. These trends, the study remarks, have affected poor single mothers in a significant, negative way.

The Dominican Republic

Estimates by the World Bank for the Dominican Republic show a decline in poverty levels from 1986 to 1998. This good performance in poverty reduction did not continue in the following years. According to the World Bank (2006a, i), "Poverty and the incomes of the poor saw virtually no improvements during the growth bonanza of 1997–2002." The same report also finds, "The 2003–2004 economic crisis brought a dramatic deterioration of real incomes and poverty levels" (World Bank 2006a, i). In 2004, an estimated 42 percent of the population was poor, and 16 percent was extremely poor.

World Bank (2006a) identifies four factors that jointly affected poverty reduction at the end of the 1990s, the subsequent decline in income, and the trends in inequality. The first factor is the pattern of unequal growth of labor incomes, which disproportionally benefited some regions, workers with a higher education (university), and sectors with lower demand for unskilled workers. This pattern of growth negatively affected other sectors, such as agriculture. The second factor is the economic damage due to the 2003–04 crisis, which affected real incomes through higher prices for food and other goods. The third factor is the low labor productivity resulting from a high dropout rate, which prevents children from acquiring the skills demanded in the labor market. The last factor is the lack of effective policies supporting the accumulation of human and physical capital in the country.

El Salvador

According to the World Bank (2005), several factors have contributed to the progress of El Salvador in poverty reduction. These factors included (a) pro-poor economic growth, (b) a significant decrease in the proportion of households whose incomes depend largely on agricultural activity, (c) an increase in remittances, and (d) more and better targeted social spending. This study also comments on the negative impacts of two large shocks: the earthquakes at the beginning of 2001 and the coffee crisis. The earthquakes had short-term impacts in the cities affected, while the coffee crisis affected real income growth of households dependent on that sector. The study argues that variations in the income growth rates of the extreme poor and the moderate poor have exacerbated inequality since 2000.

Guatemala

According to the World Bank (2009), a reduction in the levels of poverty and inequality was the result of changes in government policy in the mid-1990s. These changes were (a) the 1996 Peace Accords, which set higher targets for public social investment; (b) a restructuring of public expenditure, with less going to defense; (c) an expanded transfer program, with a significant percentage of general tax revenue transferred to the municipalities; and (d) greater attention paid to the planning process, as indicated by the preparation of a national poverty reduction strategy in 2001, followed by individual poverty reduction strategies for the munici-palities (World Bank 2009, vii). Some other factors were better road infra-structure and favorable climate and agricultural conditions (World Bank 2009, xv) in the southeast region. The study also comments that extreme poverty has not improved faster because the increase in food prices was higher than the increase in general prices and "poor infrastructure [was] coupled with adverse climate shocks . . . and low economic and agricul-tural potential" (World Bank 2009, xv) in the northeast. Regarding income, the study finds that the number of households receiving international and local remittances increased from 2000 to 2006, households diversified their income sources, and labor productivity improved. All these factors have worked together to reduce inequality and poverty levels.

Honduras

According to the most recent Honduras poverty assessment (World Bank 2006b), the fact that poverty levels did not decrease from 1998 to 2004 "can be partly explained by the combined effects of stagnant real GDP growth per capita of 0.3 percent per year, and the economy's vulnerabil-ity and exposure to external shocks and unexpected natural disasters" (World Bank 2006b, ii). However, more recent data show a further decline in poverty, which, compared to the numbers collected at the beginning of the 1990s, indicates that the country has significantly reduced poverty during the last two decades.

Nicaragua

World Bank (2008, 7) reports that the decline in inequality in Nicaragua "has been driven by two factors: an increase in consumption levels of the poor and particularly the extreme poor, and a sharp fall in consumption at the top of the distribution." However, the possible explanations for a decline in consumption in the upper-income deciles could be that "there is underreporting of income by the richer households, and the level of underreporting has increased over time . . . and that there may have been an increase in the propensity to save, which would tend to reduce consumption" (World Bank 2008, 8). It is also argued that there have been some benefits for the poor over the period 2001–05, such as an increase in labor force participation and a small increase in the income of the poor due to increases in agricultural employment (coffee, meat, maize, and beans, which are grown by small farmers) and wages. The poor also benefited from an increase in the number of family members who were working, which helped to raise income per capita. Another important factor that contributed to a decrease in poverty levels was the flow of remittances (because of an increase in migration by the poor), which are a source of income for people in this country at all levels of income.

Methodology

Winters (2003) identifies four channels through which trade openness affects welfare distribution. In this section, we concentrate on two of these channels: household consumption and labor income distribution. Goldberg and Pavcnik (2007) describe several ways in which trade openness can affect the distribution of labor income. We study those related to changes in skill premiums, transit unemployment, and industry wage premiums.

Changes in trade policy bring about changes in the relative prices of both goods (outputs) and factors of production (inputs). Therefore, trade policy affects households' welfare by affecting both income and consumption. By increasing the price of exports and by introducing new export opportunities, trade policy increases the earnings of households participating in export-oriented economic activities. However, by increasing the export prices of key consumption goods, trade policy lowers real income. In contrast, lower prices of imports allow households to purchase a given consumption bundle at a lower cost. Finally, cheaper imports may displace some of the local production at the cost of lower employment, lower wages, or lower agricultural income.

These changes affect different households differently, depending on their relative endowments of factors of production and their patterns of consumption. This is why trade policy has implications for poverty and inequality: not all households are affected the same.

The effect of changes in prices and wages on income and consumption, for a given structure of income and consumption, provides a good first-order approximation of the changes in household welfare. However, when a trade agreement such as DR-CAFTA is implemented, second-order effects—comprising changes in labor supply and substitution among consumption goods—can be important. Following the method adopted by Nicita (2004), we estimate welfare changes due to the impact of trade liberalization on consumption (first order only) and income (first and second order). The procedure consists of three steps:[5]

- Changes in employment and wages are derived using the employment models from a companion study on gender.[6]
- Changes in local prices are estimated using changes in international indexes of food and manufactured goods, together with exchange rates, local tariffs, and assuming full pass-through.[7]
- Changes in consumption and income are added up for each type of household. Then the distribution of changes in welfare is produced to describe how DR-CAFTA affects welfare according to households' income rank.

According the former motivation, we aim to study the impact of trade liberalization on household welfare distribution, taking into account both the effects on both consumption and on labor income. For this, we can start from the indirect utility function for a household h of the form:

$$V_h = V[Y_h, P]$$

where Y stands for total household income, and P for a vector of prices faced by the household. Total household income is given by the sum of each household member labor income (which is the product of wages and hours of work), and sales of goods in the market (or its market value if the good is for autoconsumption), capital/rental income, and governmental transfers.

Following Nicita (2004) and some own simplifying assumptions, we will approximate welfare changes due to trade policy as follows:

$$\frac{dV}{Y} \approx \sum_m \sigma_m dw_m - \sum_g \theta_g dp_g.$$

In other words, total change in household welfare is decomposed in two parts: one due to changes in wages (first right-hand side term) and another to changes of domestic (consumption) prices (second right-hand side term). Changes in wages, in turn, can be attributed to several factors, such as changes in skill premia, interindustry premia, and so forth. In the same way, changes of domestic prices can depend on changes in trade-related variables and other variables. Percentage changes in prices will need assumptions about the pass-through that translates international prices into local prices. Then all effects are added up for total population, or by gender, location, or some other group characteristic, which allows for estimating the distributional impact of trade liberalization.

To measure the impact of trade openness on welfare changes, several counterfactuals, or simulations, are estimated. The simulations carried out in this version can be schematically represented as follows:

$$\Delta W^j = \frac{dV}{Y} \approx \sum_m \sigma_m dw_m^j - \sum_g \theta_g dp_g^j,$$

$$w_m = f\left(T_m^j, Z_m^j\right), p_g = g\left(T_g^j, V_g^j\right)$$

where the super index j represents the different assumptions used in each counterfactual; $f(T^j,Z^j)$ represents wages as a function of trade-related variables (Z^j) and other variables; and $g(T^j,V^j)$ represents domestic prices as a function of trade-related and other variables. We hypothesize changes as if only trade variables had changed. The functions $f(T^j,Z^j)$ determining labor incomes are described in detail in chapter 11 and here we use the fitted values from those functions evaluated for each counterfactual.[8]

Data Sources

The data sets used for these simulations are labor force and other household surveys from the countries within DR-CAFTA, since the mid-1990s, as processed and harmonized by SEDLAC (Socio-Economic Database for Latin America and the Caribbean). These data sets have been harmonized by a joint team from Universidad de la Plata in Argentina and the World Bank to produce a database of comparable surveys for Latin American countries. The data sets are harmonized such that income definitions and several other variables relevant for socioeconomic analysis are comparable over time and across countries.[9]

We use both labor surveys and income-expenditure surveys. For the simulation of earnings equations that support the estimates of wage changes, we use labor force surveys for as many years as possible since the mid-1990s. For the computation of consumption shares, we use the most recent income-expenditure surveys available for each country. A summary of the data sets used is shown in table 12.1.

Results

The welfare results of the simulations depend on the size of trade-related changes in consumption prices and labor incomes. In turn, the size of the shock produces different outcomes for different households in accordance with the households' consumption patterns—in particular,

Table 12.1   Data Sources

Country and type of survey	Survey	Periodicity	Years available[a]
Survey with labor market information			
Costa Rica	Encuesta Permanente de Hogares de Propósitos Múltiples	Annual	1997, 2000–07
Dominican Republic	Encuesta Nacional de Fuerza de Trabajo	Biannual	1997, 2000–07
El Salvador	Encuesta de Hogares de Propósitos Múltiples	Annual	1998, 2000–07
Guatemala	Encuesta Nacional de Empleo e Ingresos	Annual	2000, 2002–06
Honduras	Encuesta Permanente de Hogares de Propósitos Múltiples	Biannual	1997, 1999, 2001, 2003
	Encuesta Permanente de Hogares de Propósitos Múltiples	Annual	2004–06
Nicaragua	Encuesta Nacional de Hogares sobre Medición de Niveles de Vida	Annual	1998, 2001, 2005
Surveys with income-expenditure information			
Costa Rica	Encuesta Permanente de Hogares de Propósitos Múltiples		2005
Dominican Republic	Encuesta Nacional de Gastos e Ingresos de los Hogares		2006
El Salvador	Encuesta de Hogares de Propósitos Múltiples		2007
Guatemala	Encuesta Nacional sobre Condiciones de Vida		2006
Honduras	Encuesta Nacional de Condiciones de Vida		2004
Nicaragua	Encuesta Nacional de Hogares sobre Medición de Niveles de Vida		

Source: Authors' compilation.
a. For surveys with income-expenditure information, most recent year available.

the consumption of food and nonfood items—and the composition of their income sources. The same labor income shock will have different effects according to how much income each member of a specific household obtains from unskilled or skilled labor and whether he or she is employed in the agricultural, manufacturing, or another nontradable sector.

For the specific periods under study, which vary for each country depending on the data available, the trends in price changes are shown in table 12.2. Each country records a different change in international prices, due to differences in periods. The same can be said about the trends in exchange rates and tariffs. What is common is the high correlation between the changes in the consumer price index and our indexes for international prices in local currency terms. Countries with the highest inflation also show the highest increases in our indexes. For instance, Costa Rica experienced a 275.8 percent increase in consumer prices between 1995 and 2007. For the same period, based on international prices adjusted by tariffs and exchange rates, the price of food increased 263.2 percent and the price of manufacturing goods increased in 261.5 percent. In the other extreme, El Salvador experienced an inflation rate of 32 percent between 1998 and 2007, and the price of food and manufactured goods rose 36.4 and 23.6 percent, respectively. In other words, our estimates of price increases are quite close to the actual inflation recorded, making the indexes a good approximation of actual price changes due to international prices and trade policy.

The results for the trade simulation are reported in summary format in growth incidence curves for each country in figures 12.1–12.6. Across the deciles of the population, each figure illustrates the total effect and the price and labor income effects (panel a) and the decomposition of the price effect into changes in the price of food and other products (panel b).

Starting with a consideration of the welfare effect due to a change in consumption prices, panel b of figures 12.1 to 12.6 displays a common pattern across all countries, except Nicaragua. Reductions in food prices produce positive welfare changes for all households and progressive welfare changes in three cases (El Salvador, Guatemala, and Honduras)—that is, gains for poorer people are relatively larger than gains for richer ones. The reverse is recorded for reductions in the price of nonfood items: richer people benefit from this proportionally more than poorer ones. This is because, for all these countries, when compared to people with

Table 12.2 Price Changes in DR-CAFTA Countries in Select Periods

Country and time period	Weighted index of commodity prices, current US$ (2000 = 100)	Manufactures unit value index, US$ (2000 = 100)	Exchange rate (local/US$)	Own tariff Agricultural products	Own tariff Manufactured products	Consumer price index	International price index[a] Food	International price index[a] Manufactured products	Simulated local prices[b] Food	Simulated local prices[b] Nonfood
Costa Rica										
1995	141.55	92.12	179.73	13.87	9.39	32.44	1.00	1.00	1.00	1.00
2007	184.74	119.82	516.62	10.23	5.76	121.90	3.63	3.61	0.97	0.97
% change	30.5	30.1	187.4	-26.2	-38.7	275.8	263.2	261.5	-3.2	-3.3
Dominican Republic										
1997	139.19	95.43	14.27	20.35	15.32	36.09	1.00	1.00	1.00	1.00
2007	184.74	119.82	34.62	13.45	8.61	114.18	3.04	2.87	0.94	0.94
% change	32.7	25.6	142.6	-33.9	-43.8	216.4	203.6	186.9	-5.7	-5.8
El Salvador										
1998	129.13	96.49	8.76	13.75	5.22	82.43	1.00	1.00	1.00	1.00
2007	184.74	119.82	8.75	8.55	4.82	108.8	1.36	1.24	0.95	1.00
% change	43.1	24.2	-0.1	-37.8	-7.7	32.0	36.4	23.6	-4.6	-0.4

(continued next page)

Table 12.2 (continued)

Country and time period	Weighted index of commodity prices, current US$ (2000 = 100)	Manufactures unit value index, US$ (2000 = 100)	Exchange rate (local/US$)	Own tariff		Consumer price index	International price index[a]		Simulated local prices[b]	
				Agricultural products	Manufactured products		Food	Manufactured products	Food	Nonfood
Guatemala										
2000	100.00	100.00	7.76	10.88	6.50	68.79	1.00	1.00	1.00	1.00
2007	184.74	119.82	7.67	8.23	5.16	115.05	1.78	1.17	0.98	0.99
% change	84.7	19.8	-1.2	-24.4	-20.6	67.2	78.2	16.9	-2.4	-1.3
Honduras										
1999	104.87	97.88	14.21	14.02	7.34	60.19	1.00	1.00	1.00	1.00
2007	184.74	119.82	18.90	8.11	5.16	112.9	2.22	1.59	0.95	0.98
% change	76.2	22.4	32.9	-42.2	-29.7	87.6	122.1	59.4	-5.2	-2.0
Nicaragua										
1998	129.13	96.49	10.58	8.88	4.47	57.86	1.00	1.00	1.00	1.00
2005	133.57	112.81	16.73	12.41	6.34	100.00	1.69	1.88	1.03	1.02
% change	3.4	16.9	58.1	39.8	41.8	72.8	68.9	88.2	3.2	1.8

Source: Authors' calculations.

a. Indexes of the price indicator are as follows: $Pw_j^t(1 + Tar_j^t)ER^t$, where Pw_j^t stands for international prices (for agricultural commodities and for manufactures), Tar_j^t stands for own average agricultural and manufacturing product tariffs, and ER^t is the exchange rate, for country-year t.

b. If only tariffs change.

Figure 12.1   Costa Rica: Trade Simulation

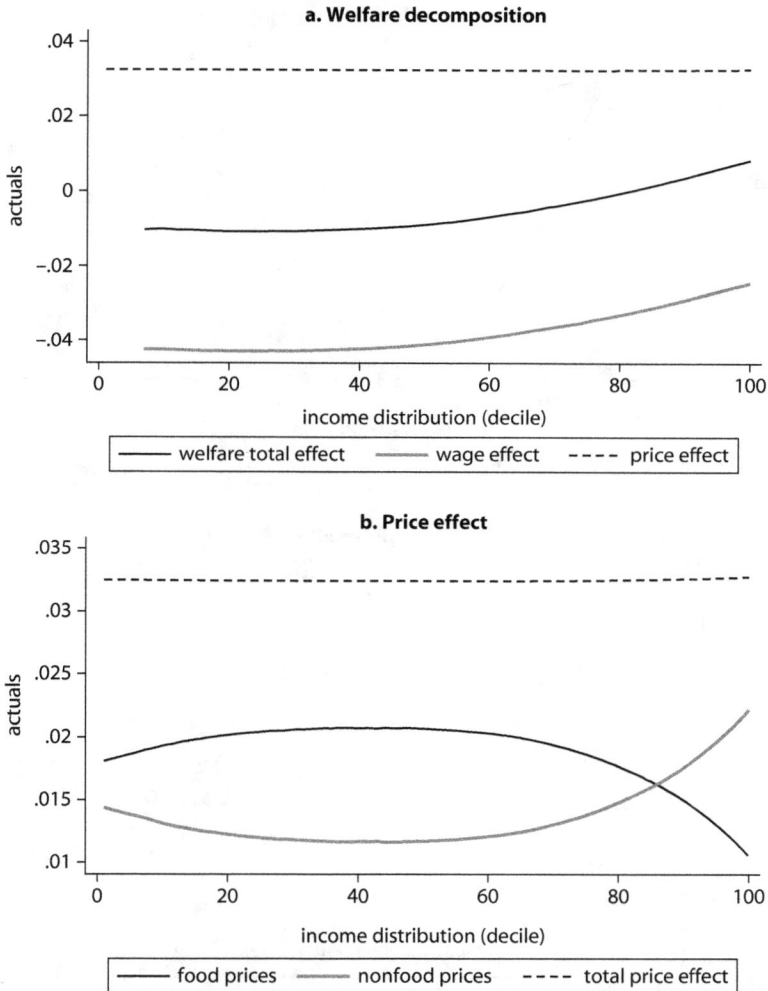

a. Welfare decomposition

b. Price effect

Source: Authors' calculations.

higher incomes, the poor tend to spend a larger share of their income on food. In general, price reductions generate welfare gains in the range of 2 to 6 percent. The case of Nicaragua appears different simply because, in the period under study, trade-related shocks push prices up instead of down. Therefore, for this country, the overall outcome of price increases is a reduction in welfare, which is a combination of large losses for the poor

Figure 12.2   Dominican Republic: Trade Simulation

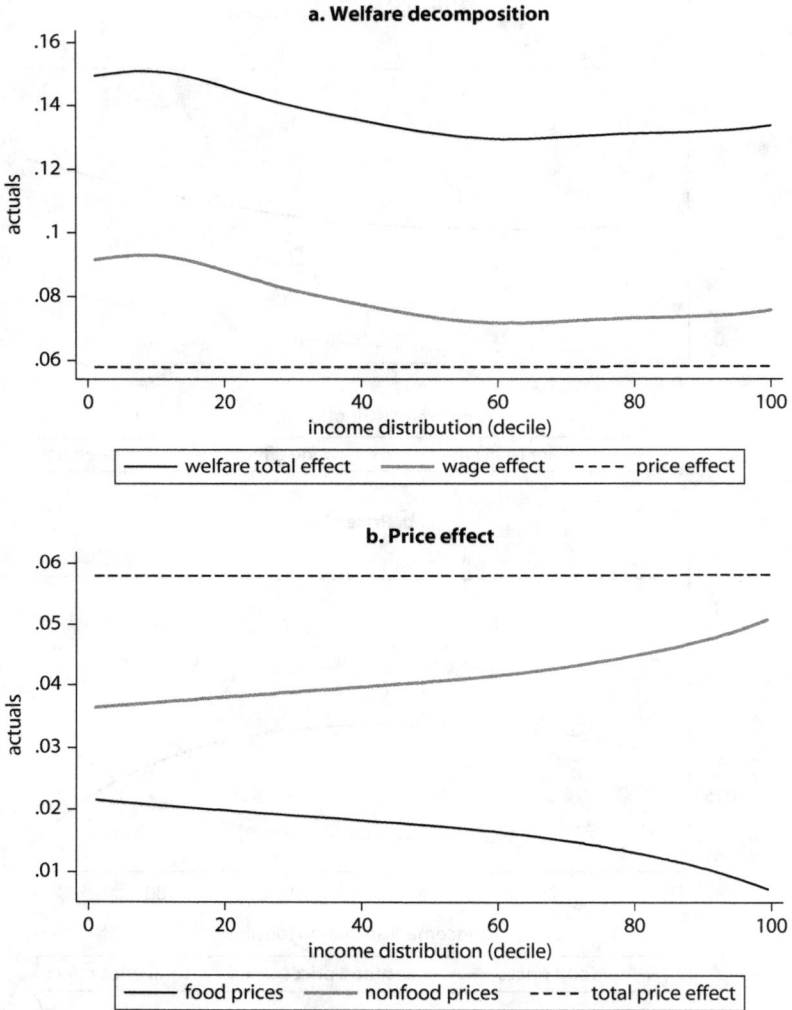

a. Welfare decomposition

b. Price effect

Source: Authors' calculations.

due to higher food prices and large losses for the rich due to higher prices
for other items. Before discussing the welfare effect of changes in labor
income, it should be emphasized that these results rely on the assumption
of perfect pass-through. In other words, a reduction of 5 percent in a
tariff on imported food translates into a full 5 percent reduction in the

Figure 12.3   El Salvador: Trade Simulation

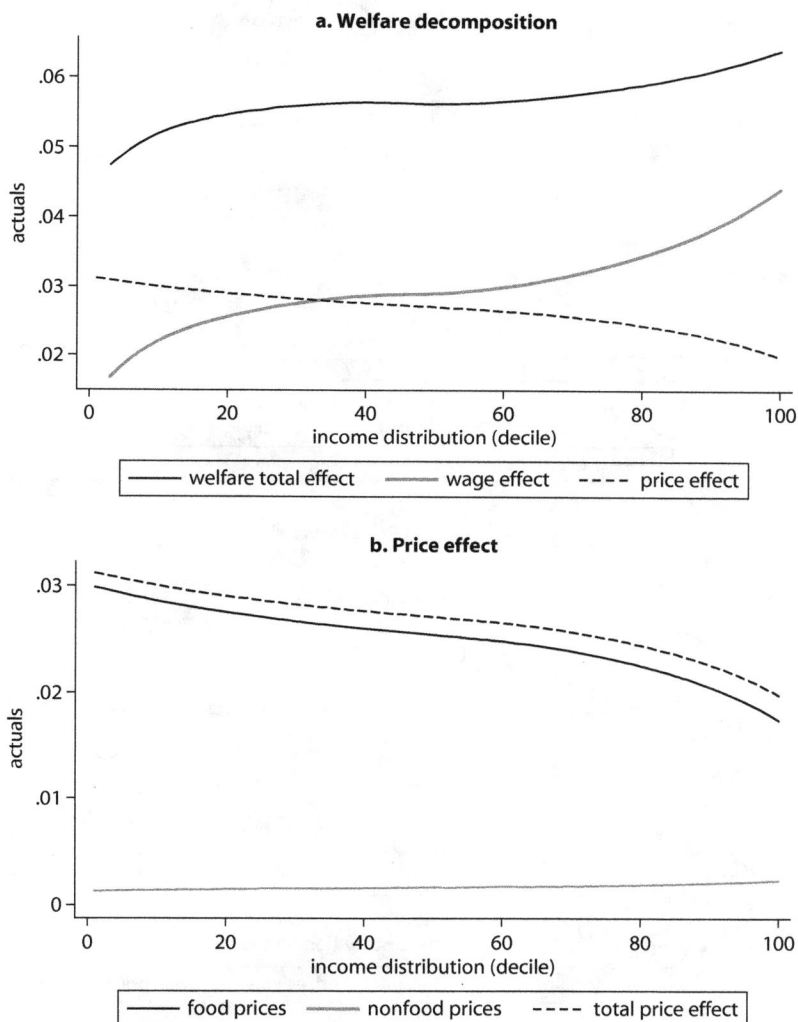

a. Welfare decomposition

y-axis: actuals
x-axis: income distribution (decile)

Legend: welfare total effect —— wage effect —— price effect ----

b. Price effect

y-axis: actuals
x-axis: income distribution (decile)

Legend: food prices —— nonfood prices —— total price effect ----

Source: Authors' calculations.

domestic consumption price of food, and this decrease benefits all house-holds in the same way. This is a strong assumption, and several studies have shown that perfect pass-through is almost never attained; therefore, the results should be considered as an upper bound on the benefits of trade-related price reductions.

Figure 12.4   Guatemala: Trade Simulation

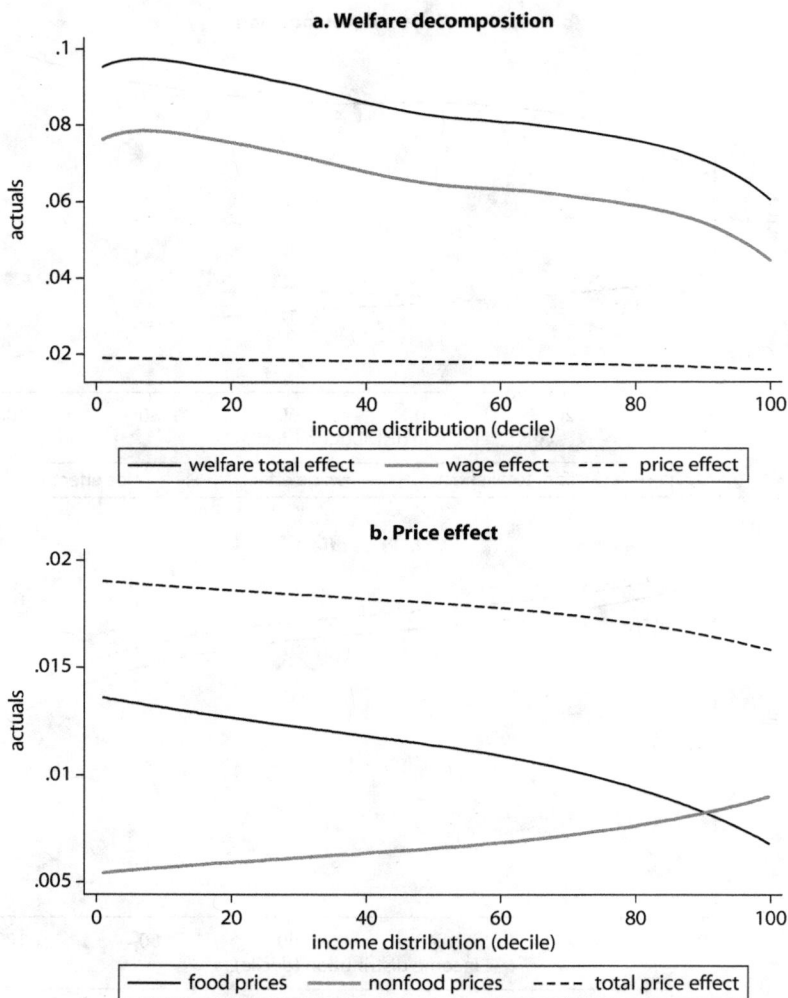

a. Welfare decomposition

b. Price effect

Source: Authors' calculations.

The welfare implications of wage changes show a higher degree of variation across the DR-CAFTA countries; however, some common patterns are still identifiable. For example, for the Dominican Republic, Guatemala, and Honduras, total welfare change is positive for all households and progressive. This total welfare change results from the combination of

Figure 12.5   Honduras: Trade Simulation

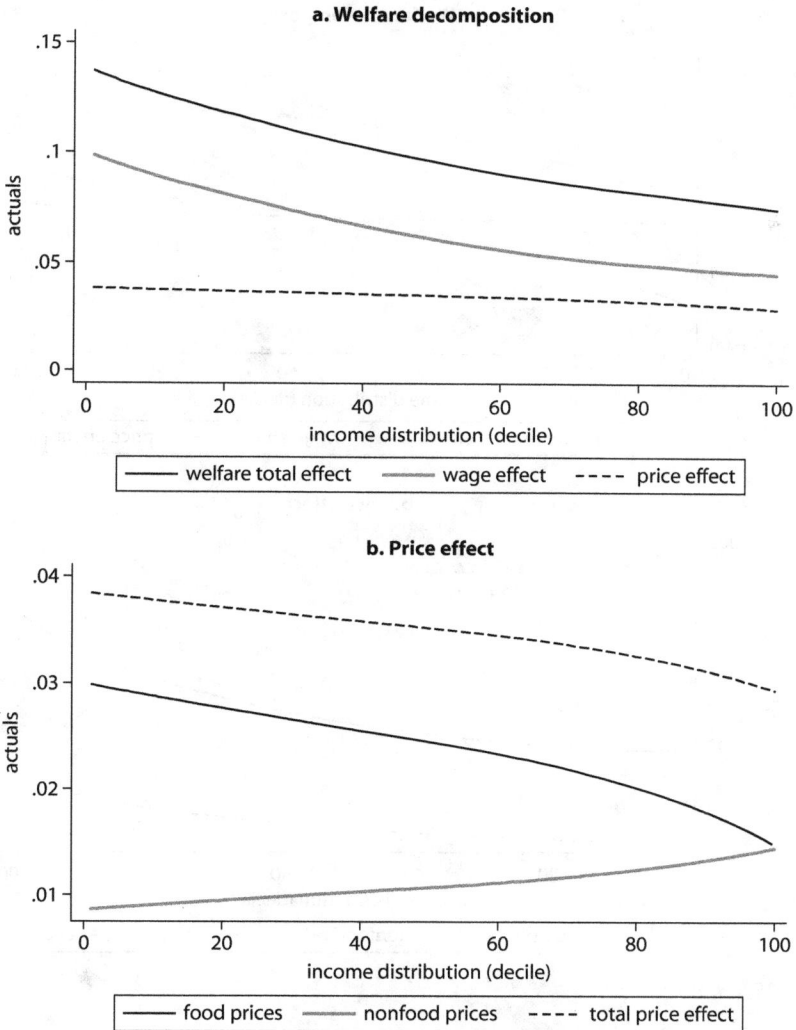

a. Welfare decomposition

b. Price effect

Source: Authors' calculations.

positive and progressive changes in labor incomes and a low positive and
distributionally neutral (flat in the figures) gain derived from price reductions. The progressivity in the changes of labor income can be attributed
to the fact that trade shocks tend to generate larger gains for unskilled
workers who, on average, are found in the lower part of the income

Figure 12.6   Nicaragua: Trade Simulation

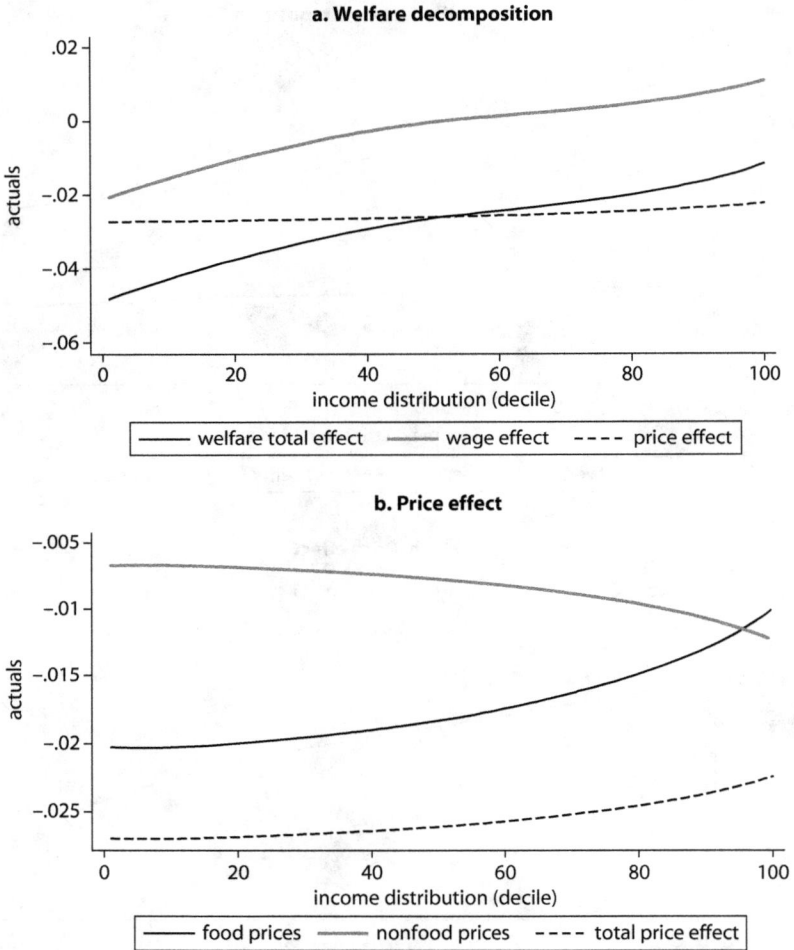

a. Welfare decomposition

| welfare total effect | wage effect | ---- price effect |

b. Price effect

| food prices | nonfood prices | ---- total price effect |

Source: Authors' calculations.

distribution. This pro-poor unskilled worker bias is not offset by the fact that trade seems to produce larger gains for the urban, and normally wealthier, population.

These trends are common for these three countries, but what differs across them is the size of the welfare change. Due to the trade shocks in the period under study, bottom (poorer) decile in the Dominican Republic enjoys a 15.2 percent welfare increase, the top (richer) decile gains about 13.2 percent, and the average household experiences a trade-related benefit of 13.6 percent. In Guatemala the bottom decile gains about 10 percent, the top gains 6.3 percent, and the average household gains 8.4 percent. In Honduras, the respective gains are 13, 7.8, and 10 percent.

The cases of Costa Rica and Nicaragua are quite different from those of the three countries mentioned above. In Costa Rica and Nicaragua, total welfare effects are negative (with the exception of the top portion of the distribution) and regressive, and this is mostly due to negative wage effects. Although trade liberalization benefits workers in tradable sectors, losses for workers in other sectors are larger. Besides, income from unskilled and rural-based jobs seems to benefit relatively less than income related to other jobs, and this translates into the regressive bias of the change in welfare. In terms of the size of the welfare change, in Costa Rica the bottom decile suffers a loss of about 1.0 percent, the top decile gains about 0.6 percent, and the average household experiences a marginal loss of 0.6 percent. In Nicaragua the same groups lose 4.0, 0.7, and 2.4 percent, respectively.

Finally, El Salvador is unique because it experiences a positive change in labor income, in contrast with the negative change in Costa Rica and Nicaragua, but this change is regressive, in contrast with the experiences of the Dominican Republic, Guatemala, and Honduras. The main explanation is that trade produces an overall positive effect on labor income, but it pushes up the earnings of skilled and urban workers relatively more than the earnings of poorer unskilled and rural workers.

Conclusions

The results of the simulations of the impact of trade openness on household welfare for the countries under study show some remarkable similarities. For all countries under study, price changes associated with tariff reductions bring about positive welfare gains. These welfare gains are either distributionally neutral or very slightly progressive in the sense that they are marginally larger for households in the bottom than in the top of the income distribution.

Regarding wage changes, three countries (the Dominican Republic, Guatemala, and Honduras) record welfare gains. These welfare gains are progressive and depend on the positive relation between trade openness and returns to unskilled workers. Consequently, lower tariffs are associated with higher returns to unskilled people, and given that these people tend to be members of poorer households, the shock benefits proportionally more households at the bottom of the distribution. The other three countries (Costa Rica, El Salvador, and Nicaragua) experience wage changes that generate regressive welfare effects. Moreover, for two countries, Costa Rica and Nicaragua, these effects are actually negative. Again this is a result of the trade shock, which, in these cases, produces adverse effects on poorer unskilled and rural workers.

For the average household, the total size of the gains is quite diverse, with countries like the Dominican Republic, Guatemala, and Honduras showing welfare gains for the average household of more than 10 percent compared to smaller gains of about 5.0 percent for El Salvador, a marginal loss of about 0.5 percent for Costa Rica, and a larger loss of 2.4 percent for Nicaragua.

The consumption price–related welfare gain is positive for all countries (except Nicaragua), and this suggests that a policy designed to compensate adverse consequences of trade opening need not develop cash transfers or subsidies for sustaining consumption among poorer groups of the population. These groups, and all of the population, get welfare gains from falling prices in consumer goods due to trade openness. These gains, however, can be easily lost if macroeconomic mismanagement leads to inflation and depreciation of the exchange rate, all of which nullifies the gains of lower prices through lower tariffs. Sound fiscal and monetary policies are very important if the goal is to keep the gains from free trade.

In the case of the countries under study, it seems that labor markets realize welfare gains from trade openness only in some cases. The lack of labor reallocation reported in chapter 11 of this volume may be the reason for these small welfare gains. Compensating this impact may require policies that facilitate the accumulation of human capital and, more important, the reallocation of labor from low-productivity to high-productivity activities.

Notes

1. In a companion study, chapter 11 of this volume explores in detail the impact of trade openness on labor gender gaps for the same set of countries.

2. To be discussed in more detail later.

3. Exports plus imports as a share of total GDP.

4. Several common principles are related to inequality and welfare, including the Pareto principle and the Pigou-Dalton transfer principle, among others. There is a vast literature regarding the relations between efficiency and

inequality and social welfare. See, for instance, Atkinson (1970); Kats (1972); Sen (1973).

5. The model is available from the authors on request.

6. The companion study presented in chapter 11 of this volume analyzes the impact of trade liberalization on gender gaps in labor market performance. The study estimates both labor participation and earnings equations for all DR-CAFTA countries, which serve as inputs for this study on welfare.

7. In other studies, price changes are derived from pass-through equations (like in Nicita 2004).

8. Chapter 11 follows a methodology based on Ferreira, Leite, and Wai-Poi (2007) and Pavcnik et al (2004). This is a two-stage procedure that, first, estimates an earnings function of wages on skill, sector of employment, and other usual human capital characteristics of workers. Second, coefficients for skill and for sector-employment premia become dependent variables in a linear regression on a vector of trade-related variables, such as faced and own tariffs, real exchange rates, import penetration, and export shares by economic sector. Then changes in wages solely due to trade are simulated using fitted wages from the first equation and fitted coefficients from the second equation, keeping workers characteristics at the initial period.

9. For more information about SEDLAC, visit the link for the Socio-Economic Database for Latin America and the Caribbean at http://www.cedlas.org.

References

Atkinson, A. B. 1970. "On the Measurement of Inequality." *Journal of Economic Theory* 2 (3): 244–63.

Attanasio, Orazio, Pinelopi K. Goldberg, and Nina Pavcnik. 2004. "Trade Reforms and Wage Inequality in Colombia." *Journal of Development Economics* 74 (2): 331–66.

Bardhan, Pranab, Samuel Bowles, and Michael Wallerstein, eds. 2006. *Globalization and Egalitarian Redistribution.* New York: Russell Sage Foundation.

Bussolo, M., and H. Niimi. 2005. "An Illustration from the Dominican Republic–Central American Trade Agreement in Nicaragua." Policy Research Working Paper 3850, World Bank, Washington, DC.

Bussolo, M., S. Freije, C. Djiofack, and M. Rodríguez. 2010. "Trade Openness and Labor Gender Gaps in DR-CAFTA Countries." World Bank, Washington, DC.

Chiquiar, Daniel. 2008. "Globalization, Regional Wage Differentials, and the Stolper-Samuelson Theorem: Evidence from Mexico." *Journal of International Economics* 74 (1, January): 70–93.

Ferreira, Francisco H. G., Phillippe G. Leite, and Matthew Wai-Poi. 2007. "Trade Liberalization, Employment Flows, and Wage Inequality in Brazil." Policy Research Working Paper 4108, World Bank, Washington, DC.

Galiani, Sebastian, and Pablo Sanguinetti. 2003. "The Impact of Trade Liberalization on Wage Inequality: Evidence from Argentina." *Journal of Development Economics* 72 (2): 497–513.

Goldberg, Pinelopi K., and Nina Pavcnik. 2007. "Distributional Effects of Globalization in Developing Countries." *Journal of Economic Literature* 45 (1): 39–82.

Jaramillo, Carlos Felipe, and Daniel Lederman. 2005. *DR-CAFTA: Challenges and Opportunities for Central America.* Washington, DC: World Bank.

Kats, A. 1972. "On the Social Welfare Function and the Parameters of Income Distribution." *Journal of Economic Theory* 5 (3): 377–82.

Nicita, Alessandro. 2004. "Who Benefited from Trade Liberalization in Mexico? Measuring the Effects on Household Welfare." Policy Research Working Paper 3265, World Bank, Washington, DC.

Porto, Guido G. 2006. "Using Survey Data to Assess the Distributional Effects of Trade Policy." *Journal of International Economics* 70 (1): 140–60.

Sen, A. K. 1973. *On Economic Inequality.* Oxford: Clarendon Press.

Winters, L. Alan. 2003. "Trade Liberalization and Poverty: What Are the Links?" in *Global Trade Policy 2002*, ed. Peter Lloyd and Chris Milner, ch. 8. Hoboken, NJ: Blackwell Publishing.

Winters, L. Alan, Neil McCulloch, and Andrew McKay. 2004. "Trade Liberalization and Poverty: The Evidence So Far." *Journal of Economic Literature* 42 (March): 72–115.

World Bank. 2005. "El Salvador: Poverty Assessment; Strengthening Social Policy." Report 29594-SV, World Bank, Poverty Reduction and Economic Management Unit, Human Development Management Unit, Latin America and the Caribbean Region, Washington, DC.

———. 2006a. "Dominican Republic: Poverty Assessment; Achieving More Pro-Poor Growth." World Bank, Caribbean Country Management Unit, Latin America and the Caribbean Region, Washington, DC; Inter-American Development Bank, Regional Operations Department 2 and Social Division Programs, Washington, DC.

———. 2006b. "Honduras: Poverty Assessment; Attaining Poverty Reduction." 2 vols. Report 35622-HN, World Bank, Washington, DC.

———. 2007. "Costa Rica: Poverty Assessment; Recapturing Momentum for Poverty Reduction." Report 35910-CR, World Bank, Poverty Reduction and Economic Management Unit, Human Development Management Unit, Latin America and the Caribbean Region, Washington, DC.

————. 2008. "Nicaragua: Poverty Assessment." 3 vols. Report 39736-NI, World Bank, Central America Country Management Unit, Poverty Reduction and Economic Management Unit, Latin America and the Caribbean Region, Washington, DC.

————. 2009. "Guatemala: Poverty Assessment; Good Performance at Low Levels." Report 43920-GT, World Bank, Central America Department, Poverty Reduction and Economic Management Unit, Latin America and the Caribbean Region, Washington, DC.

CHAPTER 13

DR-CAFTA and the Environment

Muthukumara Mani and Bárbara Cunha

The seminal work of Grossman and Krueger (1992) ignited a debate on the impact of international trade on the environment. Originally fueled by negotiations over the North American Free Trade Agreement (NAFTA), the debate remains relevant as new bilateral and multilateral agreements are formed and environmental concerns continue to rise. This chapter contributes to this recent literature by assessing the environmental implications of trade, specifically the pollution effects of the changes in production and trading patterns that followed the Dominican Republic–Central America Free Trade Agreement with the United States (DR-CAFTA).

The DR-CAFTA has a complementary policy agenda addressing local competitiveness, property rights, labor, and environmental issues. On the environmental side, the agreement emphasizes the monitoring and implementation of current environmental laws, but unlike NAFTA it pays less attention to the strengthening and harmonizing of unequal environmental standards among member countries.

The authors would like to thank Teresa Molina Millán for the excellent assistance during the preparation of this paper.

The literature on trade and the environment discusses various channels through which trade liberalization (and trade agreements) can affect pollution emissions. On the one hand, empirical evidence indicates that trade liberalization can stimulate economic growth. Scaling up (holding constant the mix of goods produced and production techniques) leads to an increase in pollution (scale effects). On the other hand, trade liberalization changes relative prices by intensifying foreign competition. As a result, the structure of production is expected to change according to relative comparative advantages—defined by both factors of production and institutional arrangements. This effect can either increase or decrease relative output in pollution-intensive sectors (composition effects). Finally, changes in production technologies (including pollution intensity by unit of output) tend to follow trade liberalization (technique effects). Technique effects can result from different forces: while trade facilitates the access to more efficient (and cleaner) technologies, stronger competition can trigger a race to the bottom of environmental standards, favoring the adoption of cheaper and dirtier technology in the short run. Nevertheless, as income grows, the demand for environmental quality tends to increase. By adopting both tighter environment policies and more advanced, cleaner technologies, countries can afford to reduce emissions after reaching a certain level of income. This inverted-U relationship between per capita income and pollution is known as the environmental Kuznets curve.[1]

Previous empirical studies on the relationship between trade and the environment have found varying results. For example, Dean (2002) uses province-level data on water pollution from China and finds support for the idea that trade liberalization has both a direct and an indirect effect on emissions growth and that these can be opposite in sign. In contrast, Grossman and Krueger (1992) examine the environmental impacts of NAFTA and find no evidence that a comparative advantage is being created by lax environmental regulations in Mexico. Using data for different countries from 1960 to 1995, Mani and Wheeler (1998) find that "pollution haven effects" are insignificant in developing countries. In a closely related study, Gamper-Rabindran and Jha (2004) analyze the empirical relationship between trade liberalization and the environment in the Indian context. Their findings indicate that exports and foreign direct investment grew in the more polluting sectors relative to the less polluting sectors between the pre- and post-liberalization periods. This evidence provides some support for concerns raised about the environmental impact of trade liberalization.

This chapter builds on this literature by assessing the pollution effects related to implementation of the DR-CAFTA. It starts by revisiting the related literature and discussing the possible implications of the agreement for Central America environmental conditions in the short and medium term. It then computes the scale, composition, and technique effects of pollution by comparing average annual emissions before and after implementation of the agreement.[2] The analysis shows, as often found in the literature, that the scale effects outweigh the composition and technique effects. Most of the variation in pollution results from a scaling up of production. Composition effects are small and vary in sign across member countries. This result suggests that environmental regulation in most DR-CAFTA countries is not a major factor influencing pollution dynamics. This idea is also supported by the findings of the second empirical exercise. The second part of the analysis investigates whether the sectoral changes in production and exports that followed the DR-CAFTA favored pollution-intensive ("dirty") industries. Consistent with the results of the first exercise, this analysis indicates that the period following negotiation of the agreement is associated with a slowdown in the relative growth and export of pollution-intensive industries.

The results indicate that all countries could benefit from closing the gaps in their environmental regulatory framework in terms of regulations, capacity, and monitoring. Countries such as El Salvador, where the agreement favored the relative expansion of more-polluting industries, should go beyond the DR-CAFTA environmental agenda and work on strengthening regulations in the short run. However, environmental reforms should be accompanied by a competitiveness agenda (including reforms to facilitate training, access to credit, and logistics) that would help to compensate for the costs imposed by the additional rigidity in the environmental laws. For poorer countries such as Nicaragua and Honduras, environmental regulations do not seem to play an important role in the current allocation of production. Nevertheless, as these economies grow, the situation will change. For this reason, these countries should start planning and implementing a medium-term environmental agenda.

The remainder of this chapter is organized as follows. First, we review the trade and environment literature and discuss the case of DR-CAFTA. Then we outline the basic exercise, describe the sample and data, and provide empirical evidence in support of the predictions of the model. A final section concludes with a discussion of the results and their implications.

DR-CAFTA and the Environment

The main goal of DR-CAFTA was to create a free trade zone for economic development, regulate investment activities, and facilitate the trade of goods and services. The agreement has a complementary policy agenda addressing local competitiveness, property rights, labor, and environmental issues. Chapter 10 and specifically chapter 17 of the agreement outline the rules, regulations, and other provisions for addressing environmental issues. Under chapter 17, each party shall, among other things, (a) ensure that its laws and policies provide for and encourage high levels of environmental protection; (b) not fail to enforce its current environmental laws; (c) ensure that judicial, quasi-judicial, or administrative proceedings are available to sanction or remedy violations of its environmental laws, that such proceedings are fair and transparent, and that tribunals that conduct or review such proceedings are impartial and independent; (d) provide appropriate and effective remedies or sanctions for a violation of environmental laws; (e) ensure that interested persons have the right to request a party's competent authorities to investigate alleged violations of its environmental laws; and (f) encourage the development and use of incentives and other flexible and voluntary mechanisms to protect or enhance the environment.

In support of these obligations, the parties entered into a separate Environmental Cooperation Agreement to protect, improve, and conserve the environment, including natural resources. The agreement establishes the creation of a Dominican Republic–Central America–United States Environmental Cooperation Commission composed of government representatives appointed by each party. The commission is responsible for identifying priorities for cooperative activities and developing a program of work in accordance with those priorities. It also examines and evaluates the cooperative activities under the agreement and recommends ways to improve future cooperation. In addition, the U.S. administration agreed to commit roughly US$40 million a year from fiscal 2006 to fiscal 2009 to help countries to implement labor and environmental provisions. To date, a total of $38.8 million has been allocated to strengthen the capacity of members to comply with the environmental provisions of DR-CAFTA and to build environmental capacity linked directly to trade in broad program areas.

Under DR-CAFTA, countries are mainly required to enforce their existing laws. Although the provision prevents a race to the bottom among member countries, there is no explicit requirement for strengthening existing regulatory frameworks. In addition, critics of the agreement point to the existence of loopholes in that provision: "Although DR-CAFTA establishes a citizen submission process to allege enforcement failures, it does not provide for any clear outcomes or actions to actually ensure that citizens of the region can achieve enforcement of environmental laws" (Sarkar 2009). Finally, existing environmental laws vary significantly across member countries. Table 13.1 compares the ranking of select environmental regulatory regimes during the DR-CAFTA negotiation period (following Esty and Porter 2005). While the environmental regimes of the United States and Costa Rica score above the international average, those of Guatemala and Honduras score among the bottom five. These differences could potentially favor the rise of pollution havens within the region.

Given the new challenges following the signing of DR-CAFTA, we review the regulatory environmental frameworks of countries to underline the differences among them. While Costa Rica has been a regional leader on environmental issues, ensuring that economic growth is not achieved at the expense of its rich natural endowments, El Salvador faces the most severe environmental degradation of any country in Central America, especially in the areas of forests and water resources. Although the four countries in the CA-4 (Costa Rica, El Salvador, Honduras, and Nicaragua) have achieved some progress in the governance of natural resources and environmental protection, more effort has to be made to even out the still largely uneven regulatory frameworks, especially with respect to pollution and emissions control.

Despite this large list of accomplishments, there are apparent weaknesses in several areas with regard to the efficiency and effectiveness of

Table 13.1   Environmental Regulatory Regime Index, 2001

Rank[a]	Country	Index
1	Finland	2.303
14	United States	1.184
36	Costa Rica	−0.078
60	Dominican Republic	−1.014
62	Nicaragua	−1.164
63	El Salvador	−1.215
66	Honduras	−1.300
69	Guatemala	−1.532

Source: Esty and Porter 2005.
a. Out of 71 countries.

environmental and natural resource management policies, as pointed out by Sarkar (2009). Areas of weakness include environmental information, environmental quality, and institutional performance; coordination between environmental authorities and other sector agencies; regulatory instruments; and compliance, monitoring, and enforcement mechanisms.

Increased trade can lead to different kinds of environmental pressures. Trade-related production specialization, linked to the reallocation of productive resources, can create additional environmental pressures. One of the main environmental problems faced by Central American countries, not addressed in this chapter, is deforestation. Future research on the topic should take into account differences in the scope of and compliance with deforestation laws, for example, in Costa Rica and Honduras, because the expansion of agricultural frontiers in less protected countries could have a role in deteriorating watersheds and decreasing biodiversity. Although beyond the scope of this chapter, climate change also could exacerbate existing conditions in some countries.

Trade and the Environment: A Review of the Literature

A few concerns are frequently present in the debate over trade liberalization and environmental policy. First, there is concern that reducing barriers to trade could reinforce the creation of pollution havens and, due to weak environmental policies, shift the composition of production and exports to more pollution- or resource-intensive sectors. Second, trade liberalization may directly affect environmental standards by encouraging a race to the bottom. While the risks of a race to the bottom in environmental standards are reduced by the environmental clauses in the DR-CAFTA, regulatory differences between countries could potentially play a role in the production and export of pollution-intensive commodities.

The political debate has been followed by an effort in the economic literature to search for theoretical underpinnings and empirical evidence to justify such concerns. On the theoretical side, works can be divided into two main groups. The first group focuses on the direct relationship between trade and the environment, and most works extend the traditional trade framework to account for pollution modeled as an input or a second output of production (Copeland and Taylor 1994; Antweiler, Copeland, and Taylor 2001; Di Maria and Smulders 2004; Péridy 2006). The second group focuses on an indirect relationship between trade and pollution, in particular, the relationship between economic growth (facilitated by international trade, among other things) and pollution (Stokey

1998; Copeland and Taylor 2003). On the empirical side, many papers attempt to assess the relationship between trade, growth, and the environment. While early works focus on testing the pollution havens hypothesis, later works try to disentangle the channels through which these variables interact (Cole and Rayner 2000; Grether, Mathys, and de Melo 2009). Copeland and Taylor (2004) provide a comprehensive review of both theoretical and empirical work on the topic. This section focuses on select works that will help us to discuss the expected effects of the trade agreement on pollution in Central America.

Copeland and Taylor (1994), in what is considered a seminal work in the trade and environment literature, develop a two-country static general equilibrium model of international trade to explain the pollution haven hypothesis. The authors focus on how differences in human capital across countries affect their income, regulation, trade flows, and pollution levels. Large differences in human capital across regions ensure that each country specializes in a set of either relatively clean or dirty goods in trade. The intuition for these results is fairly clear. Trade alters the composition of output in both countries with high and countries with low human capital because of differences in the stringency of their pollution regulations. Given the relative cost structure in autarky, a movement toward free trade shifts the production of dirty goods to the country with lax regulation and the production of clean goods to the one with strict regulation. However, the authors pay little attention to other factors that influence trade patterns and the environmental effects resulting from them. For example, a simple factor endowment hypothesis suggests that dirty capital-intensive processes should relocate to relatively capital-abundant developed countries.

Antweiler, Copeland, and Taylor (2001) extend the previous framework to account for variables such as factor costs and endowments and technological changes. The theoretical framework supports a model-based decomposition of the trade effect on emissions into *scale, composition,* and *technique* effects.[3] According to their model, while trade facilitates the adoption of more efficient (and cleaner) technologies of production, increased competition could trigger a race to the bottom on environmental standards, favoring the adoption of cheaper or dirtier technology in the short run. Nevertheless, as income grows, the demand for environmental quality tends to increase.

Recent works have built on the framework of Antweiler, Copeland, and Taylor (2001), but the main channels and effects remain similar. For example, Kahn and Yoshino (2004) consider trade among different types of partners, including North-North, North-South, and South-South, and the formation of trading blocs. The formation of trading blocs will most likely result in a shift toward dirtier industries in the middle-income country, which is moderately capital abundant but still has a relatively weak regulatory framework. These results reconcile the pollution haven and factor endowment hypotheses.

The relationship between economic development and environmental quality has been extensively explored since Grossman and Krueger (1992) suggested an inverse-U relationship between income per capita and pollution, the so-called environmental Kuznets curve (EKC). Most theoretical works agree with the idea that economic development in low-income countries is associated with industrialization and a consequent increase in pollution, but they present different explanations for the declining portion of the curve. Reasons for this inverted-U relationship include income-driven changes in (a) the composition of production or consumption (Selden and Song 1994; Hettige, Mani, and Wheeler 2000; Brock and Taylor 2004); (b) the preference for environmental quality (Stokey 1998); (c) institutions dealing with externalities (Chichilnisky 1994; López 1994); or (d) increasing returns to scale associated with pollution abatement (Bovenberg and Smulders 1995; Stokey 1998). Among the empirical studies, results seem dependent on the type of pollution analyzed.

Many contributions have empirically tested the existence of an EKC using cross-country relationships (among the others, Grossman and Krueger 1995; Stern, Common, and Barbier 1996), time-series analyses for specific countries (Egli 2004), or panel data (de Bruyn, van den Bergh, and Opschoor 1998; Dijkgraaf and Vollebergh 2004). While studies focusing on sulfur dioxide, nitrogen oxide, suspended particulates, and an aggregate measure of air pollution tend to support the existence of an EKC (Grossman and Krueger 1992; Markandya, Golub, and Pedroso-Galinato 2006), papers studying carbon dioxide emissions (Aslanidis 2009) or water pollution (Hettige, Mani, and Wheeler 2000) are less conclusive. The EKC may vary with country-specific characteristics, but studies supporting the EKC hypothesis suggest that the turning point ranges from US$2,805 (Halkos 2003) to US$9,239 (Stern and Common 2001).[4] According to these studies, with the exception of Costa Rica, all countries in Central America would currently be placed in transition or in the increasing part of the EKC.[5]

Empirical studies testing for the direct effects of trade on the environment are less conclusive. For example, Gamper-Rabindran and Jha (2004) empirically analyze the relationship between trade liberalization and the environment in the Indian context. Their findings indicate that exports and foreign direct investment grew in the more-polluting sectors relative to the less-polluting sectors between the pre- and post-liberalization periods. Mani and Jha (2006) and Akbostanci, Ipek Tunc, and Türüt-Asik (2004) find similar results for Vietnam and Turkey, respectively.

While data and methodological issues could help to explain the differences in findings, one interesting pattern arises from the literature. Consistent with the predictions of Kahn and Yoshino (2004), positive links between international trade and pollution are more frequently identified in studies dealing with middle-income countries. These and a few other findings from the literature will help to guide discussion of the possible and expected implications of DR-CAFTA for the environment in the Central America economies.

Possible Environmental Developments for the DR-CAFTA

There are significant differences among DR-CAFTA countries. Countries differ not only in their regulatory environments, but also in their level of development, income, and human and physical capital endowments. Following the predictions of EKC theory, one would guess that, even before the agreement, countries were likely to be experiencing different trends with respect to pollution emissions. Both level of income and regulatory framework suggest that Costa Rica is experiencing a decline in pollution and that Nicaragua, Honduras, and Guatemala are in the upward-sloping stages of the EKC. El Salvador and the Dominican Republic have intermediary income levels, but weak regulatory frameworks. These countries were probably approaching the turning point before the agreement.

As a consequence of these regional disparities, the medium-term environmental implications of the agreement with the United States are likely to differ among member countries. Following the framework proposed by Kahn and Yoshino (2004), one would expect that, at least in the medium term, countries like Honduras, Guatemala, and Nicaragua would tend to specialize in labor-intensive products. Despite their lax regulatory frameworks, these countries seem to have low comparative advantage in capital-intensive activities (which correspond to approximately 4 percent of GDP). One would expect a negative pollution trend after the agreement. The cases of the Dominican Republic and El Salvador are less straightforward. These countries are richer than the previous group of countries, but they still possess weak regulatory frameworks. The two countries differ, however, in their level of specialization in capital-intensive sectors, with El Salvador having a significantly larger share of capital-intensive activities (approximately 10 percent of GDP). These characteristics make El Salvador a pollution haven candidate—that is, one could expect to observe higher emissions after the agreement, not only due to an increase in production, but also due to an increase in the share of dirty industries. Finally, Costa Rica combines a relatively higher degree of specialization in capital-intensive industries with a much stronger regulatory framework (although still weaker than that of the United States). While Costa Rica would be likely to lose dirty industries to less regulated countries, it could still absorb more sophisticated industrial activities from the United States, and the stringent regulatory framework would serve to check polluting activities.

The next sections provide some empirical evidence by comparing the dynamics for different types of pollution before and after the agreement. The exercises focus on four countries: Costa Rica, El Salvador, Honduras, and Nicaragua. We start by decomposing the average variation in pollution content in both overall production and exports before and after the agreement into scale, composition, and technique effects. We then move to a systematic analysis of the patterns of change in the composition of both production and exports during the period of analysis. The formal analysis is constrained by a series of limitations in the data, including the lack of country-specific pollution data for the relevant period and the small number of observations after the DR-CAFTA (see the annex to this chapter for a detailed discussion of the data). Nevertheless we hope to provide an intuitive and initial quantitative assessment of the predictions offered above.

The Empirical Analysis

Ex ante one would expect that the most direct effect of trade liberalization on the environment would be through the composition of industries. Trade leads to specialization, and countries that specialize in less (more) pollution-intensive goods will have cleaner (dirtier) environments. For this reason, much of the literature has sought to dissect the composition effects of trade. However, the direct impacts of trade on environmental quality go beyond composition and can be divided into three main channels: the effects of trade on the overall *scale* of the economy, the *techniques* of production, and the *composition* of industries. To assess these effects in the context of the DR-CAFTA, this section proposes two simple exercises: a decomposition exercise and a sector composition exercise.

Decomposition Exercise

Following Copeland and Taylor (2003), this exercise compares average emissions before and after the trade agreement. Changes in pollution are then decomposed into scale effects (changes related to scaling up output, keeping composition and technologies unchanged); composition effects (generated by changes in sector shares, keeping total output and technologies unchanged); and technique effects based on technological improvements that affect emissions per unit of output according to the following equation:

$$
\begin{aligned}
\Delta pollution = P_t - P_0 \\
= Q_t \sum_j \alpha_{jt} P_{jt} - Q_0 \sum_j \alpha_{j0} P_{j0} \\
= \underbrace{(Q_t - Q_0) \sum_j \alpha_{jt} P_{jt}}_{Scale} + \underbrace{Q_0 \sum_j (\alpha_{jt} - \alpha_{j0}) P_{j0}}_{Composition} \\
+ \underbrace{Q_0 \sum_j \alpha_{jt} (P_{jt} - P_{j0})}_{Technique},
\end{aligned}
\tag{13.1}
$$

where P_t stands for pollution in period t, Q_t represents total output, α_{jt} represents the share of output of industry j in total output in period t, and P_{jt} measures the emissions per unit of output in industry j in period t. In addition to the comparison of pollution levels before and after the agreement, we consider changes in the average growth rate of pollution. This exercise accounts for existing trends in emissions and measures whether the agreement affects these trends. The decomposition exercise is developed taking into account air, water, metal components, and the overall level of emissions. It considers emissions resulting from manufacturing production as well as the pollution content of manufacturing exports.

The data and the methodology used to construct emissions statistics implicitly assume stable technologies (that is, no technical effects in the period). Since technical effects are found to have a significant impact on the medium-term pollution outcomes, we construct an alternative pollution scenario where the average pollution intensity per unit of output varies with time and opening to trade.

Sector Composition Exercise

This exercise investigates whether trade liberalization increases the participation of pollution-intensive industries in production and exports. In other words, it analyzes whether the agreement promotes the relative growth of "dirty" industries. The exercise estimates the following equation:

$$g^o_{jt}, g^e_{jt} = \alpha + \beta^* D_j + \gamma_A^* A_t^* D_j + \delta^* X_{jt} + \delta^* A_t^* X_{jt} + \varepsilon_{jt}, \quad (13.2)$$

where g^o_{jt} and g^e_{jt} stands for the growth rate of outputs and exports, respectively; D_j is a dummy variable indicating "dirty" industries; A_t is a dummy variable indicating the period post-negotiations; and X_{jt} is a collection of variables that can help to explain a change in composition. Regressions for the Central American region might also include country-specific fixed effects. Table 13A.1 in the annex to this chapter presents the variables included in the regression.

Data

The exercises focus on four Central American countries for which data are available: Costa Rica, El Salvador, Honduras, and Nicaragua. The study covers a 10-year period (1999–2008) and takes 2004 (the beginning of DR-CAFTA negotiations) as the threshold (1999–2003 = before; 2005–08 = after). While the ratification and beginning of implementation took place between 2005 (for the United States) and 2007 (for Costa Rica), we believe that part of the changes in the patterns of production anticipate the actual ratification. Moreover, the choice of the beginning of negotiations as a threshold is convenient because it allows for additional observations in the post-agreement period.

Annual statistics on pollution emissions are constructed using pollution intensities from the Industrial Pollution Projection System (IPPS) of the World Bank. This database provides information on pollution intensity and abatement costs at the industry level.[6] More specifically, the IPPS reports the amount of each of 14 pollutants, in pounds per million dollars of value added, that are generated from each of 459 four-digit Standard Industrial Classification (SIC) codes. The predicted pollution levels are constructed by multiplying the industry's value added by the industry's IPPS coefficient. Industries are then classified into dirty and clean industries following Mani and Wheeler (1998).

While numerous studies use the results from IPPS for countries where data are insufficient (such as Mani and Jha 2006), the data have a few shortcomings. For example, IPPS takes pollution intensities in the United States in 1987 as the base. It represents a snapshot of the technique of production, held constant in a single year and place—that is, not accounting for country-specific factors or technical changes. This could affect the accuracy of IPPS estimates outside the United States and in different periods of time. However, if the intensity rankings by sector and relative magnitudes are similar across countries and time, IPPS can still be useful for identifying pollution problems even if it does not produce exact estimates of pollution.[7]

To address this shortcoming, we propose an alternative scenario where pollution intensities change across countries and time. The scenario is constructed taking as the base the technique effects estimated by Grether, Mathys, and de Melo (2007) for 62 developed and developing countries during 1990–2000. To our knowledge, this is the only study that estimates and identifies the technique effect for a large sample of countries.[8] It does so by combining different databases providing pollution estimates at the country level. For most countries the data are available only until 2000, which prevents us from developing a full decomposition exercise. We circumvent the data problem by regressing the estimate of Grether, Mathys, and de Melo (2007) against the possible determinants of technical changes (regression results are presented in table 13A.2 in the annex to this chapter). Model selection analysis helps us to focus on two dependent variables—initial GDP per capita and ratio of trade to GDP—which allows us to project the rate of adjustment in pollution intensity for each of the CA-4 countries in the 1999–2008 period. The rates are then applied to IPSS pollution intensities to construct new emissions data series. We assume that technical changes are homogeneous across sectors.

The remaining data used in the analysis include the following indicators: value added, exports, imports, number of workers, wages of skilled workers, and wages of unskilled workers. All indicators are disaggregated at the two-digit industry level. While value added and trade data are used directly in the analysis, labor indicators are used to calculate industry-specific factor shares. Following Grossman and Krueger (1992), we assume that each industry's output is produced according to a constant returns to scale Cobb-Douglas technology using three main inputs: labor, human, and physical capital. For each industry, labor share is calculated as a product of average unskilled wages and total number of workers divided by industry output. Human capital share is calculated as the total wage bill divided by output minus the labor share. Finally, physical capital share is calculated as the residual.

While we acknowledge potential limitations of the pollution data and the analytical framework used, we believe that these exercises are in line with the literature and can help to provide insights useful for the ongoing policy debate.

Results

This section presents and discusses the results from the two quantitative exercises. In each case, we start by discussing the benchmark case (no technique effect) and move on to the alternative scenario. We present both individual-country results and the aggregate analysis for the region.

Decomposition Exercise

Figure 13.1 compares the emissions from clean and dirty industries in the period before and after DR-CAFTA assuming no technique effect. All countries experience a significant increase in pollution between the two periods. While for Costa Rica and El Salvador the additional emissions seem to come mainly from dirty industries, both type of industries played a role in the expansion of emissions for Nicaragua and Honduras. A more detailed analysis is necessary to assess the extent to which the variation in pollution relates to changes in composition and to control for underlying trends in emissions.

Figure 13.2 presents the results of the decomposition analysis under the baseline scenario for total emissions.[9] The first striking fact of the analysis is the importance of scale effects. More than 90 percent of pollution variation results from a scaling up of production. This is consistent across all countries in the sample. Composition effects not only are smaller, but vary significantly across countries. For Costa Rica and El Salvador, composition effects further expand pollution, while for the remaining countries (including the regional average), composition effects related to total emissions and metal pollution partially compensate the positive scale effect. These results go against the idea of pollution havens. Here, countries with better regulatory frameworks experience relative growth in emissions from dirty industries, while the opposite is true for countries with less stringent frameworks such as Honduras. When allowing for existing trends in emissions, we notice that in all countries, with the exception of Honduras, emissions increase after the agreement through scale effects. Nicaragua is the only country where the agreement

Figure 13.1 Average Pollution per Year, before and after DR–CAFTA Negotiations (pounds, millions)

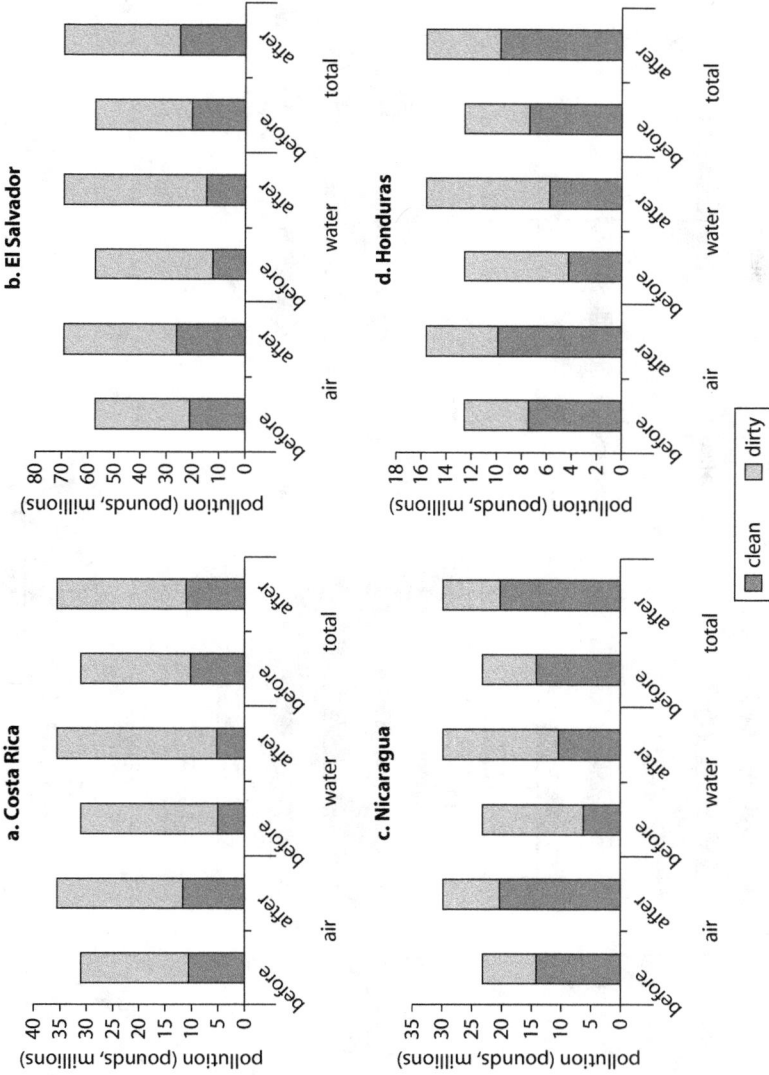

a. Costa Rica

b. El Salvador

c. Nicaragua

d. Honduras

Source: IPPS and authors' calculations.

Figure 13.2   Decomposition in Total Emissions: Baseline Scenario

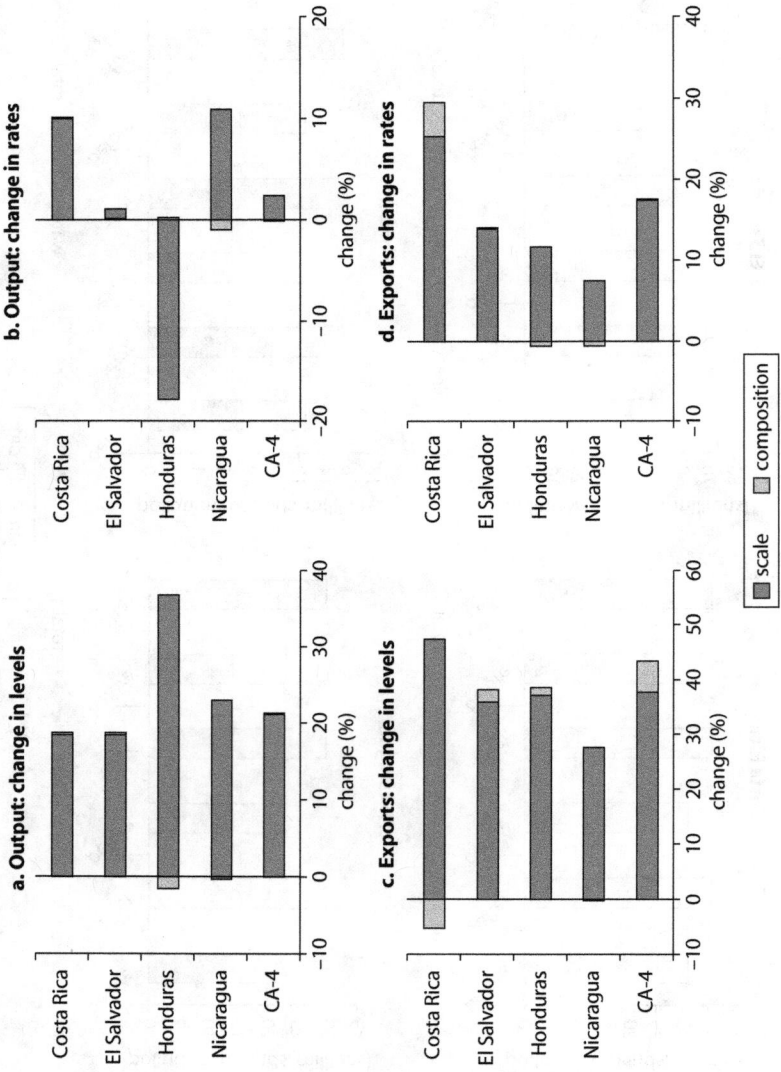

a. Output: change in levels

b. Output: change in rates

c. Exports: change in levels

d. Exports: change in rates

scale   composition

Source: IPPS and authors' calculations.

significantly reduces the rate of changes in the composition of production. Emissions from manufacturing exports significantly increase the overall production of emissions and, with the exception of Honduras, the manufacture of exports becomes "dirtier." This result probably reflects the fact that, although these economies expanded a few of the dirty activities for exports, they also increased imports from other dirty production, reducing domestic production in these segments.

Results change significantly when we allow for changes in pollution intensity. For almost all countries, the technique effect is the largest component of changes in emissions from production. Under alternative scenarios, the level of emissions in manufacturing production decreases steadily over time (see figure 13.3). Patterns of emissions from exports are less clear, although the technique effect plays a large role; the sector is still dominated by gains due to changes in scale in all countries but Honduras. When we allow for existing trends, we find only a minor increase in the expansion of pollution in production and exports after the agreement. The upward pressures related to scale gains are compensated by downward pressure from the arrival and survival of cleaner technology.

The decomposition analysis therefore suggests that the overall direction and size of changes in emissions are largely dependent on assumptions about changes in technology. Nevertheless, some interesting findings arise from the two extreme scenarios:

- Scale effects play a major role in explaining changes in emissions levels and trends after the agreement.
- Composition effects are small and vary in direction across countries.

This effect is the focus of attention of the next exercise. While there seems to be no strong evidence supporting the pollution haven hypothesis in Central America, the exercise shows significant gains from the adoption of cleaner technologies.

Sector Composition Exercise

Table 13.2 presents the results of the regression analysis measuring changes in the composition of outputs and exports, by sector, for the CA-4. The results indicate a positive trend in the relative growth of dirty industries before the beginning of DR-CAFTA negotiations. The trend disappears in the period after. Results are significant only when total pollution is taken into account. Coefficients remain significant even after

Figure 13.3   Decomposition in Total Emissions: Alternative Scenario

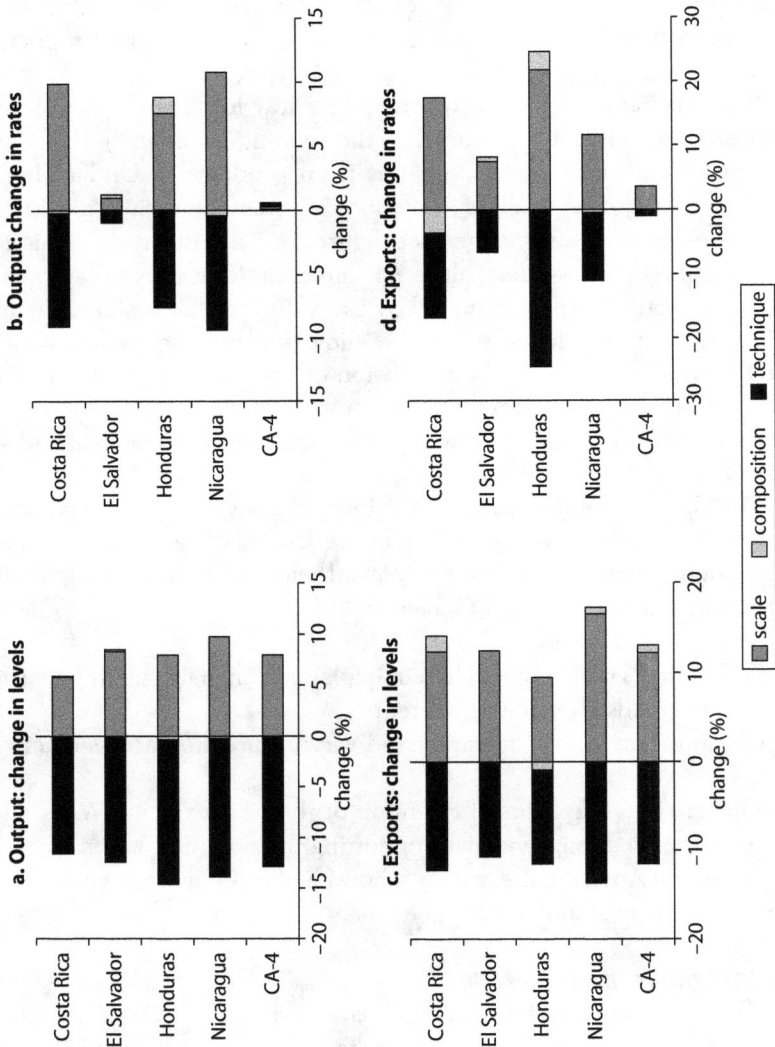

a. Output: change in levels

b. Output: change in rates

c. Exports: change in levels

d. Exports: change in rates

■ scale   □ composition   ■ technique

Source: IPPS and authors' calculations.

Table 13.2　Regression Analysis: CA-4

Variable[a]	Annual output growth per two-digit industry								Annual exports growth per two-digit industry							
	(1)	(2)	(3)	(4)	(5)	(6)	(7)	(8)	(1)	(2)	(3)	(4)	(5)	(6)	(7)	(8)
Dirty total	0.16		0.33**		0.35**		0.38**		0.81*		1.74**		1.67*		1.34	
Dirty air		0.11		0.28		0.30		0.30		0.79		17.04*		1.86		1.71
Dirty water		0.07		0.17		0.17		0.17		0.42		9.91		0.85		0.46
Dirty metal		−0.08		−0.21		−0.24		−0.25		−0.75		−14.34**		−2.11*		−2.57**
After*dirty total			−0.34*		−0.35*		−0.41*				−1.75**		−1.93*		−1.30	
After*dirty air				−0.31		−0.33		−0.33				−17.30		−1.95		−1.67
After*dirty water				−0.18		−0.19		−0.19				−10.71		−1.14		−0.39
After*dirty metal				0.24		0.25		0.26				13.00		1.45		2.31
Labor share					−0.09	−0.19	−0.14	−0.24					−1.62	−2.72	−2.00	−3.23
Capital share					0.14	0.09	0.11	0.10					−1.23	−1.69	−0.88	−1.00
After*labor							0.10	0.10							0.64	0.80
After*capital							0.06	−0.01							−0.70	−1.41
Number of observations	168	168	168	168	168	168	169	170	168	168	168	168	147	147	147	147
Country fixed	y	y	y	y	y	y	y	y	y	y	y	y	y	y	y	y

Source: Authors' calculations.

Note: The classification into dirty industries follows Mani and Wheeler (1998). y = Yes.

a. Asterisks represent the product between the two variables; see equation 13.2.

*p < .10, **p < .05.

controlling for production factor shares, which indicates that the dynamics of dirty industries go beyond traditional comparative advantages. Results for exports follow a similar path. Dirty industry exports are expanding relative to other industries before the agreement, but this trend disappears after the beginning of negotiations. The main difference regarding the composition of exports is the fact that, after crossing the DR-CAFTA dummy with the indicators of factor shares, trends in dirty industry exports become insignificant.

The results of the regression analysis for individual countries are presented in table 13.3. We focus here on the analysis of total emissions. The results for other types of pollutants are presented in the annex to this chapter. Results for Costa Rica indicate higher growth of output for dirty industries before the agreement, but this trend is partially canceled after negotiations. As for Costa Rica's exports, dirty industries expand faster during the whole period. Regressions for El Salvador indicate no significant effects of the agreement on the composition of output toward dirty industries. Growth seems to be driven mainly by factor shares, with human capital-intensive industries expanding relatively faster. El Salvador's exports behave similarly to exports for the region, that is, the higher growth of exports in dirty industries slows significantly after the agreement takes place. In Nicaragua, the agreement seems to have no impact on relatively pollution-intensive industries. During the sample period, growth favors labor-intensive manufacturing activities. Finally, in Honduras, the agreement seems to have contributed to the relative growth in the output of cleaner industries. This result remains significant even after controlling for factor shares of production. Once more, results go against the common assumptions in the policy debate.

Overall, the quantitative exercises developed in this section find no evidence to support the formation of pollution havens after DR-CAFTA negotiation. Annual levels of pollution seem to have increased after the agreement, but changes were driven mainly by the increase in production. In none of the economies analyzed do weak environmental regulatory frameworks seem to have played any part in determining comparative advantages. Changes in the composition of production are quite small and, in some cases (like Honduras), favor cleaner sectors. Nevertheless, countries should continue pursuing their environmental agenda and working to close regulatory gaps among member countries, as pollution pressures tend to increase as economies grow. The environmental agenda should be combined with

Table 13.3 Regression Analysis: CA-4 Countries

Country and variable[a]	Output growth per two-digit industry				Exports growth per two-digit industry			
	(1)	(2)	(3)	(4)	(1)	(2)	(3)	(4)
Costa Rica								
Dirty total	0.64	0.34**	1.21**	1.23*	0.33**	0.51**	0.53**	0.62**
After*dirty total		−0.34*	−1.13*	−1.10		−0.31	−0.31	−0.47
Labor share			−1.96	−1.72			−3.26*	−3.17
Capital share			−1.62	−1.02			−2.86*	−2.96
After*labor				0.33				−0.2
After*capital								−0.22
Number of observations	168	168	168	168	168	168	168	168
El Salvador								
Dirty total	−0.01	0.00	0.00	0.01	0.31	0.69**	0.69**	0.68*
After*dirty total		−0.02	−0.02	−0.06		−0.69*	−0.69*	−0.68
Labor share			−16.27*	−16.27*			3.08	3.08
Capital share			−16.23*	−16.32*			3.07	3.07
After*labor				0.02				1.00
After*capital				0.04				−0.16
Number of observations	168	168	168	168	168	168	168	168

(continued next page)

Table 13.3 *(continued)*

Country and variable[a]	Output growth per two-digit industry				Exports growth per two-digit industry			
	(1)	*(2)*	*(3)*	*(4)*	*(1)*	*(2)*	*(3)*	*(4)*
Honduras								
Dirty total	0.07	0.17*	0.08	1.08	-0.7588605	-1.004951	-0.8423495	-1.40
After*dirty total		-0.17*	-0.17*	-0.17*		0.4921811	0.49	1.60
Labor share			-3.26	1.08			-8.41*	-9.33*
Capital share			-3.83*	-4.04*			-4.35	-4.27
After*labor				-7.07**				7.8
After*capital				0.17*				-1.59
Number of observations	168	168	168	168	168	168	168	168
Nicaragua								
Dirty total	-0.07	-0.09	-0.05	-0.01	3.14	6.36**	0.07	-0.05
After*dirty total		0.03	0.03	-0.04		-6.45*	-0.48	-0.25
Labor share			0.62*	1.30**			5.81*	11.32**
Capital share			0.04	-0.03			-2.81**	-2.83**
After*labor				-1.22				-11.02*
After*capital				0.13				0.05
Number of observations	168	168	168	168	168	168	168	168

Source: Authors' calculations.

a. Asterisks represent the product between the two variables, see equation 13.2.

$*p < .10, **p < .05$.

action to improve and sustain competitiveness in the presence of higher regulatory costs.

Conclusions

The chapter analyzes the short-term and possible medium-term environmental impacts of the DR-CAFTA for the region. Following a review of DR-CAFTA environmental provisions and the existing literature on trade and the environment, two empirical exercises are carried out for assessing the initial changes in emissions for countries in the region. The first exercise decomposes the pollution effect into scale, composition, and technique effects. The second exercise focuses on changes in the composition of production and assesses whether the agreement favors the relative expansion of dirty industries. Two scenarios—no technical effect and a positive technical effect—are then considered.

Results show that the environmental developments from DR-CAFTA vary significantly across member countries. Most results are consistent with the findings in the literature. Scale effects are positive and dominate the composition effects for all countries. Composition effects vary significantly across member countries. While Costa Rica and El Salvador experience a small but positive increase in pollution as a result of changes in the composition of production, Nicaragua and Honduras (as well as the regional average) experience negative composition effects. The results indicate that factors other than a lax regulatory framework play an important role in determining the patterns of production and trade. Results change after allowing for adjustments in pollution intensity. Under this alternative scenario, levels of emissions from production seem to have decreased after the agreement. The share of pollution in exports continuously expands in the alternative scenario as well.

The findings do not suggest the existence of pollution havens in Central America. Nonetheless, countries should continue strengthening and homogenizing environmental rules in the region. The environmental agenda should be combined with an effort to improve competitiveness that helps sustain trade in the medium term as regulatory costs rise.

Annex. The Data

This annex describes how the chapter estimates the rate of changes in pollution intensity, presents the regression analysis for individual countries, and explains the ranking of the dirtiest industries.

Table 13A.1   Regression Variables

Variable	Description
Dirty Y	Dummy identifying pollution-intensive industries taking into account emission type Y
After	Dummy indicating the period after DR-CAFTA negotiations (2004–08)
Labor share	Share of unskilled labor value to GDP
Capital share	Share of physical capital value to GDP

Source: Authors.

Estimating the Rate of Changes in Pollution Intensities

Technical changes, defined here as changes in pollution intensity, are estimated based on the work of Grether, Mathys, and de Melo (2007). This is one of the few articles in the literature that identify technical effects in emissions changes for a large set of countries. The authors focus on changes in sulfur dioxide for the period 1990–2000. Given the lack of more comparable alternatives, we extend their measure to the pollutants studied here. We regress the annual changes in intensity estimated by Grether, Mathys, and de Melo (2007) against a list of variables that could potentially affect technical changes in pollution.[10] After trying different specifications, we identify the best model as the parsimonious regression presented in the text. Table 13A.1 presents the variables. Table 13A.2 presents the results. Estimated coefficients are then used to construct rates of technical changes for Central America between 1999 and 2008.

Ranking the Dirtiest Manufacturing Industries

A conventional approach to defining dirty industries has been to identify pollution-intensive sectors as those that incur high levels of abatement expenditure per unit of output in the United States and other developed economies (Tobey 1990; Mani 1996). A more direct approach is to select sectors that rank high on actual emissions intensity. Mani and Wheeler (1998) determine the high-ranking sectors by this criterion using emissions intensities of medium U.S. manufacturing firms at the three-digit Standard Industrial Classification level. They then compute average sectoral rankings for conventional air pollutants, water pollutants, and toxic substances. Similar to the conventional approach, five of the six sectors with the highest overall ranks are iron and steel, nonferrous metals, industrial chemicals, pulp and paper, and nonmetallic mineral products. The strength of their approach lies in the fact that the set of dirtiest manufacturing industries appears to be fairly stable across countries and pollutants.

Table 13A.2 Full Regression Analysis: CA-4 Countries

Country and variable[a]	Dependent variable: Annual exports growth per two-digit industry							
	(1)	(2)	(3)	(4)	(5)	(6)	(7)	(8)
Costa Rica								
Dirty total	0.64		0.34**		1.21**		1.25*	
Dirty air		0.58		1.18		1.17		1.15
Dirty water		0.34		0.66		0.64		0.58
Dirty metal		−0.49		−0.95*		−0.96		−1.03
After*dirty total			−0.34*		−1.13*		−1.20	
After*dirty air				−1.19		−1.20		−1.16
After*dirty water				−0.63		−0.64		−0.52
After*dirty metal				0.92		0.93		1.06
Labor share					−1.96	−1.56	−2.11	−1.72
Capital share					−1.62	−1.14	−1.66	−1.02
After*labor							0.31	0.33
After*capital							0.07	−0.22
Number of observations	168	168	168	168	168	168	168	168
El Salvador								
Dirty total	−0.01		0.00		0.00		0.017552	
Dirty air		−0.01		0.00		−0.01		0.00
Dirty water		−0.01		0.00		0.00		0.03
Dirty metal		−0.02		−0.02		−0.02		0.00
After*dirty total			−0.02		−0.02		−0.06	
After*dirty air				−0.01		−0.01		−0.03
After*dirty water				−0.03		−0.03		−0.07
After*dirty metal				0.00		0.00		−0.04
Labor share					−16.27*	−16.65*	−16.27*	−16.62*
Capital share					−16.23*	−16.20*	−16.32*	−16.25*
After*labor							0.02	−0.05
After*capital							0.04	−0.08
Number of observations	168	168	168	168	168	168	168	168
Honduras								
Dirty total	0.07		0.17*		0.08		0.02	
Dirty air		−0.06		−0.10		−0.08		−0.05
Dirty water		−0.01		−0.02		−0.08		−0.14
Dirty metal		0.11*		0.19**		0.11		0.04
After*dirty total			−0.17*		−0.17*		−0.07	
After*dirty air				0.05		0.05		0.01
After*dirty water				0.01		0.01		0.11
After*dirty metal				−0.14*		−0.14		−0.02
Labor share					−3.26	−3.33	0.72	1.08
Capital share					−3.83*	−3.93*	−3.96*	−4.04*
After*labor							−6.37**	−7.07**
After*capital							0.21**	0.17*
Number of observations	168	168	168	168	168	168	168	168
Nicaragua								
Dirty total	−0.07		−0.09		−0.05		−0.01	
Dirty air		−0.06		−0.10		−0.09		−0.08
Dirty water		−0.04		−0.05		−0.02		0.01
Dirty metal		0.04		0.03		0.06		0.09
After*dirty total			0.03		0.03		−0.04	
After*dirty air				0.07		0.07		0.05
After*dirty water				0.01		0.01		−0.05
After*dirty metal				0.01		0.01		−0.04
Labor share					0.62*	0.68		1.37**
Capital share					0.04	0.05		−0.02
After*labor								−1.25
After*capital								0.14
Number of observations	168	168	168	168	168	168	168	168

(continued next page)

Table 13A.2 (continued)

Country and variable[a]	Dependent variable: Annual exports growth per two-digit industry							
	(1)	(2)	(3)	(4)	(5)	(6)	(7)	(8)
Costa Rica								
Dirty total	0.33**		0.51**		0.53**		0.62**	
Dirty air		0.39**		0.50*		0.50*		0.51*
Dirty water		0.13		0.26		0.27		0.30
Dirty metal		−0.38**		−0.52**		−0.52**		−0.48*
After*dirty total			−0.31		−0.31		−0.47	
After*dirty air				−0.21		−0.21		−0.23
After*dirty water				−0.24		−0.24		−0.30
After*dirty metal				0.25		0.25		0.18
Labor share					−3.26*	−2.88*	−3.17	−2.80
Capital share					−2.86*	−2.41	−2.96	−2.47
After*labor							−0.2	−0.16
After*capital							0.2	0.12
Number of observations	168	168	168	168	168	168	168	168
El Salvador								
Dirty total				0.31	0.69**	0.69**	0.68*	
Dirty air		0.30		0.68*		0.75		0.73
Dirty water		0.16		0.40		0.36		0.30
Dirty metal		−0.28		−0.56*		−0.69*		−0.76*
After*dirty total				−0.69*	−0.69*	−0.68		
After*dirty air				−0.69		−0.75		−0.71
After*dirty water				−0.43		−0.43		−0.32
After*dirty metal				0.52		0.63		0.75
Labor share					3.08	3.08	3.08	3.08
Capital share					3.07	3.07	3.07	3.09
After*labor							1.00	5.8
After*capital							−0.16	−2.0
Number of observations	168	168	168	168	168	168	168	168
Honduras								
Dirty total	−0.76		−1.00		−0.84		−1.40	
Dirty air		−0.03		−0.08		−0.11		−0.34
Dirty water		−0.51		−0.73		−0.69		−1.19
Dirty metal		−1.42		−1.49		−1.65		−2.27*
After*dirty total			0.49		0.49		1.60	
After*dirty air				0.09		0.09		0.55
After*dirty water				0.45		0.45		1.45
After*dirty metal				0.15		0.15		1.39
Labor share					−8.41*	−10.60**	−9.33*	−10.81**
Capital share					−4.35	−5.74*	−4.27	−5.67*
After*labor							7.79	3.40
After*capital							−1.59	−2.14*
Number of observations	168	168	168	168	168	168	168	168
Nicaragua								
Dirty total	3.14		6.36**		0.07		−0.05	
Dirty air		2.97		6.09		−0.24		−0.26
Dirty water		1.66		3.62		0.01		−0.03
Dirty metal		−2.67		−4.96*		0.00		−0.14
After*dirty total			−6.45*		−0.48		−0.25	
After*dirty air				−6.24		−0.19		−0.15
After*dirty water				−3.93		−0.04		0.04
After*dirty metal				4.57		−0.25		0.03
Labor share					5.81*	5.20*	11.32**	10.61**
Capital share					−2.81**	−2.85**	−2.83**	−2.85**
After*labor							−11.02*	−10.81**
After*capital							0.05	−0.01
Number of observations	168	168	168	168	168	168	168	168

Source: Authors' calculations.

a. Asterisks represent the product between the two variables, see equation 13.2.

*p < .10, **p < .05.

Notes

1. Its proponents argue that environmental degradation is just a matter of "grow-ing pains" that will disappear with prosperity.

2. Data limitations prevent us from assessing technological changes directly, so we create an alternative scenario drawing from results in the literature.

3. Following the terminology proposed by Grossman and Krueger (1992).

4. Defined as the level of per capita income (purchasing power parity, PPP) beyond which emissions start declining.

5. Per capita GDP (US$, PPP) in 2009: Costa Rica, US$10,737; Dominican Republic, US$8,570; El Salvador, US$7,570; Guatemala, US$4,873; Honduras, US$4,282; Nicaragua, US$2,668.

6. The information is available at SIC two-digit and three-digit level of disaggre-gation.

7. $\Delta^{calculated} pollution$

$$= \Delta^{actual} pollution - \underbrace{Q_0 \sum_j \alpha_{jt} \left(p_{jt} - p_{j0} \right) + \left(Q_t - Q_0 \right) \sum_j \alpha_{jt} \left(p_{jt} - p_{j0} \right)}_{Bias}$$

$$= \underbrace{\left(Q_t - Q_0 \right) \sum_j \alpha_{jt} p_{j0}}_{Calculated\ Scale} + \underbrace{Q_0 \sum_j \left(\alpha_{jt} - \alpha_{j0} \right) p_{j0}}_{Composition}$$

8. Most papers in the literature estimate a combination of scale and technique effects.

9. The results for air, water, and metal pollution are available on request from the authors.

10. Initially, we consider a large set of variables, including per capita GDP, ratio of trade to GDP, ratio of foreign direct investment to GDP, share of manufactur-ing output, per capita income growth, ratio of trade to GDP growth, proxies for human capital, average year of schooling, secondary education attendance, and tertiary education attendance.

References

Akbostanci, Elif, G. Ipek Tunc, and Serap Türüt-Asik. 2004. "Pollution Haven Hypothesis and the Role of Dirty Industries in Turkey's Exports." ERC Working Paper 0403, Middle East Technical University, Economic Research Center, Ankara.

Antweiler, Werner, Brian R. Copeland, and M. Scott Taylor. 2001. "Is Free Trade Good for the Environment?" *American Economic Review* 91 (4, September): 877–908.

Aslanidis, Nektarios. 2009. "Environmental Kuznets Curves for Carbon Emissions: A Critical Survey." Working Paper 2009.75, Fondazione Eni Enrico Mattei, Milan.

Bovenberg, A. L., and Sjak Smulders. 1995. "Environmental Quality and Pollution-Augmenting Technological Change in a Two-Sector Endogenous Growth Model." *Journal of Public Economics* 57 (3, July): 369–91.

Brock, William A., and M. Scott Taylor. 2004. "The Green Solow Model." NBER Working Paper 10557, National Bureau of Economic Research, Cambridge, MA.

Chichilnisky, Graciela. 1994. "North-South Trade, Property Rights, and the Dynamics of Environmental Resources." MPRA Paper 8415, University Library of Munich, Germany.

Cole, Matthew A., and Anthony J. Rayner. 2000. "The Uruguay Round and Air Pollution: Estimating the Composition, Scale, and Technique Effects of Trade Liberalization." *Journal of International Trade and Economic Development* 9 (3, September): 339–54.

Copeland, Brian R., and M. Scott Taylor. 1994. "North-South Trade and the Environment." *Quarterly Journal of Economics* 109 (3, August): 755–87.

———. 2003. *International Trade and Environment: Theory and Practice.* Princeton, NJ: Princeton University Press.

———. 2004. "Trade, Growth, and the Environment." *Journal of Economic Literature* 42 (1, March): 7–71.

Dean, Judith M. 2002. "Does Trade Liberalization Harm the Environment? A New Test." *Canadian Journal of Economics* 35 (4, November): 819–42.

de Bruyn, S. M., J. C. J. M. van den Bergh, and J. B. Opschoor. 1998. "Economic Growth and Emissions: Reconsidering the Empirical Basis of Environmental Kuznets Curves." *Ecological Economics* 25 (2, May): 161–75.

Di Maria, Corrado, and Sjak A. Smulders. 2004. "Trade Pessimists vs. Technology Optimists: Induced Technical Change and Pollution Havens." Open Access Publication urn:hdl:10197/845, University College Dublin.

Dijkgraaf, Elbert, and Herman Vollebergh. 2004. "A Note on Testing for Environmental Kuznets Curves with Panel Data." Others 0409001, EconWPA. Washington University, St. Louis.

Egli, Hannes. 2004. "The Environmental Kuznets Curve: Evidence from Time Series Data for Germany," CER-ETH Economics Working Paper 03/28, Center of Economic Research, Swiss Federal Institute of Technology (ETH), Zurich.

Esty, D., and M. Porter. 2005. "National Environmental Performance: An Empirical Analysis of Policy Results and Determinants." *Environment and Development Economics* 10 (4): 391–434.

Gamper-Rabindran, Shanti, and Shreyasi Jha. 2004. "Environmental Impact of India's Trade Liberalization." Working Paper, University of North Carolina at Chapel Hill, Department of Public Policy.

Grether, Jean-Marie, Nicole A. Mathys, and Jaime de Melo. 2007. "Trade, Technique, and Composition Effects: What Is Behind the Fall in World-Wide SO_2 Emissions 1990–2000?" Working Paper 2007.93, Fondazione Eni Enrico Mattei, Milan.

———. 2009. "Scale, Technique, and Composition Effects in Manufacturing SO_2 Emissions." *Environmental and Resource Economics* 43 (2, June): 257–74.

Grossman, Gene, and Alan B. Krueger. 1992. "Environmental Impacts of a North American Free Trade Agreement." CEPR Discussion Paper 644, Centre for Economic Policy Research, London.

———. 1995. "Economic Growth and the Environment." *Quarterly Journal of Economics* 110 (2): 353–77.

Halkos, George E. 2003. "Environmental Kuznets Curve for Sulfur: Evidence Using GMM Estimation and Random Coefficient Panel Data Models." *Environment and Development Economics* 8 (4): 581–601.

Hettige, Hemamala, Muthukumara Mani, and David Wheeler. 2000. "Industrial Pollution in Economic Development: Kuznets Revisited." *Journal of Development Economics* 62 (2): 445–76.

Kahn, Matthew E., and Yutaka Yoshino. 2004. "Testing for Pollution Havens Inside and Outside of Regional Trading Blocs." *B. E. Journal of Economic Analysis and Policy* 4 (2): art, 4.

López, Ramón. 1994. "The Environment as a Factor of Production: The Effects of Economic Growth and Trade Liberalization." *Journal of Environmental Economics and Management* 27 (2): 163–84.

Mani, Muthukumara S. 1996. "Environmental Tariffs on Polluting Imports: An Empirical Study." *Environmental and Resource Economics* 7 (4): 391–411.

Mani, Muthukumara S., and Shreyasi Jha. 2006. "Trade Liberalization and the Environment in Vietnam." Policy Research Working Paper 3879, World Bank, Washington, DC.

Mani, Muthukumara, and David Wheeler. 1998. "In Search of Pollution Havens? Dirty Industry in the World Economy, 1960–1999." *Journal of Environment and Development* 7 (3): 215–47.

Markandya, Anil, Alexander Golub, and Suzette Pedroso-Galinato. 2006. "Empirical Analysis of National Income and SO_2 Emissions in Selected European Countries." *Environmental and Resource Economics* 35 (3): 221–57.

Péridy, Nicolas. 2006. "Pollution Effects of Free Trade Areas: Simulations from a General Equilibrium Model." *International Economic Journal* 20 (1): 37–62.

Sarkar, S. 2009. "A Study of the Environmental Issues Associated with the Dominican Republic–Central American Free Trade Agreement (DR-CAFTA)." *International Business and Economics Research Journal* 8 (1): 113–88.

Selden, T., and D. Song. 1994. "Environmental Quality and Development: Is There a Kuznets Curve for Air Pollution Emissions?" *Journal of Environmental Economics and Management* 27 (2): 147–62.

Stern, David I., and Michael S. Common. 2001. "Is There an Environmental Kuznets Curve for Sulfur?" *Journal of Environmental Economics and Management* 41 (2): 162–78.

Stern, David I., Michael S. Common, and Edward B. Barbier. 1996. "Economic Growth and Environmental Degradation: The Environmental Kuznets Curve and Sustainable Development." *World Development* 24 (7): 1151–60.

Stokey, Nancy L. 1998. "Are There Limits to Growth?" *International Economic Review* 39 (1): 1–31.

Tobey, James A. 1990. "The Effects of Domestic Environmental Policies on Patterns of World Trade: An Empirical Test." *Kyklos* 43 (2): 191–209.

Index

Boxes, figures, notes, and tables are indicated by *b*, *f*, *n*, and *t*, respectively.

www.ingramcontent.com/pod-product-compliance
Lightning Source LLC
Chambersburg PA
CBHW071827270326
41929CB00013B/1913

9780821387122